BIBLICAL AND HUMANE
A Festschrift for John F. Priest

JOHN F. PRIEST

BIBLICAL AND HUMANE
A Festschrift for John F. Priest

Edited by

Linda Bennett Elder
David L. Barr
Elizabeth Struthers Malbon

Scholars Press
Atlanta, Georgia

BIBLICAL AND HUMANE
A Festschrift for John F. Priest

Edited by
Linda Bennett Elder
David L. Barr
Elizabeth Struthers Malbon

©1996
Scholars Press

Library of Congress Cataloging in Publication Data
Biblical and humane : a festschrift for John F. Priest / edited by
        Linda Bennett Elder, David L. Barr, Elizabeth Struthers Malbon.
            p.   cm. — (Scholars Press homage series ; no. 20)
        ISBN 0-7885-0285-9 (cloth)
        1. Bible—Criticism, interpretation, etc. 2. Theology.
    I. Priest, John F. II. Elder, Linda Bennett. III. Barr, David L.
    IV. Malbon, Elizabeth Struthers. V. Series
    BS511.2.B565   1996
    220.6—dc20   96-22813
                                                          CIP

Printed in the United States of America
on acid-free paper

Contents

Humane and Biblical

Preface

The twenty essays in this collection are as rich in depth and as broad in scope as the man they seek to honor: John F. Priest. The presenters represent the honoree's teachers (Kee), fellow students (Borgen, Downing, Underwood), faculty colleagues (Carey, Cunningham, Seger, Spivey , Patton and Rollins), students, (Barr, Bennett Elder, Berenbaum, Charlesworth, Struthers Malbon), colleagues in the SBL (Blenkinsopp, Grant) and colleagues in the American Interfaith Institute/World Alliance of Interfaith Organizations (Eckardt, Epp and Pawlikowski). The collection is presented on the occasion of Professor Priest's retirement from the Department of Religion at Florida State University in 1996, after 28 years of service.

John Priest was born on November 19, 1929, in Gentryville, Indiana. He received his A.B. (Summa Cum Laude) from Asbury College in 1949, his B.D. (Summa Cum Laude) from Drew in 1955 and the Ph.D. from Drew in 1960. He studied at the University of Manchester, England, in 1956-57. During his academic preparation, he was honored as a Kent Fellow, Tipple Fellow, Dempstar Fellow, Fulbright Fellow, and Lily Post-Doctoral Fellow. He served the Methodist Church as a missionary in India from 1949-52. His teaching career has included full-time teaching at a church-related university, Ohio Wesleyan University (1957-62), a seminary, The Hartford Seminary Foundation (1962-66), and a large public university, Florida State University (1968-96), as well as visiting professorships at Yale University, Trinity College, Union Theological Seminary (New York), Colgate Rochester Divinity School, and Princeton University. He also served as an academic administrator: academic dean at Hartford (1966-68), Religion Department Chair (1978-84) and Graduate Humanities Program Director (1969-76) at FSU. He is a member of the American Academy of Religion, the Society of Biblical Literature, and the American Oriental Society, serving as regional president of the SBL and as national secretary, vice-president, president (1967), and executive director and treasurer (1967-78) of the AAR. His broad-ranging research has been marked by both an eclectic method and innovative results. His seminal work on the two messiahs of Qumran and on the Wisdom tradition viewed as a humanistic and skeptical strand of Jewish life have attracted wide recognition. He has sought to place biblical studies squarely in the Humanities. The brief chronicle of John Priest's academic life is filled out anecdotally by the first essay in this collection and contextually by the final essay.

The organizing topic for this Festschrift–and now its title–is "Biblical and Humane." The words are intended as a description of both the man and the book. The biblical material, especially but not exclusively the Hebrew Bible/Old Testament, has been formative in John Priest's life and work, in his scholarship and teaching. And when Dr. Priest teaches the Bible, he brings to life its stories and characters, its history and literature--usually by subtle means of understatement and juxtaposition of the biblical past and the human present. In sharing his understanding of the biblical tradition, Professor Priest has sought to help others appreciate its human dimensions as well as its divine. This concern for the human found another natural outlet in his contribution to the Graduate Humanities Program at FSU. He is fond of asking graduates students to reflect on the relationships between the human, humane, and the humanities. And it is clear that he has done so himself. In his deep interest and knowledge of a number of fields, and in his concern and respect for students, he embodies the humane as he embodies the biblical.

The essays gathered here to honor this biblical and humane man reflect the shared commitments of his teachers, students, and colleagues. Nine essays, presented under the sub-heading "Biblical and Humane," focus on specific biblical texts or broader biblical themes from the Hebrew Bible (Blenkinsopp, Seger, Patton, Bennett Elder) or the New Testament (Kee, Barr, Malbon, Charlesworth) or on approaches to biblical interpretations (Rollins). And nine essays, under the sub-heading "Humane and Biblical," focus on the human dimensions of texts and experiences from antiquity (Borgen, Epp, Grant) to the present day, including the human impact of earlier texts on later ones (Cunningham, Carey) and the impact of biblical stories and traditions on real human persons caught in the dread of modern inhumanity (Eckardt, Downing, Pawlikowski, Berenbaum). Humane and biblical remain hopes for the world.

These two sections are framed by two essays that focus on the man we honor, John F. Priest. Richard Underwood's contribution was the last work he completed before his death in October 1995. It has been revised by his widow, Joan Underwood, also a dear friend of John and Gloria Priest; and it stands as a tribute to a four-way friendship. Robert Spivey's article honors John Priest's contribution in the larger context of the Religion Department at FSU and the academic study of religion in university settings. Thus our essays aim not only to give tribute but also to give witness, both to admire and to emulate one we know as biblical and humane.

Acknowledgments

The editorial tasks of bringing together this volume have been shared. While each of us has been involved in each phase of the project, Linda Bennett Elder has been the sina qua non who kept the idea moving from inception, to soliciting papers, to editing papers, to communication with contributors, editors, and Scholars Press. Elizabeth Struthers Malbon served as advisor, edited papers, did copy-editing, and drafted the Preface. David L. Barr edited papers and prepared the camera-ready copy. Corrine Patton and Robert Spivey served as readers for three of the papers. Dianne Wienstein, former secretary to Dr. Priest, provided secretarial assistance. Each of our universities provided valuable support, both professional and financial. We give special thanks to Ronald L. Barnette, Department Head, and Tina Hodge of the Department of Philosophy at Valdosta State University; to Burton I. Kaufman, Director of the Center for Interdisciplinary Studies, and Robert C. Bates, Dean of the College of Arts and Sciences, and the Faculty Book Publishing Committee of Virginia Polytechnic Institute and State University; and to William Rickert, Associate Dean of the College of Liberal Arts, and Beverly Rowe, University Honors Program, Wright State University. This volume would not have been possible without the active support of Robert Spivey, former chair, and Leo Sandon, current chair, of the Department of Religion at Florida State University through whose generosity much of the cost of this volume was underwritten. Harry W. Gilmer and Dennis Ford of Scholars Press provided useful assistance in the process of moving from manuscript to book.

Linda Bennett Elder
Elizabeth Struthers Malbon
David L. Barr

Contributors

David L. Barr is Professor of Religion at Wright State University, Dayton, Ohio. He studied with John Priest at Florida State University, where he received his Ph.D. in 1974. He has written two books, *New Testament Story: An Introduction* (Wadsworth, 1995, second edition) and *EndStory: A Narrative Commentary on the Apocalypse of John* (Polebridge Press, forthcoming). He has been chair of the Department of Religion and Director of the University Honors Program at Wright State and currently chairs the Seminar on Reading the Apocalypse in the Society of Biblical Literature.

Michael Berenbaum (Ph.D., Florida State University, 1975) is the Director of the United States Holocaust Research Institute and the Hymen Goldman Adjunct Professor of Theology at Georgetown University. Among his books are *After Tragedy and Triumph: Modern Jewish Thought and the American Experience, The World Must Know: The History of the Holocaust As Told in the United States Holocaust Memorial Museum* and together with Israel Gutman *Anatomy of the Auschwitz Death Camp.*

Joseph Blenkinsopp (D.Phil., Oxford) is John A. O'Brien Professor of Hebrew Scriptures at Notre Dame, where he has taught since 1970. He has been involved in archaeological work in Israel and has contributed to the *Jerusalem Bible*, the *Jerome Biblical Commentary,* and *A New Catholic Commentary on Holy Scripture*, and in 1978 was rector of the Ecumenical Institute in Tantur, Israel. His book, *Prophecy and Canon* (1977), received the National Religious Book Award from the National Association of Publishers. His most recent books are *Ezra and Nehemiah* (1988) and *Ezekiel* (1989), both published by Westminster Press.

Peder Borgen President of the Norwegian Society of Sciences and Letters and President of the Editorial Board of *Novum Testamentum*, published by E. J. Brill, Leiden, is emeritus professor of New Testament and New Testament Backgrounds, University of Trondheim, Trondheim, Norway, and currently senior research fellow under the auspices of the Norwegian Research Council. He was a fellow student with John Priest at Drew University, Madison, N.J.

John J. Carey is the Wallace M. Alston Professor of Bible and Religion and Chair of the Department of Bible and Religion at Agnes Scott College, Decatur Georgia. He was on the faculty at Florida State University for 26 years (1960-86) and served as Chair of the Religion Department, Director of Graduate Studies in Religion, and Director of the Peace Studies Program at that institution. His friendship with John Priest was nurtured during the years at Florida State. From 1986-1988 Dr. Carey served as President of Warren Wilson College in North Carolina. He has written and edited nine books and chaired the Presbyterian Special Committee on Human Sexuality.

James Charlesworth is the George L. Collord Professor of New Testament Language and Literature and Director of the PTS Dead Sea Scrolls Project at Princeton Theological Seminary. From 1969 to 1984 he was a professor at Duke University and has served as Lady Davis Professor at the Hebrew University in Jerusalem.

Lawrence S. Cunningham is Professor of Theology and Chairman of the Department at the University of Notre Dame. He was a colleague of John Priest at Florida State University until 1987 and is the author of books on Catholicism, on the Western cultural tradition, and on comparative religions.

Christine Downing is Emeritus Professor of Religious Studies at San Diego State University. Her books Include *the Goddess, Women's Mysteries*, and *The Long Journey Home*. Her thirty-five year friendship with John Priest has blossomed primarily in the context of professional associations such as the American Academy of Religion.

A. Roy Eckardt, formerly editor of the *Journal of the American Academy of Religion* and before that president of the National Association of Biblical Instructors, is emeritus professor of religion studies, Lehigh University and currently senior associate fellow of the Centre for Hebrew and Jewish Studies, University of Oxford.

Linda Bennett Elder is Assistant Professor of Religious Studies in the Department of Philosophy at Valdosta State University where she is developing and expanding the Religious Studies curriculum. Her Ph.D. in Humanities and Religion under the direction of John Priest (Florida State, 1991) has resulted in several publications, including the article on "Judith" in *Searching the Scriptures* (Crossroad, 1993); "The Woman Question: Female Ascetics at Qumran" *(Biblical Archaeologist,* Dec. 94); and forthcoming articles on "Virgins, Viragos and Virtuosi: Judiths in Opera and Oratorio" (in *Biblicon*) and "Saint, Patriot or Phallic Woman: the Judiths of Artemisia Gentileschi, Friedrich Hebbel and Martha Graham" (in *The Feminist Companion to the Bible*, Sheffield Academic Press). She is a member of the steering committee of the Ascetic Impulse in Religious Life and Culture group of the AAR/SBL.

Eldon Jay Epp is Harkness Professor of Biblical Literature (since 1971) and former Dean of Humanities and Social Sciences (1977-1985) at Case Western Reserve University. He has published widely on New Testament manuscripts and textual criticism, serves as editor of *Studies and Documents* and on the Editorial Board of the *Hermeneia* commentary series (since 1966), was the New Testament Book Review Editor of the *Journal of Biblical Literature* (1971-1990) and editor of *Critical Review of Books in Religion* (1990-1994), and is a former Guggenheim Fellow. He was a colleague of John Priest in the American Academy of Religion.

Robert McQueen Grant is emeritus professor of Religion at the University of Chicago, where he had a long and distinguished career, holding the Carl Darling Buck Professorship in Humanities. He has published nearly 30 books on biblical topics and church history. He has served as a Fulbright research professor (Leiden), a Gugenheim fellow (thrice), a fellow of the American Academy of Arts and sciences, and as president of both the Society of Biblical Literature (1959) and the Society of Church History (1970). He was a visiting professor at Florida State University in 1989.

Howard Clark Kee is former Professor of New Testament and Director of Biblical-Historical Graduate Studies at Boston University. He has published numerous works on the New Testament, including *the New Testament in Context : Sources and Documents* and *Understanding the New Testament*, on the Gospels, including *Community of the New Age: Studies in Mark's Gospel* and *Jesus in History: an Approach to the Study of the Gospels*. His recent research has concentrated on the social aspects of Christian origins, with books on: *Medicine, Miracle, and Magic in New Testament Times; Who Are the People of God? Early Christian Models of Community; Christian Origins in Sociological Perspective: Methods and Resources; Knowing the Truth: a Sociological Approach to New Testament Interpretation.*

Elizabeth Struthers Malbon is Professor and Director of the Religious Studies Program within the Center for Interdisciplinary Studies at Virginia Polytechnic Institute and State University. Her Ph.D. in the interdisciplinary Humanities Program at FSU (1980), under the direction of John Priest, is reflected in two books: one on a New Testament text, *Narrative Space and Mythic Meaning in Mark* (Harper&Row, 1986), and one on early Christian art, *The Iconography of the Sarcophagus of Junius Bassus* (Princeton, 1990).

Corrine L. Patton was an Assistant Professor of Hebrew Bible at Florida State University from 1991-96, working along with John Priest. She received her Ph.D. from Yale University in 1991, and is currently teaching at the University of St. Thomas in St. Paul, MN.

John T Pawlikowski is Professor of Social Ethics at the Catholic Theological Union, Chicago. He has served by presidential appointment on the U.S. Holocaust Memorial Council since 1980. A member of the Advisory Committee on Catholic-Jewish Relations for the National Conference of Catholic Bishops, he is the author of many books and articles on the Holocaust, Christian-Jewish relations and on social ethics, including Christ is the Light of the Christian Jewish Dialogue. He shares with Dr. Priest a continuing interest in Christian-Jewish relations and in the work of the AAR.

Wayne G. Rollins is Professor of Biblical Studies and Director of the Ecumenical Summer Institute at Assumption College (1974 to the present), having formerly taught at Princeton University (1958-59), at Wellesley College (1959-66), and as a colleague of John Priest at the Hartford Seminary Foundation (1966-74) . He has served as President of the New England Section of the AAR and is currently chair of the SBL Group on Psychology and Biblical Studies.

Joe D. Seger is Professor of Religion and Anthropology and Director of the Cobb Institute of Archaeology at Mississippi State University. He was John Priest's junior colleague in Old Testament Studies at Hartford Seminary Foundation between 1964-1969. He subsequently served as director of the archaeological program at the Hebrew Union College/Nelson Glueck School of Biblical Archaeology in Jerusalem (1969-1974) and was director of the Phase Two HUC excavations at Tell Gezer (1972-1974). He has been director of the Lahav Research Project Excavations at Tell Halif, Israel, since 1976. He is Past-President of the W. F. Albright Institute of Archaeological Research in Jerusalem (1988-1994) and currently serves as President of the American Schools of Oriental Research.

Robert Atwood Spivey, after teaching at Williams College, became the first chairman of the Department of Religion at Florida State University, where he recruited John Priest in 1968. He was John's colleague from 1964-1978, serving both as faculty member and administrator. He then became president of Randolph-Macon Woman's College serving there for ten years, and is now president of the Virginia Foundation for Independent Colleges. From 1972-1975 he was executive director of the American Academy of Religion. He has published both in the field of biblical studies, particularly *Anatomy of the New Testament* with D. Moody Smith, and in the area of religion and public education.

Richard Underwood was born in Greenwich, Kansas, in 1928 and grew up in various rural, Methodist parsonages in northern Indiana while his father finished college and seminary. He was graduated from Depaw University in Greencastle, Indiana, and attended Drew Seminary and Graduate School. He taught at Stephens College in Columbia, Missouri, and Hartford Seminary Foundation before assuming the chair the Department of Religious Studies at the University of North Carolina at Charlotte. He served as fellow and on the board of ARC and as chairman of the regional AAR. At his retirement from UNCC in 1993 John Priest presented a paper, "Humanism and the Biblical Tradition." Dr. Underwood died in 1995.

John F. Priest:
A Personal Memoir of Friendship and Collegiality

Richard A. Underwood[†]
University of North Carolina at Charlotte

How to begin to write of a friendship that has flourished for more than forty years? Friendship is one of the truly marvelous and sometimes mysterious realities of human experience. A friendship that has survived for so long in a profession devoted, supposedly, to the vocation of critical scrutiny concerning some of the most puzzling aspects of human community must have something very special about it. Before going into details, therefore, I want to risk beginning with what I think is the central defining quality of John Priest's and Dick Underwood's 40 year plus friendship. It has two distinct but inter-related aspects: a sense of humor and a sense of place-of-origins. These are so intimately connected in both our lives that it is hard to separate them. But let me quit being so serious and get on with the humor-side of the essence, to use a politically incorrect word in the current climate of philosophical discourse–namely, our senses of humor.

Humor and Origins

Our senses of humor were and are decidedly two-fold and this "two-folded-ness" has something to do with our common slants on life: mostly "both-and"; rarely "either-or." As far as humor is concerned, ours is a combination of good, old-fashioned slap-stick joke telling and seemingly sophisticated word play and puns. We would sometimes on social occasions make our wives very nervous because our slap-stick side would slide into vulgarity. This nervousness, of course, would encourage John, who was less constrained by conventional standards than I. But let me give two concrete examples of our humor at work–or play!

When we were graduate students together at Drew Theological Seminary in Madison N. J. in the early 1950's, we were both active in the Inter-Seminary Movement–an ecumenical movement with an annual spring conference at members' institutions. At these meetings, lectures and symposia on current theological issues would be presented both by faculty from the host institution and notable invited guest-speakers. Following the official session, the conferees would meet for conviviality and discussion–mostly conviviality. During one such conference at Lancaster Theological Seminary in Pennsylvania, John and I, with other seminary colleagues were at an after-program party; when the group grew tired of serious theological we talk began to tell jokes from our considerable repertoire. The other people in the party, sensing competition between John and me, egged us on. John would tell a joke and I would respond and he would come back with another,–"Dueling Banjoes" with jokes.

Now it should be noted here that John had, and still does, one of the most incredible memories I've ever encountered. So after we had swapped jokes for about an hour or so, I was completely out of my stock of jokes-stories. Sensing this, but knowing that I knew he could go on for another hour or so, John graciously announced that we wanted to change the genre from joke to epic poem to conclude the evening. He then gave a dramatic recital of "Casey at the Bat." This hilarious and impeccable performance ended the evening with humor as the victor.

At the other end of the spectrum from that slap-dash sort of variety show was our interest in puns and word-play. Such must be an occupational hazard for professional scholars–especially those in the fields of biblical studies and ancient languages, as in John's case; and in philosophy and theology in mine. In both cases ordinary words are taken out of everyday contexts and loaded with specialized meanings. An example that comes to mind is the word "substance," in ordinary conversation one speaks of a "person of substance" in the history of Aristotelian-Thomistic Philosophy, the technical "substance" means the "essential unity of being that stands-under or supports the realm of appearances."

When John returned to this country after a Fulbright Scholarship year of study at the University of Manchester in England, he told me the following story he had heard while there, perhaps the most beautiful example of the art of the pun I have ever encountered. The story as John told it goes as follows. After an evening at dinner and theater in London, four Oxford dons were walking back to their hotel. They were engaged in a complicated discussion of collective nouns– such as "pride of lions," "gaggle of geese," "school of fish" and so forth. When stopped by three ladies of the evening plying their services, being of both modest means and temperament the four scholars demurred and continued on their way. One though had the bright idea of seeing what collective noun they could come up with to describe the trio of ladies whose wiles they had just rebuffed. Their answers were as follows. One said, "I would describe them as a trey of tarts." Another said, "I would describe them as a fanfare of strumpets." The third don said, "I would refer to them as an essay of Trollope's." And the fourth said, "Gentlemen, very, very good. But would you not agree that we have just encountered a vulgar but moving passage of English pros?"

Some might well say that the series of puns just recounted is itself only a variation of the slap-stick humor alluded to earlier. That contention I will not argue. But my basic point is that John and I have continued this genre of word play throughout the years of our friendship.

The second aspect of our adult-life friendship has to do with our sense of location or place of origins. We are both Hoosiers. Even though John came from the deep south of Indiana near the Ohio River at Indiana's southern boundary and I came from the rich farmlands of the northeastern part of the state, we knew what "Indiana" meant. We both loved basketball which was to Hoosiers north and south what the Dodgers and Ebbets Field were to Brooklynites and we were both Methodists. Being Methodist was for a Hoosier of those mid-century days almost as strong a bond as basketball. The tradition, however, of Southern Indiana Methodism was more "Methodist Protestant" than "Methodist Episcopal." Though the two churches had been formally joined in the 1939 General Conference to create The Methodist Church, one of the differences between the two "strands" was the policy on cigarette and tobacco use. Those of us in the old "Episcopal" strand in the north could not use tobacco. Those in the south had a more liberal policy on use of tobacco. In those pre "health consciensness" days, I was a smoker, in violation of church orders. John, too, was a smoker. When we discovered that both of us shared the filthy habit, we took it as a sign of another bond, we were mavericks of a sort. If we had not discovered earlier that we were "mavericks" in far more important ways our friendship would not, of course, have endured.

I need to emphasize the Hoosier commonality, if not down-right communion. It may seem overly romantic or nostalgic, but to discover a fellow Hoosier in the early days of my seminary student days was an important grounding for me. Even though I had been born and lived the first six years of my life on the Kansas prairie, and had had an interlude of two years in Chicago, my entire life of growth into self-awareness had taken place in Indiana Methodism. To find someone like John Priest who had just returned from three years in India as apprentice missionary-teacher and to find that he was Hoosier and Methodist was very, very, very important for me. In addition, John was much more widely read than I was so I was always learning from him and was constantly impressed with his generosity in sharing his learning and insight. It is no exaggeration to say that John Priest was a pivotal figure in my early life at Drew, helping me in the process of re-evaluating my educational goals, especially exploring whether I could do work at the PhD level.

I have now dealt, perhaps at too great length with the double-sided aspects I see at the core of John's and my friendship. I now turn to a more narrative style to show how this friendship and my deep respect for and indebtedness to John developed.

I. The Madison-Drew Years: 1951-1958

The first social adventure I remember having with John and his wife Gloria, was when my wife, Joan, and I went with them to a D'Oyly Carte production in New York City of Gilbert and Sullivan's *Pirates of Penzance*. One of the advantages of being a student at Drew University in the fifties was proximity to the Big City. Whether by the Lakawanna railroad or by automobile in normal traffic, one could travel from the campus of Drew to Manhattan in less than an hour. Life in Madison was a nearly ideal combination of the Drew campus in the forest primeval and closeness to one of the great metropolitan centers of the world. The trip to the *Pirates* was arranged by Joan and Gloria who along with Joan had a mutual passion for Gilbert and Sullivan. For my part I knew only that there were some tunes in the Methodist Hymnal that had been composed by Sullivan, so the experience of *Pirates of Penzance* was for me a whole new world of pleasure. That memorable evening marked the beginning of the long friendship of the Priests, John and Gloria, and the Underwoods, Dick and Joan, Moreover, this event led to, in addition to other gala dinners and activities in the city (as budget would allow) the sharing of a beautiful old house in Madison.

John Priest's three years in India as an apprentice missionary-teacher after graduation from undergraduate college were part of what called the "I-3 Program"–the "India Three-year Program." His teaching duties as a member of the theological faculty included teaching Greek New Testament. Legend has it that even then John was an accomplished linguist and within only a short time after his arrival was teaching New Testament Greek in the native language of Urdu.

In any event, this stint in India qualified John as a candidate for renting a house owned by Marie Searing. Ms. Searing, a remarkable woman in her mid-seventies, had left her family home in Madison to live with her sister in North Bergen, N.J. Rather than sell the old house, she made arrangements with Drew University to rent it (at an unbelievably low rate) to missionaries who for one reason or another might be studying at Drew. In the year of his arrival at Drew, John Priest was the only one to qualify as a possible renter, so he and Gloria and their newly born boy-child, John Michael, moved in. During their second year at 24 Maple Avenue, just a few blocks from the campus of Drew, and after the Priests and Underwoods had shared several social occasions they invited the Underwoods, to become co-renters. Joan and I, married only for a year, jumped at the chance and joined John and Gloria and John Michael for an 18 month venture in communal living.

Up to now I have not stressed the common intellectual academic pursuits in which John and I were engaged. These were just sort-of "there" and because a "natural" dimension of our communal life. In addition to a sense of humor and place of origins, this "third something" the precondition of our being together as friends, was for want of a better phrase and one I will want to qualify, the "life of the mind." At that time both of us would have laughed at this phase for being too pretentious and unworthy of two Indiana farm boys who did not want to "put on airs" of any kind, especially intellectual. Moreover, by temperament and by design we were constantly challenging authority. Though we respected tradition, our respect was always tempered by a healthy dose of skepticism.

The qualities John and I shared at both intellectual and emotional levels were shared also by our spouses. Gloria and Joan were as engaged in the adventures of "intellectual" pursuits as John and I, albeit not defined in terms of academic degrees. Gloria's mind was the most mathematically intuitive and accomplished of the four of us. As in the case of most persons with this particular intellectual gift, though, it was not narrowly conceived or applied. Indeed, Gloria enrolled in a seminar offered by the new Dean of the Graduate School, Stanley Romaine Hopper, on the "Life and Thought of Blaise Pascal" the 17th century French mathematician- philosopher-genius. In fact, she and I took that seminar together while we were at 24 Maple Avenue. Furthermore, at that time she was a working mother, not only the young John Michael to attend (with help from the rest of us) but also being employed at a financial office in near-by Morristown.

Joan Underwood, who had majored in English literature in her undergraduate days and recalled all she read in almost as much detail as John, at this time took a course in Biblical Hebrew from one of John's teachers, Lawrence Toombs. Though we did not have children, Joan too was a working wife with a job in the office of one of the deans at Drew. In addition to Joan's expertise in English literature, she was reasonably versed in the history out of which the literature came. That fit well with one of John's interests in political history, thus we evidenced commonality of intellectual interests in our experiment in communal living before communes became one of the marks of the revolution of the sixties.

This time together had two aspects that forged a life-long friendship—on the one hand the sharing of family life and on the other hand the deepening articulation of our bonds as students in pursuit of degrees which would make it possible for us to become life-long members of the academic community. The fact that I will now concentrate on the "intellectual" side of this bonding should not make the living together seem only incidental.

John was never one to talk ideas for ideas sake alone. If ideas could not be somehow related to the earthiness and community of human existence he was not interested. He could play the abstract-intellectual game to perfection but his real engagement seemed always to be how the life of mind and spirit had to be incarnate. This trait I attribute to his love of the biblical traditions of communal-covenantal, incarnational and historical focus. This fundamental concern of John's, growing out of his commitment to biblical scholarship, made even more interesting our developing friendship. I myself had been a philosophy major in my undergraduate days and now in seminary and graduate school I was continuing my study of the philosophy of religion. So John and I represented in our scholarly and academic pursuits precisely the themes of the western Judaeo-Christian tradition that have been in tension, sometimes creatively though at other times destructively, since the origins of Christianity–the meaning and power of reason represented by Greek philosophy on the one hand and the significance of Biblical revelation on the other. In the history of Christianity this tension was most powerfully represented and summed up by the theologian Tertullian of the 2nd Century C.E. in his infamous question: "What has Athens to do with Jerusalem? What has the church to do with the academy?" In one way or another, every major theologian since then has had to grapple with that question. The problem with Tertullian's formulation of the question was that he made the two traditions mutually exclusive. The truly creative thinkers in the tradition, beginning with Augustine in the 5th century and consummated eight hundred years later, though with some different presuppositions, by Thomas Aquinas in the late middle ages–the most creative theologians redefined Tertullian's position. This redefined position looked upon faith and reason, or revelation and philosophy, as dynamically and dialectically related, not as two mutually exclusive dimensions.

In our academic disciplines John and I symbolized this split in the tradition, a false split we both thought. John's academic interests have illustrated dramatically his attempts to reject the Tertullianic hypothesis. As early as the late fifties, in his dissertation on certain aspects of the Dead Sea Scrolls, the wisdom literature and the inter-testamental materials and as recently as January 26, 1994 when he presented a public lecture at the University of North Carolina at Charlotte John has always maintained that the Hebrew tradition has a philosophical-humanistic dimension that cannot be gainsaid. I should add as another sign of our forty-year plus friendship that the lecture John gave at the University of North Carolina-Charlotte campus in 1994, entitled "Humanism and the Biblical Tradition," was an evening dedicated to my official retirement from UNCC and the Department of Religious Studies.

Thus as a scholar of Biblical languages and literature John Priest has been from the beginning of our friendship actively, even passionately, interested in the ways in which critical reason is essential to understanding Biblical revelation and tradition. At the same time, back in those early days of our friendship, I was beginning to be deeply interested in how story, myth, and symbol were essential to understanding the history of Greek philosophy–as well as essential to the living of a truly human life.

The time that John and I were studying and living together was a time of remarkable ferment in the arena of theology and philosophy. Our lives were intertwined both academically and existentially. While doing the supper dishes together at 24 Maple Avenue we would be engaged not only on the incidental task at hand but would wash and dry those dishes, carry out the garbage and sweep the kitchen floor to a whole range of intellectual, political, theological-cultural subjects ranging from the validity or invalidity of Rudolf Bultmann and "demythologizing" to Paul Tillich and his method of correlation. But it was not all intellectual. Sometime we would get into old hymn singing contests and sing the songs we had learned from our mothers' knees–singing at the top of our voices–much to the consternation of our wives who seemed to object just as much to the quality of our singing voices as to the theological content of the lyrics. John had just as good a memory for those songs as he did for jokes and stories. In fact, a few years later when we were colleagues at Hartford Seminary I would often hear John walking through the halls singing hymns like "Bringing in the Sheaves" and "Amazing Grace."

Another common passion John and I discovered was for Western movies; on many Saturday afternoons, when the Texaco broadcast of the Metropolitan Opera on the radio was not in season we would go to the Madison movie theater, along with high school and grade school children, to watch the great old western movie stars, from Gene Autry and Roy Rogers to John Wayne. We would get caught up in the story line and marvel at the moral, theological and psychological implications of the constant and never-ending battle between the good guys and the bad guys against the backdrop of that beautiful, wild landscape.

There were two other areas in which John and I discovered a common early interest: sports and politics. Being from Indiana it was no surprise to find that we loved basketball. One of the distinctive and perhaps unique features of high school basketball in Indiana is that there is no division of teams into categories of size of town and/or school. In the annual spring-time state tournaments, as anyone who has seen the movie, *Hoosiers*, knows, a team from the very smallest or rural village can end up playing a team from a large metropolitan area.

While we were living together in Madison as students I discovered that John also loved baseball and many times he would go to the Bronx or Brooklyn to see the Yankees and Dodgers games. Like all truly avid baseball fans, John had a passion for statistics of the game. And with his marvelous memory he could recall virtually every stat he had ever read. Further he could remember crucial plays from important games and from time to time would lapse into his sport-announcer-story-telling mode and regale his listeners with a play-by-play reconstruction of a crucial play in an important game.

In another contest area of a different sort, John also loved politics, both domestic and international. Our friendship was developing during the Eisenhower era of post World War II. This time was also during and after some of the most vicious and dreadful years of the McCarthy era of anti-communist hysteria. In this context and partly because of the Methodist church's reputation for liberal social action policies, John and I both reflected the wit and wisdom contained in the maxim that goes as follows: "If you are not a liberal when you are sixteen you have no heart. But if you are not a conservative when you're sixty you have no mind." Regarding the liberal part of this maxim I was more typical than John. His ideas in politics had been considerably influenced by his experience in India during that critical period right after the war. In the area of politics John had the capacity to see the validity of alternate views and could usually be counted on to attack sacred cows when they needed prodding.   The   recounting   of   these peripheral interests should not be interpreted as taking too lightly our academic pursuits. I don't think John ever made, in either secondary or graduate school a grade under "A" or "Honors." Even though our life together was sort of a continuing seminar of both academics and "life-studies," I think we took together only one formal class–a seminar in Luke-Acts conducted by the Dean of the Theological School, Clarence Tucker Craig. John had come to Drew expressly to study New Testament literature with Dean Craig who had arrived at Drew in 1948 from Yale Divinity School. In this seminar on the books of Luke and Acts, John was clearly the one in the class who knew what he was doing. Even though I had studied classical Greek for four years as an undergraduate I was, in this seminar, clearly in over my head. Sometimes when I was in the process of translating a passage, Dean Craig would say to John, "Mr. Priest, do you think you could give your friend a little help'?" This, cut to the quick because usually John had already given me more than a little help in preparing for the class.

One of the tragedies we at Drew had to undergo during that time was the sudden and unexpected death of Clarence Tucker Criag due to a brain tumor. John, particularly hard hit, had to decide whether to continue study at Drew or go elsewhere. He decided, with the encouragement of many, to stay and study Old Testament literature with Professor John Paterson, who had come to Drew from Scotland. One of Drew's truly great teachers, Professor Paterson, had that marvelous old-fashioned professorial persona that endeared him to all. Needless to say it was great to have a good old Scots-Presbyterian to temper the overwhelming Methodist piety of the Seminary. Dr. Paterson, along with Dr. Craig, recognized John's genius as a scholar and they got on famously at all levels.

During the holiday season of 1957 John, Gloria and John Michael did not go south for Christmas and New Year's either to her family home in Donaldsonville, Georgia or to John's parents' home outside Evansville, Indiana. Moreover, Joan and I also had no plans to go to our parents' homes in New York State and Indiana. So during this particular holiday season the Priests and the Underwoods were together in Madison, New Jersey. In order to mark this occasion properly, Joan and Gloria came up with the idea of having a holiday reception at 24 Maple Avenue the week between Christmas and New Year's.

The house at 24 Maple Avenue was a marvelous, old-fashioned place that when festooned with holiday decorations and greens looked like a Currier and Ives print come to life. Joan and Gloria had come from families and traditions which had taught them how to put on magnificent traditional parties. (John and I knew about non-traditional parties, but this one was the production of Joan and Gloria, with their husbands' eager cooperation.) Gloria was from the old south where the gracious arts of hospitality had been gently nurtured. Joan had been brought up in a family of northern Presbyterian clergy persons where entertainment at the manse was meticulously observed. In addition, both women were superb cooks and pastry chefs who had learned these arts at their mothers' instruction and example and their fathers' behest.

The party was organized as a late afternoon-early evening open house with lots of food and Methodist-permitted beverages. It was all a huge success. Even the President of the university and his wife made an appearance. They were an exceptionally gracious couple and at one point in the party he enhanced the occasion with a recitation of one of his favorite poems by Emily Dickinson. Along with two deans, several faculty also appeared; as well, of course, as many graduate students and spouses who stayed long after the "official" hours of the open house for less restrained partying and clean-up that lasted into the wee hours.

In a very real sense this event summed-up all the excellent qualities of common academic interest, egalitarian comradeship, intellectual pursuit, spiritual seeking and authentic self fulfillment that in themselves constitute true collegiality and friendship.

II. The Hartford Years: 1961-1969

Between the years 1957-58 and 1964 John and I saw each other infrequently but still kept in close touch. After his year of Fulbright study at Manchester University in England, John received his doctorate and took a position in the Department of Religion at Ohio Wesleyan University. I stayed at Drew to complete my Ph.D.

While I was still at Drew and John at Ohio Wesleyan, we saw each other two or three times. I visited him at Ohio Wesleyan and attended some of his classes. I remember being impressed with the excellence of his classroom presence–not surprising since I had watched him function as a teacher during our years at Drew. What really struck me was how easily he got along with the students both in and after class; he was genuinely liked and appreciated.

By some quirk of fate the chair of the Department of Religion at Ohio Wesleyan was Robert Montgomery, who had been one of my important teachers at DePauw University in Greencastle, Indiana. His academic field was Biblical literature and I had had much contact with him at DePauw both as a student in his classes and in some extra-curricular activities associated with the Methodist Student Movement. When we saw each other during my first visit to John and Gloria's, Dr. Montgomery was both happy and surprised. He was surprised to discover I was a Ph.D. candidate in philosophy of religion because I had not in any way, shape or form distinguished myself in his classes at DePauw. He was happy because he liked and respected John and seemed glad that we were friends. He was most enthusiastic about John Priest's contribution to Ohio Wesleyan not only as teacher and scholar but in his committee work. He told me that John had been appointed to key faculty committees at an unusually early stage in his tenure at Ohio Wesleyan. Although, I did not realize it at the time, this ability to function effectively in the salt-mines, so to speak, of academic politics would be exhibited so dramatically in later years as John got involved in academic administration in his years at Hartford Seminary as Dean of the Faculty, and at Florida State University, not only as chair of religious studies but also as director of the graduate program in humanities. John's true genius as politico-scholar-academic was shown most effectively a few years later during his pioneering work in helping to make the American Academy of Religion a really important national-scholarly--professional organization.

John and I resumed our close association as working colleagues on the fourth of July, 1964 when I became visiting instructor in philosophy of religion at Hartford Seminary Foundation where John had gone in 1961 from Ohio Wesleyan.

Two or three years after John joined the Hartford faculty, the faculty member who was the philosopher of religion got an invitation from the Ford Foundation to go to Thailand on a mission to help modernize the colleges in Thailand. According to the terms of the invitation, the appointment would be for two years at the end of which the philosopher of religion from Hartford Seminary would return to his regular position. So, Hartford Seminary was looking for someone to come on a visiting basis for two years. My name was introduced into the situation, only two years out of graduate school I had achieved nothing even remotely like a national reputation, however, I was invited to Hartford for an interview in March 1964 and as a result of that interview, I was invited to go to Hartford on a visiting basis for two years.

The resulting decision was incredibly difficult for me on many grounds. Suffice it to say that at that time Stephens College, which I had gone to from Drew in 1962, was a remarkably interesting institution, especially as a member institution of "The Union of Experimental Colleges and Universities" further, in 1964 the so-called "revolution of the sixties" was beginning to take shape and I wanted to be a part of that at the college level. My training academically and my inclination by temperament were to challenge establishment patterns of institutional authority and tradition. Why then in a time of looming cultural revolution should I take what looked like a retrograde step and return to what seemed like a dying mode of education–namely theological education?

In the midst of my agonizing I blush to say that I sent John a telegram in Latin quoting Tertullian's previously mentioned query, "What has Athens to do with Jerusalem, what has the academy to do with the church, what has reason to do with faith?" In sending that telegram to John I knew I was appealing to an anti-Tertullian position that John shared. But I knew also that John had a passion for creative dialogue between faith and reason.

John did me the kindness of never responding formally to my telegram. What he did do was point out that the move to Hartford would be only for two years and that in the end, along with the granting to me by Stephens College of a leave of absence to protect my position at the college, persuaded me to say yes to the offer from the seminary. What I did not know at the time, of course, was that the two years "visiting" appointment would turn into an eleven year stay until I moved from Hartford Seminary to the University of North Carolina at Charlotte to become chair of the department of religious studies where I remained until my retirement in 1994. The following vignettes of Hartford Seminary convey the pleasures and some of the pains of being a close friend to a marvelously complex and talented person such as John Priest during some of the most convulsive years both our culture as a whole and the arena of higher education have gone through.

Our families' friendship resumed that 4th of July in 1964 just as if we had never been apart. The Priests' son, John Michael, from the Madison days at 24 Maple Avenue, was no longer an only child since Andrew had been born in Delaware, Ohio. The Underwood family now contained two children: Margaret Anne, was born in November, 1961, before her father, Dick, received his Ph.D. in June of 1962, at Drew; and Douglas Bare, born in August, 1963, at Columbia, Missouri while his father was on the faculty of Stephens College.

In the context of family life which was so important to all of us, one of the most intense of times together was around the circumstances of the birth of John and Gloria's third son, Stephen in Hartford. It had been a hard pregnancy for Gloria. When the time for birth came some complications developed, so severe as to be life-threatening to both mother and child. Gloria had been in the hospital several days and things were getting worse. On the third or fourth night I received a call from John asking if I would meet with him at an all-night grill near the hospital. John and I talked, when we met at about 11:30 p.m., our talking together was itself a form of meditation and prayer. Finally, after four or five hours, John said he was going back to the hospital to wait there, assuring me he would call me and Joan at home whenever there was something to report. When I got to my house, about a 20 minute drive from the hospital, Joan greeted me at the door. I could tell by her smile that she had heard some good word from John who had already called to report that the crisis had passed and normal labor pains had begun. And sure enough, in another four or five hours the youngest boy-child of the Priest family was alive, kicking and screaming and eating and the mother was doing just fine. The ordeal was over, thank the good Lord God.

John and I soon settled into a new version of the conversational closeness we had established at Drew. But now, of course, we were colleagues as faculty members not simply as students. I say "not simply as students" because we both realized that a very important part of teaching is the continuing activity of learning and that aspect of our professional collegiality continued to be as strong as ever, if not stronger in some ways. John and I were the only faculty at that time who had had experience teaching at the undergraduate level. He and I were in some ways better able to be confronted with the areas of dissent that began to challenge the orthodoxies of theological curricula, challenges represented in the attitudes of students who came to the seminary. John was always sensitive, first as one of the faculty leaders in the movement toward reform and later as Dean of the faculty that the seminary was a unique locus of the meeting point of clashing energies–energies of the establishment that had to slow the demands for change and maintain some continuity of authority and tradition from generation to generation and the energies of new student attitudes bursting with demands for change in the culture at-large.

All of the unrest, conflicts, struggles, victories and defeats of the "sixties" were somehow involved in this point of basic conflict or tension–that of the clash between traditional authority and burgeoning new structures of awareness. The 60's and 70's contained either explicitly or implicity the seed of every "new" movement or protest we look back upon now in the mid-nineties as part of, for better or worse, "new" modes of awareness: gay and lesbian rights, the women's movement, the civil rights movement organized around black liberation, challenge to military-industrial excesses, the ecological movement, and other contemporary variations on those themes. Every single one of these began to be manifest during the time John and I were together at Hartford.

If he and I had any difference of opinion on the magnitude of this revolutionary decade of the sixties it was differences of degree rather than of substance. With his own passion for ancient texts and cultures, John had much more concern for historical dynamics than did I. My own commitment to cultural change has sometimes been too uncritical and John has from the beginning always represented that wise sentiment preserved in the old caricature: "If it's new it's not good and if it's good it's not new." But for both of us there was always a creative dialogue between the "old" and the "new."

Ironically perhaps, John recognized the lay of the land so to speak before I did. With all his predilection toward the "old" represented by theological institutions in general and Hartford Seminary in particular, in 1969-70 he left for Florida State University - a secular institution that in many ways provided him with greater opportunity to seek the "old" than did the Seminary curriculum in the midst of radical change. So John was asked at FSU to combine the classics and modern texts in his classroom and research interest that were never available in a theological institution such as Hartford, convulsed in the throes of a constant, narcissistic reexamination of its role. Whereas I, the allegedly creative, anti-historical modernist type kept on holding to the illusory dreams that the ancient visions and text both theological and philosophical could be rescued and re-defined in a re-designed "theological" curriculum. How far John would concur in what I have said about his participation in these Hartford years I cannot say; however, the following additional vignettes describe John's style in pedagogical and administrative as well as personal terms.

Shortly after my arrival at Hartford, John and I began to meet at a diner called the Yankee Flyer. This diner was already a special place for John and was about halfway between his house in Newington, some eight or ten miles from the Seminary campus, and our home in Hartford on the very edge of the campus. Being a rurally-oriented midwesterner I never encountered the institution of the diner until I moved from Indiana to the east in New Jersey. In Madison there had been a diner named The Rose City where John and I and other graduate students would congregate from time to time to discuss the urgent matters of the day–or century, or millennium! Now here were John and I reunited in Hartford and there was another diner with the wonderfully romantic name of Yankee Flyer. When we wanted to get away where we could eat and talk unobserved by our colleagues at the Seminary, we would meet at the Yankee Flyer. Our mid-morning brunch there on Saturdays came to be something of an institution. Sometimes we would just read the sports page of the *New York Times* or exchange jokes. No topic was out of bounds, except for policy and personnel matters when he was dean. It was not an agreement we reached by way of any specific decision, for never once during all those years of close friendship and discussion do I recall our discussing a specific policy or upcoming vote in a faculty meeting or any of our colleagues. It is as if John and I both knew intuitively that any attempt to politicize our friendship would be harmful. As a matter of fact one thing that makes John Priest stand out as someone special in the halls of academe is his refusal to engage in that activity so prevalent in academic politics: gossip. If there was anything relevant to say about a professional colleague at the personal level John would say it in a very unelaborated way and just let it stand. This trait, I think, stood him in very good stead during his years at Hartford, riven as the institution was by different constituencies suspicious of one another.

By "different constituencies" I mean, of course, those represented by faculty, students, administration, trustees–and the general public represented by the various churches in the area. Within the faculty itself, though, there was deep division: the so-called old guard whose turf was the traditional disciplines and the young turks who had been brought in over a relatively short period of time. While John was at Hartford both as faculty member and Dean, new and young faculty in several key fields had been brought in: John himself in Hebrew scriptures, and in the philosophy of religion, sociology and ethics, New Testament, psychology of religion, American church history–over just a four to six year period. By and large the old guard and the young turks got along in a fairly civil manner but every once in a while the tensions simmering just beneath the surface would erupt into open hostility. At those times John would demonstrate a remarkable capacity for amelioration, a capacity rooted not only in John's sense of humor but also in his commitment to interdisciplinary programs of study. In Drew days even though his graduate field was in Old Testament, he took courses outside that area. Indeed, he considered his own field as interdisciplinary; Appropos of an especially excellent study by John of a contemporary text in a graduate seminar by Dean Hopper. John explained, "What you in religion and culture don't realize is that Biblical studies by its very nature is inter-disciplinary: you must know the language and culture out of which the text comes, you must know something of the social structures and economic dynamics of the society. "Then he paused and said, "You must also be aware of the biases you yourself, as a member of your own society, bring to the text." When I watched John confront conflicting situations of academic disciplines in competition, I knew he was reading the immediate situation as a "text" requiring, to use the technical shorthand term, "hermeneutical awareness" as well as his highly developed sense of humor.

There were numerous meetings in which motions concerning development of a revised curriculum would be discussed. One of John's "styles" was to bring issues to a vote once debate had sufficiently clarified matters. This procedure may seem to the reader all obvious and commonplace but under previous leadership the strategy had been to avoid vote because voting would divide the faculty into "yea" and "nay." The technique had been to reach consensus as if faculty discussion were like a Quaker meeting waiting for the Holy Spirit to descend and do its work of transformation–a strategy inclined to make faculty meetings interminable. John from the beginning had made it quite clear that he thought the action of voting was a more acceptable procedure.

At a particular meeting one of the most revered, by young and old alike, of the "old guard" was taking especial umbrage at a change in curricular structure being sought and pushed by the young turks. This person's objectioning was beginning to take a sort of nasty personal turn in which he was charging younger persons of the faculty with thinking he was old - and out of date. An anthropologist of German origin, as he was talking the pitch of his voice went higher and higher. At the same time John began to slouch lower and lower on his chair with his elbows on the conference table around which we were all seated, his head in his hands, looking down at the table. This characteristic pose indicated either that he was bored to death or that he was listening with rapt intensity. The anthropologically-oriented faculty member finally raised his pitch, not the volume, to its highest level and charged supporters of the motion with "pedagogical trespassing" and cited an obscure passage from the Deuteronomic law which forbade a farmer to plow his neighbor's land. At this point, without raising his head but still maintaining his concentration on the table, John's voice said, "Professor," and then began to speak in the guttural cadences of German and Hebrew, or perhaps Yiddish. As the objecting professor sat down and as John went on for just about a minute or so, the old professor's face began to broaden into a smile. Throughout John's head was still in his hands and his gaze still fixed on the table in front of him. Then, abruptly, he stopped talking, lifted his head, looked around the table and with a huge grin on his face said, "For those of you who do not understand German or Yiddish, I just told the professor that though he had the correct verse from Deuteronomy his translation was lacking. The verse in question does indeed warn against plowing land without permission but it does so by talking about using the neighbor's ass to do that plowing. I then said to the professor that all the motion under discussion sought to do was to use his ass to pull the

pedagogical plow, and that we all needed his instruction on how best to do that."
The meeting exploded in laughter, the vote was taken and we moved on to other
business. In one fell swoop John had broken the deadlock on the vote, advanced
the curricular reform being sought by the young turks and perhaps most
importantly preserved the dignity of a distinguished elder faculty member–and,
incidentally while doing that maintaining the support of the other faculty part of
the old guard.

These qualities of interdisciplinary interests were also at work constantly in
his teaching. Not surprisingly when Archibald Macleish's *J.B.* became public, John
was already using it in some of his classes and was invited to speak on the work
in comparison with its prototypical Book of Job in many churches throughout the
area. This was of special interest to me personally since many times throughout our
friendship the question of suffering in human existence had been not just a topic
of intellectual conversation but of existential concern. John's personal life had not
been free, naturally, of personal trials and tribulation, and in this area, as in so
many others, he found cliches obnoxious and shallow, no matter how inevitable.
I think what I am trying to convey here is that interdisciplinary concerns were
never a gimmick with John. He just seemed always to have a breadth of intellectual
and moral concern that was pushing the edge of ordinary academic-scholarly
boundaries. Two quick examples show this capacity.

One thing he did to set an example of inter-disciplinary concern was
establish a course on "Philosophy East and West" which he and I conducted. In all
of our years together this was the first time we ever shared the teaching of a course.
As usual he surprised me by his wide reading in both Eastern and Western sources.
One aspect of the course I remember most vividly was the discussion on
"suffering" in Buddhist teaching as compared with how suffering was interpreted
in the Stoic philosophy of the Hellenistic era and Hebrew texts such as Job and
Koheleth. One of the sharp differences John and I have had throughout our
friendship has been at the point of emphasis on commonality and unity. I have
been more of a Platonist in this regard and have sought *unity* underneath the
obvious differences between various times and places. John, on the other hand, has
always appreciated the historical *differences*. To use a conventional distinction,
that has both the advantages *and* shortcoming of most generalizations, John was
the Aristotelian while I was the Platonist. In the case of looking at the question of
human suffering at the existential level, though, John in this course, helped me see
that the Platonic-Aristotelian distinction was only a secondary verbal-intellectual
distinction. The unique quality of suffering was, he would say when rehearsing the
"Four Passing Sights" of Buddhist legend, its concrete character or quality. The
"real" commonality that bound together such seemingly disparate characters as the
Biblical Job on the one hand and the young prince Gautama in search of liberation
on the other hand was their common involvement in life-as-body. Doctrinal
answers to the questions of pain and suffering might be different but they were
rooted in a common condition–a condition that led to different cultural

symbol-systems whose uniqueness the historian is obliged to respect. Our very differences in temperament and academic methodology joined together to make for fruitful dialogue in our course on "Philosophy East and West."

His most fruitful evidence of inter-disciplinary concern was his agreement as Dean at Hartford to provide funds for a lecture series on Myth and Dream and Religion. I had conceived of the series which included invitations to such notables as Joseph Campbell and Alan Watts. The invited speakers included also Dean Stanley Hopper and David Miller from our days together at Drew, along with three people from the Hartford faculty, including John, who presented a lecture, "Dream in Old Testament Literature." John took an intellectual-academic risk in that venture.

When the series moved to New York City and was presented as a series under the sponsorship of the Society for the Arts, Religion and Culture, the list of lecturers expanded to include Norman O. Brown, Owen Barfield, Amos Wilder and Ira Progoff. Eventually published under the editorship of Joseph Campbell, the fruit of the series is still in print.

Newington was not only the town in which the Priests made their home while John was on the faculty at Hartford Seminary. It was also the place where John made a foray into local politics by running for and being elected to two terms as town committeeman (as the office was referred to in those gender-restricted days). One of my most memorable sights of John was watching him at a political rally at the Newington Polish-American Club during one of his runs for office on the Democrat ticket. John has always had the Irish gift of gab and when he wanted to could out talk anyone and out-think them on any issue in public debate. At this particular rally at the Polish-American Club all the speeches had been made and it was time for dancing to the music of a local band. As the evening wore on I think John danced with every woman voter in the hall. When it was about time for the band to pack up and go the band leader announced over the loudspeaker that the evening's finale would consist of a special treat: Committeeman Priest had agreed to do a solo dance of a polka as his tribute to the voters of Newington. There was much applause and John went to the center of the dance floor, a spotlight was turned on him, the music of the band began and John Priest did a beautifully athletic version of a Polish polka in solo. It was an amazing performance at the end of which, what began as vigorous applause for him now ended as an ovation by all those standing in a circle watching. When the election returns were announced in about two weeks, John once again was victorious over his opponent by an almost two-to-one margin.

There were other ways John served the public interest of the greater Hartford area and enhanced the reputation of Hartford Seminary. For years John had been a devoted reader and fan of Mark Twain who had built and lived in a beautiful Victorian house in Hartford, on Farmington Avenue just a few blocks from the Seminary. There was an active Mark Twain Society in the area and John was a speaker at many of their meetings. He was always fascinated by Twain's character as an author: that peculiar combination of qualities which made him prominent as a humorist in American letters *and* the "dark side" of the humorist's persona as represented in such books as *The Mysterious Stranger.* In this context of holding together of opposites I think it not irrelevant to observe that in virtually every endeavor John found himself most attracted to those which combined in a perhaps uncanny degree both aspects: the comic absurd and the tragic absurd. Unlike virtually anyone else I have known, John had this deeply rooted antagonism to the superficiality of easy answers to anything. Nothing could inspire his ire as much as trivialization of the painful contradictions of life with the attempted facade of easy answers.

There is one other aspect of John's career that transcends his service at particular institutions such as Ohio Wesleyan, Hartford Seminary and Florida State. His work at those institutions in and of itself has been noteworthy, especially covering the broad spectrum of institutions of higher learning from small, denominational, private college and seminary to the large, secular "mega-university." His responsibilities at each of these has ranged from undergraduate to graduate teaching and administration at the highest academic levels. While doing all of this–and fulfilling visiting appointments at such graduate institutions as Yale, Union in New York City, and Princeton–John also compiled an impressive list of publication in his special area of Biblical studies. Because of these achievements he does indeed deserve the recognition demonstrated by the Festschrift volume in which my "memoir" appears. Beyond all of this there is, however, one other accomplishment of John's that should be emphasized. I refer to his yeoman service on behalf of helping to bring into being the American Academy of Religion.

There were others, of course, but without John's tireless work in the early years between 1963 and 1973, it is no exaggeration to say that his efforts to establish the American Academy of Religion as the professional organization of teachers and scholars in all fields and disciplines relating to religious studies were absolutely essential. At one point John's wife, Gloria, became an essential adjunct to the organization by serving as Treasurer after the move to Florida State. Building on her experience and knowledge of financial complexity, Gloria instituted procedures of accounting and financial responsibility that are in effect, I believe, to this day.

John's service to the Academy of Religion during those formative years was an example of that combination of intellectual acumen, ability to articulate in public forum, dedication to inter-disciplinary concerns and sheer political savvy that John showed in all of his other activities. Anyone who was around national meetings of AAR in the early years marvels at its growth. There are now regional meetings which count greater numbers of registrations than national meetings in the early days. Of course, this phenomenal growth has brought its own kind of problems and it seems to me that current leadership in the Academy is doing a fine job of meeting those challenges. I am just pleased to have been close to John Priest during those times thirty years ago when he was present at the creation, so to speak, and helped to chart a course that turned into a professional organization which has survived and flourished so spectacularly.

In conclusion, what more can I say regarding my friendship with John during five decades from the 1950's to the 1990's. Soren Kierkegaard was one of the theological-philosophical psychological giants of the 19th century being rediscovered during those years when John and I were in process of forging our friendship. One of S.K.'s more radical statements that generated all kinds of excitement and some new understandings of the human condition was: "Truth is subjectivity."

Well, John Priest, mustering all of the subjectivity I can, I say, "I salute you. May your tribe increase. Oh yes, and thank you for helping me to understand what friendship is."

"We Pay No Heed to Heavenly Voices": The "End of Prophecy" and the Formation of the Canon

Joseph Blenkinsopp
University of Notre Dame

I

Since I shall be dealing in this paper exclusively with the Hebrew-Aramaic Bible, it will be well to note at the outset that the term "canon" originated in a Christian environment. With reference to a catalogue of biblical books, the word shows up no earlier than the fourth century, the earliest references occurring, as far as I have been able to determine, in the *Decrees of the Synod of Nicaea* and the *Festal Letter* of Athanasius, the former around 350, the latter seventeen years later. While lists of biblical books were in circulation in Christian circles from the second century,[1] no comparable compilation is attested in Jewish sources prior to the familiar passage in the Babylonian Talmud (b.B.Bat. 14b-15a) that lists titles and authors. By now everyone knows that the conventional view about the role of the "men of the Great Assembly" (*'anše kenesset hagg^{e}dôlâ*) and the "Council of Yavneh/Jamnia" in establishing the canon is anachronistic and misleading. The process eventuating in the biblical canons acknowledged today (Jewish, Protestant, Catholic, Eastern Orthodox, etc.) was long and complicated and can be reconstructed only tentatively. Rather than go over this well-worn ground again, I propose instead that we reflect on some implications of this matter

---

[1] One of the earliest is the list in the Didache MS published by Bryennios, on which see J. P. Audet, "A Hebrew-Aramaic List of Books of the Old Testament in Greek Transcription," *JTS* n.s. 1 (1950) 136.

of canonicity that are relatively underdeveloped in current scholarship. These reflections are offered as a small tribute to John Priest one of whose many interests is this issue of "the end of prophecy".

The familiar passage in Josephus' *Against Apion* (1:37-41) will serve us as a useful point of departure. In Henry St. John Thackeray's translation it runs as follows:

It therefore naturally, or rather necessarily, follows:

> (seeing that with us it is not open to everybody to write the records, and that there is no discrepancy in what is written; seeing that, on the contrary, the prophets alone had this privilege, obtaining their knowledge of the most remote and ancient history through the inspiration which they owed to God, and committed to writing a clear account of the events of their own time just as they occurred) – it follows, I say, that we do not possess myriads of inconsistent books, conflicting with each other. Our books, those which are justly accredited, are but two and twenty, and contain the record of all time.
>
> Of these, five are the books of Moses, comprising the laws and the traditional history from the birth of man down to the death of the lawgiver. This period falls only a little short of three thousand years. From the death of Moses until Artaxerxes, who succeeded Xerxes as king of Persia, the prophets subsequent to Moses wrote the history of the events of their own times in thirteen books. The remaining four books contain hymns to God and precepts for the conduct of human life.
>
> From Artaxerxes to our own time the complete history has been written, but has not been deemed worthy of equal credit with the earlier records, because of the failure of the exact succession of the prophets.

Here we have something of a list, though no book is actually named. There are twenty-two books; no more, no less. The first five are attributed to Moses and cover the period from creation to the author's death. (b. B. Bat. 15a will avoid an obvious problem by attributed the account of Moses' death in Deuteronomy 34 to Joshua). The next thirteen are of prophetic authorship and comprise a history from Moses' death to Artaxerxes, presumably Artaxerxes I nicknamed Long Hand (465-424 BCE). The final four contain liturgical and didactic-moralistic material. What sets all of these books apart is prophetic authorship; and what makes the difference between the "myriads of inconsistent books" of the Greeks and the strictly limited number of duly accredited (*dikaios pepisteumena*) compositions of the Jews is the requirement among the latter that only prophets may compile official records since they alone enjoy the privilege of divine inspiration (*epipnoia*).[2]

All twenty-two books are therefore inspired and prophetic, but the corpus is presented as essentially a historical record, one which includes the giving of the law. Since the last four, the "hymns and precepts", cannot be other than Psalms, Proverbs, Ecclesiastes and the Canticle, the remaining hagiographa (Ruth, Chronicles, Ezra-Nehemiah, Esther, Job and Daniel) must be subsumed under the rubric of history. We note further that the composition of fully inspired and

---

[2] Josephus notes elsewhere that the prophet has direct contact with the deity (*Ant.* 8:327) and is possessed by God in a way transcending reason (*Ant.* 6:223).

accredited writings is limited to the historical epoch that ends with the reign of Artaxerxes in the fifth century BCE. To a fixed number of canonical books, therefore, there corresponds a canonical epoch, one which is brought to a close by the failure of the prophetic succession (*diadoche*).

It is fairly clear that Josephus' presentation of the literary patrimony of the Jews is polemical and tendentious. One of his principal aims in writing the treatise was to refute Apion and others who had criticized his own historical writing and questioned his arguments for the great antiquity of the Jewish people. This led him to contrast the records of his own people with those of the Greeks, which he described as self-contradictory, often mendacious, and vitiated by their failure to keep *public* records (*demosia grammata*, 1:21). But it is obvious that his contrast between the myriads of Greek books produced without quality control and the strictly limited number of Jewish compositions is not only unfair but absurd; for he is contrasting the entire corpus of Greek literature with a small selection from the literary output of the Jews. It would have made better sense to compare the Homeric poems with the Jewish texts he catalogues - both incidentally composed of twenty-two items - with respect to their canonical status and function, but this would not have served his purpose.[3]

The cutting off of the prophetic succession in the reign of Artaxerxes, first of that name, can be explained by referring to Josephus' chronology of the biblical period in the *Antiquities*. For Josephus, Artaxerxes is the Ahasuerus (Asueros) of Esther 1:1 and *passim*. The story recorded in this book, which Josephus retells at inordinate length as a piece of historiography contemporary with the events recorded in it (*Ant.* 11:184-296), concludes the biblical part of his narrative. This suggests that the topos of the end of prophecy is a construct derived from the prior acceptance of certain books as scriptural or canonical. Later Jewish tradition will justify the inclusion of Esther in the canonical collection either by elevating the heroine to prophetic status (*S. 'Olam Rab.* 21) or by declaring Mordechai to be the author of the book and identifying him with the prophet Malachi (b. Meg 15a). Neither of these options occurred to Josephus, though they would have been consonant with the position he adopts in *Against Apion*. From this point on, at any rate, he refrains from using the term *prophetes* of any individual who otherwise might have seemed to merit it, though he does not hesitate to brand contemporary failed messiahs as *pseudoprophetai*. And when speaking of his own prophetic gifts, opportunely discovered or activated as he awaited capture and possible execution in the cave at Jotapata, he is careful to note that they derived from his priestly status and descent, exegetical skill, and expertise in dream interpretation (*Wars* 3:351-4). While, therefore, remaining faithful to his announced views on the prophetic tradition, he managed to insinuate his own qualifications as

---

[3]See the remarks of J. Barr, *Holy Scripture: Canon, Authority, Criticism* (Philadelphia: Westminster Press, 1983) 58.

continuator of that tradition. He refrains, nevertheless, from calling himself a *prophetes*.[4]

II

The idea that prophecy ended at a specific point in the past was not a product of the fertile brain of Josephus; it is alluded to on numerous occasions in attributions to Tannaitic and Amoraic sages. Thus, R. Abba states that "after the last prophets Haggai, Zechariah and Malachi had died, the Holy Spirit departed from Israel but they still availed themselves of the *bat qôl*" (b. Yoma 9b; also t. Sota 13:2 and b. Sanh. 11a). Here and in similar contexts the "Holy Spirit" (*rûah haqqodeš*) is identical with the "spirit of prophecy" (*rûah hannᵉbû'â*), and the *bat qôl* (heavenly voice; literally, echo) is the standard surrogate for prophetic mediation now no longer available.[5] Periodizing by reference to the death of the last prophet makes a reasonably good fit with the reign of Artaxerxes as terminus, especially in view of the drastic telescoping of the two centuries of Persian rule in later Jewish historiography.[6] It was evidently established at an early date that Haggai, Zechariah, and Malachi stood at the end of the prophetic series (*sôp nᵉbî'îm*, b. B. Bat. 14b).

An alternative view placed the terminus at the destruction of the First Temple when, as Abdimi of Haifa noted, prophecy was taken from the prophets and given to the sages (b. B. Bat. 12a). This opinion recalls the topos of the five things present in the First and absent from the Second Temple. Though there are slightly different versions of the list, they all include the Holy Spirit (b. Yoma 21b; b. Sota 48a). It resulted that, in the post-prophetic dispensation, not even the holiest and most learned, such as R. Akiba, could claim inspiration by the Holy Spirit, and not even the most charismatic, such as R. Hanina ben Dosa, could claim to be a prophet.[7] Inspiration and guidance for living were not to be a matter of miracle-working, divine voices, and oracular utterances, but were entrusted exclusively to the sages and their teaching–a point made famously in the dispute

[4]See my "Prophecy and Priesthood in Josephus," *JJS* 25 (1974) 240-1. Restriction of the term *prophetes* to biblical prophets in Josephus is contested by David Aune, "The use of PROPHETES in Josephus," *JBL* 101 (1982) 419-21, but his objections do not seem to me to be decisive. Cleodemus, author of a *History of the Jews*, is called *prophetes* (*Ant.* 1:240), but the appellation occurs in a quotation from Alexander Polyhistor. Josephus says that John Hyrcanus combined in his person the supreme political office, the high priesthood, and prophecy, but the designation *prophetes* is not used of him, and it is clear from what immediately follows that Josephus is speaking of a very specialized faculty, that of prediction by virtue of the high priestly office (*Ant.* 13:299-300; *Wars* 1:68-69). Also, he does not regard the Seventy as on a par with inspired biblical authors (*Ant.* 12:103-5).

[5]P. Schäfer, "Die Termini 'Heiliger Geist' und 'Geist der Prophetie' in den Targumim und das Verhältnis der Targumim zu einander," *VT* 20 (1970) 304-14.

[6]Due to failure to distinguish clearly between the two rulers named Darius, three Artaxerxes, and two Xerxes; see, for example, S. 'Olam R. 30 which shrinks the Persian period to thirty years.

[7]On Hanina and his refusal of the title "prophet" see G. Vermes, "Hanina ben Dosa: A Controversial Galilean Saint from the First Century of the Christian Era," *JJS* 23 (1972) 28-50; 29 (1973) 51-64.

about the Oven of Akhnai from which the title of this paper is taken (b. B. Mes 57b).

Let us note, in passing, that the *theologoumenon* of the end of prophecy would also have served to counter the Christian claim to have inherited the prophetic mantle from Judaism, a claim put forward by Justin in the second century among others. We do not know who the third century Amora R. Johanan had in mind in enunciating the dictum that, since the destruction of the temple, prophecy had been taken from the prophets and given to fools and children (b. B. Bat. 12a). It could have been applied to Christians *inter alios*, and it is curiously reminiscent of the so-called Johannine logion (Matt 11:25) in which revelation is vouchsafed not to the wise but to babes. At any rate, the idea that prophecy ended at a specific point in the past has roots older than either the rabbis or Christianity. The author of 1 Maccabees informs us that at the rededication of the temple (164 BCE) the priests dismantled the desecrated altar and stored the stones until there should come a prophet to tell them what to do with them (1 Macc 4:46). Then, some years later, during the temporary triumph of the Syrian general Bacchides, we hear that there was such distress in Israel as had not been since the time prophets ceased to appear among them (9:27), a point also emphasized by Josephus (*Ant.* 13:5). Later still, Simon was appointed military commander and high priest until such time as a trustworthy prophet should arise, which of course implies that none was available at that time (14:41). The lament for the absence of prophecy in the Prayer of Azariah (Dan 3:38, LXX) confirms the idea of a kind of mediation that was available in the past, will be again in the latter days, but is currently absent.

It may be objected at this point that laments for the absence of prophetic guidance are characteristic of periods marked by crisis, disorientation, and anomie. The author of Lamentations, for example, grieves that after the sack of Jerusalem prophets obtain no vision from Yahweh (Lam 2:9). Psalm 74, of uncertain date, voices a similar complaint. This may be conceded, but it seems fairly clear that the statements in 1 Maccabees reviewed a moment ago envisage something more than a temporary loss of prophetic mediation. On the contrary, they convey the impression of being programmatic, of a conviction about a qualitative difference between past and the present. 1 Macc 9:27 in particular speaks of a precise point in time when prophets ceased to appear in Israel (*aph'hes hemeras ouk ophthe prophetes autois*).[8]

By now we may be beginning to suspect that this restriction of prophecy to an epoch in the past is an ideological construct designed to sustain the worldview and hegemonic position of a distinctive social class. In any group in which specifically religious legitimation is considered essential, control of the

---

[8]This seems to be conceded by J. Barton, *Oracles of God: Perceptions of Ancient Prophecy in Israel after the Exile* (New York & Oxford: Oxford University Press, 1986) 107-8, who doubts that these texts refer to an eschatological prophet.

"redemptive media," and therefore of the process of mediation, translates very readily into social control. It is characteristic of prophets to claim authorization to speak and to be heard outside of officially sanctioned channels; hence the relegation of prophecy to the past would, if successful, remove a powerful irritant for those whose authority rested on a more traditional basis, and especially on a written law, the right to interpret which they restricted to themselves.

As a matter of fact as opposed to theory, however, prophetic figures and prophetic phenomena continued to be attested in Israel and early Judaism after the point at which, according to the requirements of the thesis, prophecy should have passed from the scene. Some of the older biblical commentators used to speak of prophecy having "dried up" after the Babylonian exile,[9] but they omitted to explain why it "dried up" then rather at some other time. The "end of prophecy" thesis cannot, therefore, be explained simply as reflecting what actually happened to prophecy, but it is nevertheless itself a historical datum calling for an explanation in the context of political, social and religious changes in the later period of Israel's history. To grasp these changes will, I believe, bring us closer to understanding how the idea of canonical texts emerged within the biblical period itself.

III

We begin with Deuteronomy since, as Julius Wellhausen put it, "the connecting link between old and new, between Israel and Judaism, is everywhere Deuteronomy."[10]   Even on a fairly superficial reading, this book reveals indications of being a canonical document. It contains a strict injunction against adding to it or subtracting from it (4:2; 12:32); the ruler must have an official copy by him and be governed by the law which it contains (17:18-20); it is to be deposited in the sanctuary and read from publicly on certain stated occasions (31:10-13,26), a ruling which seems to have been followed (2 Kgs 23:1-3; Neh 7:73-9:5; 13:1-3). It is therefore pre-eminently a public and official document. Deuteronomy is also the first biblical text to speak of "the Torah" or "the book of the Torah" as a single but complex entity, and it is presented as a patrimony to the people, a last will and testament, in the lawgiver's own words. Its intent is to provide a comprehensive and binding blueprint for the commonwealth that is to be established after settlement (or resettlement) in the land. It defines, *inter alia*, the scope and function of public offices (monarch, judges, priests, prophets), the operation of the cult and the judicial system, and qualifications for membership and suffrage in the community.

---

[9]E.g. "The inward flame which had inspired the [prophetic] movement until now is growing dim, and may soon be extinguished" (A. Lods, *The Prophets and the Rise of Judaism* [London: Kegan Paul, Trench, Trubner, 1937] 205).

[10]J. Wellhausen, *Prolegomena to the History of Israel* (Edinburgh: A. & C. Black, 1885; reprinted Atlanta: Scholars Press, 1994) 362.

What, then, does Deuteronomy have to say about prophecy? By speaking of it in the section of the law dealing with the organs of statecraft (16:18-18:22), it betrays a concerfn to bring it within the institutional grid of the ideal commonwealth (18:15-22).[11] In keeping with the nationalistic and ethnocentric character of the book, prophecy is understood to be a uniquely Israelite phenomenon, in contrast to such foreign "abominations" as divination and necromancy (18:9-14). More to our purpose, it is redefined as "Mosaic," that is, patterned on the ministry of Moses, understood as the fountainhead of prophecy in Israel. The principal function of the prophet, therefore, is to proclaim the law and warn against the consequences of non-observance; and the same function is illustrated in the Deuteronomistic History (hereafter Dtr) (e.g. 2 Kgs 17:13). Where Deuteronomy speaks of other aspects of prophecy, especially predicting the future, the tone is unmistakeably deterrent. Unauthorized prophets and, *a fortiori*, those who speak in the name of deities other than Yahweh, are subject to the death penalty (13:1-5; 18:20). Prophets are bracketed with dreamers (13:1), and those whose predictions turn out to be wrong automatically lose their prophetic credentials (18:21-22).

Whatever conclusion is reached on the origins and authorship of Deuteronomy, a subject of interminable debate, its production cannot be adequately explained without postulating a class of scribes with responsibility for drafting and probably also interpreting laws. Unhappily, we know too little about scribal activity and scribal schools in Israel to enable us to reach any definite conclusions. We may reasonably surmise that the fall of the Northern Kingdom in the eighth century BCE would have led to a more concentrated attempt to preserve the common patrimony, including the legal patrimony, no doubt in written form. Prov 25-29 is attributed to "the men of Hezekiah," the first Judean ruler without a counterpart in Samaria, and a rabbinic tradition (b. B. Bat. 15a) expands the activity of these people to take in the compiling and editing of the sayings of Isaiah, and even the Canticle and Qoheleth. During that same period, incidentally, the Homeric poems were being put together, and similar attempt to preserve the national heritage in written form were going on in contemporary Egypt and Mesopotamia.[12]

Some scholars have suggested that an early draft of Deuteronomy may have been part of the literary activity going on during the reign of Hezekiah. This may be so, but the connections of the book with the reign of Josiah and the period subsequent to 586 BCE are more clearly in evidence, however the connection with Josiah's reforms is understood and formulated. The period between these reforms and the fall of Jerusalem witnessed a crisis within the ranks of the prophets and in

---

[11]For a different reading of this passage see H. M. Barstad, "The Understanding of the Prophets in Deuteronomy," *SJOT* 8 (1994) 236-51.

[12]On scribal activity and the scribal ethos at the time of Hezekiah and in connection with Deuteronomy see my *Sage, Priest, Prophet: Religious and Intellectual Leadership in Ancient Israel* (Louisville: Westminster Press, 1995) 28-41.

the prophet's relation with his (less commonly her) public, a situation well documented in prophetic writings from that critical period (e.g. Jer 23:9-40; 28-29; Ezek 13). It seems to me that one aspect of that crisis is traceable to tension between prophet and law scribe. If the point of view of the latter is detectable in what Deuteronomy has to say about prophecy, the contemporary prophetic attitude to such scribes comes to expression in Jeremiah's disparaging allusion to religiously insensitive "handlers of the law" (*tos^{e}pe hattôrâ*, Jer 2:8) and his denunciation of scribes who have falsified the law with their lying pens (8:8-9).[13] The contrast in this last saying between alleged scribal wisdom and appeal to the word of Yahweh, meaning the prophetic word, reinforces the impression that we are dealing with conflicting claims to authority in the religious sphere, involving the prophetic word on the one hand, and the drafting and interpreting of law on the other. This situation illustrates a point made by Max Weber, that tension is "characteristic of any stratum of learned men who are ritually oriented to a law book as against prophetic charismatics."[14]

If the first compilation of prophetic writings was assembled during the exilic period by adherents of the Deuteronomic school, a hypothesis which has much to recommend it,[15] the line of argument advanced here would be strengthened. The existence of an official and authoritative corpus of prophetic writings does not in itself exclude the possibility of ongoing prophetic activity, but it will tend inevitably to shift the weight from the present to the past, from the spoken to the written word, and from direct prophetic utterance to the interpretation of past prophetic texts. That this is what actually happened will be apparent from a reading of late prophetic material. It is also significant in this respect that, in spite of Jeremiah's criticism of scribes and handlers of the law, his book has received by far the heaviest overlay of Deuteronomic editing of any of the prophetic books. The reasons is, I believe, that the editor(s) thought of him as standing at the end of the prophetic *didache* as Moses stands at its beginning. The parallelism between the call of Moses and that of Jeremiah is noted in all the commentaries, and the connection is further strengthened by the forty years of prophetic activity editorially assigned to Jeremiah in the opening verses (Jer 1:2-3 corresponding to 627-587 BCE). The many prose passages in the book of unmistakeable Deuteronomic vintage refer often to "his servants the prophets" who throughout the history of the nation have preached observance of the law and threatened disaster as the inevitable consequence of non-observance.[16] The same expression

---

[13]These passages are discussed in my *Prophecy and Canon* (Notre Dame & London: University of Notre Dame Press, 1977) 35-39.

[14]M. Weber, *Ancient Judaism* (New York: The Free Press, 1952) 395.

[15]Freedman has argued for an exilic prophetic collection put together as a supplement to Dtr; see his "The Law and the Prophets," VTSup 9 (1963) 250-65 and "The Earliest Bible," (ed. M. P. O'Connor and D. N. Freedman; *Backgrounds to the Bible* (Winona Lake, IN: Eisenbrauns, 1987) 29-37.

[16]Jer 7:25; 25:4; 26:5; 29:19; 35:15; 44:4.

(*ᵃbadaw hannᵉbî'îm*) occurs often in Dtr,[17] and this kind of retrospective allusion suggests that prophecy, or at least the kind represented by Jeremiah, is now a thing of the past. The thesis of a prophetic *didache* from Moses to Jeremiah would also explain why the the last section of Dtr (2 Kgs 24:18-25:30) also serves as the conclusion to the account of Jeremiah's career (Jeremiah 52).

With the publication of the Deuteronomic *oeuvre* in its several parts we therefore have the following situation: (1) a document claiming immunity from later editorial intrusion and containing a law and constitution that may not be altered; (2) the delineation of a normative epoch ending with the death of Moses the lawgiver; (3) a definition of the role of Moses as prophetic[18] and, correspondingly, a redefinition of prophecy as "Mosaic," that is, as continuing the work and mission of Moses; (4) a collection of Mosaic-prophetic books, the exact contents of which are unknown,[19] but which ends with Jeremiah, last of "his servants the prophets". I submit that we have here the essentials of canonicity, which I take to consist in the element of *closure* and the neutralization, by redescription and redefinition, of claims to new revelations. The history of Judaism and Christianity, not to mention Islam, testifies, needless to say, to the difficulty of sustaining this kind of claim.

I have been able to do little more than hint at the social and political situation that precipitated this ideological enterprise of the Deuteronomists. Conflicting claims to divinely warranted authority, to control of the "redemptive media," surface sooner or later in any social entity that has achieved a certain level of cohesion and organization and in which religious symbols play a strongly integrative function. Indications of such a conflict surface with unmistakeable clarity during the last decades of the Judean monarchy, involving prophets and legal specialists. In such situations appeals to the past, and to a significant figure in the past like Moses, are standard ways of validating claims to authority, and are by no means confined to Israel. W. G. Lambert refers, for example, to a Babylonian concept of canonicity exemplified in the *Babyloniaka* of Berossus in the third century BCE, but in operation certainly much earlier. The basic idea was that all revealed knowledge was handed down once and for all to the antediluvian sages in the first age of humanity.[20] Contact with the Mesopotamian intellectual tradition in the Neo-Babylonian period may, one suspects, have encouraged this appeal to a normative antiquity and the production of a corpus of authoritative and

---

[17]1 Kgs 14:18; 15:29; 18:36; 2 Kgs 9:7, 36; 10:10; 14:25; 17:13, 23; 21:10; 24:2.

[18]Deut 18:15, 18; 34:10; cf. Hos 12:13. Josephus (*Ant.* 2:327; 4:329) also regards Moses as a prophetic figure.

[19]The synchronized reigns of Northern and Southern rulers in the titles of Hosea and Amos suggest a Deuteronomic hand, but for the rest we must rely on the uncertain procedure of identifying editorial passages in the Deuteronomic style or reflecting Deuteronomic ideology. Isaiah 36-39 (with the exception of 38:9-20), taken from Dtr or drawing on the source on which the corresponding Dtr passage drew, presents an Isaiah very different from the author of the sayings in chapters 1-35.

[20]W. G. Lambert, "Ancestors, Authors and Canonicity," *JCS* 11 (1957) 1-14. See also F. Rochberg-Halton, "Canonicity in Cuneiform Texts," *JCS* 36 (1984) 127-44.

allegedly ancient texts. We see a similar process behind the production of the pseudepigraphal Jewish writings of the Greco-Roman period. Attributed as they are to such ancient worthies as Enoch, Shem, and even Adam, they were motivated by the same concern to validate a certain world view over against competitors. And the book of Deuteronomy itself is, after all, a pseudepigraphal work.

IV

In spite of its claim to finality, Deuteronomy came to form part of a much larger complex of narrative and law. The narrative span of the book takes in only one day, the last day in the life of Moses, and the historical reminiscence that the author puts into the mouth of Moses goes no further back than the giving of the first law at Horeb. The framework in which the Deuteronomic narrative and law came to be located begins, on the other hand, with creation and includes the settlement in the land, its division among the tribes, and the setting up of the wilderness sanctuart at Shiloh.[21] All the indications are that this Priestly narrative (P), with its strong interest in cultic matters, was put together either with a view to or subsequent to the re-establishment of worship in the rebuilt Jerusalem temple during the reign of Darius I in the late sixth century BCE.[22] Disagreement continues as to whether it was composed independently of existing narrative material–conventionally designated JE–or as either a new and expanded version of the same or a later redactional level. For our present purpose, all that needs to be said is that it covers a time span beginning before and extending beyond that of Deuteronomy.

At some stage the two works, Deuteronomy and the P account of human and national origins, were amalgamated, resulting in a significant modification of the overall structure. It is not difficult to see how this combination was effected. The date at the beginning of Deuteronomy–"in the fortieth year, in the first day of the eleventh month" (1:3)–is reckoned from the exodus calculated according to the P chronology, as is tolerably clear from other P chronological markers (Exod 12:40-41; 19:1; 40:17; Num 10:11). The addition of this date brought the entire book, with its homilies and laws, elegantly and economically into the carefully periodized framework of the more inclusive P historical narrative. But it then became necessary to transpose the commissioning of Joshua and death of Moses from their original position in the P narrative (Num 27:12-23) to the end of Deuteronomy (32:48-52 + 34:1, 7-9[23]) in order to allow Moses to promulgate the Deuteronomic law and preside over a new covenant-making before dying in Moab on the eve of the occupation of the land. A synoptic reading of the two

---

[21]See my article "The Structure of P," *CBQ* 38 (1976) 275-92.

[22]A minority opinion shared by some Israeli and North American scholars posits a pre-exilic date for the compilation of P, generally in allegiance to the thesis of Yehezkel Kaufmann.

[23]Deut 32:48-52 has been separated from 34 by the insertion of the blessings on the tribal eponyms in chapter 33.

passages–Num 27:12-23 and Deut 32:48-52 + 34:1, 7-9–will, I believe, confirm the impression that the latter, also attributed to P, is a revised version of the former, with the addition of the death of Moses displaced from its original location in the wilderness narrative.[24]

In terms of structure, the result was that the overall narrative was extended back in time to an absolute beginning in creation, but that the last section, consisting in the conquest of Canaan, was omitted. The result, i.e., the Pentateuch, therefore represents a compromise between quite different ideologies inscribed in the narrative, legal, and protreptic material of the Deuteronomists and the Priestly school respectively. In the next and final section we will consider some of the implications of this new "canonical" structure.

V

First, with respect to the chronological parameters: beginning with creation and the early history of humanity permitted alignment with a mythographic-historiographical pattern well attested in the ancient Near East and Levant according to which technologies, institutions, and practices, including religious practices, were grounded in antecedents of unimpeachable antiquity. In this respect Genesis 1-11 may be read as an Israelite version of a literary genre and literary conventions attested from the *Atrahasis* epic, elements of which go back to the second millennium BCE, to the *Babyloniaka* of the Babylonian priest Berossus writing in the Seleucid period. According to this Israelite version, then, the covenant, sabbath, the prohibition of eating bloody meat, and much else besides, received the sanction of high antiquity. Taking in the history of early humanity also permitted the introduction of a universalistic note conspicuously absent from Deuteronomy. All humanity is now accorded a religious qualification and destiny as created in the divine image (Gen 1:26-28), receives the first moral guidance from God, the so-called Noachide laws of rabbinic tradition, and is the recipient of the first covenant (Gen 9:8-17). But perhaps the most significant, and most neglected, aspect of the P history is that it undermines the contractual basis of covenant, so fundamental to the Deuteronomists, even those who had experienced the political and religious disasters of the late seventh and early sixth centuries BCE. The P account of the Sinai event does not include the making of a covenant, and though the Priestly authors clearly believe in the regulation of human life by law, they lay down no conditions on either early humanity or early Israel on the observance of which God's fidelity and God's intervention on their behalf are contingent.

We would very much like to know the circumstances that, presumably some time during the two centuries of Persian rule, dictated closure of the foundational

---

[24]See my *The Pentateuch: An Introduction to the First Five Books of the Bible* (New York: Doubleday, 1992) 229-39.

narrative with the death of Moses. It would be natural to attribute the exclusion of the conquest and settlement of the land to prudent regard for Persian imperial sensitivities, but there must have been more to it than that. If from one point of view the Pentateuch may be regarded as a life of Moses the lawgiver with a long introduction, ending with his death would emphasize that the life of the emerging commonwealth must be based on a revealed law, including ritual law,[25] rather than on other forms of mediation, which in one way or another had come up short during the time of the kingdoms. In this respect the concluding statement, the *excipit*, of the Pentateuch is significant: "there has not arisen a prophet since in Israel like Moses whom Yahweh knew face to face" (Deut 34:10). The point is clear: there is a qualitative difference between the kind of revelation vouchsafed to Moses and prophetic communications in the epoch following his death. Guidance for living must draw on this face-to-face revelation at Sinai-Horeb rather than on the sporadic, problematic, and often disruptive phenomenon of prophecy. This is the point of the famous oven of Akhnai story from which the title of this paper is taken: authoritative guidance and solutions to ethical and ritual problems are not to be sought in miracles or even in direct communication from heaven in the form of the *bat qôl*, but rather in the law given at Sinai and its duly authorized interpreters.

It remains for us to note that the final formulation of early Judaism's foundational myth and law affected ongoing literary activity, as also the understanding of prophecy in general. Former Prophets (Dtr) retained its authoritative status by virtue of its close links with a "canonical" Deuteronomy. If, as is sometimes argued, Chronicles was written to supersede Dtr, the attempt did not succeed. The Deuteronomic prophetic collection, discussed earlier, continued to be expanded, in the first place with Ezekiel, whose links with the Priestly matter in the Pentateuch, however formulated, are incontrovertible. Other prophetic writings, or writings purporting to be prophetic, from the period of the Second Temple were added, and existing prophetic books were edited and expanded down into the Greco-Roman period which witnessed the first essays in commentary distinct from the books themselves.

Study of additions and editorial modifications in these prophetic books, especially in Isaiah, reveals a thrust in the direction of an eschatological worldview, a direction, in other words, away from officially sanctioned redefinitions of the prophetic role attested in the literature surviving from the Second Temple period. One of these roles, that of historiography, is illustrated by the author of Chronicles who lists so many prophets among his sources as to leave little doubt that he regarded the writing of history as a prophetic activity.[26] As we

---

[25]If the division of the Pentateuch into five books is exegetically significant, rather than just a matter of scroll length, the central position of Leviticus, the shortest of the five, may not be accidental. See my *The Pentateuch* 42-47.

[26]See my *Prophecy and Canon* 124-38, and for the different transformations affecting prophecy in the Second Temple period see Barton, *Oracles of God* (n.8).

saw at the beginning of our inquiry, Josephus was of the same opinion. We may find a certain resolution of this tension between officially sanctioned forms of prophetic activity and understandings of prophecy, originating with Deuteronomy, and the new eschatological prophecy in the final paragraph of Malachi (Mal 3:32-34 [Eng. trans. 4:4-5]). This statement, which inculcates observance of the law of Moses while anticipating the revival of prophecy with the return of Elijah, serves as the *excipit* to both Law and Prophets. By going beyond the coda to the Priestly-Deuteronomic Pentateuch, it restores the tension between institution and charisma, between the claims of the past and those of the future.

From Heroic Individual to Nameless Victim: Women in the Social World of the Judges

Corrine L. Patton
Florida State University

T he period of the Judges narrates a time of immense social change in ancient Israel.[1] From the first tenuous land holdings in the sparsely populated hill country to the brink of tribal unity under a national monarch, political changes belie immense sociological variations. While the book of Judges overtly depicts the political fluctuations of this turbulent period, the individual narratives are driven by the social unrest played out in the lives of the individuals depicted. The political focus relativizes the stories of women in the book by failing to record names or lineages, by depicting women as narrative devices rather than full characters with lives outside of the text.[2] An analysis of the sociological background of the period, however, helps to "re-relativize" the stories of these women as portraying the inherently essential nature of social change on the micro-level effecting macro-political upheaval.

---

[1] Since I have been a member of the faculty at Florida State University, Prof. John Priest has been conducting courses and doing research in the burgeoning field of sociological criticism. With great respect for his work, I offer here a modest attempt to investigate the intersection of sociological and feminist studies.

[2] For a recent discussion of male and female authorship in the Bible see A. Brenner and F. van Dijk-Hemmes, *On Gendering Texts: Female and Male Voices in the Hebrew Bible* (Biblical Interpretation Series, 1; Leiden: E. J. Brill, 1993) 17-29.

Sociological analysis of the pre-monarchic period has been at the forefront of the method's utilization. The pioneering works of G. Mendenhall and N. Gottwald have brought much light to our understanding of the period.[3] These scholars have examined Israelite kinship relationships in order to reconstruct the interplay of economic production, kinship organization, and social structure. Study of primitive societies has shown that primitive societies with domesticated animals and sedentary agriculture develop a tribal structure wherein extended families band together to share labor and production.[4] This structure is relatively egalitarian, with little specialization of labor or centralization of political power. The basic economic and political unit is the family, with differentiation in authority dependent only on age and gender. More complex social groups can evolve from this tribal arrangement, including the chiefdom and the state, both of which include specialization of labor in which the chief or head of state regulates trade and the sharing of production. Such social organization is economically superior to the tribe, although clearly hierarchically structured with increasing systems of rank and class.[5]

Gottwald notes that Israelite society in the time of the Judges reflected neither the tribal structure nor the chiefdom in their pure states.[6] The basic unit of social and economic power was the immediate family (*bêt 'ab* בת אב) with little of the decision-making resting in the clan or tribe. In addition, Israelite clans were probably not kinship groups, but resident coalitions, i.e. groups of families who banded together for mutual support and protection without relinquishing the power of the immediate family.[7] According to Gottwald, such a hybrid structure arose out of historical circumstances: Israel did not evolve from the ground up, but devolved as groups of peasants fighting the hierarchical structure of the Canaanite land owners. Their experience of oppression led the early Israelites to resist all attempts at complex social structure.[8]

---

[3] See especially G. E. Mendenhall, *The Tenth Generation: The Origins of the Biblical Tradition* (Baltimore: Johns Hopkins University Press, 1973) and N. K. Gottwald, *The Tribes of Yahweh: A Sociology of the Religion of Liberated Israel, 1250-1050 B.C.E.* (New York: Orbis, 1979).

[4] E. R. Service, *Primitive Social Organization: An Evolutionary Perspective* (2nd ed.; Studies in Anthropology; New York: Random House, 1971) 99-132.

[5] Service, 133-69.

[6] See especially N.K. Gottwald, *Tribes of Yahweh*, 237-340. Gottwald has written extensively on the social world of early Israel. Some of this work has been collected in *The Hebrew Bible in its Social World and in Ours* (SBLSS; Atlanta: Scholars Press, 1993).

[7] C. J. H. Wright sees the clan as both a territorial unit and kinship group (*God's People in God's Land: Family, Land, and Property in the Old Testament* [Grand Rapids: Eerdmans, 1990] 48-53).

[8] For further discussion of kinship organization in ancient Israel see R. R. Wilson, *Genealogy and History in the Biblical World* (Yale Near Eastern Researches, 7; New Haven: Yale University Press, 1977) 11-55; *Sociological Approaches to the Old Testament* (Guides to Biblical Scholarship; Philadelphia: Fortress, 1984) 30-53; J. W. Rogerson, *Anthropology and the Old Testament* (Growing Points in Theology; Oxford: Blackwell, 1978) 86-101; and V. H. Matthews and D. C. Benjamin, *Social World of Ancient Israel, 1250-587 BCE* (Peabody, MA: Hendrickson, 1993) 7-9.

This approach has been critiqued and modified by F. S. Frick.[9] While Mendenhall and Gottwald have both been influenced in part by Marxist social theory, Frick examines a number of different sociological methods to determine their applicability to ancient Israel. While most sociological analyses of ancient Israel show dependence on an evolutionary model that posits set factors in a fixed hierarchy of importance for state formation, Frick prefers a "multilineal" approach that recognizes the complexity of social change and state formation. While environmental changes are among these factors, so are such variables as excess production, influence from surrounding cultures, and coordination of building projects. In addition, multilineal approaches have illuminated the sociological factors underlying sudden social collapse or change, factors not dependent on invading forces or internal revolt.[10] Leadership in a collapsed society tends to favor charismatic authority, especially during the threat of war. Also evident is the mixture of social devolution to more primitive stages of social structure with the retention of various elements from the preceding, more complex organization, a situation already observed by Gottwald. An additional result of the analysis of social collapse has been the clarification of later traditions about such sudden change that arise within the social group itself. Reflections on the collapse tend to stress individuals and their heroic deeds, rather than the larger social factors that contributed to the change.[11] While Frick does not apply such conclusions to the book of Judges, he notes its evident applicability.

Since the work of Frick and Gottwald, changes in archaeological methods have also clarified reconstructions of this time period. Stager has noted that archaeological evidence suggests a more complex social unit than is presented by Gottwald.[12] While in the Iron II period single-family homes were the rule, in Iron I in Syro-Palestine homes were complexes of approximately three family units organized around a central courtyard. Thus the *bet 'ab* consisted of two to four family units headed by a senior family member (*'ab*) who was responsible for production, distribution, and justice within the compound.[13] Such architecture reflects a growing complexity within the family unit in the period of the Judges.

Advances in sociological and archeological analyses have been utilized by biblical scholars to fill out the portrayal of Israelite women. Steinberg has examined the ways in which the texts in Genesis reflect the reality of problems in inheritance within the kinship structure, and the strategies the texts proffer to deal

---

[9] F. S. Frick, *The Formation of the State in Ancient Israel: A Survey of Models and Theories* (SWBA; Sheffield: Almond, 1985) 13-50.

[10] See C. Renfrew, "Systems Collapse as Social Transformation: Catastrophe and Anastrophe in Early State Societies," *Transformations: Mathematical Approaches to Cultural Change* (ed. C. Renfrew and K. L. Cooke; New York: Academic, 1979) 481-506.

[11] Renfrew also notes the tendency of modern historians to accept the testimony of later traditions at face value (482-85).

[12] L. A. Stager, "The Archaeology of the Family in Ancient Israel," *BASOR* 260 (1985) 1-36.

[13] Stager, "The Archaeology of the Family," 18-23.

with problems such as infertility or different status levels among various wives.[14] Meyers has used data from the settlement period to elucidate the creation texts in Genesis.[15] Working from the conclusions of Gottwald and Stager, she points out the function of Israelite women, both in labor-intensive terraced farming and in child-bearing to meet the family needs of an accessible labor force. In addition, women controlled food distribution within the household, thereby controlling a significant percentage of the economic resources of the family. Such control gave women a great deal of power in pre-monarchic Israel, although they still did not hold positions of authority within society.[16]

These two studies have used the reconstruction of the period of the Judges to clarify the book of Genesis. Few biblical scholars have turned their attention to the book of Judges for a similar analysis. The notable exception is the work of M. Bal.[17] Bal combines sociological method and literary critique in her analysis of the book of Judges. Utilizing a method of reading she terms "counter-coherence," a reading that exploits the narrative's subtexts and ideological assumptions, Bal is able to examine the social presuppositions that drive the treatment of women in the book of Judges. Noting the designation of the woman in Judges 19 as *pylgs*, Bal concludes that the term does not mean "concubine" or secondary wife, but refers to a wife who continues to reside with her father's family, rather than with her husband's family (patrilocality instead of virilocality). The struggle between these two social structures underlies the tensions between men and women in Judges, a struggle that has disastrous effects for the women. However, the existence of patrilocality in ancient Israel has been seriously doubted since its proposal by Morgenstern, thus undermining Bal's conclusions.[18]

In this study I will examine the portrayals of three Israelite women, Deborah, Jephthah's daughter, and the Levite's concubine, in light of sociological reconstructions of the period. The prominence of women in the narratives of the pre-monarchic era suggests that a different social matrix existed behind these stories than in subsequent periods of Israelite history, a social matrix that does not retain a strict division of power and authority, private and public. This social reconstruction accords well with what is known of pre-state societies. The question then is raised, to what degree do the stories of these three women belie social structures and conflicts in the period of the Judges?

While the project looks like a simple one, the fact remains that the book of Judges is not the product of the pre-monarchic period. The book clearly has a late

---

[14] N. Steinberg, *Kinship and Marriage in Genesis: A Household Economics Perspective* (Minneapolis: Fortress, 1993) esp. 35-86.

[15] C. Meyers, *Discovering Eve: Ancient Israelite Women in Context* (New York: Oxford University Press, 1988) 14-16.

[16] Meyers, 41-45 and 139-40.

[17] M. Bal, *Death and Dissymmetry: The Politics of Coherence in the Book of Judges* (Chicago Studies in the History of Judaism; Chicago: University of Chicago Press, 1988).

[18] J. Morgenstern, "Additional Notes on *Beena* Marriage (Matriarchat) in Ancient Israel," *ZAW* 49 (1931) 46-58.

overlay. Scholars have long recognized the complexity of the redaction of the book, its retention of old traditions, including its encapsulation of perhaps the oldest literature in the canonical collection, the Song of Deborah.[19] The narratives within the Deuteronomic framework may well contain clues to the social world about which they report. The question remains, however, to what degree does the later redactional activity manipulate, filter, and alter the stories as we have them? Gottwald notes that the social configuration of the pre-monarchic period is unlike anything expected by sociologists. This conflation of social stages may be due to one of two factors: either it reflects the fact that Israel did not evolve as a primitive society, but devolved from urbanized Canaanite society, or it is a by-product of the redactional layers in the texts at hand, a possibility not considered by Gottwald. Such redactional layering might result in either anachronistic elements in the portrayal and/or incomplete representation of elements that have been handed down but not fully understood. In addition, Renfrew notes the tendency of traditions about social collapse to fail to recognize the macro-level social factors of such change. This study will consider the possible effect of redactional overlays on the sociological background that can be reconstructed from this analysis.

Deborah and Jael

The story of the war against Sisera in Judges 4-5 prominently features two of the strongest, most positive female characters in the Hebrew Bible: Deborah and Jael.   The text enhances the prominence of these two women by giving them names, dialogue, self-motivating action, power, and, in the case of Deborah, two of the highest social positions in pre-monarchic Israel: prophet and judge.[20] These titles are proffered without apology, suggesting the presence of other female prophets and judges in ancient Israelite society. The dual biblical accounts of the battle in chapters 4 and 5 also offer the modern biblical scholar a rare opportunity to explore redactional activity in the text. Accepting the early date of Judges 5 enables a truly pre-monarchic view to be examined.[21]

The poem in Judges 5 affords poor material for analysis of sociological structure. There are numerous references to kings (vv 3 and 19), but these are probably not Israelite figures. Instead, in the enumeration of the regions,[22] the Israelites, called "people" (*m*, vv 2, 9, 11, 13, and 18), "peasants" (*przwn*, v 7 and

---

[19] For a recent analysis of the redactional issues underlying the book of Judges see U. Becker, *Richterzeit und Konigtum: Redaktionsgeschichtliche Studien zum Richterbuch* (BZAW 192; Berlin: de Gruyter, 1990).

[20] For a discussion of the interrelationship of status, gender, and relative contributions, see C. Meyers, "Procreation, Production, and Protection: Male-Female Balance in Early Israel," *JAAR* 51 (1983) 569-93.

[21] For a recent discussion of the date of the poem and brief review of scholarship, see J. Gray, *Joshua, Judges, Ruth* (NCB; Grand Rapids: Eerdmans, 1986) 261, and L. D. Schloen, "Caravans, Kenites, and *Casus belli*: Enmity and Alliance in the Song of Deborah," *CBQ* 55 (1993) 20-21.

[22] The word "tribe" (*sbt*) is never used in the poem with that sense.

11),[23] are led by chiefs (*srym*, v 15), commanders (*hwqqym*, v 9), and noblemen (*'dyrym*, v 13). The decision-making process, when reflected in the text, seems to reside with the largest social unit, the tribe. Whether this group is an actual kinship organization, or just nominally related, the ideal of kinship is reflected.[24] Economically the Israelites appear to be involved in more than just agriculture; in fact, agrarian interests play little part in the poem. While Reuben is said to "tarry among the sheepfolds," reflecting pastoral activity, Dan and Asher are involved in maritime activity. In addition, Israelite involvement in trade is implied at the outset of the piece; Schloen argues that certain Israelite tribes had been guarding and protecting caravan travel, an occupation interrupted by the Canaanites, thus leading to the war.[25] Fighting occurs in "gates," presumably of fortified cities, although these cities may not be Israelite. Although there may be one reference to terraced farming in the poem (Judg 5:18),[26] there are no concerns for fertility of either crops or humans here, nor insinuation that participants may have been reluctant to fight due to the labor-intensity of terraced farming. All told, social structure appears to reflect the more complex chiefdom, rather than a simple tribal structure. As such the prominence of women in the text is rather surprising, since among the groups whose status is customarily adversely affect by a more marked rank and class system are women.

Deborah and Jael reflect two conflicting reflexes of war. On the one hand, Yee points out that in pre-monarchic Israel the whole household would have been involved in defending its territory.[27] There was no specialized class of male soldiers, but everyone worked in whatever capacity possible to defend the family's holdings. In such a situation, fighting did not occur at a remove from the private or domestic sphere, involving women in war in rather complex ways. The figure of Jael in particular has her personal tent pitched within close proximity to the fighting. The proximity of Deborah and Jael are contrasted with the distant urban location of Sisera's mother. However, Deborah must travel outside of her tribal home to accompany Barak, while Jael, clearly does not permanently reside in a tent in the confines of Naphtali.

The author of the song includes a notice that Jael is married.[28] Such a notice, nominal as it is, serves no overt function in the text, but rather reflects the woman's need to be attached to some male, either husband or father. The sexual nuances

[23]L. E. Stager, "Archaeology, Ecology and Social History: Background Themes to the Song of Deborah," *Congress Volume: Jerusalem 1986* (ed. J. A. Emerton; VTSup 40; Leiden: E. J. Brill, 1988) 224-27.
[24]Wilson, *Sociological Approaches*, 37-38.
[25]Schloen, "Caravans, Kenites, and *Casus belli*," 18-38. See also Stager, "Archaeology, Ecology, and Social History," 221-34.
[26]Meyers, *Discovering Eve*, 59.
[27]G. A. Yee, "By the Hand of a Woman: The Metaphor of the Woman Warrior in Judges 4," *Sem* 61 (1993) 110-14.
[28]Although her husband's name, Heber, may not have originally been a proper name (Gray, *Joshua, Judges, Ruth*, 258), it is presented as such in this final redaction.

surrounding the killing of Sisera in the text suggest sexual knowledge and manipulation by Jael.[29] While such knowledge is not consistent with a young unmarried girl, the text makes clear that she was also no prostitute but has acquired sexual knowledge through her marital status. Thus, Jael's status as wife lends her an air of respectability, while at the same time provides for the source of her plan.[30]

Alternatively, in the poem Deborah is never once regulated by a male. She is no one's daughter, no one's wife, but only a "mother in Israel." As such, however, she is also no one's mother.[31] In fact, the poem relates no earthly role for this female figure: she is neither a prophet, nor a judge,[32] and her only activities are that of "waking" (v 7), "arising" (v 12), and uttering a song (v 12), all of which precede the mustering of troops.[33] She is not insinuated into the battle, and, like Barak, does not appear in the second half of the poem. Such scanty material allows little reconstruction of her social function.[34] Craigie has noted several parallels between the language used to describe Deborah within the poem and that of the Ugaritic goddess, Anat, including the epithet of "mother," the implied reference to Deborah as *raham*, and the accompaniment of stars into the battle.[35] If the language used of Deborah in the earliest literary stratum, then, utilizes divine metaphors, either literally or figuratively, the subsequent prose account consciously avoids such language, replacing the hyperbole with descriptions that clearly "demythologize" Deborah, including giving her a husband and locating her in a concrete geographical setting.[36]

While the poem might reflect a social world that includes women in battles to defend their territory, Deborah and Jael seem to be women far removed from the agrarian setting of Meyer's Eve. This is even more apparent in the later prose

---

[29] Y. Zakovitch, "Sisseras Tod," *ZAW* 93 (1981) 364-74; R. Alter, *The Art of Biblical Poetry* (New York: Basic Books, 1985) 43-49; S. Niditch, "Eroticism and Death in the Tale of Jael," *Gender and Difference in Ancient Israel* (ed. P. L. Day; Minneapolis: Fortress, 1989) 43-57, and *War in the Hebrew Bible: A Study in the Ethics of Violence* (New York: Oxford University Press, 1993) 113-17; and D. N. Fewell and D. M. Gunn, *Gender, Power, and Promise: The Subject of the Bible's First Story* (Nashville: Abingdon, 1993) 125.

[30] Alternatively, see D. N Fewell and D. M. Gunn, "Controlling Perspectives: Women, Men, and the Authority of Violence," *JAAR* 58 (1990) 394-96.

[31] Both R. G. Boling (*Judges* [AB 6; Garden City: Doubleday, 1975]   118) and Meyers (*Discovering Eve*, 159-60) view the epithet as indicative of Deborah's prophetic power. J. C. Exum relates the title to her attributes as leader ("'Mother in Israel': A Familiar Figure Reconsidered," *Feminist Interpretation of the Bible* (ed. L. M. Russell; Philadelphia: Westminster, 1985) 74.

[32] Gray believes the titles in the prose account are Deuteronomic additions (*Joshua, Judges, Ruth*, 255).

[33] Boling interprets the language of these verses as both a call to war (*Judges*, 119) and as the victory song at the end of the battle (111).

[34] F. van Dijk-Hemmes suggests that Deborah is not an historical figure but is "a literary creation inspired by the song of Deborah" (*On Gendering Texts*, 65).

[35] "Deborah and Anat: A Study of Poetic Imagery," *ZAW* 90 (1978) 374-81.

[36] Many scholars do not want to read Judg 4:4 literally. Boling thinks "Lapidoth" is another name for Barak (*Judges*, 95), an explanation that fails to account for his need to travel to consult her. Exum reads the husband's name as an epithet, translating that Deborah was a fiery woman ("'Mother in Israel,'" 85). See also Fewell and Gunn, *Gender, Power, and Promise*, 122-23.

narrative. Deborah can be found under a tree, presumably a sacred tree where she dispenses oracles. Such activity suggests a degree of specialization seen in the more socially complex chiefdoms. Neither Deborah nor Jael, while nominally married, function as wives, nor does either have off-spring.[37] Additionally, issues of childbirth and fertility are nowhere addressed.

Finally, all figures in this pericope act alone as individuals. While clearly the war involved troops, tribes, and clans–given their oblique mention especially in the poem–Deborah has no entourage. Barak has no armor-bearer, accompanying officers, or even clan elders who assist him in arriving at the decision to fight. Such isolation serves to highlight the power struggle between Deborah and Barak, a power struggle that makes clear that final authority rests in the female prophet, not the male warrior. Jael is noticeably alone, a solitary figure at the opening of her tent, apparently not in the midst of a bustling camp. Without such isolation, Sisera would not have thought it a safe haven to hide. The overall impression left by the text is of a very simple society, with few mechanisms for waging war, coordinating intertribal activity, or even approaching God. The individuality of the characters in the prose narrative heightens the dramatic movement of the tale by illuminating the dual heroines but also hinders an attempt to reconstruct the lives of these heroines beyond the text. They were each somebody's wife, but where they permanently lived, how they related within the larger family structure, how these families supported themselves, even the basic question of how normative their lives were for pre-monarchic Israelite society all remain in obscurity. While the obscurity surely rests in part on later traditions emphasizing the heroic individual over the social group, the isolation of these figures is heightened by a later urbanized redactor who very well might have viewed such activities as isolated, aberrant, and extraordinary.

Jephthah's Daughter

Kinship relations frame and permeate the stories of Jephthah in Judges 11-12. The narrative of this judge is set in motion by his failure to inherit. Kinship irony is played out within the stories of Jephthah's battles with the Ammonites. Disinherited by family with the support of town elders,[38] because of the social status of his mother, Jephthah returns to social prominence at the instigation of those very elders and family. Jephthah's own family structure is unknown throughout the first part of the text. His daughter is introduced only after we know she is doomed. His wife remains non-existent, and the text unambiguously informs us he had no other children.

---

[37] Oddly, Fewell and Gunn see the two women as maternal figures (*Gender, Power, and Promise*, 123-26).

[38] R. Alter, *The World of Biblical Literature* (New York: HarperCollins, 1992) 60.

Socially, the story of Jephthah accords well with the expected social matrix of pre-monarchic Israel. Decisions seem to rest primarily with the family or residential unit (*bet-'ab*) with some collaboration by the larger social support group, here elders of the area or tribe. The economic base for the group seems based on land use since this is the heart of Jephthah's rejection. In addition, once Jephthah is disinherited, he makes his living outside of that social matrix, by raiding with a group of social outcasts in a foreign land. At his return he negotiates not just for the temporary military leadership offered him, but for a prominent, permanent position as "head" (*r's*).

A sure result of this position implied in the text is possession of a "house," presumably attached to land. Without such possession, Jephthah's vow makes little sense. Of course, the tragic irony of the text lies in the fact that his vow leads him to sacrifice the only heir to the inheritance he has worked so shrewdly to regain, his daughter. While at the beginning of the story the brothers attempt to disinherit Jephthah, near the close of the narrative Jephthah has effectively disinherited himself.[39] As Exum notes, at the close of the Jephthah cycle, the tribe of Ephraim is unaware how anti-climactic is their threat to burn down Jephthah's house.[40]

Within this social world, the daughter acts in perfectly acceptable ways. Even without the sacred vow, a daughter lived under the authority of her parents, especially her father.[41] The sacred vow, even without parental authority, again, would have sealed her fate. Thus Jephthah's daughter is doubly doomed, a fate she clearly recognizes.[42] The ritual interlude emphasized the social effect of the sacrifice of Jephthah's daughter: she mourns her virginity. In a society where offspring were at a premium, enhancing economic status of the primary social unit, the family, complete annihilation of a family line meant failure by the father (*'b*) who had a variety of means to insure against such an outcome, including polygamy, concubinage, and adoption.[43] However, as a disinherited raider it may

---

[39] Boling (*Judges*, 197-98), J. A. Soggin (*Judges: A Commentary* [OTL; Philadelphia: Westminster, 1981] 204), Gray (*Joshua, Judges, Ruth*, 314), and P. Trible (*Texts of Terror: Literary-Feminist Readings of Biblical Narratives* [OBT; Philadelphia: Fortress, 1984] 94) believe Jephthah's father was unknown. However, the story of the disinheritance makes better sense if the text is read literally.

[40] J. C. Exum, "Murder They Wrote: Ideology and the Manipulation of Female Presence in Biblical Narrative," *The Pleasure of Her Text: Feminist Readings of Biblical and Historical Texts* (ed. A. Bach; Philadelphia: Trinity, 1990) 56.

[41] Note that narratively this daughter is functionally motherless. In addition, she has no brother to defend her case in lieu of or against their father as did Dinah and Tamar. Thus she is completely within Jephthah's power.

[42] I do not think she could have been saved in the same manner as Jonathan. In fact, I read the passage in 1 Samuel 14 as part of Saul's negative characterization. If one follows M. Brettler reading Judges as a pro-Davidic, anti-Saulide text, this text is one more way that Saul is denigrated ("The Book of Judges: Literature as Politics," *JBL* 108 [1989] 395-418).

[43] For the literary significance of Jephthah's childlessness, see J. C. Exum, "The Centre Cannot Hold: Thematic and Textual Instabilities in Judges," *CBQ* 52 (1990) 420-22.

not have been economically advantageous for Jephthah to have had many offspring. Since he had returned to inheritance only recently, he would not have had time to adjust his own familial structure to suit his new social standing. Nevertheless, Jephthah was a fool not just for being in a position of having only one heir, but for making such a vow that put this solitary heir at risk in this circumstance.

The perennial question arises with any discussion of this text, just what did Jephthah expect to come out of his door to greet him?[44] Answers to this question range from an animal who would have been housed on the bottom floor of his house, to a human, perhaps of lesser status.[45] While the rabbinic texts have already noted the ritual problem of vowing an unspecified animal who may or may not be ritually acceptable, I would add that those animals that are most commonly sacrificed, bovine and sheep, are not those most inclined to greeting their masters. If Jephthah expected a human out of his door, and if he resided in a single-family domicile, then he was vowing either a servant or his wife, assuming, as the text shows that he did not consider that it would be his daughter.[46] The lack of any servants in these texts is notable and may be the result of the relative egalitarian quality of Jephthah's social world. As Meyers notes, servitude at this time was simply not economically feasible.[47]

If, however, as Meyers and Stager point out, most "houses" of this day were complexes where brothers and their families dwelled together, then Jephthah may have headed a residential unit that included his half-brothers and their families. Jephthah, then, may have been vowing to sacrifice one of his brothers' family members (assuming the brothers themselves accompanied him into battle), which would have diminished the claims on the inheritance owed to his family line. Such a conjecture is not far-fetched. For instance, Jephthah may have assumed women other than his daughter, women of higher status, would have led the victory song.[48] After all, both Miriam and Deborah, who also lead victory songs, clearly held status positions in their communities. Thus an older, more established female member of the extended family might have been the expected leader of the song.

Unlike Deborah and Jael, the characters in these stories rarely act alone. Rather they are intimately bound to their social groupings. When Jephthah's daughter sets off to mourn her virginity, she is accompanied by her "companions." These companions are the ones who continue the annual commemoration of the daughter's act, presumably in part because, as a member of their social group, she

---

[44] For a discussion of the deliberate ambiguity of the text see D. Marcus, *Jephthah and His Vow* (Lubbock, Texas: Texas Tech Press, 1986).

[45] For a review of scholarship, see T. W. Cartledge, *Vows in the Hebrew Bible and the Ancient Near East* (JSOTSup 147; Sheffield: JSOT, 1992) 175-85.

[46] Note, however that Fewell and Gunn suggest that the vow was public knowledge. Therefore, Jephthah's daughter chooses to confront her father with the fulfillment of the vow (*Gender, Power, and Promise*, 126-27).

[47] Meyers, *Discovering Eve*, 132-37.

[48] For the muting of the victory song, see Brenner, *On Gendering Texts*, 37-38.

represented what could have happened to any of them.[49] These same companions could well have included female cousins and relatives, women who very easily could have been the first out that fateful door. This renders their participation in her lamentation even more poignant. In this reading of the text, God does not provide a substitute for Jephthah's daughter as a sacrificial victim as God had done with Isaac, because this daughter *was* the substitute for the implied more innocent victim of her father's vengeful vow.

Redactional activity seems to have had little effect on the tale of Jephthah. Kinship issues permeate the text and the odd details in the story seem to make better sense when read against the background of archaeological and sociological research in the period of the Judges. Yet, these stories did not create social tension with the world of the redactor in the same way as the traditions of Deborah. Even in the monarchy, women remained under the jurisdiction of their fathers, and virginity was still a state to be mourned. However, unlike the expected traditions of social collapse, these stories, while presenting a charismatic military leader, do so against the background of an increasingly complex social structure.

The Levite's Concubine

The social world of the Levite and his concubine in Judges 19-21 represents an even more complex stage than does the story of Jephthah's daughter. The narratives all occur in urban settings: the Levite travels from city to city, and the spaces in between those cities seem to be wilderness, not pasture land. Danger comes not in the form of pastoral disaster such as drought, famine, lack of fertility, but in the form of urban danger with the aggression by male citizens against an "outsider." The social structure is more obviously hierarchical: the Levite has a servant, and there are degrees of marriage. There is more overt attention paid to who is the insider and who the outsider, preparing the reader for the chapters that follow in which the Benjaminites define Israelites not belonging to their tribe as "outsiders" or sojourners.[50]

This increasing social complexity leads to decreasing autonomy for all the characters, including the women. Here not only is the concubine anonymous, but even her father and husband are unnamed.[51] She is not only a nobody, but she is the daughter of a nobody and the secondary wife of a nobody. She is raped by a

---

[49]For a discussion of the commemoration as a rite of passage, see Bal, *Death and Dissymmetry*, 46-68, and P. L. Day, "From the Child Is Born the Woman: The Story of Jephthah's Daughter," *Gender and Difference in Ancient Israel*, 58-74. For the communal identification with the daughter, see Fewell and Gunn, *Gender, Power, and Promise*, 127-28, and J. C. Exum, *Tragedy and Biblical Narrative: Arrows of the Almighty* (Cambridge: Cambridge University Press, 1992) 45-69.

[50]See Trible, *Texts of Terror*, 71.

[51]While various scholars have noted the denigrating effect of the concubine's anonymity, little attention has been paid to the fact that all figures in this story remain nameless. The final redactor therefore sees this degradation as a general human condition by this time in the story line.

nameless crowd, and her dismembered body is sent to nameless tribal leaders.[52] She has no status, no rights, because those who should defend and protect her, i.e. her husband and father, fail to do so. Her situation brings the message of the text to the fore: the need for the monarchy. One of the primary duties of the king was to protect the rights of the "widow, orphan, and resident alien." As is known, these categories refer to those elements in society who have no one to plead their case in Israel. I would contend that, functionally, the Levite's concubine fits all three categories. First, the Benjaminites would surely view her as a resident alien. Second, since her father has sent her out of his house, she is no longer under his protection, rendering her an orphan. Finally, her status as concubine, rather than wife, limits the Levite's responsibility toward her.[53] Like Ruth, without a king to guarantee her rights, this woman is completely vulnerable. In this way the text clearly reflects the monarchic view.

The complexity of social structure is also evident in the level at which authority resides. Only decisions of "marriage" are determined at the family level, and even these decisions are rather ineffectual. The story begins with the concubine leaving the house, a sign of the powerlessness of this family head at the most fundamental level. Similarly, the woman's father is ineffective in influencing his guest's travel plans. Finally, the Ephraimite host in Benjamin is completely powerless to protect his guests from harm. In this narrative the power of the *bet 'ab* has completely disintegrated.

All other authority, as seen in the narratives of war that follow the rape of the concubine, resides with the clans that constitute the building blocks of the tribes. Therefore, when the assemblies are called to decide the fate of Benjamin, the tribes are gathered by clans, who then all participate in both the consultation with God and the decision to engage in battle. The effects of the battles are clearly felt at the level of tribe and clan. The tribe of Benjamin is almost annihilated, a situation remedied by forcible seizure (rape) of girls from two different towns or clans.

In addition, the text projects the clearest veneer in the book of pan-Israelite activity.[54] All eleven tribes gather to decide the fate of Benjamin. They all act in concert, displaying military effectiveness at a time when it is most self-destructive.[55] The overlay of pan-Israelite activity clearly reflects a later time period, a period that idealized Israel as a unity of twelve, and only twelve, tribes. If this story retains any social *Kern* it would be of the period immediately

---

[52] For an exploration of the themes of rape and social disintegration, see A. A. Keefe, "Rapes of Women/Wars of Men," *Sem* 61 (1993) 79-97, and J. C. Exum, *Fragmented Women: Feminist (Sub)Versions of Biblical Narratives* (Valley Forge, PA: Trinity, 1993) 176-88.

[53] For the status of the concubine see Steinberg, *Kinship and Marriage*, 15-17.

[54] Boling suggests that the purpose of the story was to express the importance of pan-Israelite unity to a community in exile (*Judges*, 293-94).

[55] Like the story of Jephthah's daughter, the tribes are almost successful in disinheriting one of their own relatives, but here at the tribal level, rather than at the familial level!

preceding the monarchy. The increased urbanization, the loss of individual identity replaced by simple tribal designation, the increased specialization, the level at which decisions are made all point to a complex society in need of strong central leadership.

There is ample evidence, however, that the story in its current form displays signs of at least heavy redactional activity, if not outright authorship by the final redactor. Overt parallels to Genesis 19 require a date post-dating that text.[56] Further parallels with the Saul narratives suggest either the activity of a single Deuteronomic redactor or an author later than the traditions now contained in 1 Samuel.[57]The book of Judges portrays the growing social complexity as spontaneous, natural, and uncontrolled. Yet it is this very complexity, with its inherent abuses, that inevitably leads to the necessity of central authority yielded under God, i.e., the monarchy. The redactor casts the final story of the rape of the concubine and the subsequent inter-tribal wars against the background of a complex social structure that closely mirrors monarchic Israel: this casing of the story expresses the inevitability of monarchy, not as an ideal in and of itself, but as a necessary evil in a society unable to protect its citizens or adjudicate inter-tribal disputes.

Conclusion

The final redaction of Judges then expresses the theme of the need of a king within an ever-increasing complex society. As long as charismatic individuals such as Deborah could effectively handle Israel's enemies, a king appeared to be rather superfluous. Yet, while Jephthah could arise and defeat the Ammonites, the system of families and elders controlling inheritance clearly showed signs of easy abuse and the need for a king had begun to appear arguable. Finally, with the complexities of the society of the concubine, the simple world of the charismatic judge had long since disappeared, replaced by abuse on the grandest scale imaginable. The vehicles of authority and power were so far removed from the individual that one cannot imagine even a Deborah having the ability to right the abuses of the system.

I suggest that this schema does not consciously reflect the actual social development of ancient Israel but is a literary device employed by the redactor to render this message unavoidable. While the story of Jephthah's daughter displays little evident re-working, redactional activity in Judges 4 substantiates such conclusions. The final author or redactor wants to show that charismatic authority can only work in a society in which individuals have power. While this may have been the situation at the earliest stages of Israel's settlement, it was a world to

[56] S. Lasine, "Guest and Host in Judges 19: Lot's Hospitality in an Inverted World," *JSOT* 29 (1984) 38-41.

[57] Lasine, "Guest and Host," 41-43, and Brettler, "The Book of Judges," 395-418.

which Israel would not return. In a unified Israel, an Israel of twelve tribes, power and authority rested in the monarch who stood outside the congregation whose clan leaders gathered as political and military leaders before God and the ark. The individual is sacrificed to the nation, who is the sole heir of the land promised by God.

The women in the book share in the fate of the whole society in such social upheaval. The difference is that they are the first to suffer the negative effects of such change.   They lose more power, more permanently than their male counterparts within the monarchic structure. They are the first to lose their names, lose their voices, and lose their lives as a result of the increasing social complexity. When national identity becomes corporate identity, it becomes male identity. Women then are the nameless other, relegated to a private sphere whose power has been curtailed by the corporate nation. Yet, the book of Judges depicts the increasing social complexity as a social reality outside of the control of human political power. This social complexity threatens the lives and safety of all Israelite members, especially the women. The longing for a king in Judges is not a utopian ideal, but rather a necessary response to a social structure inherently out of control. The book of Judges shows that with increased social complexity comes systemic abuse in which women lose their power, their names, their voices, their lives, and ultimately their individuality.   While the author of Judges may fondly remember a time when women were prophets and judges, he portrays the nation as incapable of returning to that stage.   By the end of the book these women can only hope for some basic protection of their lives and rights, a hope only a king can insure.

A Note on the Early Antiquity of the Song of Hannah[1]

Joe D. Seger

Mississippi State University

While few of the critical problems respecting the background and date of the Song of Hannah (I Sam 2:1-10) have been finally solved, the bent of recent study has steadily tended toward more serious consideration of an early preexilic origin for the piece.[2] This note aims to advance

---

[1] Knowledge is cumulative! The principal insight offered in this textual note emerged from exchanges in a graduate Old Testament seminar at Hartford Seminary Foundation in 1966 in which John Priest participated along with the author and doctoral student Rev. Joseph Hakes. In the light of recent studies emphasizing the early use of the asseverative particle within Ancient Near Eastern sources, e.g. T. Muroaka, *Emphatic Words and Structures in Biblical Hebrew* (Leiden: E.J. Brill, 1983) cf. 113-123; J. Huehnergard, "Asseverative *la* and Hypothetical *lu/law* in Semitic," *JAOS* 103 (1973) 569-93; and D. Sivan and W. Schniedewind, "Letting your 'Yes' be 'No' in Ancient Israel: A study of the Asseverative *la'* and *halo'*," *JSS* 38 (1993) 209-26; and the appearance of new seminal studies on the text of I Samuel 2:1-10, e.g. W. F. Albright, *Yahweh and the Gods of Canaan* (Garden City, NY: Doubleday, 1986) cf. 20-22; J. T. Willis, "The Song of Hannah and Psalm 113," *CBQ* 35 (1973) 139-54; P.K. McCarter, *I Samuel: A New Translation with Introduction, Notes and Commentary* (Garden City, NY: Doubleday, 1980) cf. 67-76; and J. Watts, *Psalm and Story: Inset Hymns in Hebrew Narrative* (Sheffield: JSOT, 1991), it seems appropriate to retrieve this suggestion and add it to the growing corpus of other references. Doing this as a special means of honoring John Priest, a well respected colleague and suppportive friend, whose influences on my early academic career were most formative, and whose seminal help is remembered with warm and most sincere appreciation, makes it doubly appropriate.

[2] Eissfeldt's comment still reflects the contemporary climate, "the possibility of genuineness (i.e., of its being original with Samuel's mother) can hardly be seriously considered with reference to the Song of Hannah . . . though this does not by any means imply that it must have been inserted at a late date in the Samuel narrative and may not already have been taken up by E." Cf. O. Eissfeldt, *The Old Testament, an Introduction* (trans. by P. Ackroyd, New York: Harper and Row, 1965) 281, with parenthetical

48 Biblical and Humane

this view by suggesting that another remnant example of the archaic asseverative particle *lu'* is to be found in the Hebrew text of verse three, and that its recognition helps resolve one of the principal difficulties encountered in translating the verse's final bi-colon.

The Massoretic Text of verse three reads:

'l trbw tdbrw gbhh gbhh	Do not multiply proud speech,
ys' 'tq mpykm	Nor let arrogance come from your mouths.
ky 'l d'wt yhwh	For the Lord is a God of Knowledge,
wl' ntcnw 'llwt	And deeds are not weighed.[3]

The principal *crux interpretum* is found in the last bi-colon where the consonantal text *wl'* apparently indicates the negative, i.e. *welo'*. However, the contextual difficulties with this reading are clear, and problems of translators are reflected both in the history of the text versions and in the efforts of subsequent commentators.

The Massoretes themselves resolved the matter by instructing the reading (*qere*) *welo*, i.e., "And by Him (i.e. God) deeds are weighed." That this was the authoritative reading tradition from an early time is also borne out by the Vulgate which renders: *et ipsi praeparantur cogitationes*, i.e., "And by Him (alone) plans are prepared." [4]

The Greek texts provide a slightly different solution, possibly indicating an alternative *Urtext*. The main LXX uncials and virtually all of the cursive MSS read together *kai theos hetoimazon epitadeumata autou*, i.e., "And God is preparing his ways."[5] As suggested by Kittel's notes, a separate Hebrew *Vorlage* with *w' l* in place of MT *wl'* may be represented here.[6] But this is not a necessary conclusion. Indeed, unless we are to assume a double origin for the piece (which is extremely dubious), it would seem less likely for the more difficult MT *kethib* to have developed (via scribal error?) from some *Vorlage* to be assumed for the Greek, than to suppose the converse, i.e. that the Greek is interpreting an enigmatic Hebrew and conforming to the pressures of what the context demands, or perhaps

---

comment added. See also the similar, more recent, opinion in McCarter, *I Samuel*, 75.

[3] Most of the critical problems of this verse were cogently discussed early in the century by Paul Dhorme, *Les livres de Samuel* (EB Paris: J. Galbalda, 1910) whose work builds on the comment of his predecessors, especially O. Thenius, *Die Bücher Samuels* (KeH 4. Leipzig: S. Hirzel, 1842), S. R. Driver, *Notes on the Hebrew Text of the Books of Samuel* (Oxford: Clarendon, 1890), and K. Budde, *Die Bücher Samuel* (KHC VIII. Tübingen: J.C.B. Mohr, 1902). Except for the final bi-colon we follow his reading and translation here.

[4] *Biblia Sacra iuxta Vulgatam Clementinam* (Rome: Typis Societatis S. Joannis Evang., 1956).

[5] Cf. A. E. Brooke, N. McLean, and H. St. J. Thackeray, *The Old Testament in Greek* (Cambridge, 1909-40) Vol. II, Part I, *ad loc.* Reading with BAMNa-i,m-q, st(v)w-c₂,e₂, Armenian, (Boharic¹), Sahidic s(w), Ethiopic, Old Latin b(esv). The minor variants include the replacement of *hetoimaz□n* with *hetoima* in M, and of *autou* with *aut□n* by the Adg group.

[6] R. Kittle, *Biblia Hebraica* (Stuttgart: Privileg Württ. Biblanstalt, 1937) *ad loc.* note b. The Greek *epitᴐdeumata autou* may reflect a Hebrew *Urtext* with *'llwtw*, cf. McCarter, *I Samuel*, 69.

more simply just reflecting a case of audile confusion, hearing *la'* for *lu'*. Still, the almost absolute consistency of the Greek evidence, as reflected also in the Old Latin and Syro-Hexaplaric versions which follow from it,[7] does not allow for easy dismissal of the possibility of an alternative *Urtext.*.

However, some instances where the versions do seem to reflect the received MT can be cited. In view of the otherwise monodic Septuagint witness, the fact that even one Greek fragment can be noted in this connection is the more significant. The citation in question comes from Symmachus and reads: *kai ouk eisi par auto prophaseis*, i.e., "And there are no excuses before Him." [8] That we have in *kai ouk* a reflex of *wl'* seems clear, though the exact text behind *par auto* remains in question. [9] In company with this is the Syriac rendering "and deeds are not ordered before Him."[10] Again here the MT *kethib* must be presupposed, with the reading of the negative being preserved inspite of severe contextual difficulties. Finally, an additional witness is found in an isolated fragment from the Latin works of Origen. Reading *non emendaverunt excusantes, i.e.,* "Those pleading have not corrected themselves" or "Those excusing themselves have not changed"[11] this may be the clearest direct reflection we have of the MT received text.

As suggested initially, this survey of textual evidence underscores the interpretive problem of the bi-colon.[12] None of the versions provide a satisfactory key to resolve the dual demands of both the text and the context preserved in the MT *kethib*. Moreover, neither is the abstruseness of these data relieved by the efforts of subsequent scholars. The older commentators failed to achieve consensus, though a variety of interesting suggestions were forwarded, [13] and

---

[7] See. Brooke, McLean, Thackeray, *ad loc.* Also see the following works by P. A. H. De Boer, "A Syro-Hexaplaric Text of the Song of Hannah," pp. 8-18 in *Hebrew and Semitic Studies* (ed. by W. Thomas and W. D. McHardy: Oxford: Clarendon Press, 1963); "*Confirmatum es Cor Meum*, Remarks on the Old Latin Text of the Song of Hannah," *OTS* 13 (1963) 173-92: "Once Again the Old Latin Text of Hannah's Song," *OTS* 14 (l965) 206-13.

[8] Cf. Brooke, McLean, Thackery, *ad loc.*

[9] For *prophaseis* as translation for *'lylh* cf. also Ps. 140(141):4.

[10] Cf. A. M. Ceriani, *Translatio Syra Pescitto Veteris Testamenti ex Codice Ambrosian*, (Milan, 1876-83) cf. folio column 81r. It is quite possible that the Syriac here has been corrected in the direction of a Greek text like Symmachus.

[11] Cf. Brooke, McLean, Thackeray, *ad loc.*

[12] The text history of the Song of Hannah as a whole is further complicated by its character as an independent unit. Apart from Samuel it is also preserved as one of the collection of Odes that are appended to the Psalms in some Greek MSS and in the Old Latin and Syro-Hexaplaric versions. The Targum, on the other hand, omits the poem completely and substitutes a totally different text in its place.

[13] E.g. Thenius, *Die Bücher Samuels*, translates the bi-cola with the MT *kethib*, "nicht festgestellt sind Freveltaten." But "freveltaten," i.e. "mischievousness," is not necessarily implied in *'aliylah*. While Driver, *Notes on the Hebrew Text of the Books of Samuel*, reads with the *qere*, Budde, *Die Bücher Samuel*, allows that both the *qere* and the Greek evidence offer possibilities, and then offers dubious support for the latter with the suggestion that the original text might have begun with *w'elohim*. P. Dhorme's rendition in *Les livres de Samuel* is perhaps the most original: "et (ses) gestes son sans Reproche."

more recent translations and commentaries have settled for the solution indicated by the MT *qere* and/or by the LXX majority tradition. [14] Accordingly the enigma of the text at this point remains unabated.

It is argued here that this interpretive impasse can be bridged by the recognition that *wl'* should be read, not as a negative, but as the asseverative particle *lu'*, i.e. "indeed" or "verily." The use of this particle has been clearly demonstrated in other Semitic languages including Ugaritic, as well as elsewhere in the Biblical text itself.[15] Employing this usage, the final cola of verse three would read: "For the Lord is a God of Knowledge, Verily deeds are weighed" (or "deeds are surely weighed," or the like). [16] Such a rendering not only satisfies the demands of the received text but also offers clearer contextual and theological sense.

Moreover, if this is taken as the proper original reading, it is not difficult to understand how the complications illustrated by the history of the text might arise in later times when the asseverative particle was no longer widely employed or understood.[17] Implicit here is a conclusion about the dating of the Song of Hannah, i.e. that it is definitely preexilic in origin and most likely belongs, at least in part, with that corpus of early Hebrew poems which predate the ninth century B.C. [18] Both the formal structure of the Song and its vocabulary show strong

[14] Cf. e.g. RSV: JPS (1955); Jerusalem Bible (1961); also G. Bressan, "Il cantico di Anna," *Biblica* 33 (1953) 67-89; and McCarter *Samuel I*, 69.

[15] Cf. F. Nötscher, "Zum Emphatischen Lamed," *VT* 3 (1953) 372-80: W. L. Moran, "The Hebrew Language in its Northwest Semitic Background," pp. 60-61, 69 in *The Bible and the Ancient Near East* (ed. by G. E. Wright, Garden City, NY: Doubleday, 1961); Also J. Huehnergard, "Asseverative **la* and Hypothetical **lu/law* in Semitic"; T. Muraoka, *Emphatic Words and Structures in Biblical Hebrew*; D. Sivan and W. Schniedewind, "Letting your 'Yes' be 'No' in Ancient Israel: A Study of the Asseverative *la'* and *halo'.*"

[16] An alternative translation which would also both honor the *kethib* and preserve the negative force would involve reading the final bi-colon as a question, i.e. "and are not actions weighed?" Cf. A. F. Kirkpatrick, *The First Book of Samuel* (Cambridge: Cambridge Bible, 1930) 53 n. 3. The semantic correlation with our suggested reading is obvious. Nötscher's observations regarding the semantic interchange between the negative rhetorical question and the clause with asseverative force clearly apply at this point (cf. "Zum Emphatischen Lamed," 374-75). This points also to a possible explanation for the morphological correspondence between the negative and asseverative particles in Semitic.

[17] It is now quite clear that the ancient versions were almost totally unfamiliar with the several archaic particles (including especially enclitic *mem* and emphatic *ki*, as well as emphatic or asseverative *lamed*) whose preservation in Hebrew poetry, and elsewhere in the Biblical text, has now been made clear by Ugaritic studies. Another addition to the body of evidence in this regard is provided in the study of M. Dahood, "Vocative Lamedh in the Psalter," *VT* 16 (1966) 299-314, where the failure of the versions to recognize the related "vocative lamed" particle is indicated.

[18] Cf. D. N. Freedman, "Archaic Forms in Early Hebrew Poetry," *ZAW* 72 (1960) 101-07 and esp. 101 n.l, where a useful bibliography referent to this corpus is provided. Also see D. N. Freedman, "Divine Names and Titles in Early Hebrew Poetry," 55-107 in *Magnalia Dei: The Mighty Acts of God. Essays on the Bible and Archaeology in Memory of G. Ernest Wright* (ed. by F. M. Cross, W. E. Lemke, and P. D. Miller, Jr., Garden City, NY: Doubleday, 1976).

correspondences with other early poetic pieces as is testified to in more recent treatments.[19]

Finally, though without pretending to resolve the issue of primary authorship in any way, a case for the inclusion of the poem as part of the original composit of Samuel can be made on the basis of the fact that several of the other recognized occurrences of the asseverative particle also occur within the Samuel text (cf. e.g. II Sam 18:12; 19:7).[20] Notably these examples appear within the so-called "Court History" (II Sam 9-20, I Kings 1-2) which is generally regarded to stem from the early monarchy. That the poem itself, in its final form, comes from a period not before the beginning of the monarchy seem to be indicated by the final cola of verse 10, i.e. "And He will give strength to His King, and exalt the horn of His anointed."[21]   However, on the basis of the evidence here discussed, it is clearly possible that in some part it may have enjoyed even a slightly earlier history.

---

[19]Cf. Willis, "The Song of Hannah and Psalm 113"; Albright, *Yahweh and the Gods of Canaan*, 20-22; McCarter, *I Samuel*, 75-76.

[20]Cf. D. Sivan and W. Schniedenwind, "Letting your 'Yes' be 'No' in Ancient Israel: A Study of the Asseverative *la'* and *halo'*," 219-20.

[21]This final bi-colon, however, may be seen as an addition to a still earlier form of the poem; so A. Klosterman, *Die Bücher Samuelis und der Konige* (SZ III Nördlingen, 1887) *ad loc*, though Budde is probably correct in arguing that they are integral to the poem in its present construction (cf. Budde, *Die Bücher Samuels*, 16). McCarter (*I Samuel*, 75-76, and n. 5-7) provides a concise summation on the current status of the chronological discussion. He provisionally dates the Song of Hannah to the late tenth or early ninth century B.C., while Freedman, "Divine names and Titles in Early Hebrew Poetry," concludes that a date *ca.* 1000 B.C. would be appropriate.

Judith's *Sophia* and *Synesis*: Educated Jewish Women in the Late Second Temple Period?

Linda Bennett Elder
Valdosta State University

In 1983, in a discourse on Women in Judaism before 70 *CE*, Elisabeth Schüssler-Fiorenza lamented the lack of feminist critical analysis of Jewish literature in the Second Temple Period "between the Bible and the Mishnah."[1] A decade later, at the Ninth Berkeshire Conference on the History of Women, classicist Sarah Pomeroy suggested that the next major locus for exploration of women's history in the ancient world is the Hellenistic period.[2] Pomeroy's comment aroused an animated exchange among classicists at the conference about frustrations and complexities that attend research in this period. For many of the reasons cited in response to Pomeroy's challenge, the quest to discover evidence for Jewish women's history in the Hellenistic era has attracted little attention. Yet, although Judaisms in the Hellenistic and Greco-Roman worlds continue to be re-defined, Schüssler-Fiorenza's lamentation has become a clarion call to a handful of feminist scholars.

---

[1] E. Schüussler-Fiorenza, *In Memory of Her* (Boston: Beacon, 1983) 108.
[2] S. B. Pomeroy, "The Social and Sexual Politics of Martrilineality in Classical Greec," Ninth Berkeshire Conference on the History of Women, Vassar College, Poughkeepsie NY, June 1993. Professor Pomeroy's remarks about the Hellenistic world were made during her response to questions concerning her paper.

Astute considerations for the analysis of Jewish Women in the Greco-Roman world are aptly described in recent monographs and anthologies.[3] A. J. Levine presents a particularly valuable overview of theoretical and methodological considerations represented in this research.[4] Historical reconstructions and narrative analyses that are related to Jewish women in the Late Second Temple period, however, want more synchronous and culture specific discussion. The present paper intends such an inquiry.

Methodological Concerns

A prinicpal methodological premise adopted for this endeavor maintains that characterizations of Judith are shaped and influenced by representations and realities of women in the author's cultural ambient. Social location is a category of inquiry that facilitates both narrative analysis in the Book of Judith and reconstructions of the social reality of Jewish women in the historical milieu of the author. For purposes of this study social location is defined as the subject's relationship to external (social) aspects of reality within the community that determine and define her status and influence within that community. In a broad context these aspects might include station within the family unit, marital status, property ownership, ethnicity, class, occupation, education, religious affiliation and praxis. The three aspects of Judith's social reality that are most clearly articulated in the text include her widowhood/inheritance (Jdt 8:4, 7), asceticism/religious praxis (Jdt 8:5-6) and education. The latter category, which is by far the most speculative, is the subject of the present inquiry.

While I grant that there may indeed be historical roots for the Judith figure in Jewish folk tradition, I concur with scholarly consensus that affirms her identity as a fictional character. My arguments, however, proceed from the premise that regardless of historical roots, Judith was a "viable" female protagonist to audiences of popular fiction in Hellenistic Palestine. Current scholarship on Judaisms in the Hellenistic age supports the hypothesis that the author of Judith writes based upon an experience of certain Hellenistic influences as normative in Jewish life, especially among wealthy Jews in Palestine. The Book of Judith was probably written by a Palestinian Jew in the Hasmonean period (142-63 *BCE*), by which

---

[3] A.J. Levine, ed., *Women Like This: New Perspectives on Jewish Women in the Greco-Roman World* (Early Judaism and Its Literature; Atlanta: Scholars Press, SBL, 1991); R. S. Kraemer, *Her Share of the Blessings* (New York: Oxford University Press, 1992); C. A. Brown, *No Longer Be Silent* (Louisville: Westminster/John Knox, 1992).

[4] Among issues under consideration Levine includes: public and private spheres; symbolic use of the female as metaphor, allegory, exemplar; gender considerations; cross cultural comparison; the prescriptive or descriptive nature of texts; Hellenistic and Hebraic conjunctions; temporal displacement; conditions of a document's authorship, production and audience reception. (Levine, *Women Like This* xi-xvii).

time many norms of Greek education and culture had been absorbed and assimilated. [5]

In the eighth chapter of the Book of Judith the author introduces Judith, a young widow who appears to have possessed an unusual authority to counsel the *gerousia* (Magistrates/Elders) of her city (Jdt 8:11-27). Her status as wealthy and propertied and as a religious ascetic would have had a bearing on this authority. Attentive readings of the text, however, suggest that Judith's authority resided as well in a wisdom, intelligence and sophisticated theological sensitivity that proceeded from an educated person.

My premise that representations and realities of women in the author's cultural ambient shape characterization of Judith prompts questions about whether the author of the Book of Judith (possibly as late as 63 *BCE*) intended for the audience to understand that this fictional protagonist was educated. If so, might the author's characterization of Judith provide clues about the education of some Jewish women in the Hellenistic world? Considering the myriad arguments about what constituted "education" in the Hellenistic world, it is of paramount importance to articulate that this paper proposes *descriptors* of education not definitions.

The question of Judith's social location as an educated woman has not previously been addressed in scholarly discourse.[6] Despite quite viable arguments that could be advanced for an un-educated Judith's sagacity and understanding, I argue here that the author intended for the audience to perceive that Judith was educated. Several strata of contextualization converge to undergird my argument. In the larger project from which the present paper is derived, a brief description of Hellenistic education is followed by evidence for educated women in the Hellenistic world.[7] Texts, archives, inscriptions and iconographical images are cited as evidence for educated women among Hellenistic queens, philosophers,

---

[5]C.A.Moore, *The Book of Judith* (AB Garden City, New York: Doubleday, 1985) 49-56. Moore provides a comprehensive discussion of scholarship on the dating of Judith.

[6]Modified and abbreviated versions of this paper have been presented in the Hellenistic Judaism Section at the Annual Meeting of the Society of Biblical Literature, Washington D.C., November 1993 and at the Eastern Great Lakes Biblical Society, Canton, Ohio, April 1994.

[7]L.Bennett Elder, "Transformations in the Judith Mythos: A Feminist Critical Analysis," unpublished diss., Florida State University, Tallahassee, Fl. 1991. Two studies on education in the ancient world that were immensely helpful include J. T. Townsend, "Ancient Education in the Time of the Early Roman Empire" in *The Catacombs and the Colosseum*, S. Benko and J. O'Rourke eds. (Valley Forge: Judson, 1971); H. I. Marrou, *A History of Education in Antiquity* (New York: Sheed and Ward, 1956); W.V. Harris, *Ancient Literacy* (Cambridge, Ma: Harvard University Press, 1989). Harris cautions against overly optimistic speculations about literacy in the ancient world. It is important to note concerning the present study my interests reside in *paideia* and education among the Jews Harris frequently neglects to distinguish the similarities and differences between literacy and education. It is also worthy of note that Professor Harris' study does not address the proliferation of literature among the Jews in the Second Temple period.

physicians, religious functionaries, poets, musicians and painters.[8] As my focus
narrows to Jewish education in the Hellenistic period this study follows S. J. D.
Cohen in assuming that

> all Judaisms of the Hellenistic period of both the diaspora and the land of Israel were
> Hellenized, that is, were integral parts of the culture of the ancient world. Some varieties
> of Judaisms were more Hellenized than others but none was an island unto itself.[9]

Education Among the Jews in the Hellenistic Period

The issue of education among the Jews in the Second Temple period is
fraught with ambiguities, many of which proceed from conflicts among scholars
concerning "varieties of Judaisms."[10] In the present paper a brief review of the
status of education in the cultural ambient of the author of the Book of Judith
follows Martin Hengel's argument for the gradual introduction of formal education
among Jews in Palestine.[11] Hengel proposes connections between threats posed
by an encroaching Hellenistic influence upon Judaism and the experienced
necessity among the Hasidim to engage the whole people of Israel in the study of
Torah. From the time of the Hasidim, and the concurrent influence of Hellenistic
paideia, there occurs in Judaism an increased emphasis on education. Two
principal factors that bear upon Hengel's arguments are the extensive evidence for
Greek language in Jewish culture and the presence and persistence of Greek

[8]Over the last fifteen yeats myriad texts, epigraphs and inscriptions from the Greco-Roman world
(including Hellenistic texts) that attest women's participation in culture have been identified and brought
into the discourse. A representative sample of works that present these texts in translation include: S. B.
Pomeroy, *Goddesses, Whores, Wives and Slaves* (New York: Schoken, 1975), *Women in Hellenistic
Egypt* (New York: Schoken, 1984), "Technikai kai Musikai" *American Journal of Ancient History* 2
(1977); M. Lefkowitz and M. B. Fant, *Women's Lives in Greece and Rome* (Baltimore: Johns Hopkins
University Press, 1982); G. H. Macurdy, *Hellenistic Queens* (Baltimore: Johns Hopkins University Press,
1932); R. S. Kraemer, *Maenads, Martyrs Matrons and Monastics* (Philadelphia: Fortress, 1988); C.
Averil and E. Kuhrt eds. *Images of Women in Antiquity* (Detroit: Wayne State University Press, 1981);
B. Geller-Nathanson "Reflections on the Silent Woman of Judaism and Her Pagan Roman Counterpart,"
The Listening Heart: Essays in Wisdom and Psalms in Honor of Roland Murphy, O.Carm. K.Hoglund
ed. JSOTSup 58 (Sheffield: Sheffield Academic Press, 1987); M. Meunier, *Femmes pythagoriennes:
Fragments et lettres Theano, Perictione, Phintys, Melissa et Myia*, (Paris: 1932); S.K. Heyob, *The Cult
of Isis Among Women in the Graeco Roman World* (Leiden: Brill, 1975); M.E.Waithe, *A History of
Women Philosophers*, V.1 (Dordrecht, Boston, Lancaster: Nijhoff, 1987).
[9]S. J. D. Cohen, *From the Maccabees to the Mishnah* (Philadelphia: Westminster Press, 1987)
37.
[10]For a multiplicity of perspectives on scholarship in Early Judaism see: E. Bickerman, *Jews in
the Greek Age* (Cambridge MA: Harvard University Press, 1988), Cohen *Macabees*; M. Hengel *Judaism
and Hellenism* 2 Vols. (Philadelphia: Fortress, 1974); J. H. Charlesworth, ed., *OTP*, 2 vols.(Garden City,
New York: Doubleday, 1985); G. W. E. Nickelsburg, *Jewish Literature Between the Bible and the
Mishnah* (Philadelphia: Fortress, 1981); G. W. E. Nickelsburg and M. E. Stone, *Faith and Piety in Early
Judaism* (Philadelphia: Fortress, 1983).
[11]Hengel, *Judaism* vol.1., 78-83..

thought in Jewish literature of the Late Second Temple period before, during and after the Maccabean revolt against Hellenism in Jerusalem.[12]

In addition to traditional scribal schools that were closely related to the cult, by 180-175 *BCE* the *bet-midrash* of Sirach and a Hellenestic *Gymnasium* supported by the Jewish upper classes prospered in Jerusalem. [13]

Uzziah remarks in Jdt 8:29 that Judith was known for her wisdom and understanding from the time that she was a child. Questions about the education of Jewish children, informed by the work of Cohen, John T.Townsend, Joseph Kaster and David Goodblatt indicate, however, that precise dating for the development of Jewish elementary schools is problematic.[14] Talmudic texts propose both Simeon b. Shetah (y *Ketub.* 8.2) in the first century *BCE* and Joshua b. Gamala (b. *B Bat* 21) in the first century *CE* as first to decree compulsory education for all Jewish children.[15]

Although the historicity of these sources is debatable the gradual introduction of elementary schools, which may indeed have begun under the tutelage of early Hasidic scribes, became a more formal process during the first century *CE*. Townsend suggests that in Palestine and the Diaspora, pedagogical methods and curricular format that became normative for education at this level exhibit striking Hellenistic influence.[16] For instance, Greek education proceeded according to three stages: Primary, Secondary and Advanced. Under the instruction of the *didaskolos* students at the Primary level began schooling at about seven years of age. They completed secondary school under the instruction of their *grammatikos* in the mid to late teens. Those few students who received advanced training, the *ephebetes*, usually finished within two years time (18-20 years).[17]

After the advent of formal elementary schools for Jewish children the *bet sopher* or primary school was presided over by a *sopher* or scribe. Curriculum included the study of scripture and instruction in Jewish liturgies.[18] By the time of the rabbis, Jewish students, moved to a *bet midrash* or secondary school for study of the Oral Torah.[19] This process had its genesis in the Hellenistic period

---

[12] Hengel *Judaism* vol.1, 58-65.

[13] "So they built a Gymnasium at Jerusalem according to Gentile custom . . ." I Mac 1:14); See Hengel *Judaism*, 65 vol.1, for a discussion of the gymnasium. Also see J. T. Townsend, "Ancient" 154-157;. R. Doran, "Questions About Education," Presented at the Sociology of the Second Temple Group, Annual Meeting of the *SBL*, San Francisco, CA. 1992. Doran discusses Sirach (1-5), Jewish education in Alexandria (5-8), the Gymnasium in Jerusalem (8-11). See also R. Doran, "Jason's Gymnasium" in *Of Scribes and Scrolls*, H.Attridge, J.Collins eds. (Lanham, Md.: University Press of America, 1990).

[14] J. Townsend, " Ancient" 24 141; Cohen, *Macabees*, Chapter 5; D. Goodblatt, "The Beruriah Traditions" *JJS* 26 1/2 75. 82-83; J. Kaster, "Education O.T." *IDB* New York: Abingdon 1962.

[15] Cohen, *Macabees*.

[16] Townsend,"Ancient" 154-157.

[17] J.Townsend, "Education N.T." *AB Dictionary*, D.N.Freedman ed. (New York: Doubleday, 1992). See also H.Marrou 102-115.

[18] Townsend, "Ancient" 155-156.

[19] Townsend, "Ancient" 155.

where Sirach's *oikia paideia* (Sir 51:23) functioned as a secondary school in pre-Maccabean Jerusalem.[20] Among earliest evidence of a formal school for Jewish children in Palestine is the reference to the "children's class" among the community at Qumran (1QSa 1.8) probably in De Vaux's Qumran Period 1B, in the second half of the first century *BCE*.[21] Considering the plethora of texts discovered at Qumran it is reasonable to assume that "Secondary" and "Advanced" training among the community who generated these writings consisted in the knowledge of and meditation upon a variety of types of texts. Thomas Conley attests that in Alexandria the education of the Jewish philosopher, mystic, theologian, Philo (20 *BCE* to 50 *CE*) included elements of Hellenistic *encyclios paideia* as well as knowledge of the Law and the Prophets of Israel.[22] Hengel suggests that during the Late Second Temple period

> anyone who belonged to the people of God, even the proselyte, was invited to study Wisdom and provided that person had the application and the aptitude, the person had the possibility to become a great teacher of the Law.[23]

Increased emphasis on education in Israel was attended by an elaboration of new liturgies consisting of prayer, recitation and the study of scripture. As Cohen reminds us, there also developed in this period a regimen of private prayer and worship previously un-attested in Pre-exilic Israel.

The word of God was the object of constant study and meditation, the very act of study was deemed an act of worship. Commandments of Torah were expanded and elaborated thus affording the individual Jew an opportunity for demonstrating his [or her] loyalty to God.[24]

The new emphasis on education, piety and devotion elucidates, at least in part, a plausible context for the subsequent development of sectarian movements,

---

[20] Townsend, "Ancient" 156-157.

[21] R. De Vaux, *Archaeology and the Dead Sea Scrolls* (London: Oxford University Press, 1973.

[22] T. Conley "General Education in Philo of Alexandria," *Proceedings of the Center for Hermeneutical Studies in Hellenistic and Modern Culture*, January 1975 (Berkeley: University of California Press, 1975). Respondents to Conley's paper include J. Dillon, D. Winston and an assortment of scholars from Classics, Rhetoric and Assyriology. Conley begins by citing Philo's references to general education: *Cong.* 15, 74; *Cher.* 105; *Agr.* 18; *Ebr.* 49; *Somn.* I. 205, and notes the importance of both Greek and Jewish education in Philo's thought. Philo's works indicate that the writings he studied included Homer, Hesiod, Euripedes, Menander, Sophocles, Aeschuylus, Pindar, Solon and Theognis. (15) In his discussion of *paideia*, Conley notes grammar, rhetoric, music and geometry, along with arithmetic and dialectic. More detailed and varied lists are also noted by Robert Grant, "Carpocratians and Curriculum," *Christians Among Jews and Gentiles* G. E. W. Nicklesburg and G. W. MacRae, S.J., eds. (Philadelphia: Fortress, 1986). One tetrad is said to consist of agronomy, medicine, rhetoric and military science! Other lists that illustrate the perspectives of various thinkers over several centuries include: architecture, harmony, astronomy, logic, law, painting and sculpture. For another discussion of Philo's education see also D. Winston, *Philo of Alexandria* (New York: Paulist 1971).

[23] Hengel, *Judaism* vol.1. 80; See also W. F. Albright, *From the Stone Age to Christianity* (Baltimore: Johns Hopkins University Press, 1940) 355; E. Bickerman, *RB* 59 (1952) 53.

[24] Cohen, *Maccabees* 22.

formal schools, houses of prayer, synagogues, and a large literary corpus that characterize the Late Second Temple period. I would argue that Judith's pious devotion and theological intensity are also representative of that tendency.

Evidence for Educated Jewish Women in the Hellenistic Period

In recent years there has been greater recognition among scholars that Jewish women were more prominent in public life during the Hasmonean Dynasty.[25] Yet, whereas studies by Henri Marrou and Pomeroy attest to the education of female children and adults in Greece, Rome and Hellenistic Egypt, the education of Jewish females in the Second Temple period does not receive attention in scholarly discourse. It should, however, be apparent that in the context of the emphasis on education in Hellenistic culture in general and in Judasim in particular, some Jewish women in the Second Temple period were educated. The following cursory overview attempts to remain within the chronological margins of the Late Second Temple period that define the present study.

Among Jewish women advanced as viable candidates for our consideration I would include the Hasmonean Queen, Salome Alexandra (76-67 *BCE*) (Josephus *J.W.* I 112-113), as well as her grandaughter Alexandra, who was one of the *dramatis personae* in the Herodian intrigues (Josephus *Ant.* XV 43-49).

Female Theraputae are praised by Philo for their ardent study of wisdom and their advance of the study of philosophy (Philo *V.C.* II. 5-6). Theraputae seek wisdom from the holy scripture and from the writings of their ancestral philosophy, which they interpret allegorically. In addition to contemplation they compose hymns and psalms to God in a variety of metres and melodies (Philo *V.C.* III. 29). In my work on female ascetics at Qumran, I argue that Daughters of Truth and the Venerable Women from 4Q 502 are educated.[26]

Bernadette Brooten's evidence for women leaders in ancient synagogues ranges in date from the last quarter of the first century *BCE* to the sixth century *CE* and is primarily outside the province of the present study.[27] Nonetheless, Brooten's descriptions of the titles for female Heads of Synagogues and Elders, in particular, and her conclusions concerning their incumbent duties, present another instance in which it is apparent that the women who bore these titles would have been educated. Brooten cites a female Head of Synagogue, Sophia of Gortyn at Kisamos, Crete, in the first or second century *CE* whose dates are within the parameters of the present study.

---

[25] J. B. Segal, "The Jewish Attitude Towards Women," *JJS* 30 2 4/79 135.

[26] L. Bennett Elder, "The Woman Question and Female Ascetics Among Essenes" *BA* 57/4 1994.

[27] B. Brooten, *Women Leaders in the Ancient Synagogues* Brown Judaic Studies 36 (1982). See also S. J. D. Cohen "Women in the Synagogues of Antiquity," *CJ* 34 2 (Nov/Dec 1980) 23-29 on the inscriptive evidence for female leadership in the synagogues.

Daniel Harrington's treatment of Pseudo-Philo (135 *BCE*-70 *CE*) situates these texts in the milieu of the synagogue and notes concerning the treatment of women "interesting plays on O.T. cliches from what would now be described as a feminist perspective."[28] Following an analysis of Hannah texts in Pseudo- Philo, Joan E. Cook concludes that if the Pseudo-Philo corpus was written to be read in the synagogues "the listening congregation acknowledged and respected women as wise teachers in the community."[29] I would argue that the figures of Deborah (*Bib. Ant.* 30-33) and Seila, daughter of Jepthah (*Bib.Ant.* 40:1-9) as they are depicted in Pseudo-Philo also affirm Cook's hypothesis.[30]

Judith and Questions about Education

Now, enter with me if you will, the world of the fictional Judith as protagonist in a dramatic narrative. In this analysis I abandon customary characterizations of Judith that focus primarily on her role as a female assasain, a theological "answer" to Esther, a metaphor for Judas Maccabeus or a Type of the People of Israel.[31] Here, Judith is *subject*. The author's complex characteriztion attributes to Judith elements of self formation that invite, for the feminist historian, irresistable questions about education as an aspect of Jewish women's social reality in this cultural ambient.

Speculations about Judith's Education during Her Childhood

We turn now to the enigmatic text in Jdt 8:29 in which Uzziah declares that Judith has been known for her "wisdom" from the beginning of her days.

---

[28] D. Harrington, "Pseudo-Philo" *OTPs* 300.

[29] J. E. Cook "Pseudo Philo's Song of Hannah: Testament of a Mother in Israel," *JSP* 9 (1991) 103-114.

[30] Following Cook's paradigm I introduce a discussion of these two figures in the synagogue setting suggested by Harrington. (L.Bennett Elder "Transformations" chap. 3, for Deborah see 156-158, for Seila see 158-160.

[31] M. S. Enslin, *The Book of Judith* (Leiden: Brill, 1972). S. Zeitlin's "General Introduction" to Enslin's commentary and translation advances Judith's persona as an asassain and explores in some depth the relationship between Judith and Esther from several perspectives, including the issue of inclusion in the Hebrew canon. Zeitlin argues that the author of Judith wrote his narrative as an "answer to Esther." Zeitlin also posits Judith as a metaphor for Judas Maccabeus (28-30). A. J. Levine "Sacrifice and Salvation: Otherness and Domesticationin the Book of Judith," in *No One Spoke Ill of Her* (Atlanta: Scholars Press, 1992). Levine joins a host of scholars who objectify Judith as a metaphor for the Jews /community of faith. For a comprehensive discussion of the variety of interpretive frameworks that have captured the imagination of Judith scholars see C. A. Moore, *Judith* 64-66. See also Bennett Elder, "Transformations." The Judith mythos is analyzed from the perspective of Judith's social location in the ambient of the author of the Book of Judith as well as interpretations of Judith by biblical scholars and theologians from the first century *CE* to the present. This study also considers transformations of the Judith mythos in the arts and humanities from the eighth century *CE* to the present.

. . . today is not the first time your wisdom (*sophia*) has been shown but from the beginning of your days, all of the people have known your intelligence/understanding (*synesin*) for the disposition of your heart is good.

Because Uzziah's comment follows immediately upon Judith's theological and historical instruction and her exhortation to the Elders of the city, it seems clear that these demonstrate, at least in part, the *sophia* and *synesis* to which he refers. It is, however, more difficult to postulate an arena in which all of the people would have been aware of Judith's wisdom, intelligence and nobility of heart. The text itself proffers nothing. Anything that can be suggested will be highly speculative. The following imaginative reconstructions for this enigmatic pericope, however, suggest possible means by which the fictional character Judith (and, by analogy, historical women in the Late Second Temple period) might have acquired an education and have come to be known for her wisdom from the "beginning of her days."

I think most scholars would argue that, if indeed Judith was educated, she would have been educated exclusively by private tutors. I concur. Imaginative reconstructions that lend credence to Uzziah's statement, however, reduce the prospect of a private tutor. Theories might include a situation wherein a *bet sopher* was engaged for Judith and all of the children on a family estate.[32] Such a master instructed little girls like Judith and the female child of a family servant who later became Judith's trusted *abra* (female servant). Judith's *abra* was indeed sufficiently literate (and educated?) to serve as steward of the estate Judith inherited from her husband (Jdt 8:7b, 10). In an informal *bet sopher* on the family estate, Judith studied with other children and acquired a reputation for wisdom "from the beginning of her days."

In a second scenario, I suggest that men like Judith's father, Merari (Jdt 8:1), followed an injunction proclaimed by Jose ben Jo'ezer, a contemporary of Sirach, to "bring wise men into your home and drink their knowledge thirstily"(*Abot* I. 4 IA; *Gen. Rab.* 65.22). During such visits, animated instruction in the scripture by a Hasidic sage was common in Merari's home. In this setting it was expected that one would find Merari's sagacious daughter, Judith, seated at the feet of the old sage, absorbing his wise teachings.

My interest in the synagogue/*proschue* (house of prayer) as a site for Judith's early education was prompted by I. Sonne's suggestion that elementary schools were frequently attached to the synagogue/*prosuche*.[33] This keen interest

---

[32] This assumes that in an agnatic line of inheritance Judith's father, Merairi, was as wealthy as her late husband and kinsman, Manasseh.(Jdt 8:1-2)

[33] I. Sonne, "Synagogue," IDB 1962. The synagogue was indeed a site for instruction in Torah. Sonne suggests that when elementary schools were instituted they were frequently attached to or adjacent to the synagogue (477). He also notes that there is no clear ruling for, or evidence of, the separation of the sexes in the synagogues in early rabbinic sources (486). On the basis of Sonne's arguments it is not unreasonable to suggest that until schools were built, villages that had a synagogue/*prosuche* educated their youngsters there.

has been tempered a bit, however, by Lester Grabbe's article cautioning toward later dates for a pervasivenesss of synagogues in Palestine.[34]

Judith as an Educated Woman

More substantive arguments for an educated Judith are grounded in her instruction to the Elders in Jdt 8:11-28. The proposition that only an educated Judith would direct theological exhortation to the Elders of her city constitutes my principal thesis. Studies by Goodblatt and Robert Doran facilitate my analysis of the Judith narrative.

Goodblatt's article " The Beruriah Traditions" provides a methodological paradigm.[35] Goodblatt contends that whether or not Talmudic Beruriah texts are good biographical data, they nevertheless contain valuable evidence about the possible educational achievements of women in rabbinic society. He determines the provenance of relevant passages and the degree of formal education attributed to Beruriah in the sources. Goodblatt isolates pericopae that could have been the provenance of any woman brought up in a rabbinic household, explores the remaining texts, identifies their contexts and finally demonstrates that Beruriah possessed interpretive and exegetical skills that could only be acquired at advanced levels of education.[36] Goodblatt's appraisal of texts demonstrates Beruriah's advanced education on the basis of both the specific content of her discourses and the particular settings in which the discourses are delivered.

Although Goodblatt's study reviews Talmudic texts that emerged over several centuries, I find his methodology instructive for my proposal that the author of the Book of Judith intends a formally educated protagonist. Just as in Goodblatt's analysis of the Beruriah texts, we find in the Book of Judith that both the substantive content and physical contexts are constituative elements of the author's exposition of Judith's theology, her knowledge of history, military strategy, liturgical composition and prayer that presuppose formal study or instruction.

Doran's discussion of criteria for what constitutes education among Jews in the Second Temple Period also assists my analysis.[37] His argument that education at the Gymnasium in Jerusalem would have included both Greek *and* Jewish curriculum is immensely instructive. Doran reminds us that the High Priests' regard for their Jewish constituency in developing their curriculum is only reasonable:

> Given the developing literary education curriculum among Jews in Alexandria as well as attempts by Sirach to include Greek . . . for the education of young Jews, I would

[34] L. Grabbe, "Synagogues in Pre-70 Palestine: A Reasessment," *JTS* 39 (1988) 159-189.
[35] D. Goodblatt, "The Beruriah Traditions," *JJS* 26 (Spring /Autumn 1975) 69-85.
[36] Goodblatt, "Beruriah" 84.
[37] R. Doran, "Questions" 1-11.

argue that a Roman rather than an Athenian model should be applied to Jerusalem. The literary education of young Jews in Jerusalem would have remained an education in the laws, language and literature of Judea . . . alongside this education in Greek language and rhetoric would have taken place.[38]

Doran extrapolates Sirach's references to "education" and contends that for the sage, Sir 6:27-32; 8:8-9 and 39:1-5 are descriptive of Sirach's criteria for education. A selective composite of these criteria indicates as foremost, the student's devotion to a Wise Teacher(s). The student is also instructed to search out the wisdom of the ancients (Sir 39:1 b), to take a stand in the throng of elders (Sir 6:34), to return an answer in time of need (Sir 8:9), to pray (Sir 39:5), to be prepared to serve before the great rulers(Sir 39:4a) and to travel through lands of strange peoples to test the good and evil among them (Sir 39:4b). Those conversant with Judith will recognize that this protagonist meets each of the criteria of Sirach outlined above, save the first. I return to Sirach's criteria following an explication of Judith's theology, knowledge of history, military expertise, liturgical composition and prayer.

Theology

Moore maintains "with some justification one might describe Judith as the sole female theologian in the OT."[39] The authorative character and theological nature of hortatory and didactic injunctions directed by Judith to the *gerousia* in Jdt 8:14-27, confirm Moore's assertion. Both the contextual conditions and the substance of these injunctions are revealing. In the midst of a national crisis when their city is under threat of seige and destruction, a young, wealthy, widowed ascetic summons the Elders of her city to her rooftop hermitage and they respond affirmatively to her call (Jdt 8:10-11). A dialogue commences in which Judith challenges the Elder's understanding of the relationship between God and humankind and chastises them for their presumptions and arrogance before God. Judith asks the leaders of her city " Who are you to put God to the test . . . in doing this you are setting yourselves up in the place of God, among the sons of men" (Jdt 8:12-13). Judith's instructions on the nature of God and the limitations of human beings that follow (Jdt 8:14-15) indicate Judith's perceived authority among these men. In a pericope reminiscent of Job 38, Judith's reminds the leaders of her city:

> you cannot plumb the depths of the human heart nor find out what a man [sic] is thinking . . . How do you expect to search out God, who made all these things and find out God's mind or comprehend God's thought (Jdt 8:14).

[38] Doran, "Questions" 9.
[39] Moore, *Judith* 186.

Following George W. E. Nickelsberg I also identify the didactic and exhortatory function of Judith with Israel's Wisdom tradition.[40] An association of the rational, empirical character of Judith's theological erudition and her marked anthropological and ethical perspective is consistent with Wisdom in Israel. If this association, posited as well by J. C. Dancy, E. Schüssler-Fiorenza and Anitra Bingham-Kolenkow, was intended by the author, the probability that the fictional Judith received formal instruction becomes more tenable.[41] Cohen contends that in the Late Second Temple period people "claim political and religious authority on the basis of their scriptural expertise."[42]

Judith's instruction of the magistrates in Jdt 8:18-20 reflects her expertise as an exegete. Her discourse here does not elaborate specific encounters but in explicit allusions to paradigmatic events she graphically articulates the fate of apostates. These exhortations may be informed by texts such as 2 Kings 19 and the threatened capture of Jerusalem under Hezikiah or Judg 9:57 and the curse of Jotham upon the Schechemites, in which "all of their wickedness would fall back upon their heads." In Jdt 8:26-27 Judith makes deliberate references to the trials, ordeals and testings of the heart endured by Abraham (Gen 14 - 21), Isaac (Gen 21- 28) and Jacob (Gen 27- 37).

Judith's instruction to the principal Elders of Bethulia requires knowledge of traditional interpretations of Deity reflected in Deuteronomic thought. This female protagonist, however, also demonstrates a moving beyond formulaic interpretations of God to those which demand living in and accepting the ambiguities of reality. Judith's theology is consistent with an emphasis on the action and reponsibility of the individual that is characteristic of the Hellenistic *Weltanschauung*. She indicates as well a familiarity with Wisdom traditions reflected in Koheleth and Job. The political and religious authority implicit in Judith's exhortations, her theological erudition and the Elder's acquiesence to her injunctions in Jdt 8:11-35 demonstrate an expertise acquired through some process of education.

History

Among principles for education in ancient Judasim, J. Kaster specifies the transmission of the *historical* heritage of the Hebrew nation, embracing the saga

---

[40] Nickelsburg, *Jewish Literature* 107.

[41] J. C. Dancy, "Judith" *The Shorter Books of the Apocrypha* (Cambridge: Cambridge University Press, 1972) 99; Schussler- Fiorenza, *In Memory* 109; A. Bingham-Kolenkow (L. Alonso-Schokel "Narrative Structures in the Book of Judith" Proceedings of the Protocol Series of the Colloquies of the Center for Hermeneutical Studies in Hellenistic and Modern Culture 12.15 (March 1, 1974) (Berkeley: University of California Press, 1974) 66-67.

[42] Cohen, *Macabees* 27. It has been interesting to observe that it is female exegetes who specifically discuss authority as a descriptor of Judith's character. See Schüssler-Fiorenza, *In Memory*, 116; T. Craven, *Artistry and Faith in the Book of Judith* (Chico, CA: Scholars Press, 1980) 110; Geller-Nathanson, "Reflections" 265.

of the workings of the covenant in subsequent history.[43] This is analogous to Sirach's description in Sir 39:1-3, of the educated person as one who

> seeks out all of the wisdom of the ancients, and is concerned with prophecies; he preserves the sayings of the famous and penetrates the subtleties of parables; he seeks out the hidden meanings of proverbs and is at home with the obscurities of parables.[44]

In the Hellenistic period a variety of pseudepigraphical and apocryphal apocalypses, testaments, revelations, and histories reflect continued concern for the history of Israel. With few exceptions, however, biblical versions of historical events are notably re-cast and reconfigured to reflect contemporary ideologies, as we observe in Judith below.[45] Kaster also notes that among pedagogical methods, parable, allegory, and metaphor ... all illustrating truth or principle by analogy ... were common teaching devices.[46]

As noted above, Judith freely instructs the magistrates of Bethulia by allusions to events recorded in the history of Israel and by appropriating specific analogies for the testing of their faith from the experience of Abraham, Isaac and Jacob (Jdt 8:26-27). Judith's connection to her foremothers Miriam, Deborah and Ja`el are included in an analysis of the Victory Ode in chapter 16, as discussed below.

Judith commences her prayer in Jdt 9:2-4 by describing, as an analog to her present situation, events from the Genesis account of the rape and subsequent vindication of Dinah (Gen 34). Although, in keeping with practices outlined above, the author of Judith provides the protagonist with a somewhat modified interpretaion of Genesis 34, from Judith's point of view (as subject) this story proceeds from within her personal genealogy.[47] Judith displays an internal logic indicative of acquired skills for allegory and metaphor. In a sensitive and sophisticated image (Jdt 9:7-9), Judith equates, metaphorically, the devastation of her foremother Dinah and the revenge perpetrated upon Dinah's captor with the present threat of the Assyrians upon the Temple and the Sanctuary (Jdt 9:7-10). Judith identifies with both Dinah and Simeon. She provides insight into the inner-landscape of a patriotic woman who appropriates knowledge from her personal ancestry to her refusal to be victim either sexually or politically.

---

[43] J.Kaster, "Education O.T.," *IDB* (1962).

[44] History is not usually a component of the Wisdom tradition. Consider, however, the Psalms of Solomon (first century *BCE*) that present echoes of Isa 60:21, 63:16, 64:7; Ps 120; Ezek 39:23 and references to David in Ps 17.

[45] J. H. Charlesworth, *OTP*. Introductions to Pseudepigraphical texts provide detailed descriptions of the nature of variences from their canonical counterparts.

[46] Kaster, "Education" 34.

[47] Judith's genealogy in Jdt 8:1 hearkens back to Jacob/Israel, includes at least sixteen ancestors and is the longest genaeology for any woman in the bible. See Moore's commentary on the genaeology in *Judith*, 187-188.

Military Strategy

The author of Judith validates the female protagonist's cognizance of military strategy by the very agency ascribed to her for the military victory of Israel over the Assyrians. In her exhortation to the Elders, Judith (Jdt 8:21) understands precisely the political and religious consequences of defeat by the Assyrians. Her prayer reveals concerns about the increase in the Assyrian forces, the designated personnel, the weaponry they employed (Jdt 9:7), and their objective to defile the Sanctuary at Jerusalem (Jdt 9:8).

Judith understands as well the crucial responsibility of Bethulia to intercept and overcome the oppressors; her very prayer as she decapitates Holofernes (Jdt 13:4b) illustrates a comprehension of the political consequence of her action for "the exaltation of Jerusalem."

After Judith's triumphant return to Bethulia with the severed head of Holofernes (Jdt 13:11-20) it is her detailed military instructions (Jdt 14: 2-4), to the citizens of that city that pilot the successful rout of the Assyrian army (Jdt 14:11-15).

Speculative proposals for literary sources on military strategy that might have been familiar to an educated Palestinian Jew in the Hellenistic period are as varied as Homer and the Hellenistic and Hasmonean queens. Grace Harriet Macurdy discusses the military expertise of several queens. Among the most provocative is Arsinoe II Philadelphus, whose husband, Ptolemy II, relied upon "her strength and brains" to manage his second war against Syria.[48] Josephus (*J.W.* V.2) attests to the military decisions made by queen Salome Alexandra (d. 76 *BCE*). Hengel discusses in some detail the importance of Homer in Greek education in Palestine.[49] The possible knowledge of Herodotus among educated Jews is suggested by Arnaldo Momigliano and Mark Stephen Caponigro.[50] Instruction about the "Woman Warriors" Deborah, Ja'el and Miriam are part of Judith's Jewish heritage; their status in the history of Israel would have been studied by an educated Judith.[51]

---

[48] Macurdy, *Queens* 119-120.

[49] Hengel, *Judaism* vol.1.; Doran "Questions" 9-11.

[50] M. S. Caponigro, "Judith as a Hellenistic Jewish Text," Paper presented at Annual Meeting of the SBL, November 20, 1988, (It is in this un-published version of his paper that Caponigro most effectively relates to Momigliano's thesis). A. Momigliano, "Biblical Studies and Classical Studies: Simple Reflections About Historical Method," *BA* 45 (1982) 227-228.

[51] The Prophet Miriam (Exodus 20:21 and Numbers 12) who was an administrator of the Law at Kadesh, (Murray Newman, *People of the Covenant* (Nashville: Abingdon, 1962) 94), led the Victory Ode at the Sea of Reeds. Deborah (Judg 5) and Judith also led their communities in Victory Odes following great battles. Deborah accompanied Barak into battle against Sisera (Judg 4:7-10). Judith gave detailed instructions as to how the rout of the Assyrians was to take place. As professional religious functionaries both Deborah and Miriam were" schooled" adequately to successfully execute their duties. To what extent their education also included knowledge of military strategy can only be surmised. But it is not unlikely that knowledge of her Jewish foremothers would have been part of Judith's education.

Liturgical Composition and Prayer

Analyses of liturgical texts by James H. Charlesworth and Andre Dupont Sommer inform my contention that the prayer of Judith in chapter 9 shares characteristics of other prayers from the late Second Temple period. There are striking similarities in Judith's prayer to concepts of Deity expressed in IQH I.[52] This is demonstrated in the spontenaeity of her prayer, and the fact that the prayer expresses Judith's individual concerns but indicates no interest in material resources.[53] Yet, in a manner which corresponds to many of the Hodayot from Qumran, Judith's prayer does affirm God as the God of the oppressed.[54] Whereas these similarities obviously reflect the literary and theological awareness of the author of the Book of Judith, the ascription of these qualities to the prayer of a woman implies that at least this woman was familiar with contemporary conventions of spirituality and prayed within their parameters.

Considering the proliferation of liturgical texts from the Second Temple period we must assume that they were composed by people who were educated. Given our premise about representations and realities of women in the cultural ambient of an author, and given Judith's agency within the Victory Ode in Chapter 16 of the Book of Judith, it is germane to approach this Hymn in the context of Judith as an educated woman.

The great Hymn of Thanksgiving, which functions as a Victory Ode, is the object of considerable discussion among Judith scholars. Numerous comparisons note similarities between this Hymn and Miriam's Song of the Sea in Ex 15:20-21 and Deborah's Victory Ode in Judges 5.[55] We also find correspondences between this hymn and liturgical literature in the Late Second Temple period. [56] Charlesworth notes some of the elements of the process by which this literature took shape and form. He mentions that

> the movement from private instantaneous prayer to formalized, sometimes cultic, prayer was accompanied both by injunctions not to make any prayer a fixed form *and* by the appearance of communal fixed prayers and hymns ....[57]

The Hymn of Thanksgiving in chapter 16 of the Book of Judith can be compared to Hymns from Qumran created for corporate worship that are representative of a fixed form and include both parallel constructions and lines of disperate lengths.[58]

---

[52] A. Dupont Sommer, *Essene Writings From Qumran* (Cleveland and New York: The World Publishing Co. 1962) 202-204.

[53] J. H. Charlesworth, "Jewish Hymns, Odes and Prayers,"*Early Judaism and Its Modern Interpreters* (Philadelphia: Fortress, 1986) 423.

[54] Dupont Sommer, *Essene Writings*, 206-209. Hymns C, D and E, are examples of this genre.

[55] Moore, *Judith* 84. See also 251 on the Song of Deborah; Song of the Sea: 192-193, 249, 256.

[56] Charlesworth, "Jewish Hymns" 413, 422.

[57] Charlesworth, "Jewish Hymns" 412.

[58] Charlesworth, "Jewish Hymns" 422.

These structural similarities also obtain for Deborah's Victory Ode in Judges 5.[59]
First person, present tense construction is also characteristic of Judges 5 and
certain Hodayot from Qumran. Some of these Hodayot are attributed to a single
author as a personal statement made within a corporate setting as in Jdt 16:1-2; 7-
11; some represent the single voice of the community. In Judith's Victory Ode six
of the seventeen verses are first person, present tense constructions (Jdt 16:1, 4, 11,
12, 13, 17). These texts evoke a sense of immediacy and capture a highly personal
intensity within a corporate setting.

Moore suggests that in chapter 16 Judith is identifying with Miriam and
Deborah, and that several references to the LXX Song of the Sea (Ex 15:3) are
quoted in the Victory
Ode.[60] Moore's position supports my contention that the author of the fictional
Judith ascribed to her a knowledge of history that she appropriated by analogy in
her present celebration.

Whether or not the author of Judith composed the entire hymn, the
selection of first person, present tense construction within the Victory Ode
attributes authorship of the Hymn to Judith and conveys the heroine's skill as a
liturgist.[61] The author's inference that Judith did compose the Hymn invites our
comparison of Judith as a composer of hymns to composition of hymns by female
Theraputae. Female Theraputae, like their male counterparts, engaged in
allegorical interpretations of scriptural texts and composed hymns of varying
melodies and metres (Philo *V.C.* III. 29). Comparisons between Judith and these
female ascetics further support arguments for Judith as an educated woman.

Conclusion

Sirach's criteria for an educated person are somewhat early for Judith, but
they are not late! And, whereas the *bet midrash* of the Sage in Jerusalem
functioned for the edification of male pupils, it is instructive to consider
correspondences between Sirach's criteria for education and Judith's agency within
her community. The Elders of Bethulia take counsel from Judith (Jdt 8 10-29); the
young female ascetic takes her stand in the midst of the Elders (Sir 6:34/ Jdt 8:11-
25) and returns an answer in time of need (Sir 8:9/ Jdt 8: 32-34). She prays (Sir
39:5/Jdt 9) and having searched out the wisdom of the ancients (Sir 39:1b/Jdt 8:25-
26), she counsels her Elders (Jdt 8:27). Judith devises a plan in which she serves
Israel by going before a great general among strange peoples to test the good and
evil among them (Sir 39:4/Jdt 10:11-13:12).

A review of Judith's encounters with the *gerousia* and with Holofernes and
the Assyrians, reveals that she commands respect and affirmation within her own

[59] S. A. White, "In the Steps of Deborah and Jael: Judith as Heroine," *No One Spoke Ill of Her*
(Atlanta: Scholars Press, 1992) 11.
[60] Moore, *Judith* 236.
[61] Moore, *Judith* 246-247.

community and among foreigners as an authoritative woman. The author of the Book of Judith substantiates ratification of Judith's authority within her community in areas customarily traditioned by formal study or instruction, namely theology, history, military expertise and liturgical composition. A curriculum comprised of these subjects, especially as they were explicated in the Judith narrative, is consistent with Doran's discussion of a curriculum for Jewish students in a *bet midrash* that included the "language, laws and literature of Judea . . . festivals of the God of Judea" and Greek curiculum as well.[62]

The preceding historical reconstruction and narrative analysis proffers little definitive evidence about education as an aspect of the social reality of Jewish women in the Late Second Temple period. It is interesting to note, however, that among the historical women who were postulated as educated, namely female Theraputae, Daughters of Truth and the Venerable Women of 4Q502, all share the fictional Judith's social location as female ascetics. In a manner not dissimilar to that of Judith, the fictional characters Hannah, Deborah and Seila from Pseudo-Philo function in a didactic capacity to edify, enlighten and counsel members of their communities within the synagogue. Religious praxis and education are social loci common to each of these figures.

Considering the substantial corpus of Jewish literature that emerged within the parameters of the Late Second Temple period, it is disconcerting that so many issues concerning education among Jews in this period remain a mystery. We affirm with certainty only that some people *wrote*, some people *read* and some people *listened*. There is scholarly consensus about authorship for some Hellenistic Jewish texts. It is with far less certainty, however, that we suggest who read and with less certainty still that we propose theories about the pervasiveness of both scribal and oral traditions. Questions of Jewish women's experience in these contexts have been infrequently and inconclusively addressed. The data are meager. Yet, even provisional insights derived from their analysis and critique support proposals for further research and estabish some foundations in this avenue of inquiry. It is my hope that hypotheses advanced in this inquiry might initiate further dialogue and invite us to enter more deeply into the question of Jewish women's social reality in the Late Second Temple period.

My advent into the world of Religious Studies came late in my personal journey. For many years, in my work as a stage director, interpretation of texts consisted in interpreting operatic libretti. As both teacher and mentor, John Priest's embodied wisdom in the humanities and biblical studies has opened for me an ever widening universe. His legacy to me is multifaceted . . . but I am especially indebted to him for encouraging my burgeoning interests as a feminist historian, for suggesting and advocating pragmatic and eclectic methodologies to facilitate my research and for all he has taught me about accepting ambiguities in a multitude of life's arenas.

---

[62] Doran, "Questions" 9.

Facing the Future: Common Themes
in Jewish Apocalyptic and Stoic Philosophy

Howard Clark Kee
Bryn Mawr

M any scholars in the field of biblical studies seem to suffer from a chronic case of what might be called "abortive Hegelianism." The symptoms of this ailment are that its victims feel compelled to establish a pair of conceptual dichotomies, but instead of working toward a new synthesis, they try to make a case for one option over against the other. Nowhere is this more evident than in the analyses of wisdom and apocalyptic, earlier in studies of the Jewish scriptures, but more recently in New Testament studies as well. Fortunately, the protracted debate as to whether apocalyptic developed out of prophecy (as asserted by H. H. Rowley,[1] among others) or out of the wisdom tradition (as maintained by von Rad [2]) has been answered by mediating voices seeking to show how both factors contributed to the rise of apocalypticism.[3] More recently, however, the rich complexity of the situation has been more fully demonstrated in brilliant essays that have shown that Jewish apocalyptic had counterparts in non-Jewish literature of the hellenistic and Roman periods and that it was powerfully

---

[1] In *The Relevance of Apocalyptic* (2nd ed.; London: Lutterworth, 1947).

[2] In *Wisdom in Israel* (Nashville: Abingdon, 1972).

[3] E.g., P. D. Hanson, *The Dawn of Apocalyptic*. Philadelphia: Fortress, 1975; W. McKane, *Prophets and Wise Men* (SBT 40). London: SCM, 1965.

influenced by mantic wisdom that can be documented in later material from the
Near East.

I

A pioneer in this approach was Jonathan Z. Smith, whose essay on "Wisdom
and Apocalyptic" first appeared in 1975 [4]. He begins by affirming a declaration of
H.D. Betz that "Jewish and subsequently Christian apocalyptic cannot be
understood from themselves or from the Old Testament alone, but must be seen
and presented as peculiar expressions from the entire development of hellenistic
syncretism" [5]. We shall see that features analogous to those of apocalyptic are
evident in a wide range of both hellenistic and Roman documents. In his
illuminating article Smith concentrates on apocalyptic-type elements as evident in
a Babylonian historian and three Egyptian writings. Berossus, the Babylonian
historian who was writing in Greek at the time of Alexander drew on astronomical
and astrological material, and as mythographer and historian writing in relation to
the Babylonian sibyl, he compiled "a history of the cosmos and a people from
creation to final catastrophe which is dominated by astrological determinism"[6].
From Egypt come three apocalyptic writings: The Demotic Chronicle, The Curse
of the Lamb, and the Potter's Oracle (which we shall examine later in some detail).

J. Gwyn Griffiths and Walter Burkert, in essays contributed to the Congress
on Apocalyptic in Upsala,[7] point to the documents mentioned by Smith but also
to philosophers–especially Hesiod and Plato–where the course of history is seen
as divinely determined and moving toward cosmic renewal. It is in David Aune's
excellent monograph, *Prophecy in Early Christianity and the Ancient
Mediterranean World*,[8] however, that the fullest account is provided of the similar
features of prophetic speech in the Greco-Roman world and that of post-biblical
Judaism and early Christianity. Aune analyzes in detail the various forms of
prophetic utterance in the Greek world and the roles performed by diviners,
especially by the sibyls and the collections of their oracles so highly prized over
the centuries down into the Roman era. Included is a description of what he terms
"eschatological prophets", such as Virgil in his Fourth Eclogue, and other utopian
visions of the future from the seventh century BCE to the third century CE,[9] with
oracle collections known from Herodotus (fifth century BCE) to Plutarch and
Pausanias in the first and second centuries CE. The Sibylline oracles disclosed the

---

[4]In *Religious Syncretism in Antiquity*, ed. B. Pearson, 131-56. Reprinted in *Scriptures, Sects and
Visions*, ed. J. Neusner. Philadelphia: Fortress, 1980, 101-120.
   [5]In ZThK 63 (1969) 155.
   [6]J. Z. Smith, "Wisdom and Apocalyptic," 108.
   [7]J.G. Griffiths, "Apocalyptic in the Hellenistic Era," in *Apocalyptic in the Mediterranean World
and the Near East* (ed. D. Hellholm; Tübingen: Mohr, 1983, 273-293. W. Burkert, "Apokalyptik in früher
Griechentum: Impulse und Transformation", 235-53.
   [8]Grand Rapids: Eerdmans, 1983.
   [9]Aune, *Prophecy in Early Christianity*, 43.

purpose of the gods in the present but looked back to divine activity in the past and forward to the accomplishment of a divine purpose in the future, in both cases linked with the role of rulers. Plato affirmed the validity of these inspired oracular instruments to deal with questions and responses.[10]

Two very different studies of the Sibylline Oracles show how documents that in their present form were preserved by Jews are basically products of hellenistic culture as adopted and adapted by the Romans. John J. Collins' study of *The Apocalyptic Imagination*[11] includes at the outset a useful definition of apocalyptic developed by the SBL Genres Project [12] : "A genre of revelatory literature with a narrative framework in which a revelation is mediated by an otherworldly being to a human recipient, disclosing a transcendent reality which is both temporal, insofar as it envisages eschatological salvation, and spatial, insofar as it involves another, supernatural world." In *The Old Testament Pseudepigrapha*, [13], Collins' translation of the Sibylline Oracles and notes demonstrate in detail the author's (or authors') use of imagery from the Bible but also from older Near Eastern and Greco-Roman sources, with the result that motifs are transferred from one context to another.[14] In apocalyptic writings, Collins writes, wisdom is not inductive, as in Proverbs or Ben Sira, but *mantic*, as in the Babylonian tradition. Its language is expressive rather than referential, symbolic rather than factual.[15] The course of history is viewed in light of transcendent reality, which enables the beneficiary of this disclosure to see the hidden world that is shaping the present as well as the ultimate destiny of the favored group.

Another extremely useful analysis of the Sibyllines is that of D. S. Potter in *Prophecy and History in the Crisis of the Roman Empire: A Historical Commentary on the Thirteenth Sybilline Oracle.*[16] He shows how the single Sibyl of the late fifth century BCE is transmuted into a series of sibyls from Babylonia across the Mediterranean world following Alexander's conquests, and how other cultures appropriate the sibyl as a prophetess among their own people "in their efforts to claim intellectual respectability in a Greek context."[17] By the first century BCE, she was linked with official collections of oracles in Rome and "elevated to the position of the greatest prophetess of antiquity." An official committee was assigned to preserve and interpret her oracles, which bore directly on the conduct of wars and public policy. Victors were identified with Ares, and thus received divine sanction for their exploits.[18] The Thirteenth Sibylline Oracle concerns the

---

[10] Plato, *Timaeus*, 71c-72b.

[11] Sub-title: *An Introduction to the Jewish Matrix of Christianity* (New York: Crossroads, 1989).

[12] Published in *Semeia* 14 (1979).

[13] "The Sibylline Oracles" in OTP 1, 317-472 (ed. J.H. Charlesworth, Garden City: Doubleday, 1983).

[14] Collins, *Imagination*, 16.

[15] *Imagination*, 14.

[16] Oxford: Clarendon Press, 1990.

[17] Potter, *Prophecy*, p. 109.

[18] Pp. 138-39.

struggle for political and cultural power in the eastern empire at the great city of Palmyra in the third century, when Persia was threatening to resume control over this region. The reigns of the various emperors are evaluated on the basis of their military and economic impact on the region. Far from being an esoteric treatise for intellectually and culturally fringe people, this oracle is dealing with the most basic issues that confronted the Roman empire and its leaders in the crisis of the third century.

James C. Vanderkam's fine study, *Enoch and the Growth of an Apocalyptic Tradition*,[19], while carefully differentiating Mesopotamian mantic material from Israel's prophetic tradition, notes that the former "provided a considerable part of the context from which Jewish Enochic literature arose and grew,"[20] with possibly additional contribution from Persian eschatology. The length of Enoch's life–365 years–and the contents of the Astronomical Book (*Enoch* 72-82), as well as details in the Book of Watchers (*Enoch* 1-36), show how central for apocalyptic was the cosmic order of the universe as evident in the movement of the heavenly bodies.[21] Although Vanderkam notes the absence of several typical features of apocalyptic, it is in this Astronomical Book that Enoch "assumes the role of antediluvian sage who still experiences intimate contact with the divine realm and who bridges the gap between human and divine by conveying his special knowledge to humanity,"[22] like the role of the Mesopotamian *apkallus*.

George Nickelsburg, in addition to his useful analyses of the Jewish literature of the hellenistic period,[23] has made an important methodological contribution to the area of our investigation by calling attention to "The Social Aspects of Palestinian Jewish Apocalypticism."[24] Noting the generalizations about apocalypticism that have been made on the basis of inadequate evidence or by imposition of modern sectarian models, Nickelsburg raises a long series of substantive questions to be addressed to the texts by those analyzing them. These questions concern the political, economic, cultural and religious circumstances of the writer and his potential readers, the response of the writer to the crisis that he and his community confront, the self-definition of the community expecting divine action on its behalf, and the distinctive features of each apocalypse as compared with others. As a test case, he raises these questions with regard to *1 Enoch* 92-105, the so-called *Epistle of Enoch*, which sketches the history of Israel in the Apocalypse of Weeks. His proposal for a date is the early second century BCE. Possibly this work was produced at Qumran, since it shares with the Dead Sea Scrolls the critique of the Jerusalem priesthood. His questions require the

[19] (CBQMS 16) Washington, D. C.: Catholic Biblical Association, 1984.

[20] Vanderkam, *Enoch*, 70.

[21] Vanderkam, *Enoch*, Chap. 4.

[22] Vanderkam, *Enoch*, 106.

[23] *Jewish Literature between the Bible and the Mishnah* (Philadelphia: Fortress Press, 1981).

[24] In *Apocalyptic In the Mediterranean World and the Near East*, 641-654.

interpreter to take into account the diversity of details represented in apocalyptic literature in order to see how they shed light on the origins of each document.

David Winston's superb commentary on *The Wisdom of Solomon*[25] has been supplemented by an essay, "The Sage as Mystic in the Wisdom of Solomon."[26] He shows that wisdom is concerned with the entire scope of human and cosmic history, and the search for wisdom is described in mystical, even erotic, language (7:25-26, 29-30; 8:2-3, 9), for which he notes analogies in Philo, especially in his "On Mating with Preliminary Studies." Wisdom is seen as essential not only for the immortality of the soul but also for the effective rule of monarchs (6:17-21). The goal, therefore, is not the attainment of timeless proverbial truths but achieving personal union with wisdom (6:12-16), for which the analogy is union with Isis as in Apuleius' *Metamorphoses* 11:23, 25, 29.

II

In spite of these important insights and the availability of newly-recovered sources that document the shared concerns of apocalyptic literature and wisdom of the Greco-Roman period, there has developed in New Testament studies in the past decade a counterpart to the false wisdom/apocalyptic dichotomy that once pervaded studies of Jewish sources. Some scholars are now seeking to show that the apocalyptic features of the gospel tradition are later accretions, behind which can be discerned Jesus' authentic words of wisdom[27]. The latter are said to be purely aphoristic in style and timeless in intent. They allegedly mirror the style of Cynic-Stoic philosophers of the Greco-Roman era. The theory runs that it was later dull-witted early Christian editors who emended these texts and supplemented them with apocalyptic and miracle-working features, in accord with popular but intellectually inferior religious impulses of the era, and thus produced the gospels as we have them in their canonical form. The new model for the historical Jesus fits this wisdom-purveying construct.

---

[25] *Wisdom of Solomon* (AB). Garden City, NY; Doubleday, 1979.

[26] In *The Sage in Israel and the Ancient Near East* (ed. J. G. Gammie and L. G. Perdue; Winona Lake, IN: Eisenbrauns, 1990), 383-97.

[27] This assumption is basic to the analyses of Q (1) by the group calling itself The International Q Project; (2) by Helmut Koester (in *Ancient Christian Gospels: Their History and Development* [Philadelphia: Trinity Press International, 1990]), (3) by James M. Robinson in an essay, "The Q Trajectory: Between John and Matthew via Jesus" for the Koester Festchrift (*The Future of Early Christianity: Essays in Honor of Helmut Koester*, ed. B. A. Pearson, *et al.*, [Minneapolis: Fortress, 1991] 173-94), who pictures the original Q as devoid of apocalyptic or christological features, and (4) by Burton L. Mack (in *The Lost Gospel: The Book of Q and Christian Origins*. San Francisco: Harper, 1994). All simply posit a radical disjunction between wisdom and apocalyptic in the developing Jesus tradition. Although Robinson appeals to R. A. Piper's study, *Wisdom in the Q Tradition* (SNTSM 61; Cambridge University Press, 1989) for support of his position, Piper notes the links in Q between aphorisms and eschatological pronouncements, and observes the continuity implied between past, present, and "the nature of the eschaton which confronts [the author of this source]" (154-55), and between aphoristic wisdom and revealed knowledge (178-79).

It was just over a century ago (in 1891) that Albert Schweitzer posed the problem of apocalyptic in early Christianity when he published his analytical survey, *Das Messianitäts und Leidensgeheimnis: Eine Skizze des Lebens Jesu*,[28] with its portrait of the thoroughly apocalyptic Jesus. Schweitzer's conclusions were more systematically formulated a few years later in his critical survey of scholarly analyses of the life of Jesus, *From Reimarus to Wrede: A History of Research on the Life of Jesus*, which is of course better known in its English translation as *The Quest of the Historical Jesus*.[29] In both works Schweitzer developed the evidence for a thoroughly apocalyptic framework for Jesus' self-understanding and career, and asserted that Jesus' eschatological view of himself and his work "can only be interpreted by the aid of the curiously intermittent Jewish apocalyptic literature of the period between Daniel and the Bar-Cochba uprising".[30] Having arrived at these results of his investigation–which he regarded as incompatible with the intellectual values of his own post-enlightenment training and orientation and which the subsequent history of early Christianity proved to have been wrong –Schweitzer adopted two tactics: (1) He affirmed a Jesus who was "absolutely independent of historical knowledge" (including his apocalyptic outlook) and who "can only be known by contact with his Spirit which is still at work in the world."[31] (2) He turned from theological and biblical studies to medicine, and devoted the rest of his life to noble humanitarian service among indigenous Africans.

Among the other escape routes from apocalyptic taken by scholars in the earlier decades of this century were the reductionist modes of (1) Adolf von Harnack, for whom the essence of Jesus' message was (in pre-feminist days) the fatherhood of God, the brotherhood of man, and the infinite worth of the human soul,[32] and (2) Rudolf Bultmann, for whom the essence of Jesus was his existentialist call to radical decision, to which the Jesus tradition could be conveniently reduced by demythologization.

III

As we have seen, however, more recent analyses of documents from the Greco-Roman world puts the eschatological mode of the gospel tradition in a very different historical light from that assumed by those engaged in the flight from apocalyptic throughout the present century of scholarly inquiry. Instead of Greco-Roman wisdom providing a refuge from apocalyptic, it is now evident that

[28] Subsequently published in Tübingen (J. C. B. Mohr, 1901.

[29] A. Schweitzer, *The Quest of the Historical Jesus* (New York: Macmillan, 1910).

[30] *Quest*, 367.

[31] *Quest*, 401.

[32] A. von Harnack, *What Is Christianity?* (trans. T.B. Saunders; New York: G.P. Putnam, 1900; reprinted New York: Harper and Row, 1957). The title is an inaccurate rendering of the German original, *Das Wesen des Christentums* = "The Essence of Christianity".

precisely among the intellectual and political leaders of the emergent Roman imperial world were to be found the very issues that–differently formulated and drawing on different mythological tradition–are represented in the apocalytic documents of Judaism and early Christianity. Politicans, poets, and philosophers of the late Roman Republic and early Empire are dealing with just these issues. The assumptions of some recent scholars about an exclusively aphoristic mode of Cynic-Stoic wisdom in this period may be shown to be in fact a mixture of inaccuracy and anachronism. The questions about human destiny which in spite of cultural differences are evident in both the Jewish/Christian apocalyptic and the Roman literature (especially the Stoic sources) may be formulated as follows:

(1) Concern for the maintenance of cosmic order.
(2) Conviction about human moral accountability before the gods.
(3) Confidence in oracular disclosure of the divine purpose.
(4) Belief in divine choice of human agents to fulfill the divine purpose.
(5) Use of traditional mythic imagery to depict the course of human destiny and the consummation of the divine purpose.

What is called for in responsible historical analysis of Christian origins is to highlight the various facets of the religious and philosophical literature of the centuries before and after the turn of the eras with the aim of discerning how certain aspirations and claims about human destiny were shared by Greco-Roman philosophers and leaders *and* Jewish and early Christian writers. As noted above, the answers will differ in imagery and in detail, but the basic human questions are common features. Our analysis of the evidence will involve an examination of the divinatory and oracular sources preserved from the wider Greco-Roman world in the period from second century BCE to second century CE, and then–more briefly–from Jewish and early Christian sources. Next we shall move to an examination of some of the most important philosophical and literary sources of this period. On the basis of these lines of investigation, we hope to demonstrate the presence of common issues in Jewish and Greco-Roman sources, in spite of the obvious differences in cultural and mythological tradition drawn upon by each.

The "Potter's Oracle" as an Apocalyptic Document

The sub-title of Ludwig Koenen's analysis of the Potter's Oracle is of fundamental significance: "A Prophecy of World Renewal Becomes an Apocalypse."[33] The document shows the "intellectual resistance on the part of Egyptian national groups to Greek hegemony and of the aspiration enkindled among these groups by the bloody strife in the royal house [Ptolemaic] about 130 B.C." Eschatological prophecy projects the myth and rite of enthronement into the

---

[33] "The Prophecies of a Potter" is the main title, in *Proceedings of the Twelfth International Congress of Papyrology*, ed. D.H. Samuels, 1970; 248-254.

future during a period of desperation.[34] The collapse of the order of nature will be followed by political, social, and economic chaos, from which deliverance will come through a savior-king, who is described in imagery drawn from Egyptian mythology (Horus/Isis). Koenen notes a similar mode of expectation of a king-deliverer on the mythological model in the "Demotic Chronicle"[35], who appears as "a long-awaited savior-king after a period of domination by godless foreigners."[36] (251). Later interpretations of the Potter's Oracle, after differences were settled between the Egyptians and the Ptolemies, recast the prophecies in a cyclical mode, projecting the hope of fulfillment into the future in true apocalyptic style.[37]

The Imperial Roman Adoption of Astrology as an Official Mode of Divine Confirmation

Too often overlooked by biblical scholars is the pervasive and widely-valued role of astrology in the thought and literature of the Greco-Roman period. Frederic H. Cranmer, in *Astrology in Roman Law and Politics*,[38] notes the discussion of astrology by Plato's student, Eudoxus [39] and by Aristotle, whose view of the structure of the stars and planets was used by early astrologers. Alexander's successful invasion of Persia was accounted for by Chaldean astrologers (Diodorus Siculus 17.112.2ff). Stoicism fostered the surge of hellenistic belief in "the science of fatalistic astrology" [40]. According to Josephus, it was Berossus who introduced priestly astrology among the Greeks, and Pliny tells how he was honored at Athens "on account of his divine prophecies" (*Natural History* 7.37, 123). Refinement of astrology by the Greeks took place in 300-150 B.C.E., with two goals: mystical participation in the divine purpose, and scientific, mathematical calculation of the course of the universe.[41] Dozens of existential questions–about family, love, prosperity, journeys–were answered by an appeal to astrology.[42] Through the concept of cosmic cycles, in which various planets were successively dominant, there was foreseen an eternal sequence of fiery consummation (*ekpyrosis*) and rebirth (*palingenesis*), with the interval between these events known as The Great Year.[43]

---

[34] Koenen, "A Prophecy," 248.
[35] From Papyrus # 215 in the Bibliotheque Nationale, Paris. Published by W. Spiegelberg, "Die sogennante demotische Chronik..." in *Demotische Studien* (Leipzig: J. C. Hinrichs, 1914).
[36] Koenen, "Prophecy," 251.
[37] Koenen, "A Prophecy," 252-53.
[38] American Philosophical Society, Vol. 37. Philadelphia, 1954.
[39] Quoted by Cicero, *De Divinatione*. 2.87.
[40] Cranmer, 13.
[41] Cranmer, 15.
[42] Cranmer, 19-24.
[43] Cranmer, 25.

An initial period of skepticism about astrology on the part of philosophers gave way at the end of the Roman Republic to the affirmative point of view articulated by Posidonius of Apamea, so that with the establishment of the Empire the rulers sought and gained support of astrologers in the belief that the stars controlled human destiny–a view which was dominant from Augustus to Domitian. Varro and Virgil, in his Fourth Eclogue (as we shall note below), affirmed the controlling effects of the astrological powers).[44] Julius Caesar promoted astrology to gain popular support, and on the basis of it revised the calendar. Octavius (or Octavianus) exploited the appearance of a comet to prove the heavenly assumption of Julius Caesar and his own placement in power by the gods.[45] Astrology provided a link between mundane causality and the cosmic laws that regulated the movement of the stars and of human history. This reliance on astrology reached its zenith in the Julio-Claudian and Flavian houses. The divine powers were perceived to be directly and effectively at work shaping human destiny and the history of the state in a larger cycle of cosmic renewal–features that are shared formally with the apocalyptic world-view.

James H. Charlesworth has assembled the evidence for credence in astrology on the part of Jewish writers from the first century BCE down to the Talmudic period [46]. In one section of *1 Enoch* astrology is denounced as demonic (8:3), but in the portion known as the Astronomical Book (72:1-37; 75:3), the features of the zodiac are prominent, as they are in *2 Enoch*. The first century BCE *Treatise of Shem* is an astrological tract that seeks to show how human fortune, the fertility of the land, and the movement of the stars are all dependent on the powers resident in the houses of the zodiac.[47] Fragment 4Q 186 from Qumran is a horoscope based on astrological beliefs in the powers that shape human life and character [48]. Surveys of the iconography of Palestinian synagogues more recent than that of Charlesworth show that those of the third and fourth centuries CE regularly had the signs of the zodiac at the center of the hall, with Yahweh pictured as Helios, driving the chariot of the sun. One must acknowledge that the astrological symbolism was not merely decorative, but was an expression of the conviction that the God of Israel was responsible for the ordering of the universe and the course of human events. That conviction also found expression in the early Roman imperial period through the writings of Stoic philosophers, to which we turn.

---

[44] Cranmer, 61-65.

[45] Cranmer, 78.

[46] "Jewish Astrology in the Talmud, Pseudepigraha, the Dead Sea Scrolls and Early Palestinian Synagogues," HTR 70 (1977), 183-200.

[47] J.H. Charlesworth in *the Old Testament Pseudepigrapha*, Vol. 1, 473-486.

[48] Geza Vermes, *the Dead Sea Scrolls in English*. London: Penguin Books, (1987), 305-307.

Historical Determinism and Stoic Philosophy in the Roman Period

Largely neglected by scholars dealing with the factors of wisdom and apocalyptic in the Greco-Roman period is the discussion of this dimension by Stoic philosophers of the period. We select for examination here the writings of two philosophers who were directly involved at the political center of the Roman Empire: Cicero at the time of its establishment and Seneca when the crisis arose at the end of the Julio-Claudian succession of emperors. Both were central wisdom figures at the political heart of their world.

The importance of the issue concerning a divine purpose at work in human history is highlighted in Cicero's treatise *On the Nature of the Gods* and is then more directly adddressed in his work *On Divination*. Although he makes an assertion that he does not share the conviction that the divine purpose for the world is communicated through oracles, dreams, and other modes of divination, Cicero documents fully how deeply engrained these beliefs were in the minds of Stoics of the first century BCE. Balbus, who presents the Stoic position in *De Natura Deorum*, first makes a case for the rational ordering of the universe by the gods. In the course of describing the spherical form of the divine nature, he pictures the movement of the world as also spherical, and corresponding to it is the "great year" when the heavenly bodies complete their prescribed courses and return to their original relative positions. Only humans have been granted prophecy and divination: through auguries, oracles, dreams and portents "the power or art or instinct has clearly been bestowed by the immortal gods on man, and on no other creature, for the ascertainment of future events" (II.65). Oracles, including the Sibyllines, show that the gods disclose the future as a warning and a counsel to humanity (II.3-4). That the stars are divine, and that they possess consciousness and intelligence, is evident in their orderly motion. Divine nature is spherical and its motion is rotary. Hence the "great year" is the span of time when the heavenly bodies will return to their same relative positions as at the beginning (II.15-20). Only human beings have been granted "this power or art or instinct" to discern the future and avoid its dangers (II.65).

In *De Divinatione*, Cicero, writing in the middle of the first century BCE, notes the universality of the belief among Assyrians, Babylonians, Greeks that the gods communicate concerning the future through divinatory signs. He describes the importance of augurs in Rome since its founding by Romulus, the practice of consulting the *auspices* on all important state issues, and the appointment of the ten supervisors of the Sibylline Oracles to shed light on major decisions. He recalls the accuracy of dreams and oracles that foresaw the future of Greece and Rome, and the support for this understanding of divine communication on the part of Socrates, Plato, and Aristotle. The reputation for reliablity is well-deserved by the oracles at Delphi and Cumae. Throughout history, divination has flourished in the best-regulated states, as evident in the Senate's regular, official consultation of the Sibyl. Central to this are God, Fate, and Nature, but especially *heimarmene*, which is the orderly succession of causes. The gods know what will happen; humans presage the future by certain signs, which include the movement of the stars and the entrails of sacrifices. Effect follows cause; sign precedes event. The study of these signs is divination. Cicero recounts a scathing critique of this Stoic point of view by Cotta, who denounced the whole enterprise as superstition, but then Cicero commends the Stoics for the skill of their arguments and leaves to the thoughtful inquirer the judgment concerning the truth.

Writing in the middle of the first century CE, Seneca shows no trace of the skepticism—or more accurately, ambivalence—of Cicero on the subject of divine disclosure of the future of the cosmos. In his *On Providence*, Seneca affirms the universality of the divine order, so that the stars and their revolutions are ruled by eternal law (I.1). Humans differ from the gods only in relation to time: they are pupils of the gods, imitators and true offspring. The highest god holds them to account for their moral behavior (I.5). Difficulties humans experience are part of the process of divine discipline, and adversities are for the good of those who endure them: "God hardens, reviews and disciplines those whom he approves, whom he loves" [49]. He quotes with approval Ovid's *Metamorphoses* (2:79 ff.) on the hero's following the divinely prescribed track of testing and struggle through the signs of the Zodiac (V.11).

In his letter *To Marcia on the Death of her Son*, Seneca describes how the world renews itself over and over within the bounds of time, with cyclic conflagrations and renewal of the creation (21.1-3). Death is not the end of existence, but the journey to the gods, who far aloft throughout the universe look down with detachment on human affairs (23.1). The soul struggles for release from the body in order to ascend to the place from which it came (24.5), a place of eternal peace, where all is bright and pure. The stars and all the fiery matter of the world will be "caught up in a common conflagration. Then also the souls of the blest, who have partaken of immortality, when it shall seem best to God to create the universe anew—we, too, amid the falling universe, shall be added as a tiny fraction to this mighty destruction and shall be changed again into our former elements" (26.6). In *On the Shortness of Life* (19.1) Seneca asks about the fate that awaits the soul, "where nature lays us to rest when we are free from the body"—a hope that recalls that of Paul in 2 Cor 5:8: "Absent from the body, present with the Lord." Writing his mother from exile, in *Helvia on Consolation* (20.1-2) Cicero says that his philosophical thoughts transport him "to the heights above" where he can enjoy "the noblest spectacle of things divine," and his soul, "mindful of its own immortality, proceeds to all that has been and will ever be throughout all ages to come."

The divine determination of the course of history was affirmed in Roman culture at the outset of the empire by Virgil as well. In his *Aenid* he traced the origins of Rome back to Troy, thereby demonstrating the continuity of the purpose

---

[49] The theme here recalls Heb 12:6, which quotes Prov 3:11.

of the gods in human history. More enigmatic but also more complex is his *Fourth Eclogue*, in which he describes the birth of Caesar Augustus as a divinely-ordained child ("offspring of the gods, mighty seed of Jupiter") who in maturity will bring in a new and joyous era of human existence, recalling the reign of the Olympian deities. All this has been heralded through the Sibyl at Cumae: the new age of peace, prosperity and plenty is about to begin. Studies of Stoic cosmology [50] have shown that the Stoics depicted the cosmos as a living animal, ensouled and possessing a mind and reasoning powers. The world-soul is identified with *pneuma*, which is an air/fire mixture permeating the universe.[51] The present cosmic order will perish in the *ekpyrosis*, but it will come into existence again and individuals will reappear. The themes of cosmic fire and cyclical periods derived from Heraclitus by way of Aristotle. The continuity of the human species is affirmed. The rational seeds (*spermatikoi logoi*) of this process were described by Zeno,[52] but it was Chrysippus (late fourth century) who described the *pneuma* as the principal cosmic agent which controls the movements of the cosmos, as is evident in the astrological forces that shape human destiny. Seneca articulates a Roman intellectual's version of this view of cosmic purpose shaping history and individual destiny.

IV

Three Jewish writers who give evidence of basic influence from Stoicism are Ben Sira, Josephus, and the author of the Testaments of the Twelve Patriarchs. David Winston, in an article on "Theodicy in Ben Sira and Stoic Philosophy," notes that in dealing with the difficult problem of theodicy, Ben Sira "seems to have consciously followed in the footsteps of the Stoics," especially "their self-satisfied and supremely optimistic faith in a perfect, all-embracing Nature."[53]

In his *Contra Apionem*, Josephus points out parallels between the Law of Moses and Greek philosophy. Moses is concerned primarily for piety and virtue. His view of God emphasizes just those qualities (unbegotten, eternal, immutable, superior to all mortal conceptions) that are described by the Pythagoreans, the Platonists, and the Stoics. Similarly, the chief religious virtues–justice, fortitude, temperance, universal laws–match those of Greek philosophy. Like Plato, Moses insisted on achieving the true commonwealth in which all people obey the laws. According to Josephus, the reason that the philosophers parallel the insights and requirements of the Jewish law is that they all derived their insights from Moses,

[50] D. E. Hahm, *The Origins of Stoic Cosmology* (Columbus, OH: Ohio State University Press, 1977). M. Lapidge, "Stoic Cosmology and Roman Literature", in ANRW II, 36.3 (1379-1429).
[51] Hahm, 137.
[52] *Stoicorum veterum fragmenta*, ed. J. von Arnim (Leipzig, 1903-24; Repr. Stuttgart, 1966; New York, 1986), 1.98.171.
[53] In *Of Scholars, Saints and their Texts: Studies in Philosophy and Religious Thought* (Ed. R. Link-Salinger, New York: Lang, 1981), 239-246.

who taught the "truest piety in the world" (II.40-42). From this perspective, there is no basic difference between the law revealed to Moses and the insights of the philosophers, including the Stoics. From the Jewish side there are some criticisms of reliance on dreams and divination (as in Sirach 34:1-7), but the basic convictions are shared about universal law, divine disclosure through historical events and through the prophets, moral accountability to the divine, and an ultimate consummation of the divine purpose.

In the *Testaments of the Twelve*, moral requirements of the Jewish people are identified with the Stoic concept of living "according to nature" (T. Napht. 3). From the opening lines of IV Maccabees (dating from the first or second century CE), the story of the struggle of the Maccabees is retold as a philosophical lesson, with emphasis on the Stoic virtues: self-control, courage, justice and temperance. Obedience to the Law of Moses enables one to perceive and embody these cardinal moral qualities. The correspondences between this point of view and Paul's appeal to universal natural law in Romans and to the Stoic virtues as manifestations of the fruit of the Spirit in Galatians are obvious.

In both Jewish and early Christian writings–as in Stoic writings of the first century–what scholars often have differentiated as "wisdom" in contrast to "apocalyptic" (understanding the latter to be divinely revealed insight as to the moral and cosmic ordering of the universe) are in both bodies of literature different facets of analogous comprehensive worldviews. Thus Paul in the very letter where he describes Christ as the "first fruits" of the dead and the one who will destroy "every ruler and authority and power" (1 Cor 15:20-28) also refers to him as "the power of God and the wisdom of God (1 Cor 1:18-30). Similarly, in the Q source, where Jesus is depicted as one whose wisdom is greater than that of Solomon, it is in a context of universal eschatological judgment and implies the clear superiority of Jesus to both Solomon as bearer of wisdom and Jonah as prophet of divine judgment (Lk 11:29-32). Neither in Paul nor in Q is the truth about God and his activity in the world in behalf of his people conveyed in timeless aphorisms, any more than it is in Stoic wisdom contemporary with these early Christian writers.

The communication of wisdom through aphorisms does take place in one body of literature that some New Testament scholars have pointed to as the historical prototype of the teaching of Jesus: Cynicism. The assumption is that there was a philosophical school of the Cynics, reaching back to the time of Diogenes (fifth/fourth century BCE) and extending down into the Byzantine period, that sought to expose the falsity of accepted patterns of life and norms of human behavior and did so by the use of clever witticisms and aphorisms. Its devotees adopted a mendicant style of life in protest to the social and economic values of their epoch. Donald R. Dudley, in his *History of Cynicism*[54]–which remains a landmark in this field of historical inquiry–declares that "it would be an

---

[54]London: Methuen, 1937.

exaggeration to speak of any Cynic 'school' in the regular sense of organized teaching and a common body of doctrine."[55]. He describes the shift away from the philosophical systems of Plato and Aristotle as follows: "From the noble quest to satisfy the curiosity of the intellect it descended to become Daily Strength for Daily Needs". The earlier Cynics described the ideal ruler, which they saw embodied in Cyrus, who was not only efficient as a ruler but also manifested courage, helpfulness, and self-control, and whom they characterized as shepherd of the flock. Dio Chrysostom recounts that Heracles was made ruler of the world because he resolved to follow the divine model of *paideia*, which is the gift of the gods, and serves as a guard against human folly, producing divine and royal virtue (*he theia kai basilike phusis*).[56] As a result, Heracles is characterized by the royal values of peace, law, and right reason; he is made king and savior of all humanity but chastises savage and wicked humans and crushes the power of tyrants. The gods will reward and sustain the king who honors virtue, is humane, and is characterized by prudence (*phronesis*), temperance (*sophrosune*), justice (*dikaiosune*), and courage (*andreia*).[57]

Although the Cynics may initially have been in conversation with the Stoics, by the time of Cleanthes (330-240) and Chrysippus (291-205) Stoicism distanced itself from the more popular Cynic features, turning instead to physics and logic in the tradition of *egkyklia mathemata*. As Dudley puts it, "The new Stoicism was determined to have no truck with Cynicism in its own day."[58] By the second and first centuries B.C.E., Cynicism did little more than gain a footing in Rome, was unknown elsewhere in the West, and survived in obscurity in the eastern half of the Mediterranean world.[59] The issues of royal authority and social responsibility which had been addressed by the earlier Cynics were taken up by the Stoics in the early Roman period. A surge of Cynicism came only well into the Common Era, in the period from Vespasian to Marcus Aurelius (69-180). It was only then that the Cynic Epistles were produced–all of them pseudepigraphic, and all seeking to lend authority to their ideas by purporting to come from the classical period of Greek philosophy.

It is evident, therefore, that Cynicism did not provide Jesus or his earliest followers or any other pre-70 Christians with a specific model for attracting a wide popular following or for communicating wisdom in the form of Cynic-Stoic-style aphorisms. Instead, the oldest layers of the early Christian tradition disclose thinkers and writers engaged in their own version of answers to the pervasive human questions that were indeed being addressed from a different cultural point

[55] Dudley, *Cyncism*, 36-37.
[56] Dio Chrysostom, *First Discourse on Kingship* (I.65).
[57] Dio Chrysostom, *Third Discourse on Kingship*, 45-47. An insightful study of the kingship theme in Cynicism is that of R. Hoistad, *Cynic Hero and Cynic King: Studies in the Cynic Conception of Man* (Uppsala, 1948).
[58] Dudley, *Cynicism*, 102.
[59] Dudley, *Cynicism*, 124.

of view by the popular Stoic philosophers of this epoch. It is to some of the points of correspondence between the Stoic and Jewish-Christian sets of responses to the central human issues that we turn in conclusion.

Conclusion

Reviewing the agenda of Greco-Roman philosophers and oracles, as well as that of Jewish and Christian writers in the period before and after the turn of the eras, we may repeat our summary of the main themes:
Concern for the maintenance of cosmic order.
Conviction about human moral accountability before the gods.
Confidence in oracular disclosure of the divine purpose.
Belief in divine choice of human agents to fulfill the divine purpose for the universe.
Use of traditional mythic imagery to depict the course of human destiny and the consummation of the divine purpose.
We have seen that by the time of the establishment of the Roman Empire in the first century BCE these were major issues among philosophically inclined Romans as well as among Jewish thinkers concerned about the prophetic promises and the current state of political impotence and moral ambiguity of the Jewish people. How would the cosmic order be renewed? How would the traditional deities/deity accomplish this? How would human beings be called to account for their moral behavior? Who were the agents through whom this renewal would come?

The answers to these questions were believed to be in process of disclosure through certain chosen instruments for the benefit of the people, and especially for the guidance of their leaders. Dreams, portents, cosmic signs, and especially oracles–with proper interpretations–were the instruments through which the divine purpose was being revealed. The actual renewal was to be achieved through divinely empowered agents, who were identified with the ancestral figures of mythological and historical tradition: for example, Horus and Osiris; the Cumean Sibyl and the reign of Jupiter or Saturn; the new Israel and the royal heir of David. These ancient hopes were now to be achieved through contemporary historical figures.

These promises of social and political renewal, with their corollaries of hope for personal meaning and moral vindication, were represented across the Greco-Roman world. Far from dismissing these Stoic visions as meaningless or idolatrous, the Jewish and early Christian visionaries presented their own alternative responses to these longings for renewal and order. Pagans, Jews, and Christians in this period would have subscribed to the declaration in the Letter of James that true wisdom is "from above" (Jas 3:17). While they would have also agreed with Paul that the wisdom of God was "mysterious, hidden, and predetermined before the ages," they would likely have dissented from his claim that "none of the rulers of this age" perceived that wisdom (1 Cor 2:7-8). Formally speaking, the intent and the mode of communication of divine wisdom were shared by Jews and Christians with the contemporary Greco-Roman culture. The crucial divergence came in the specific content of each of the cultural systems, which derived from their respective historical and cultural heritages, and which produced significantly different parameters by which the enlightened community was defined.

Blessed Are Those Who Hear:
John's Apocalypse as Present Experience[1]

David L. Barr
Wright State University

μακάριος ὁ ἀναγινώσκων καὶ οἱ ἀκούοντες τοὺς λόγους τῆς προφητείας καὶ τηροῦντες τὰἐν αὐτῇ γεγραμμένα, ὁ γὰρ καιρὸς ἐγγύς.

Blessed the one reading aloud and the ones hearing the words of this prophecy and keeping the things written herein; for the time is near

(Revelation 1:3).

When I first met John Priest, at the very beginning of my graduate education, I would have read this sentence as a religious declaration, a kind of abstract and pious sentiment. But Priest was somewhat impatient with both abstractions and piety (not to mention sentimentality), and as he taught us to study the biblical writings he constantly pressed us to discover what such words would have meant in the lives of actual men and women. He taught us to think of theology as also anthropology: it tells us as much about its human formulators as about its putative subject. His constant admonition was: translate, translate, translate. He was the first to show me the Wisdom tradition as a

---

[1] This article is a synthesis and development of my earlier consideration of these themes: "How Were the Hearers Blessed: Literary Reflections on the Social Impact of John's Apocalypse," *Proceedings of the Eastern Great Lakes and Midwestern Biblical Societies* 8 1988: 49-59.

humanistic tradition in Israel and the first to introduce me to Peter Berger and the Sociology of Knowledge.[2] This paper is dedicated to John, and I trust he can see his hand guiding mine as I write. My goal is to translate this seemingly abstract statement (blessed . . . the ones hearing . . ..) into the life situation of real men and women and so understand how the hearing of these words was meant to produce blessedness.

The emphasis is on hearing and we must do full justice to the aural nature of this experience; the Apocalypse of John was meant to be heard, not silently read and studied the way we do in the university, and definitely not allegorized into a parable of the politics of nuclear confrontation as is so popular in some circles today. It was primarily an experience of very powerful language, a kind of language we have learned to call apocalyptic, a subdivision of symbolic speech. Our task is to discover how such speech would have functioned in the specific social context in which John enunciated it. I will briefly review the various suggestions of how we might understand that social situation and then explore what a holistic view of language might indicate about the blessedness of the hearers.

Happiness Threatened: The Social Context

There is no good reason to dismiss the traditional dating of this work, and most scholars agree that at least the final edition of Revelation was published around 95–in the last years of Domitian.[3] A few argue for an earlier date, either in the reign of Nero or shortly after his death in 68.[4] But at most the evidence they point to suggests that some parts of Revelation may have originated earlier. I see the visions of Revelation as the work of a life-time edited into their present form near the end of the first century. The work convincingly locates itself along the Hellenistic coast of Asia Minor, probably centered in the wealthy port city of Ephesus. So the question becomes what problems confronted the Christians in the Hellenistic cities of Asia Minor in the last third of the first century? Various scholars have seen Revelation as a response to one or more of the following issues: persecution, relative deprivation, anomie, assimilation. Revelation, as a response to these issues, is then seen as: encouragement, catharsis, community building, boundary making.

---

[2] A discipline I resisted all the while he tried to teach me, but which eventually I came to see as enormously helpful; see P. Berger and T. Luckmann, *The Social Construction of Reality: A Treatise in the Sociology of Knowledge* (Anchor/Doubleday, 1966).

[3] For a good review of the question with some new arguments see A. Y. Collins, *Crisis and Catharsis*, (Westminster, 1984) 54-83.

[4] For modest challenges to the accepted dating see C. Rowland, *The Open Heaven*, Crossroads, 1982: 403-13 and J. C. Wilson, "The Problem of the Domitianic Date of Revelation," *NTS* 39 1993: 586-605.

Persecution/Encouragement

The traditional understanding of the context of Revelation has been Roman persecution. Since the late second century it has been supposed that Domitian was a great persecutor of the Christians, a second Nero.[5] This tradition probably originates from Revelation itself, which does speak a good bit about tribulation and war–as well as John's apparent banishment (*relegation*) to Patmos. Nearly all the Introductions[6] and a number of specialized studies[7] assume that this is the basic contextual issue that determines the rhetoric of the book.

If persecution is the problem, how might a reading of Revelation be the solution? Surely such a hearing would not make the persecution go away, but it might help the hearers to endure it. A basic function of apocalyptic literature is to see behind the veil of ordinary experience and to reveal things as they truly are. Thus Revelation allows the believer to see that God is ultimately in control of history and that, in the end, justice will prevail. They must have the courage to prevail. This is certainly a major theme in the Revelation (e.g., 2:7, 11, 17; 12:11; 15:2).

The difficulty with this view is that there is so little evidence to support the assertion of Roman persecution.[8] The problems that can be identified–a

---

[5] Irenaeus, *Against Heresies* 5.30.3.

[6] Including even H. Koester's ambitious, *Introduction to the New Testament* (Fortress, 1982): "The book thus had its origin in a time of persecution, more specifically in a time of persecution which seemed to threaten all Christians" (II:250). See also W. G. Kümmel, *Introduction to the New Testament* (14th ed., Abingdon, 1966) 328; R. A. Spivey and D. M. Smith, *Anatomy of the New Testament* (3rd ed., Macmillan, 1982) 441; E. D. Freed, *The New Testament: A Critical Introduction* (Wadsworth, 1986) 360; H. C. Kee, *Understanding the New Testament* (4th ed., Prentice-Hall, 1983) 342-44, is somewhat more cautious.

[7] This thesis was popularized by W. Ramsay, *The Letters to the Seven Churches of Asia*, Armstrong, 1905, and followed by writers like R. H. Mounce, *The Book of Revelation* (Eerdmans, 1977}; B. M. Metzger, *Breaking the Code: Understanding the Book of Revelation* (Abingdon, 1993) 16. Elisabeth Schüssler Fiorenza seems to adopt a similar perspective when she calls Revelation a "letter from prison" (*The Book of Revelation*, Fortress, 1985:8-9 and see 194ff). It is somewhat surprising to see Adela Yarbro Collins claim that the something "radically amiss" in John's world is "the persecution of Christians by Rome" (*Crisis and Catharsis*, 115-16), for her general analysis is not built on the persecution hypothesis. Some see the persecution as more local: R. W. Wall, *New International Biblical Commentary: Revelation* (Hendrikson, 1991) 10f; M. E. Boring, *Revelation* (John Knox, 1989) 13ff.

[8] L. L. Thompson, *The Book of Revelation: Apocalypse and Empire* (Oxford: Oxford University Press, 1990) presents a sustained and convincing critique of the persecution hypothesis. For a general discussion, see A. Y. Collins, *Crisis and Catharsis*, 69-73. For an authoritative summary of "The Early Persecutions and Roman Law,"see A. N. Sherwin-White, *The Letters of Pliny: A Historical and Social Commentary* (Oxford: Clarendon Press, 1966) 772-87. J. Plescia argues that the very wording of Pliny's inquiry to Trajan proves there was no legal basis for a persecution under Domitian: "On the Persecution of Christians in the Roman Empire,"*Latomus* 30 (1971) 120-32. For a careful reconsideration of the evidence see L. Thompson, "A Sociological Analysis of the Tribulation in the Apocalypse of John,"*Early Christian Apocalypticism: Genre and Social Setting (ed.* A. Y. Collins, *Semeia* 36, Scholars Press, 1986) 147-74.

flourishing imperial cult and local hostilities[9]–seem either too pervasive or too provincial to warrant the sweeping drama of Revelation. We must, of course, heed Schüssler Fiorenza's admonition that the situation might look different if we adopt a "perspective from below" rather than ask what was objectively the case.[10] Pliny's Letter surely establishes that there was some earlier persecution of Christians in these provinces.[11] To the extent that these Christians needed some explanation for the hostilities they encountered, the hearing of the Apocalypse would be experienced as an informative event in which they could learn the answer to this question of why God's people suffer. The evidence of history would lead me to hypothesize that this was a subordinate function of the hearing, not the primary cause of their happiness.

Relative Deprivation/Status Reversal

Many scholars have turned away from the assumption of an historical persecution under Domitian,[12] focusing instead on sociological proposals–which at least have the virtue of being harder to falsify. Building on the study of contemporary millenarian movements, these scholars have suggested that the problem of John's communities was one of social deprivation.

The classic case is the Cargo Cult Movement in Melanesia, where, quite obviously, the social deprivation of the islanders led to millenarian expectations of a reversal of the present order.[13] Viewed this way, Revelation represents the response of a socially disadvantaged group imagining what life will be like when the tables are turned. The language functions to create an alternative world for them, a world in which they imagine themselves (and their God) to be in control, a world in which their enemies will grovel at their feet (3:9).

This is a very powerful and revealing theory with which I have a great deal of sympathy. But it is not without problems. For one, it seems impossible, at this distance, to demonstrate that the constituency of Revelation was any more deprived than others in Asia Minor. But sociologists are resourceful and have developed a concept of *relative deprivation*: "a negative discrepancy between

[9]See the careful study of S. J. Friesen, *Twice Neokoros: Ephesus, Asia and the Cult of the Flavian Emperors* (Leiden: E. J. Brill, 1993) or the summary of E. Schüssler Fiorenza, *The Book of Revelation* (Fortress, 1985) 192-94.

[10]*The Book of Revelation*, 8.

[11]For a translation of Pliny's famous letter to Trajan asking how to conduct trials of the Christians denounced to him see A. N. Sherwin-White, *The Letters of Pliny: A Historical and Social Commentary* (Oxford: Clarendon Press, 1966) 772-87.

[12]At a recent meeting of twenty scholars participating in the Seminar on Reading the Apocalypse (Society of Biblical Literature, 1994) I asked who still thought persecution was the major factor in the writing of Revelation. No one was willing to defend this view.

[13]See the classic study of P. Worsley, *The Trumpet Shall Sound: A Study of "Cargo" Cults in Melanesia* (Second edition, Schocken Books, 1968).

legitimate expectation and actuality."[14] That is to say, people no worse off than others may *feel* deprived if they have a legitimate expectation, based on some standard, that they should have more than they actually have. This is a very slippery concept that begins to look like the manufacture of data to fit a theory, for we lack any of the economic and statistical data that might give meaning to the modifier "relative."[15]

Such invention is perhaps the primary danger of historical sociology. For when the object of our investigation is no longer available we are left with applying models developed in the modern situation, hoping they illuminate what data we have. Nothing guarantees that a pattern found in a modern millenarian movement also existed in an ancient one, let alone in *all* ancient ones.[16] A further danger lies in the tendency of social theories to engage in what we may call the causal fallacy: that the social situation causes the religious or literary experience. This is especially pernicious when we must reconstruct the social setting from the literature.

I have an increasingly difficult time entertaining theories of deprivation to explain the Apocalypse. John chose to write to seven of the most powerful cities of Asia, six of them being the capitals of their region.[17] Nor were these hard times; this region was at the height of its prosperity.[18] The number of new public buildings undertaken in the first and second centuries is quite astonishing: my own rough count shows twenty-two at Ephesus and eleven at Pergamum, the only two sites for which we have a sufficiently large number of datable structures to hazard a count.[19] While John's audience contained both poor (2:9) and wealthy (3:17), it is likely that they were all better off economically than they had been and that their prosperity was increasing.

I have no doubt that the audience of Revelation suffered certain social disadvantages and that this story functioned to alleviate some of that suffering. But I do not think we have adequate evidence, either from Revelation or from what

[14]D. F. Aberle, "A Note on Relative Deprivation Theory as Applied to Millenarian and Other Cult Movements,"*Millennial Dreams in Action: Essays in Comparative Study* (ed. S. L. Thrupp, Hague: Mouton & Co, 1962) 209-14.

[15]B. McGinn, "Response to Adela Yarbro Collins, *Crisis and Catharsis: The Power of the Apocalypse*," unpublished presentation to the Early Christian Apocalypticism Seminar, SBL Annual Meeting, 1984, p. 5

[16]Similar cautions are urged by G. W. E. Nickelsburg, "Social Aspects of Palestinian Jewish Apocalypticism,"*Apocalypticism in the Mediterranean World and the Near East* (ed. D. Hellholm, Mohr, 1983) 641-54, esp., 648.

[17]A. H. M. Jones, *The Cities of the Eastern Roman Provinces* (Oxford: Clarendon Press, 1971) 73-83. Only Philadelphia, the easternmost city, was not a capitol, being included in the Coventus of Sardis. Nevertheless, Philadelphia was the dominant city of its area, ruling an extensive territory in the Cogamis valley.

[18]T. R. S. Broughton, "Roman Asia,"*An Economic Survey of Ancient Rome* (ed. T. Frank, Pageant Books, 1959).

[19]Based on information in E. Akurgal, *Ancient Civilizations and Ruins of Turkey* (Istanbul: Haset Kitabevi, 1985).

can be known of the social situation from other sources, to posit this as the basic issue addressed.

Anomie/Order

A third view sees the basic threat faced by these Hellenistic Asian Christians as their movement between social worlds, not once but twice.[20] These movements can be discerned in the work itself. The first movement was their conversion from the world of Hellenistic Roman culture to a Christian Jewish culture. We do not, of course, know who converted them or how recently. Nor do we know whether they represent a distinctively Johannine Christianity (associated in some way with the Gospel of John) or whether they were Christians of a Pauline, prophetic, or more sectarian type. Perhaps a mixture of all these. But we do see them concerned with some of the same issues that Paul faced in the first generation of Gentile converts: idol meat, association with outsiders, and emperor worship.

Only Gentile Christians would have had to struggle with whether they should eat sacrificial meat.[21] The dietary laws, however laxly observed, would prevent the problem from arising among Jews, for there would be a ready supply of nonsacrificial meat available for those wealthy enough to afford meat. But the regular supply of meat to Gentiles would often have been sacrificial meat, and the normal occasions on which common people would have had access to meat would have been the religious festivals of the city.[22] John's strict injunction (never eat it) in comparison with Paul's more lenient attitude (eat but do not worship) implies that this community was conservatively Jewish in its cultural orientation.

This same dynamic (Gentiles being asked to behave like Jews) seems to underlay a second problem, associating with outsiders. Some accepted the Nicolaitans and the followers of the Prophetess of Thyatira, who called for broader association, but John calls for their total exclusion.[23] Again Paul faced similar issues. John seems to call for isolation from the pagan world; it is doubtful whether one following the Johannine way could belong to one of the guilds so prominent in these cities. Paul's followers probably did (see 1 Cor 5:9). Again, we see a conservative, Jewish cultural orientation.

A third issues emerges in the latter part of Revelation, though it is strangely absent in the letters, namely the imperial cult. Our understanding of the imperial

---

[20] This was the thrust of my earlier article "How Were the Hearers Blessed"; see note 1.

[21] Since most publicly available meat in the cities would have been the product of some sacrifice, this was a pervasive problem. See the study of W. L. Willis, *Idol Meat in Corinth: The Pauline Argument in I Corinthians 8 and 10* (Scholars Press, 1985). For a general overview see G. Theissen, *The Social Setting of Pauline Christianity: Essays on Corinth* (Philadelphia: Fortress Press 1982). See also M. Detienne and J. Vernant, *The Cuisine of Sacrifice among the Greeks* (University of Chicago Press 1989).

[22] See D. E. Smith, *Social Obligation in the Context of Communal Meals: A Study of the Christian Meal in I Corinthians in Comparison with Graeco-Roman Meals* (Th.D. dissertation, Harvard University, 1980) 12.

[23] See the harsh rhetoric in the messages to the seven churches, especially 2:6; 2:14ff; 2:20ff.

cult in this region has been greatly advanced in recent years;[24] still much remains obscure. Who participated in it, on what occasions, and with what means and rites is not always clear. It seems certain that Jews were officially exempt, though local exceptions are known.[25] Again we have an issue that would not have confronted Jews; only Gentiles pretending they were Jews would have needed the stern warnings that John administers.

This evidence points to a community of Christians who have moved from the world of Greco-Roman Hellenism to that of Jewish practices and attitudes. Many first-generation Christians made that move in the first few centuries of our era. But John's communities have made a second move, equally dramatic.

This second movement can be discerned in the extreme bitterness toward ethnic Jews in the Apocalypse, a bitterness that can only point to a major schism, most likely expulsion from the synagogue.[26] It seems most likely that the hearers of the Apocalypse were Gentiles who abandoned their Gentile ways and became Christians within the context of the large and prosperous Jewish communities of these cities. Within this enclave they were protected from the issues discussed above. But now, dislodged from their Jewish environment, they are forced to confront these issues on their own. It is not surprising that different answers to the question of how one would live in this culture as a Christian emerge: Balaam, Jezebel, Nicholas, John.[27] John represents the conservative call to preserve their Jewish ways, even without the resources of the Jewish community. This probably meant almost no access to meat, perhaps the loss of employment, and certainly the loss of standing by operating outside the guilds, as well as challenges to their patriotism as they refuse to participate in city and imperial cults.

Such a tenuous position, outside the boundaries of the recognized worlds of their day, would have threatened the security and happiness of the hearers of the Apocalypse. The function of Revelation, then, would be to draw new boundaries and create a new world. Whether this is the central question for Revelation remains to be proven, but it certainly seems to be an issue. We will ask below how words heard might address a need for an alternative social world. One weakness with this view is that not everyone seems to have been willing to take up the stance of outsider.

---

[24] For an excellent overview see S. R. F. Price, *Rituals and Power: The Roman Imperial Cult in Asia Minor* (Cambridge: Cambridge University Press, 1984). S. J. Friesen has made a careful study of how the cult functioned in the province of Asia in *Twice Neokoros;* see note 9.

[25] Josephus' *Antiquities* 19.6.3. For a general discussion of the "Sacred Figure of the Emperor," see J. Ferguson, *The Religions of the Roman Empire* (Cornell University Press, 1970) 88-98.

[26] John's bitterness is reflected in 3:9 where he calls them "a synagogue of Satan" who "say they are Jews, but are not" and predicts that they will be made to "come and bow down before your feet". See also 2:9.

[27] John seems to lump these other three into one mass, but that does not mean we should. Bob Jones does not differentiate between Jerry Falwell, Billy Graham, and Robert Schuller because they are all far to his left. See the analysis of David Aune, "The Social Matrix of the Apocalypse of John,"*BR* 26 (1981) 16-32, especially 28-29.

Assimilation/Identity

The same issues addressed above (emperor worship, association, and meals) can be construed to indicate a somewhat different problem: to what degree should this community assimilate to its culture? Because social institutions in ancient cultures were undifferentiated, our distinctions between religious questions and cultural questions would not be intelligible. Religion did not exist as a separate institution but was embedded in other institutions, primarily the family and the government. Thus to be in a family, in a city, or in an empire also meant to have certain religious obligations. One owed certain degrees of honor to those in these institutions, and "piety" consisted in giving honor to whom honor was due. Religion was also embedded in all other aspects of Greco-Roman culture. The theater was devoted to Dionysus, and every performance would begin with a sacrifice. Athletic contests were celebrations of religious holidays. Education was founded on reading and interpreting Homer and the stories of the ancient Gods and heroes. Even business involved the Gods, for every craft, guild, and profession would have its patron deity to whom appropriate honors were due—even if it be only the spilling of a little wine in libation at the beginning of a guild or social meeting.

In the light of such interpenetration of religion and culture, Christians would inevitably debate the propriety of their participation, and the issues identified above (emperor worship, associations, sacrificial meat) would be centers of controversy. John clearly stood against any participation, but not all agreed. In fact, in each case one could make the case for Christian participation, often grounded on the writings of Paul, who was instrumental in the founding of the churches of this area.

Paul admonished his followers to pay their taxes and more—to give due honor to those who hold public office:

> For the same reason you also pay taxes, for the authorities are God's servants, busy with this very thing. Pay to all what is due them—taxes to whom taxes are due, revenue to whom revenue is due, respect to whom respect is due, honor to whom honor is due. (Rom 13:6-7).

The respect and honor due the emperor, it could be argued, involved recognizing his special status.

In the same way, Paul was shocked by those who would withdraw completely from association with those who might be considered immoral because they worshiped other Gods. When some at Corinth misinterpreted his admonition to separation to mean isolation, he responded vigorously:

> I wrote to you in my letter not to associate with sexually immoral persons—not at all meaning the immoral of this world, or the greedy and robbers, or idolaters, since you would then need to go out of the world. But now I am writing to you not to associate with anyone who bears the name of brother or sister who is sexually immoral or greedy,

or is an idolater, reviler, drunkard, or robber. Do not even eat with such a one. For what have I to do with judging outsiders? (1 Cor 5:9-12).

Clearly Paul envisioned his followers carrying on many of their former associations and business relationships, in spite of any compromises this might entail.

Paul even permitted the of eating sacrificial meat–provided it was not eaten in a context of worship or in a way that would undermine another's faith. Clearly participation at the altar was wrong in Paul's view, but the prohibition did not include public and private spaces:

> Eat whatever is sold in the meat market without raising any question on the ground of conscience, for "the earth and its fullness are the Lord's." If an unbeliever invites you to a meal and you are disposed to go, eat whatever is set before you without raising any question on the ground of conscience. (1 Cor 10:25-27).

Whether the prophets John labeled "Jezebel" and "Balaam" (2:14, 20) saw themselves as following the Pauline tradition or whether they took even more radical assimilationist positions, we can no longer know. Certainly there is a pervasive syncretistic approach to religion in this world; only Jews and Christians, and not all of them, took an exclusive view of religion.

The author of Revelation is surely such an exclusivist, and those who see such tensions as the central theme of the work would see it functioning in ways similar to those movements that resist westernization today. The writing would intend to persuade its hearers to resist assimilation, to give an exclusive commitment to this new community, and to live outside the dominant culture. To do this one must establish an overwhelming sense of identity with the community and must also portray those outside the community as foreign, depraved, and even demonic.

Let us now turn to a second line of inquiry and ask just how language functions so that we can consider how the reading of the Apocalypse could function to produce happiness in hearers who faced such issues.

Happiness Restored: How Might Revelation Solve the Problem?

Our common sense notion suggests that language functions to communicate information from a speaker to a hearer. This is probably true in some basic way of all speech–except, perhaps, singing in the shower. If I say, "I would like a glass of water," it is quite plain that I am seeking to communicate information to you, and (if we speak the same language) you will no doubt bring me a glass of water. In fact, if said within a specific context (in a restaurant, for example) this expression is the equivalent of an order, "bring me a glass of water." This suggests two important facts. First, language can do more than provide information, it can function to produce action on the part of the hearer. Second, language is contextual and may shift both meaning and function as it shifts context. These two facts suggest a third: language can also function to express something about the speaker–for example, that I am thirsty. In fact, if said within a specific context (lost in the desert, perhaps) its *primary* function would be to express my feeling of thirst (and perhaps even despair). We may represent these observations thus:

Process: **Speaker**   →   **Statement** →   **Hearer**
Functions: *Expressive*   →   *Informative* →   *Performative*

The Functions of Language

Thus, while language seeks to communicate something from a speaker to a hearer, the nature of the "something" varies with the context of the language: expressing something about the speaker, informing the hearer of some information, or calling on the hearer to perform in some way.

G. B. Caird's reflections on the nature of language[28] allow us to enhance this model in two ways. First, he observes that statements may be of two distinct kinds: simple information or concepts and ideas, for the informative function of a genealogy is quite different from that of a letter like Galatians. We might say that some information requires only that we grasp it, absorb it, while other information demands that we wrestle with it until it takes hold of us. We might call the former information descriptive and the latter reflective.

Second, Caird makes the important observation that communication most often occurs in community and achieves in the hearers not only a performance but also a cohesion. It binds them together as a community. While it may be possible to consider this a certain kind of performance, it seems more cogent to regard it as an additional function, the cohesive function of language. When a group of civil rights protesters sing "We Shall Overcome," the primary function of the language is to bind the group together, though, of course, it also expresses their idealism (expressive), calls for commitment (performative), and provides information to the guardians of the status quo who hear them (informative).

One further consideration is necessary to complete our model of the function of language, a reflection of the functional power of the contexts of communication. We saw above that the meaning of the simple sentence, "I would like a glass of water" can shift significantly with its context (your home, a restaurant, a desert). And communication can fail entirely if we are not speaking the same language *Bir su istiyorum* might fail to get a response in Tallahassee, but it would get you a glass of water in Turkey. But it is also possible to "speak a different language" in other ways, as anyone with teenagers understands.

In fact, language not only is spoken in context, it has the power to create contexts for itself. Roman Jacobson has identified three ways language itself

[28] *The Language and Imagery of the Bible* (Westminster, 1980).

functions to provide the context in which it is to be understood. In addition to the informative function (or referential in his terms), Jacobson distinguishes the poetic, the phatic and the metalingual functions of language.[29] By poetic function he means language's ability to call attention to itself; meter and rhyme being two obvious examples. I will call this the aesthetic function. By phatic function he means the use of language to insure that the channels of communication are open. When we say "good morning" we are not giving a weather report (informative function); we are establishing a contact through which further communication might proceed (phatic function). I will call this the connective function. By metalingual function he means the use of language to create various codes in which certain communications are transmitted: at its broadest, a language code, but also genres, idioms, symbols. I will call this the regulative function. These three functions may be grouped together as *determinative functions* that shape the ways we perceive the meanings of statements. Such language determines the context in which it is to be understood.

We may now draw a more comprehensive model:

Speaker   →   **Statement**   →   **Hearer**
Expressive   *Informative*   *Performative*
                        Descriptive   *Cohesive*
                        Reflective
                    Determinative
                        Aesthetic
                        Connective
                        Regulative

It is likely that every significant communication event will involve all these functions but that one or the other will dominate, depending on the historical, social, and linguistic contexts.

The Apocalypse certainly manifests all these functions, and, in fact, one can point to a correlation between the various analyses of the life setting of the Apocalypse and the perception of the dominant linguistic function of the work.

The Linguistic Functions of Revelation

Clearly, we will construe the function of Revelation differently depending on what we see as the problem addressed.

Persecution. Those who see the social context as persecution see the function of Revelation as providing encouragement. Proponents of this view have often seen Revelation as providing the hearers with information that they did not have before–telling them what they needed to know in order to be able to

---

[29] "Closing Statement: Linguistics and Poetics," *Style in Language* (ed. T. A. Sebeok, M.I.T. Press, 1960) 350-77.

persevere. Most often this was understood as information about the end of the world, namely, that it is near.[30] Viewed this way the message of Revelation was "hang in there; your trials will soon be over" with the added promise that those who endure will be suitably rewarded. Alternatively, those less inclined to take Revelation at face value might describe the information being communicated as a proclamation of the sovereignty of God.[31] In either case, the primary function of the work is to provide the hearers with some needed information. This new information would give them the courage to live in their difficult circumstances.

Relative Deprivation: Social. To the degree that this remains a social theory,[32] our attention is directed toward a social function of literature–the performative and cohesive. The happiness of the hearers results from their hearing the Revelation because that very hearing results in the social construction of a new reality.[33] In the terms of Berger and Luckmann, the hearing of Revelation creates a "finite province of meaning," an enclave within the paramount reality of everyday life.[34] Within this enclave new rules apply, new meanings are apprehended, new views of the world are internalized. Berger and Luckmann compare this experience to being on a journey; one goes away and comes back. Such a journey does nothing to change the reality to which one comes back–our work is still waiting for us when we return from our vacations. But we may say that we have come back refreshed and ready to work. We have changed.

Viewed this way, the function of Revelation is to provide the hearer with an experience of an alternative reality. It is not a matter of getting new information but of having a new experience. And this experience is a shared experience, so Revelation also functions cohesively to build the community. Again, the analogy of a group trip is apropos, for such experiences bind people together.

Relative Deprivation: Psychological. Another possibility has developed from the conception of a social deprivation with its notion of feeling deprived. One scholar has recently taken the notion of *feeling* in a new direction, developing a psychological interpretation of the Apocalypse.[35] Yarbro Collins argues that the real crisis facing the communities of the Apocalypse was psychological: the experience of fear and resentment at the power of Rome, leading to feelings of

---

[30] "At the same time John offers the church comfort and hope. It should know that the powers opposing God will soon have exhausted themselves and that the ultimate victory of God, which is already reality in heaven, will also soon be made manifest on earth." J. Roloff, *The Revelation of John: A Continental Commentary,* translated by J. E. Alsup (Minneapolis: Fortress Press 1993) 10.

[31] See, for example, M. E. Boring, "The Theology of Revelation: 'The Lord Our God the Almighty Reigns'," *Int.* 40 (1986) 257-69.

[32] The next section will discuss its transformation into a psychological theory.

[33] The seminal work is J. Gager, *Kingdom and Community* (Prentice-Hall, 1975); see also the last chapter of Schüssler Fiorenza's *The Book of Revelation* and my article, "The Apocalypse as a Symbolic Transformation of the World: A Literary Analysis," *Int.* 38 (1984) 39-50.

[34] P. Berger and T. Luckmann *The Social Construction of Reality,* 25; see note 2).

[35] See A. Y. Collins, *Crisis and Catharsis*, 106, 144, 152-61. This development was already implicit in Gager's seminal work with his concept of Revelation as mythic therapy, 50-55.

envy and a desire for vengeance. In fact, she rather reverses Gager, speaking not of a mythic therapy but of a mythically induced schizophrenia. But rather than being disabling, this schizophrenia works to the good of the hearers, for it allows them to feel the forbidden emotions and so overcome them. She suggests that the hearing of Revelation resulted in a purgation of the emotions, as Butcher interpreted Aristotelian catharsis,[36] so that the emotions of envy and vengeance are aroused by the work and symbolically experienced, draining them of their debilitating effects. Here language functions primarily in a expressive mode, expressing first the emotions of the author and then of hearers who identify with this author. Happiness is attained by means of an emotional involvement in the oral performance of the Apocalypse.

While it may be admitted that the hearing of the Apocalypse would have been a very powerful emotional experience, it does not seem to me that it would have worked quite this way. To begin with, the response she alleges seems to rest on a sort of Laurencian reading of Revelation as a blood-thirsty, unchristian call for vengeance,[37] a reading I find quite unpersuasive. Close examination of John's symbolism shows that in every case where images of power and vengeance are used they are subverted into images of suffering and endurance, even as the lion of the tribe of Judah is transformed into the lamb slain.[38] In addition, I am not convinced that a hearing of the Apocalypse would arouse and purge fear of Rome. Never for a moment is there a scene in which the outcome is in doubt; there is not even a report of a battle scene whose outcome we must await. All is given; it is done.

The real strength of Yarbro Collins approach, however, is to force us to consider the psychological impact of such language. Its function is not to convey information but to express the convictions and emotions of the author. It is the experience of the Apocalypse that is important. Yarbro Collins has provided a framework within which we can consider the expressive function of the Apocalypse as a demonstration of John's feelings of anger, vengeance, and a cry for justice against Rome.

Anomie. The anomie inherent in the social position of those who have ceased to be Gentiles without becoming accepted in the Jewish community would likely lead to various social solutions. Some would abandon this new way for the safety of the old order; some would seek compromises; some would attempt to create a new order. John is in the latter group, and the Revelation was his effort to give validity to the new order. In this view, the function of Revelation is

---

[36] S. H. Butcher, *Aristotle's Theory of Poetry and Fine Art* (4th ed., Dover Publications, 1951) 240-57. For a challenge to this view see L. Golden, "The Clarification Theory of Katharsis," *Hermes* 104, Band 4 (1976) 437-52.

[37] D. H. Lawrence, *Apocalypse* (Viking Press, 1982). See Yarbro Collins, *Crisis,* 169.

[38] For a fuller discussion see my article, "The Apocalypse as a Symbolic Transformation of the World,"41-42.

performative and cohesive: to create a new community based on a new vision of life.

Jean-Pierre Ruiz has called the Apocalypse a ritual text, a text that encodes a rite.[39] As an oral text enacted in a public assembly (1:3), Revelation functioned to enhance the sense of community–a basic function of much ritual activity. Such ritualized social dramas provide a means for reflecting on the nature of the community and for solving its basic conflicts.[40]

If we ask *how* this is done, two answers present themselves. First, John uses a variety of boundary-marking devices, such as the assignment of praise and blame (throughout chapters 2-3), name-calling (2:9, 14, 20), and secret knowledge (13:18; 17:5). These devices clearly mark who is "in" and who is "outside" (22:15). Second, John constructs an alternative world. Under the technique of "apocalyptic" unveiling, John looks behind the apparent reality of Roman power to an alternative understanding in which power destroys itself, slain lambs and martyrs rule, and the whole creation gathers in worship before the heavenly throne. By telling a convincing story to the community gathered for worship, John provides both legitimation and plausibility structure for his alternative worldview.[41] The primary functions of Revelation in this view would be cohesive and performative, but there is also an informative function.

However, the information Revelation communicates is reflective not descriptive. Not facts but an attitude toward life lies at the heart of its message.

Assimilation.   A response to assimilation would share much with a response to anomie, for the two problems would be strongly interrelated. In fact, assimilation might be one answer to anomie, an answer John rejected. And to make his rejection palatable, he would have to develop alternative ways of dealing with anomie. Thus, much of what was said above could be repeated here, for the two moves are required: to drive a wedge between the audience and the dominant culture and to enhance the sense of community. But the emphasis shifts when we concentrate on assimilation as the basic problem.

The primary difference would be the need to demonize Greco-Roman culture, to show it is not the innocent (or beautiful) thing some claim. Such a purpose would enhance the informative function of Revelation, for John would have to show how evil is the enemy. Does Rome seem tolerant? Remember it was Roman power that crucified Jesus. Does the emperor seem majestic? Remember he is a dragon (13:11). Does the culture seem impressive (17:6)? Remember the rapacity and inhumanity on which it is founded (18:11-13). Have the Jews rejected us? Remember they are a synagogue of Satan (2:9). It is perhaps not too much to

---

[39] J. P. Ruiz, "Betwixt and Between on the Lord's Day: Liturgy and the Apocalypse," *SBLSP* (1992) 654-72, reference to 663.

[40] See J. J. MacAloon, ed. *Rite, Drama, Festival, Spectacle: Rehearsals toward a Theory of Cultural Performance* (Philadelphia: Institute for the Study of Human Issues, 1984).

[41] These terms are from P. Berger and T. Luckmann, *The Social Construction of Reality.* They refer respectively to the theoretical justifications and the social support for knowledge.

say that all the images and actions of John's story contribute to this sense of willful alienation from culture.

Conclusion.   Each of these scenarios has some insight to offer for understanding Revelation, though each leads us in somewhat different directions. When persecution is seen as the context, emphasis tends to fall on the informative function; social crises theories are more likely to concentrate on the performative function, though some reflective-informative function must be considered; and emphasis on the expressive function correlates with a psychological approach. A holistic view of language recognizes that it functions on all these levels at once, with one or the other dominating in any given utterance; a holistic picture of Revelation will require some attention to each of these functions. We must ask, in other words, how the very hearing of this story itself might constitute a blessing?

Blessing the Hearers: The Language of the Apocalypse as Experience

The happiness of the hearers of the Apocalypse was threatened on a number of fronts, and John's task was to provide an imaginative response that would be equally comprehensive. The hearers of John's story seem to have faced (modest) persecution, (relative) deprivation, and feelings for vengeance (or perhaps justice), all of which rest on the basic issue: they are an alternative community unsure of what ought to be their proper relationship to Roman culture and Roman rule. John chose to address these (and possibly other) issues by telling them an apocalyptic story as they gathered together for worship. Let's consider this act in greater detail.

Telling.   While John is not actually present with them, this story is intended to be read aloud to the audience. Now recent writers have convincingly argued that the oral/aural experience is substantially different from the silent reading experience.[42] The oral experience penetrates the audience, speaks as an inner voice, manifesting itself as a subjective event. My own classes regularly report that the experience of hearing the whole of the Apocalypse read aloud speaks more directly to them than all of the more objective study we have engaged in. An oral narrative will engage the audience, move them emotionally and psychologically. Orality emphasizes the expressive and performative functions of language. Such a telling experience would meet their need to feel different about their situation.

---

[42]I am especially indebted to the work of W. Ong, *The Presence of the Word: Some Prolegomena for Cultural and Religious History* (University of Minnesota, 1967); *Interfaces of the Word: Studies in the Evolution of Consciousness and Culture* (Cornell University Press, 1977); and *Orality and Literacy: The Technologizing of the Word* (London: Methuen, 1982). Ong's work has been extended by W. H. Kelber, *The Oral and the Written Gospel: the Hermeneutics of Speaking and Writing in the Synoptic Tradition, Mark, Paul, and Q* (Fortress, 1983). See also E. A. Havelock, *Preface to Plato* (Harvard University Press, 1963); and "The Oral and the Written Word: A Reappraisal,"*The Literate Revolution in Greece and its Cultural Consequences* (Princeton University Press, 1982) 3-38. See also L. H. Silberman, ed., *Semeia 39: Orality, Aurality and Biblical Narrative* (Scholars Press, 1987).

Story.   Stories only appear to be simple. They are often very complex events capable of a great variety of very subtle social meanings.[43] Stories are commonly used to establish group cohesion, enhance a sense of identity, regulate social hierarchies, and educate newer members of the group. A good story, well told, translates one into another reality, and in this other reality one is not only challenged to think about the world in new ways (informative and reflective functions), but one also experiences this other world as a present reality (performative function).   In this story one learns one's place in the world, including one's relationships with others–and one especially learns who the enemy is. But this learning is not merely the acquisition of new information; it is the gaining of a new experience, because one reenacts the drama.

Apocalypticism. Apocalypticism is inherently a sectarian movement, for it rests on the essential distinction between insiders and outsiders, those who possess the hidden knowledge and those who do not.[44] Thus whatever else apocalyptic literature is about it is also about community formation. Again, performative language dominates. And because the community that reads apocalyptic literature takes on the traits of an apocalyptic community, they reenact the apocalyptic story in their own social situation.[45]

Gathered Community. While not beyond dispute, the gathered community is most likely the community at worship. Pliny gives us a glimpse of worship customs in Asia Minor when he reports to Trajan that they gathered before sunrise to sing and then went about their work, reassembling for a ritual meal (almost certainly in the evening).[46] If the Apocalypse is read to the gathered community, it would surely be in the context of this evening assembly, and the meal would be the Eucharist.[47] In such a context John's language about the blood of Jesus and the coming of Jesus takes on new significance, and the final affirmation of Jesus ("Surely I am coming soon,"22:20) will be realized without delay. The story John tells explains and interprets the Eucharist, showing how sharing in Jesus' life and death leads to true happiness–in fact, speaks that happiness into being.

---

[43] On the general problem see L. Degh, "Some Questions of the Social Function of Story Telling,"*Acta Ethnographica* (1957); and also her *Folktales and Society: Story Telling in a Hungarian Peasant Community* (Indiana University Press, 1969). For applications to biblical stories see M. W. G. Stibbe, *John as Storyteller* (Cambridge University Press, 1992); D. B. Howell, *Matthew's Inclusive Story: A Study in the Narrative Rhetoric of the First Gospel* (Sheffield Academic Press, 1990); and D. R. MacDonald, *The Legend and the Apostle: The Battle for Paul in Story and Canon* (Philadelphia: Westminster Press., 1983).

[44] See R. R. Wilson, "This World–and the World to Come: Apocalyptic Religion and the Counterculture,"*Encounter* (1977).

[45] See the provocative rhetorical analysis of apocalypticism, especially in America, in S. D. O'Leary, *Arguing the Apocalypse: A Theory of Millennial Rhetoric* (Oxford: Oxford University Press, 1994) on reenactment see 200-206.

[46] See Pliny, *Letters* 10.96.

[47] See my "The Apocalypse as a Symbolic Transformation of the World" and J. Roloff, *The Revelation of John,* 252-53.

Many have noted that the Apocalypse contains not only narratives about God's coming rule but also portrayals of that rule in the extensive use of liturgical elements.[48] Liturgy is the service of God and as such reestablishes the divine order. The Apocalypse goes one step further. When seen in this liturgical context the Apocalypse itself becomes a liturgical act. Thus the story does more than describe the coming of God's rule (the narrative); it does more than portray God's rule (in its liturgical elements); it functions to bring God's rule (it is the liturgy).

Viewing the Apocalypse as liturgy allows us to synthesize the literary and social aspects of this imaginative work. For it is the total experience of the Apocalypse–verbal, psychological, social, and religious–that functioned to bless the hearers. The blessing promised in the opening statement (1:3) was attained in the present experience of hearing the Apocalypse read aloud. Their happiness did not depend on their theology or on some future event. The effectiveness of the Apocalypse did not depend on whether or not the putative end of the world was near. Obviously it was not near. This blessing came as they listened to, participated in, experienced the words of this prophecy. Hearing the Apocalypse provided a drama they could both feel and live. It formed their identities and shaped their attitudes toward their culture and toward all those who sympathized with that culture. It enabled them to see behind the veil of ordinary experience to the extraordinary reality of John's vision. As imitators of Jesus, they would face suffering in the light of Jesus' suffering. And so they are transformed (and blessed) by the very act of "hearing the words of this prophecy."

[48] Well argued by L. L. Thompson, "Cult and Eschatology in the Apocalypse of John," *JR* 49 (1969) 330-50.

Literary Contexts of Mark 13

Elizabeth Struthers Malbon
Virginia Polytechnic Institute and State University

For the past quarter-century one of the liveliest debates in New Testament scholarship has been between critics raising new literary questions of the gospels and critics pursuing primarily historical questions in the tradition of *Formgeschichte* and *Redaktionsgeschichte*. Early on in the debate the two approaches seemed to many to be irrevocably opposed, with New Testament studies (at least in the USA) echoing the battles fought between North American traditional, historically oriented literary critics and the New Critics. Attention to the text in its historical context and attention to the text in itself seemed to be either/or options. Initial antagonism, with "new" literary critics challenging "old" historical critics in the field of gospel interpretation, has mostly given way to a shared sense of the interrelatedness of historical and literary questions and the complexity of a text's multiple contexts. Although, given the human limits of individual scholars, most New Testament researchers still tend to be primarily historical or primarily literary in their approaches, most also understand their work as part of a larger whole. In addition, a newer focus (with older roots) on the sociological dimensions of texts has enriched the overall field. From my own religious, philosophical, and epistemological standpoint, I understand the requirements of the present situation of biblical studies not as the affirmation of consensus but as the appreciation of complexity.

As a small contribution to such an appreciation of complexity, which is to be distinguished from an acceptance of confusion, I have presented elsewhere "a typology of contextual foci of interpreters."[1] My starting point was a collection of essays by intellectual historian Dominick LaCarpa in which he argues persuasively that one must refer to the contexts of a text, not its singular context. "For complex texts," LaCapra writes, "one has a set of interacting contexts whose relations to one another are variable and problematic and whose relation to the text being investigated raises difficult issues in interpretation."[2] It would be an impossible task to enumerate all the contexts of a text, but a simplified typology of contextual foci may be of use in registering the different interests, approaches, and assumptions of interpreters of texts and their contexts. After locating my own approach within this typology I wish to exemplify my approach by, first, suggesting several internal literary contexts of Mark 13 within the Markan gospel, and, second, commenting on a number of literary aspects of Mark 13 as a unit. This self-conscious exercise in literary interpretation is intended to compliment, complicate, challenge, and be challenged by the explicitly historical interpretations of other New Testament interpreters.[3]

A Typology of Contextual Foci of Interpreters

My proposed typology is formed by the intersection or crossing of two familiar distinctions: internal/external and literary/historical. Murray Krieger's famous images of the text as mirror and the text as window[4] suggest metaphorically what is meant here by the "internal" and the "external" contexts of a text. When an interpreter focuses on the text's "internal" context (text as mirror) he or she looks to "the text itself"–its words and sentences, its characters and settings, its plot and action, its rhetoric and imagery–for the text's meaning and significance. When an interpreter focuses on the "external" context of a text (text as window) she or he looks through the text in some larger world–whether cultural, political, religious, or literary. As already noted, "literary" and "historical" have often been characterized as two distinctive (if not opposing) approaches to texts. To focus on the "literary" context of a text is to concentrate more on how the text

---

[1] E. S. Malbon, "Text and Contexts: Interpreting the Disciples in Mark," *Semeia* 62 (1993) 81-102; see esp. pp. 82-85.

[2] D. LaCapra, *Rethinking Intellectual History: Texts, Contexts, Language* (Ithaca: Cornell University Press, 1983) 35.

[3] An earlier version of this paper was distributed to the members of the Seminar on the Gospel of Mark of the Studiorum Novi Testamenti Societas for its 1995 meeting in Prague. In addition to my paper, the Seminar discussed papers on Mark 13 by Adela Yarbro Collins and Joel Marcus. I was privileged to present a synopsis of this paper to faculty, students, and friends of the Department of Religion at Florida State University in June 1995. John Priest's presence there reminded me of something I had learned from and about him when I was his student; this remembrance is incorporated into my conclusion here.

[4] M. Krieger, *A Window to Criticism: Shakespeare's Sonnets and Modern Poetics* (Princeton: Princeton University Press, 1964).

is read than on why it was written, more on function–perhaps in relation to the conventions of a genre–than on intention. To focus on the "historical" context of a text is to investigate its place in societal/cultural processes of continuity and change. *The quotation marks enclosing the four main terms of the typology are intended to indicate the problematic nature of the terms and the impossibility of their pure manifestation except as abstractions.*

Crossing the "internal"/"external" distinction with the "literary"/"historical" distinction results in four contextual foci of interpreters of texts (see diagram): A, the interrelations of the elements of the text; B, the interrelations of the text with other texts; C, the immediate societal/cultural situation of the text (especially its origin and/or preservation); D, the broader societal/cultural situation of the text. It is here assumed (although it will not be discussed) that "the text" is an abstraction employed to refer to the communication process involving an author (real and implied), a text (variously transmitted), and an audience (real and implied).[5] The audience of particular concern here is the community of scholarly interpreters. The community of scholars could and should look at all texts with (at least) all four foci. The distinction of the four foci is meant to be *descriptive* of how individual interpreters tend to sub-divide this enormous task into more approachable ones. No one of the four foci is intended to be *prescriptive* for any particular text.[6] The parentheses around "of interpreters in the title of the diagram indicates that the role of the interpreter (reader, literary critic, historian), although integrally involved with a text's multiple contexts, is not the focus of this typology. Yet it is important to note here that these are contextual foci *of interpreters*. The interpreter is omnipresent in interpretation. My *Semeia* 62 article concluded with a brief explicit consideration of the role of the interpreter in relation to text and contexts. My present task is to locate my own work as a Markan interpreter within this typology of contextual foci.

---

[5] Thus I am in agreement with Paul B. Armstrong (*Conflicting Readings: Variety and Validity in Interpretation* [Chapel Hill and London: University of North Carolina Press, 1990]) that "A text is not an independent object which remains the same regardless of how it is construed. The literary work is not autonomous but 'heteronomous'" (p. 11), that is, "paradoxically both dependent and independent, capable of taking on different shapes according to opposing hypotheses about how to configure it, but always transcending any particular interpreter's beliefs about it" (p. x).

[6] I make this clarification on the basis of helpful questions raised by my SNTS respondant, Peter Müller.

Contextual Foci (of Interpreters)

	"internal" context	"external" context
"literary" context	**A** the interrelations of the elements of the text	**B** the interrelations of the text with other texts
"historical" context	**C** the immediate societal/cultural situation of the text (esp. its origin or preservation)	**D** the broader societal/cultural situation of the text

One might say that as a Markan scholar I have not yet gotten off square one! My foci have been consistently "literary" and "internal." I have investigated the interrelations of the elements of the Markan text–especially spatial references and the characters around the Markan Jesus. As a narrative critic I have been intrigued by interrelations of the narrative elements of settings, characters, plot, and rhetoric. I could not have avoided, nor would I have wished to avoid, making assumptions about the Markan gospel's historical contexts: for example, although the current debate about orality and textuality calls for a total rethinking of the presuppositions underlying our synoptic source theories, I still find Markan priority sensible; and, although my reasons are more literary than historical, I suspect Mark's gospel was reduced to writing in the wake of the temple's destruction in 70 CE. And, or course, I begin my work with a *koine* Greek text, which demands some knowledge of historical contexts even to read. However, history and realities external to the Markan text are not the focus of my research and writing.

It once seemed odd to me that, as a New Testament literary critic, I spend a fair amount of time in my classes of undergraduates discussing the historical contexts of New Testament books. It no longer seems so. It has become obvious to me that those who start with the assumption that the gospels were written in English to speak without mediation to twentieth-century North American Christians cannot even embark on meaningful *literary* interpretation of the gospels.

I hope it is becoming increasingly obvious to the community of scholars that those who start with the assumption that literary elements–from genre to characterization, from plot to poetics–are not central and essential to a text's significance cannot even embark on meaningful *historical* interpretation of the gospels. Historical and literary approaches are mutually interdependent.

Internal Literary Contexts of Mark 13

The internal literary contexts of Mark 13 are the ways in which this chapter is situated in the gospel as a whole. As a literary critic I am always investigating the interrelations of parts and wholes, although what is a part in one literary context may be a whole in another and *vice versa*. The following observations on Mark 13 were initially made not on the basis of concentrated study of chapter 13 but as a result of looking at some other aspects of the Markan gospel. In terms of its internal literary contexts, Mark 13 is (1) framed by two stories of exemplary women in contrast with villainous men; (2) paralleled in two ways: (a) in its form as an extended discourse of Jesus by chapter 4, the parables discourse, and (b) in its role in the plot as a foreshadowing of the passion of the community by chapters 14-16, the passion of Jesus; and (3) linked with many other Markan passages in its manifestation of the anti-temple theme.

Framed by Stories of Exemplary Women

It was in looking at a number of narrative contexts, that is, internal literary contexts, of Mark 12:41-44, the story of the poor widow, that I was particularly impressed by an instance of Markan framing that others have also noted: the story of the poor widow's gift of her last two coins serves with the story of the unnamed woman's anointing of Jesus as a frame around chapter 13.[7] The poor widow symbolizes Jesus' death by giving her whole life (*holon ton bion autēs*, 12:44); the anointing woman prepares for Jesus' death by anointing his body beforehand for burial (14:8).[8] Chapter 13, the eschatological discourse, is intrusive within the larger story of Jesus' passion in Jerusalem, which begins in chapters 11-12 and culminates in chapters 14-15. Thus chapters 11-12/13/14-16 form a very large-scale intercalation. As with smaller scale Markan intercalations, so here too the frame and the middle are to be interpreted together. However, one can skip from the end of chapter 12 to the beginning of chapter 14 with no obvious gap in the story line; that is, chapter 13 is smoothly rounded at both ends.

---

[7] E. S. Malbon, "The Poor Widow in Mark and her Poor Rich Readers," *CBQ* 53 (1991) 589-604; see esp. pp. 598-99. See also E. S. Malbon, "The Major Importance of the Minor Characters in Mark," *The New Literary Criticism and the New Testament* (ed. E. S. Malbon and E. V. McKnight; Sheffield: Sheffield Academic Press, 1994; Valley Forge: Trinity Press International, 1994) 58-86; see esp. 67, 76-81.

[8] Malbon, "Minor Characters," 67.

This central discourse is framed not simply by two stories of exemplary women but exemplary women in contrast with villainous men. The Markan Jesus' condemnation of the scribes' typical actions (12:38-40) and his commendation of the poor widow's exceptional action (12:41-44) immediately precede chapter 13; the accounts of the chief priests' and scribes' plot against Jesus and the woman's anointing of Jesus immediately succeed chapter 13.[9] One woman gives what little she has, two copper coins; the other gives a great deal, ointment of pure nard worth 300 denarii; but each gift represents self-denial. It is, of course, ironic that the poor widow's gift occurs in the doomed temple; and it is ironic that the anointing of Jesus Christ, Jesus Messiah, Jesus the anointed one, takes place not in the temple but in a leper's house (14:3), and not at the hands of the high priest but at the hands of an unnamed woman. A further irony is manifest in the juxtaposition of the unnamed woman, who gives up money for Jesus and enters the house to honor him (14:3-9), and Judas, the named man, even "one of the twelve," who gives up Jesus for money and leaves the house to betray him (14:10-11).

These particular ironies involving exemplary women who are minor characters and villainous men who have larger roles to play in the plot form the frame for the Markan Jesus' eschatological discourse to four significant male characters, Peter, James, John, and Andrew, not so much exemplary disciples as archetypical ones. Within this frame, chapter 13 moves from the men's conventional (and, as it soon turns out, ironic) admiration for the temple, the tradition's chief religious structure, to a challenge not only to that structure's continued existence but to the continued existence of all the structures of the universe. The four disciples are not villainous (as are the scribes, the chief priests and scribes, and Judas); nor are they exemplary (as are the two women). They stand betwixt and between—between villainy and exemplary service, between the secure past of "these great buildings" (13:2) and the uncertain future of "not one stone . . . upon another" (13:2)–and thus mark the place of the Markan hearer/reader of the eschatological discourse and its narrative frame: "And what I say to you I say to all" (13:37a).[10]

Paralleling the Parables Discourse

A second internal literary context of Mark 13 is manifest by its strong parallels with the Markan Jesus' parables discourse in chapter 4. Chapter 4, actually 4:1-34, and chapter 13 are the longest connected discourses of Jesus in Mark's gospel. Both speeches are introduced with minimal scene-setting and minimal (or indirect) dialogue. Yet the minimal scene-setting for each speech involves one shift resulting in greater intimacy. At the beginning of chapter 4 the

---

[9] See Malbon, "Poor Widow," p. 599 n. 48, for relevant scholarly literature.
[10] Unless otherwise noted, all English translations are from *The New Revised Standard Version,* copyright 1989, by the Division of Christian Education of the National Council of Churches of Christ in the United States of America.

Markan narrator manages to use the word *thalassa* (sea) three times in one verse in order to establish Jesus as on the sea (sitting in a boat), teaching the crowd; the scene shift occurs at 4:10, not with a spatial marker but with a change in characters: "When he was alone, those who were around him along with the twelve asked him about the parables." At the beginning of chapter 13 the Markan Jesus (and his disciples) are coming out of the temple, where they had been since 11:27; the scene shift occurs at 13:3, marked with both spatial markers and a change in characters: "When he was sitting on the Mount of Olives opposite the temple, Peter, James, John, and Andrew asked him privately . . . ." These are two of only three occasions in Mark's gospel where Jesus is explicitly said to be sitting; the third is 12:41, where Jesus is reported to sit down opposite the treasury (in the temple). Sitting is the authoritative position of the rabbis while teaching; rabbi Jesus teaches about the coming reign of God through parables and about the coming end of the age through sayings and parables.

Minimal dialogue sets up the eschatological discourse: the disciples extol the temple buildings (13:1); Jesus contradicts them with a reference to the temple's future destruction (13:2); then four disciples, a more intimate group, ask Jesus "when will this be . . . ?" (13:4); Jesus responds with the full eschatological discourse (13:5-37). Dialogue implied by indirect speech sets up the more intimate (and longer) portion of the parables discourse: after Jesus' telling of the parable of the sower, the narrator reports that the distinctive grouping of "those who were around him along with the twelve asked him about the parables" (4:10); Jesus responds with the parables discourse (4:11-32). Mark 4:11-32 and 13:5-37 stand out and stand in parallel as the Markan Jesus' longest monologues.

In addition, both the parables discourse and the eschatological discourse are rounded-off units; after the narrative pause for each speech, action resumes *almost* where it left off. Progress is obvious in the movement beyond Galilee to foreign, Gentile regions after the parables discourse (4:35-8:21), and in the thickening of the plot leading to Jesus' crucifixion in Jerusalem after the eschatological discourse (chaps. 14-16).

Finally, both speeches are concerned explicitly with how one is to understand things–how one is to hear mysteries of the kingdom and to see the unseen future as it becomes present. As reference to hearing punctuates chapter 4 (4:3, 9, 12, 15, 16, 18, 20, 23, 24, 33), so reference to seeing punctuates chapter 13 (13:1, 2, 5, 9, 14, 21, 23, 26, 29, 33, 34, 35, 37). "Let anyone with ears to hear listen!" (4:9 and 23). "And what I say to you I say to all: Watch" (13:37, *RSV*). Hear and see, listen and watch, perceive and understand–these are the imperatives of the two parallel teaching discourses of the Markan Jesus.

The two discourses are also parallel in the way in which they fit into the overall structure of Mark's gospel. Of the making of outlines of the structure of Mark there is and shall be no end! I have argued, as have others, that the interpreter's goal is not to provide *the* definitive outline but rather to appreciate the various dimensions of the text, some of which can be best featured by one outline,

some by another.[11] One outline I have developed in teaching the Gospel of Mark
serves well to feature the parallel positions of chapters 4 and 13; in addition, this
outline utilizes a number of divisions that have achieved a high level of scholarly
consensus (4:1-34; 8:22-10:52; 11-12; 13; 14-16) and treats as larger divisions two
portions of the text where no such consensus has formed (1:1-3:35; 4:35-8:21).
My working outline is as follows:[12]

> ⌈ 1:1-3:35   powerful Messiah: kingdom + community (old and new)
> | 4:1-34   powerful words: parables of the kingdom
> ⌊ 4:35-8:21   powerful deeds: toward a new community
>   8:22-10:52   discipleship on the way
> ⌈ 11-12   passion of Jesus: rejection by and of old community
> | 13   passion of the community: powerful words of the end
> ⌊ 14-16   passion of Jesus: rejection of Jesus; toward a new community

As the parables discourse is enclosed by the narration of Jesus' powerful
deeds in Galilee and beyond, so the eschatological discourse, in which the passion
of the community is foretold, is enclosed by the narration of the passion of Jesus.
These two larger units, 1:1-8:21 and 11-16, these two panels of the diptych as it
were, are connected by 8:22-10:52, which serves as their hinge. In this center
section of the entire gospel, the disciples, and the hearers/readers who are looking
over their shoulders, struggle to bridge the gap between Jesus as powerful Messiah
and Jesus as suffering Messiah, with consequent implications for themselves. In
the center of each half of the gospel we hear and see a speech of Jesus on the theme
of understanding. The first half ends with a direct question from Jesus to the
disciples: "Do you not yet understand?" (8:21). The transitional middle section
ends with the newly sighted Bartimaeus following Jesus "on the way" (10:52).
The final half ends up in the air, with an implied question from the narrator to the
narratee (or the hearer/reader): Jesus is on the way to Galilee; the women "said
nothing to anyone, for they were afraid" (16:8), and yet I have said all this to you;
what will *you* say and what will *you* do? Not a bad ending for a narrative that titles
itself "The *beginning* of the gospel of Jesus Christ, the Son of God" (1:1, *RSV*)
    A more careful look at the material preceding each of the two parallel and
centered, or even intercalated, speeches reveals a broader pattern of functional
parallels.[13] The overarching pattern is controversy–cooperation–example (negative
and positive)–implications:

---

[11] See E. S. Malbon, *Narrative Space and Mythic Meaning in Mark* (New York and San
Francisco: Harper & Row, 1986; Sheffield: Sheffield Academic Press, 1991), and J. Dewey, "Mark as
Interwoven Tapestry: Forecasts and Echoes for a Listening Audience," *CBQ* 53 (1991) 223-36.
    [12] Cf. E. S. Malbon, "Echoes and Foreshadowings in Mark 4-8: Reading and Rereading," *JBL*
112 (1993) p. 216 n. 11.
    [13] These parallels were initially suggested to me as I was investigating how the stories of the
minor characters in Mark serve as "narrative punctuation," marking where the audience is to pause,
reflect, connect. See Malbon, "Minor Characters," esp. 72-81.

2:1-3:6	controversy	11:27-12:27
3:7-19	cooperation	12:28-34
3:20-35	example	12:35-44
	(negative and positive)	
4:1-34	implications	13:1-37

First, both 2:1-3:6 and 11:27-12:27 narrate controversy stories, the former in Galilee, the latter in the Jerusalem temple. Secondly, both 3:7-19 (3:7-19a in the English text) and 12:28-34 present a break in the pattern of controversy: in the former situation a great crowd follows Jesus; unclean spirits, who certainly are opposed to Jesus, surprisingly fall down before him, saying "You are the Son of God"; and Jesus chooses twelve of his followers to be disciples (or apostles) in sharing his work of preaching and healing; in the latter situation an exceptional scribe is in surprising agreement with Jesus, who commends him, saying "You are not far from the kingdom of God." Thirdly, in 3:20-35 (3:19b-35 in the English text) and 12:35-44 a character or characters juxtaposed with scribes (Jesus' family/the poor widow) culminates the series of encounters in an exemplary way. Who will be followers of Jesus? Not the established religious leaders (2:1-3:6 and 11:27-12:27) and especially not the scribes (3:22-30 and 12:35-40)–with a notable exception (12:28-34). Not–or not just–the biological family of Jesus (3:31-35).[14] The disciples are indeed especially chosen followers (3:13-19). But "whoever does the will of God" (3:35), whoever gives "her whole life" (12:44, my translation), is kin to Jesus, part of his new metaphorical family! Finally, in chapters 4 and 13, a longer discourse of the Markan Jesus follows the example scene, bringing out its implications not only for the characters within the narrative but also for the implied audience at its border.

Participating in the Anti-Temple Theme

A third internal literary context of Mark 13 is its participation in the anti-temple theme of the Markan gospel. A number of Markan scholars have discussed the anti-temple theme in Mark, most particularly Werner Kelber, but also John Donahue, Donald Juel, and myself.[15] Certainly Jesus' disparagement of the disciples' admiration of the temple buildings in 13:1-2 and his cryptic use of the phrase from Daniel, "the desolating sacrilege," in 13:14 play an important part in the unfolding of the anti-temple theme in Mark. The theme begins early, as "the

---

[14] For a further explanation of this reading of the passage about family, see Malbon, "Minor Characters," 79.

[15] W. H. Kelber, *The Kingdom in Mark: A New Place and a New Time* (Philadelphia: Fortress, 1974) 109-28; J. R. Donahue, S.J., *Are You the Christ? The Trial Narrative in the Gospel of Mark* (SBLDS 10; Missoula: SBL, 1973) 113-35; D. Juel, *Messiah and Temple: The Trial of Jesus in the Gospel of Mark* (SBLDS 31; Missoula: Scholars Press, for SBL, 1977) 127-39; Malbon, *Narrative Space*, 106-68. See also E. Lohmeyer, *Lord of the Temple: A Study of the Relation Between Cult and Gospel* (Edinburgh and London: Oliver and Boyd, 1961), chap. 2.

scribes who came down from Jerusalem" at 3:22 engage in controversy with the Markan Jesus. Controversy with "scribes who had come from Jerusalem" recurs at 7:1. When the Markan Jesus goes up to Jerusalem, controversy with religious leaders in the temple is repeated with the so-called "cleansing" of the temple scene (11:15-19, actually a proleptic disestablishment of the temple system) and prolonged with Jesus' extensive teaching in the temple (11:27-12:44), which leads up to chapter 13. In some ways chapter 13 marks the culmination of the anti-temple theme: the temple's destruction is explicitly foretold by the Markan Jesus, a reliable and almost omniscient character. In other ways the anti-temple theme culminates with the narrator's remark at Jesus' crucifixion, implicitly foreshadowing the temple's dysfunction or destruction: "And the curtain of the temple was torn in two, from top to bottom" (15:38).

While some scholars, including Juel and Donahue, consider that the anti-temple theme in Mark is reversed finally as the community becomes the new temple, I do not find this to be the case *in Mark*.[16] The saying that "I will destroy this temple that is made with hands, and in three days I will build another, not made with hands" is attributed to the Markan Jesus by witnesses whose falsity is mentioned three times in two verses (14:56-57). As I have argued elsewhere, the Markan architectural symbol for the new community is not the temple, not the synagogue, but the house.[17] The anti-temple theme, of which chapter 13 is a part, is unrelieved.

Paralleling the Markan Ending

Observation of the participation of Mark 13 in the gospel's anti-temple theme prepares us for recognition of a fourth, and for now final, internal literary context of the eschatological discourse. Chapter 13, with its foreshadowing of the passion of the community in the words of Jesus, parallels the Markan ending, with the narrator's words on the passion of Jesus, in chapters 14-16. A number of scholars have made observations that move us toward this interpretation.[18] Some time ago R. H. Lightfoot noticed a number of parallels between chapter 13 and chapters 14-15 of the Gospel of Mark.[19] Later Norman Perrin suggested that Mark 13 and Mark 14-16 are parallel, that "the passion and the parousia of Jesus stand in a certain tension with each other," that Mark's gospel draws to a close with a "twin climax of the apocalyptic discourse . . . and the passion narrative."[20] This

---

[16] See Malbon, *Narrative Space*, 135, and Donahue, *Are You the Christ?*, 108-109, and Donahue, *The Theology and Setting of Discipleship in the Gospel of Mark* (Milwaukee: Marquette University Press, 1983) p. 62 n. 46.

[17] Malbon, *Narrative Space*, 106-68.

[18] For what follows, see Malbon, *Narrative Space*, 151-52 and pp. 199-200 nn. 6-7.

[19] R. H. Lightfoot, *The Gospel Message of St. Mark* (Oxford: Clarendon, 1950) 48-59.

[20] N. Perrin, *The New Testament: An Introduction* (New York: Harcourt Brace Jovanovich, 1974) 148, 159.

idea has been further developed by John Donahue, who has depicted the double ending as "the passion of Jesus and the passion of the community."[21]

The positions of Perrin and Donahue represent developments, based on more detailed literary analysis, of the more historically oriented positions of Etienne Trocmé and Rudolph Pesch. Trocmé holds that Mark 1-13 made up the earliest form of the Markan gospel, and that later this work was editorially combined with an independent document that we might call the "Passion according to Saint Mark" (Mark 14-16), to form the canonical Mark. Thus the New Testament Gospel of Mark may be understood as "the 'second edition, revised and supplemented by a long appendix' of an earlier Gospel."[22] Pesch, on the other hand, posits that Mark 13 was added after the gospel was complete in order to counter a false eschatology.[23] My observations concerning the double ending of Mark are in line with the literary analysis of Perrin and Donahue and do not judge the issue of the historical creation of the Gospel of Mark as suggested by Trocmé and Pesch.

The content of the Markan Jesus' eschatological discourse is, in narrative time, a flashforward. Jesus speaks of the world's end just prior to his own end; because he knows his own end is at hand he must speak now; he claims no certainty about when the world will end (v. 32) but warns his followers that, before that time, his trials and suffering will be echoed by their own: "As for yourselves, beware; for they will hand you over to councils; and you will be beaten in synagogues; and you will stand before governors and kings because of me, as a testimony to them" (v. 9). Thus Jesus' passion will be paralleled by that of the community of his followers. The implied author of Mark seems to ask: How can the community understand and withstand its suffering?, for the Markan narrator seems to supply the answer by placing the foreshadowed trials of the community literally in the middle of the story of Jesus' final days in Jerusalem. It is for the implied audience to complete the thought metaphorically–to see its own suffering in the context of the suffering of Jesus.

At the close of the passion of the community (chap. 13), Jesus says from the mountain, "And what I say to you I say to all: Keep awake" (13:37). At the close of the passion of Jesus (chaps. 14-16), the young man says from the tomb, "'He has been raised; he is not here . . . But go, tell his disciples and Peter that he is going ahead of you to Galilee . . .'" (16:6-7). "Keep awake" (*NRSV*) or "Watch" (*RSV*; *grēgoreite*, from *grēgoreō*) and "raised" (*ēgerthē*, from *egeirō*) have a linguistic root in common and thus, perhaps, have some elements of meaning in common. *Grēgoreō* was a new formation in Hellenistic Greek from *egrēgora*, the perfect of *egeirō*;[24] their shared significance is "to be awake." Both the surprising

---

[21] Lectures given at the Vanderbilt Divinity School, Fall 1977.

[22] E. Trocmé, *Formation of the Gospel According to Mark* (Philadelphia: Westminster, 1975) 215-29; quotation from 240.

[23] R. Pesch, *Naherwartungen: Tradition und Redaktion in Mk 13* (Düsseldorf: Patmos, 1968).

[24] W. F. Arndt, F. W. Gingrich, and F. W. Danker, trans. and eds., *A Greek-English Lexicon of the New Testament and Other Early Christian Literature* (2nd ed.; Chicago and London: University of

experience of the empty tomb (chap. 16) and the surprising experience of the ruined temple (chap. 13), both the resurrection (chap. 16) and the parousia (chap. 13), call forth wakefulness from the followers of Jesus. Both the disciples of whom Jesus is "going ahead . . . [on the way] to Galilee" (16:7) and the later disciples who "flee to the mountains" (13:14) must "keep awake" (13:37). The double endings of Mark, chapter 13 and chapters 14-16, parallel each other in a number of ways, and both endings are open-ended.

Mark 13 as a Literary Unit

We have considered four internal literary contexts of Mark 13, four ways the part (chap. 13) fits into the whole (the Markan gospel); Mark 13 is (1) framed by stories of exemplary women in contrast with villainous men, (2) paralleled by the parables discourse and (3) also by the Markan ending, and (4) it participates in the Markan anti-temple theme. But we shift our focus now to consider Mark 13-as-a-literary-unit the "whole." There is a high level of scholarly consensus that Mark 13 may be considered such a whole, a rounded-off unit–from historical and redaction critical as well as literary points of view. If Mark 13 is the "whole," what are the "parts"? I have looked at a number of outlines of Mark 13, usually based on content or theme, and I have discovered a number of ways of designating these "parts." Here I will take another tack: I will investigate several elements or levels or aspects of Mark 13 as a literary unit. The result will not be a thematic outline but a literary "score," as it were. This score, like a musical score for an ensemble of instruments or voices, will allow us to follow each of several elements (voices) from 13:1 through 13:37 before listening again, with keener hearing, to their combined effect, which makes the music of Mark 13. Thematic outlines of Mark 13 are generally thought to be competitive with each other; in my analysis, the patterns of the various elements or aspects are complimentary. At each level of elements or aspects, what draws our literary attention are shifts.

Shifts in Settings

Mark 13 presents three types of shifts in settings: spatial, temporal, and those having to do with the characters present. Mark 13:1 signals a spatial shift from the relatively long temple scene, 11:27-12:44–with explicit spatial markers at 11:27, "walking in the temple"; 12:35, "teaching in the temple"; and 12:41, "sat down opposite the treasury." The opening spatial marker of chapter 13 is transitional: "As he came out of the temple . . . " No new space is yet indicated; the old space is simply left behind. This is, of course, the perfect setting for the transitional dialogue in which Jesus' disciples extol the old space and Jesus disparages it. According to the narrative's central character, the old space left behind in the narrative is to be destroyed (deconstructed?!) beyond the narrative's temporal boundaries. Mark 13:3 signals another spatial shift, and here a new space is entered: "When he was sitting on the Mount of Olives opposite the temple. . . ." The first thing to notice about this new setting is its opposition to the old setting, which is made explicit in the text (cf. the explicit contrast of "on the sea" and "beside the sea on the land" at 4:1). The second thing to notice about this new setting is that, while it is marked by a specific place name, Mount of Olives (rare in the earlier parts of Mark's gospel but more frequent in the larger passion story, chaps. 11-16), it also partakes of the connotations of the generic mountain. A mountain is where humanity, earth-bound creatures, and God, from on high, approach one another.[25] His location on a mountain lends the Markan Jesus the authority of one who speaks with and for God. His location on the Mount of Olives, opposite the temple, confirms that this authority contrasts that of the temple officials–chief priests, scribes, and elders. The seated position of the Markan Jesus, like that of the rabbis when teaching and like that of Jesus earlier in the boat for the parables discourse and most recently while observing the poor widow contribute to the temple treasury, indicates the competition between the Markan Jesus and the traditional teachers of Israel (Pharisees, scribes). These spatial shifts set up the audience for what follows in the eschatological discourse.

Although time is of central importance in the eschatological discourse, all references to time are incorporated into the speech of the main character; the narrator gives no explicit temporal signals of the passage of story time. A dramatic temporal marker opens chapter 14, helping to establish the literary break: "It was two days before the Passover and the festival of Unleavened Bread." With this temporal shift the narrator initiates the specificity on the temporal plane that had been introduced on the spatial plane at 11:1 with the piling up of proper place names: Jerusalem, Bethphage, Bethany, Mount of Olives. Earlier temporal references were generic: "on the following day" (11:12) and "in the morning" (11:20). The spatial and temporal specificity of the Markan passion narrative gives it the effect that slow motion and zooming-in have in film. It is intriguing to note that the final pericope before the beginning of specific temporal markers at 14:1, the final passage in the section of Mark generally lacking such specific time references, is focused on the Markan Jesus' denial of knowledge of specific time references for the end time: "But about that day or hour no one knows, neither the angels in heaven, nor the Son, but only the Father" (13:32). Perhaps the absence of temporal markers in chapter 13 sets the scene for Jesus' eschatological discourse equally as well as the presence of spatial markers.

A third type of scene-shifting that occurs in Mark 13 is a change in the characters present for a scene. For most of the extended teaching in the temple scene of 11:27-12:44 the disciples are in the background; in the foreground are Jesus and groups of traditional religious leaders, one by one. The disciples re-

[25] Malbon, *Narrative Space*, 84-89.

entered Jerusalem with Jesus at 11:27 as a part of a "they" (a third person plural verb ending), but at 12:43 Jesus "called his disciples" in order to comment to them on the poor widow's giving. The opening verse of chapter 13, which we have already noted as transitional at the spatial level, is also transitional at the level of characterization. One of the silent disciples steps out of the background to speak, eliciting a spirited response from Jesus, and setting up a short dialogue. However, before the dialogue can continue, a spatial shift (to the Mount of Olives) occurs, and a parallel shift in characters present is indicated. Now it is no longer "one of his disciples" but the big four, Peter, James, John, and Andrew, who continue the dialogue with Jesus. (It is, naturally enough, an unequal dialogue: the four speak as one for one verse; Jesus responds with 33 verses.) This group of four disciples, or three of them (Peter, James, John), appear at various times in the Markan narrative, giving a greater intimacy to certain scenes. The hearer/reader, of course, is invited into *all* the scenes–a position of intimacy indeed. In addition, the four disciples, the leaders among the followers who are to be leaders, take the place of the passing groups of traditional religious leaders who are Jesus' dialogue partners and audience in the temple scenes. The new leaders listen in a new space. Spatial and temporal shifts, and shifts in characters present to speak and listen, establish an appropriate setting for the eschatological discourse of the Markan Jesus.

Shifts in Narrative Form

We have already observed one narrative form present in Mark 13–dialogue; other forms are monologue, narration, and narrative aside. The chapter opens with narration–the third-person "telling" of the reliable and omnipresent narrator. In Mark as a whole there is much of such narration, but in Mark 13 as a whole there is very little, all of it giving place references or indicating who is speaking to whom. Such narration is so minimal that it can be presented here in its entirety: "As he came out of the temple, one of his disciples said to him, . . . " (v. 1a). "Then Jesus asked him, . . . " (v. 2a). "When he was sitting on the Mount of Olives opposite the temple, Peter, James, John, and Andrew asked him privately . . . " (v. 3). "Then Jesus began to say to them, . . . " (v. 5a). In Mark 13, narration simply sets the stage and brings on the characters. A similar dearth of narration and dominance of discourse occurs in the immediately preceding temple scenes (11:27-12:44). The resumption of narration at 14:1, after 33 verses of discourse, underlines the literary break at that point.

The discourse (or speech of the characters) of Mark 13 is either dialogue or monologue. Characters speaking are signs of the narrator's "showing" rather than "telling." As is conventional in ancient literature, only two speakers appear at a time–one or even both of whom may be groups speaking with one voice. In Mark 13 the dialogue opens with the exclamation of one of Jesus' disciples: "Look, Teacher, what large stones and what large buildings!" (v. 1b). The speech suggests that the speaker expects the concurrence of the one addressed. Jesus' response, however, reverses this expectation: "Do you see these great buildings? Not one stone will be left here upon another; all will be thrown down" (v. 2). In addition, Jesus' response opens with a question: "Then Jesus asked him, 'Do you see these great buildings?'" Obviously this is a rhetorical question, and Jesus, without waiting for an answer, continues with a statement. Then the four disciples, speaking with one voice, pick up the dialogue by offering an inquiring question to Jesus; they "asked him privately, 'Tell us, when will this be, and what will be the sign that all these things are about to be accomplished?'" (v. 4). Although their words could be read as two separate questions, the apparently double question is probably just an example of Markan redundancy (not unlike "very early . . . when the sun had risen" at 16:2). As Jesus answers them he continues the dialogue, but after a while, as we begin to realize that the disciples are not going to break in again, we realize dialogue has become monologue.

Verses 5b-37 are a monologue of the Markan Jesus, broken but once–and not by the dialogue of an intruding character but by a narrative aside of the intruding narrator. In response to Jesus' mention of "the desolating sacrilege set up where it ought not to be," the narrator interjects his now famous "let the reader understand" (v. 14). Historically oriented Markan critics explore carefully the possible historical referents of this verse. It is my purpose to call attention to it as one of a handful of Markan asides, all serving, from a literary point of view, both to pull the audience into the narrative and to underline the reality that the audience is in fact outside of the narrative. Such narrative asides call attention to the act of narrating.

Thus, in terms of narrative form, Mark 13 is comprised of these sections:

1a	narration
1b-2	dialogue
	one of disciples: exclamation
	Jesus: rhetorical question, statement
3	narration
4-5ff.?	dialogue
	4 disciples: inquiring question
	Jesus: answer
5-37	monologue
	Jesus
(14	broken by narrative aside)

Thus demarcation by shifts in narrative form represents an elaboration of the simpler twofold division suggested by shifts in setting: vv. 1-2, coming out of the temple, with disciples; vv. 3-37, sitting on the Mount of Olives, with four named disciples. However, since all but four verses of chapter 13 are included in the monologue of the Markan Jesus, this material calls for further analysis, which will be given below.

Shifts in Theme

My third, and for now final, category of shifts within Mark 13 as a literary unit is not as clear-cut as the previous two. Indicators of setting (spatial, temporal, or by means of characters present) and basic narrative forms (narration, dialogue, monologue, narrative aside) are fairly obvious among interpreters–not that all interpreters have observed them on their own (literary critics would be more likely to be looking for such aspects) but that, once pointed out, their presence in the narrative (if not always their significance) does seem obvious to many. Yet shfts in setting and in narrative form do not take us very far in interpreting much of chapter 13, for vv. 3-37 occur in one narrative setting (the Mount of Olives) and vv. 5-37 in one narrative form (monologue). Shifts in theme focus attention on this material undifferentiated by setting or narrative form. However, shifts in theme are less obvious, not only because there is no widely agreed upon delineation of themes in Mark 13, but also because there is no universal definition of the elastic term "theme." I too find I must stretch the term "theme"–here to include parables and short sayings (perhaps more properly called forms) as well as the temple, the Coming One, disasters, and followers–all of which receive treatment at least twice in Mark 13. Although some of my thematic categories overlap with those of interpreters presenting "an outline" (or even "*the* outline") of Mark 13, my way of applying them is different. I am trying to suggest not how the text can be divided up into smaller sense units but what subjects are treated where, what categories of content are repeated and in what pattern.

With a desire to label dominant and recurring themes in Mark 13 I have come up with six categories: the temple, the Coming One, disasters (political, earthly, cosmic), followers, parables, and short sayings. The recurrence of these themes in the 37 verses of Mark 13 is indicated in the following chart.

A	B	C	D	E	F
Temple	Coming One	Disasters	Followers	Parables	Sayings
1-4	5-6	7-8	9-13		
———	———	———	———	———	———
14a			14b-20		
	21-23	24-25			
	26-27				
———	———	———	———	———	———
				28-29	
					30-31
					32 (-33)
				(33-) 34-37	

The overall pattern may be indicated as A B C D / A D B C B / E F F E, which is analogous to the musical form, theme/variations/coda.

The first four verses, whose main function seems to be establishing the setting and the dialogue, also introduce the theme of the temple–its current glory, its future destruction. The temple theme is unambiguous in vv. 1-3, but v. 4, the question of the four disciples, is highly ambiguous: "Tell us, when will this be, and what will be the sign that all these things are about to be accomplished?" Mark's grammar is often maligned, but I suspect this unclear pronoun reference is intentional; in any case it is effective because "this" and "these things" in all their indefiniteness can be applied to the rich variety of "things" about which the Markan Jesus does in fact speak in answer to their question.

Jesus' first response presents the theme of the Coming One–in vv. 5-6 in the form of "many" who "will come" in Jesus' name, saying "I am he," and thus leading astray Jesus' followers. This theme is followed immediately by the theme of disasters–in vv. 7 and 8a, political disasters (wars), and in v. 8b, natural disasters on the earth (earthquakes and famines; famines, of course, being a frequent corollary of wars in the ancient world). At v. 9 a grammatical shift from third person ("they") to second person ("you") underlines the shift to a new theme: followers. In the broader sense this section too is about disasters, societal disasters between believers and traditional religious and political leaders and personal disasters within the family and families of believers. But the disaster theme is such an important part of eschatological thinking that it could easily swallow up all other distinctions, even though they might prove helpful. Thus it seems useful to suggest that four themes are presented in rapid succession: the temple, the Coming One, disasters, and followers.

At v. 14a it would appear that the first theme, the temple, recurs, although its occurrence, like its referent, is somewhat cryptic: "But when you see the desolating sacrilege set up where it ought not to be (let the reader understand) . . . ." Presumably this phrase from Daniel is being reused to refer the understanding reader (the implied reader) to a contemporary recurrence of the desecration of the temple. This appearance of the temple theme is fleeting, for the desolating sacrilege ushers in a crisis for the *followers* of Jesus, "the elect" (v. 20). Various images are employed to communicate the urgency of the situation for followers: there will not be time to go down from the housetop to the house, to pick up one's coat in the field; it will be hard on women who are pregnant or nursing, and hard on everyone if it is winter; such suffering has not been known since the time of creation. Fortunately, God has "cut short those days" for the sake of the elect followers (v. 20). Thus two sections on the theme of followers, vv. 9-13 and vv. 14-20, are contiguous except for the brief allusion to the temple theme in 14a. (Note that, in terms of shifts in narrative form, the narrative aside of v. 14 intrudes into the monologue of vv. 5-37.) The first section (vv. 9-13), however, employs second person ("you"), while the second section (vv. 14-20) employs third person ("they") after its opening reference to "when you see," despite its direct address to "the reader" in 14a.

Verses 21-23 echo vv. 5-6 with the theme of the Coming One. As before the warning is against false ones who will come to lead astray the followers–here "false messiahs and false prophets" (v. 22). The reference to false coming ones at vv. 5-6 was followed by word of future political and natural disasters on the earth. The reference to false messiahs and prophets at vv. 21-23 is followed by word of cosmic disasters: sun, moon, stars, and the powers in heaven will all be disabled or dislocated (vv. 24-25). Verses 26-27 continue these cosmic overtones (clouds, four winds, the ends of the heavens) but reiterate the theme of the Coming One, this time, the third time, with a positive valence of affirmation of the true Son of Man rather than a negative valence of warning of false ones who will come. Thus each of the themes introduced in 13:1-13 recur at least once in 13:14-27, although not exactly in the same order, and one theme, the Coming One, occurs twice–once negatively and once positively. The pattern is A B C D / A D B C B, a Markan theme and variations on traditional eschatological themes.

Within this musical metaphor, vv. 28-37 are a coda–new material is presented, but it serves to bring the composition to completion (if not resolution). A pair of parables enclose a pair of sayings. (Verse 33 joins the saying in v. 32 to the parable in vv. 34-37 and can easily be read with either.) These four elements are actually distinctive in form rather than in theme; their shared theme makes explicit the theme of the entire chapter; thus it is their form that marks a shift. The parable of the fig tree (vv. 28-29) opens the coda; the parable of the householder on a journey (vv. 34-37 or 33-37) concludes it. One image is from the natural/agricultural world, the other from the social world; the first parable may suggest that one can predict the time; the second parable insists that one cannot. In between the two parables are sandwiched two short sayings: the first saying (vv. 30-31) asserts that "this generation" will not outlast the taking place of "all these things" but that Jesus' words will outlast heaven and earth; the second saying (vv. 32-33 or 32) proclaims that no one–not the angels, not the Son, but only the Father–knows when the time will come. The overarching theme of chapter 13 becomes more explicit in the coda and most articulate at the coda's core, vv. 32-33: "But about that day or hour no one knows, neither the angels in heaven, not the Son, but only the Father. Beware, keep alert; for you do not know when the time will come."

Thus the Markan Jesus, who has been answering the disciples' question about when this will be "and what will be the sign that all these things are about to be accomplished" for about thirty verses so far, concludes that he does not know! Verse 32 pulls the rug out from under anyone who was taking vv. 5-31 too prosaically. It is at this point that the implied reader realizes that the eschatological discourse of the Markan Jesus is deconstructing itself! And it is for this reason that I refer to Mark 13 as the eschatological discourse rather than the apocalyptic discourse. Although traditional apocalyptic themes–the present and future temple; false heralds and the true Coming One; political, natural, and cosmic disasters; the trials and tribulations of followers–are woven together in Mark 13, their presentation does not lead, in the end (pun intended), to the "uncovering" or "revealing" (*apokalypsis*) of the end time that is the hallmark of apocalyptic. The theme of Mark 13 is eschatological (*eschatos* meaning "last"), but it is not apocalyptic, and (depending on one's definition of apocalyptic) it might even be said to be anti-apocalyptic. If apocalyptic proclaims that the end is at hand and you will know it by these signs, Mark 13 proclaims: The end is not now, not yet, not known; so keep alert, endure, and be saved![26]

This expression of the eschatological theme does not come as a complete shock at the close of chapter 13; it has, in fact, been woven as a scarlet thread throughout the dialogue and discourse. As I tried to delineate specific themes in Mark 13, my categories were repeatedly challenged by statements that seem to stand out from their specific context with a more general coloring. I have not been able to describe rigid criteria for such generaliztions, and I present the list of candidates here with acknowledgement of the subjective nature of this observation: vv. 4, 7b, 8b, 10, 13b, 14a–(let the reader understand), 19-20, 23, 30-31, 32, 33, 37. Thus, at the same time as traditional apocalyptic themes are being presented (A B C D) and re-presented (A D B C B) as theme and variations, a descant is being sung softly but insistently until it takes over in the coda (E F F E).

"Tell us, when will this be, and what will be the sign that all these things are about to be accomplished?" (v. 4). *The end is not now.* ". . . but the end is still to come" (v. 7b). *The end is not yet.* "This is but the beginning of the birthpangs" (v. 8b). *The end is not known.* "But about that day or hour no one knows . . ." (v. 32). *So keep alert.* " . . . be alert; I have already told you everything" (v. 23). " . . . keep alert; for you do not know when the time will come" (v. 33). "And what I say to you I say to all: Keep awake" (v. 37). *Endure.* "And the good news must first be proclaimed to all nations" (v. 10). *And be saved.* "And if the Lord had not cut short those days, no one would be saved; but for the sake of the elect, whom he chose, he has cut short those days" (v. 20). " . . . the one who endures to the end will be saved" (v. 13). *The end is not now, not yet, not known; so keep alert, endure, and be saved.* " . . . (let the reader understand). . ." (v. 14). "Heaven and earth will pass away, but my words will not pass away" (v. 31). *And my words are these: the end is not now, not yet, not known; so keep alert, endure, and be saved.*

Conclusion

Mark 13 deconstructs itself as an anti-apocalyptic eschatological discourse. It moves not from no knowledge to uncovered knowledge, but from presumed knowledge to no knowledge.[27] Rather Mark 13 challenges one type

---

[26] But cf. the conslusions of David Barr about the Apocalypse of John presented in Barr's contribution to the present volume.

[27] I am grateful to several Religion students at Florida State University and to my SNTS respondant Peter Müller for raising questions about this statement that have led to the following clarification.

of knowledge of the eschaton–a revelation of the time of the end through signs–by another type of knowledge in the face of the eschaton–living in the present as the unknown future impinges upon it. Perhaps one could speak of ontological knowledge being challenged and replaced by existential knowledge. Such a pattern is entirely in keeping with the internal literary contexts of Mark 13, especially its paralleling of the parables discourse and the Markan ending. In chapter 4 the Markan Jesus states that the disciples have "been given the mystery [alternate translation of *mysterion*] of the kingdom of God" (4:11). As it turns out, being given a mystery is more like being given questions than answers. In chapter 16 the Markan narrator leaves the implied audience up in the air as the women "said nothing to anyone, for they were afraid" (16:8). Still questions more than answers. The ending of the eschatological discourse claims that Jesus' words will not pass away, but his next reported words are that no one knows the day, the hour, or the time. The stories of the two exemplary women that frame chapter 13 suggest that self-giving actions best reflect the words of Jesus and of Mark.

Thus Mark 13 is parenetic in function and present- (rather than future-) oriented. That is what is *anti*-apocalyptic about it. *The end is not now, not yet, not known; so keep alert, endure, and be saved!* What is not known is what one might expect (and what many of my undergraduate students do indeed expect!) apocalyptic literature to "uncover"–the time of the end. This knowledge Mark denies, offering instead the knowledge that one can survive without knowing that "information"; one can live fully, in the words of my undergraduate and graduate professor John Priest, as a "practicing agnostic"–existentially responsible, although ontologically uncertain. These terms are contemporary, but they are in continuity with the terms of the Markan Jesus: "But about that day or hour no one knows . . . And what I say to you I say to all: Keep awake" (13:32, 37).

This look at Mark 13 as a literary unit (that is, as a whole) and at Mark 13 in its internal literary contexts (that is, as a part of the whole Gospel of Mark) is offered as a test case, as one possible literary approach to this intriguing text. It is in many ways incomplete. It may well be in some ways incorrect. I trust it is not incoherent. It is my hope that this self-consciously literary interpretation will compliment, complicate, challenge, and be challenged by the alternative literary and explicitly historical interpretations of other interpreters. My goal has not been to establish consensus but to highlight complexity. Thus I feel a certain kinship with a book that calls itself "the beginning" and ends up in the air and with a professor who approaches scholary theories–and perhaps life itself–as a "practicing agnostic."

Solomon and Jesus:
The Son of David in Ante-Markan Traditions
(Mk 10:47)

James H. Charlesworth
Princeton University

According to Mark 10 a blind man named Bartimaeus calls out to Jesus "Son of David, Jesus, have mercy on me," (Υἱὲ Δαυὶδ ᾽Ιησοῦ, ἐλέησόν με.), and then again "Son of David, have mercy on me," (Υἱὲ Δαυίδ, ἐλέησόν με.). He appeals to Jesus, urging him to restore his sight. The pericope seems truncated from an early story, and it is not easy to understand in its present form.[1] For centuries commentators have customarily interpreted Bartimaeus' exhortation as a recognition of Jesus' Messiahship. Scholars have tended to dismiss the problems inherent in these words, by passing over the question of whether a title is meant and if it is messianic. They fill commentaries on the Gospel of Mark with such comments as the "title is Messianic and implies the

---

[1] My focus for this essay is on Mk 10:47-48; attention should also be drawn to Mt 15:22. In Mt 15 the Canaanite woman approaches Jesus because her daughter is suffering from an evil demon; wishing her daughter to be healed, she salutes Jesus with the words: "have mercy on me, O Lord, the son of David" (Ελέησόν με, κύριε υἱὸς Δαυίδ).

nationalistic hopes which centred on a Davidic king,"[2] and as our "Geschichte ist die erste, in der das Messias-Geheimnis ausdrücklich gelöst wird."[3]

The purpose of this essay is to question this exegesis–in light of so-called intertestamental writings and especially new perspectives and methods–and to raise another possible approach and interpretation of Bartimaeus' cry. What is the meaning of Bartimaeus' cry to Jesus: Υἱὲ Δαυίδ, ἐλέησόν με? Who does he think Jesus is, and what does he mean by "have mercy on me"? Can we be certain "son of David" is a title and one that denotes the Messiah? In light of the now vast amount of Jewish writings from the time of Mark, and earlier, I have my doubts.

Did Mark present Bartimaeus as announcing that Jesus was the Messiah? If so, then why did he not have Jesus exhort silence as he does customarily with such confessions?[4]   C. E. B. Cranfield, reflecting on this issue, offered this opinion:

> If the title was both intended by Bartimaeus as messianic and also sure to be understood in that sense by the crowd, it is remarkable that Jesus apparently did nothing to silence him–contrast viii.30.[5]

If, however, Mark inherited a tradition that portrayed Bartimaeus as claiming that Jesus possessed the miraculous powers of Solomon,[6] then his narrative does not have this apparent problem. As is well known, the Evangelist Mark does not portray Jesus' confession that he is the Messiah (or Christ), and contains a pericope that suggests that the Messiah (Christ) is not "the son of David" (Mk 12:35-37). In light of Marcan redactional tendencies, it is evident that "Son of David" in chapter 8 is apparently not a messianic title. As will become apparent, the non-messianic meaning of "Son of David" is a a pre-Markan tradition.

[2] V. Taylor, *The Gospel According to St. Mark* (New York: St. Martin's Press, 1966 [2nd ed.]) 448.

[3] J. Schniewind, *Das Evangelium nach Markus* (Göttingen: Vandenhoeck & Ruprecht, 1937) 137. [Our "story is the first in which the Messianic Secret is solved explicitly." eds.]

[4] See W. Wrede, *The Messianic Secret*, trans. J.C.G. Greig (Greenwood, S.C.: Attic Press, 1971 [also Cambridge, London: James Clarke, 1971]. See the anthology of discussions on this issue edited by C. Tuckett under the title *The Messianic Secret* (Issues in Religion and Theology 1; London: SPCK; Philadelphia: Fortress, 1983).

[5] C.E.B. Cranfield, *The Gospel According to Saint Mark* (The Cambridge Greek Testament Commentary; Cambridge: CUP, 1963) 344-45.

[6] I wish to express appreciation to Dr. Richard K. Fenn, Maxwell M. Upson Professor of Christianity and Society at Princeton Theological Seminary, with whom I teach courses on sociology and the New Testament. Discussions with him on the social dynamics of the popular Jewish lore behind the earliest traditions in the Testament of Solomon stimulated my thinking on the possible links between "Son of David" and Solomon, David's son. See now Fenn's *The Death of Herod* (Cambridge: CUP, 1992) in which he asks how sociological observations on the crisis of succession in society, especially of society's need to reproduce itself, helps us understand the crises arising after the death of Herod the Great.

We should explore the possibility that healing is central to the pericope. It does not seem to be a redactional addition by the Evangelist Mark, since the preceding and following passage is not about healing but about the request of James and John (10:35-45) and the triumphal entry (11:1-11). If it is—and if we wish to consider what portions of the narrative may go back to Jesus' time—then we should contemplate how, and in what ways, the story makes sense in the assumed historical setting that antedates Mark's by decades. Any conclusion will have to be built upon the demonstration that Solomon was considered not only the paradigm of the wise man, and not only an exorcist (as is so clear from the Testament of Solomon and other early Jewish traditions), but also that he was able to control physical illnesses, including healing someone who was blind.

It is a pleasure to dedicate these reflections to John Priest, who introduced me to biblical research in the late fifties and early sixties at Ohio Wesleyan University. I began my formal training in Early Judaism, and the study of the Dead Sea Scrolls and Old Testament Apocrypha and Pseudepigrapha in his classes. It was at that time that I began to be critical of scholars who tended to read messianic ideas into early Jewish texts when they referred to other figure, including the Son of Man, the Elect One, and the generic "the Coming One."

New Perspectives and Methods

With the abundance of new perceptions into the origins of Christianity some methods and conclusions need modifying and sometimes altering.[7] The new perceptions derive from the vast increase in literary data that antedate the Bar Kokhba Revolt (132-135 CE). In the early sixties when we considered the Old Testament Pseudepigrapha we usually meant 17 documents, but in the nineties we frequently mean at least 65.[8] Then we examined about 12 Dead Sea Scrolls, but now well over 400.[9]

In the sixties archaeologists held out little hope of finding something significant from the first century CE by which to reconstruct the Herodian and later periods. The last twenty-five years have altered that perception. Our

---

[7] A perceptive use of rabbinic sources, and an authoritative study of first-century culture in Galilee, has been published by Shmuel Safrai. See his "The Jewish Cultural Nature of Galilee in the First Century," *Immanuel* 24/25 (1990) 147-86. He demonstrates that Galilee had close ties with Jerusalem and the Temple. See also the publications in L.I. Levine, ed., *The Galilee in Late Antiquity* (New York, Jerusalem: Harvard University Press, 1992).

[8] See Charlesworth, ed., *The Old Testament Pseudepigrapha*, 2 vols. (Garden City, New York: Doubleday, 1983-1985).

[9] See Charlesworth, et al., *Graphic Concordance to the Dead Sea Scrolls* (The Princeton Theological Seminary Dead Sea Scrolls Project; Tübingen: Mohr [Paul Siebeck], Louisville: Westminster/John Knox, 1991), and Charlesworth, et al., *Rule of the Community and Related Documents* (PTSDSSP 1; Tübingen: Mohr [Paul Siebeck], Louisville: Westminster/John Knox, 1994).

understanding of Jerusalem and Lower Galilee have been considerably modified,[10] and this reevaluation is primarily due to unexpected archaeological discoveries.[11]

Hand in glove with the vast amount of realia now available from the time of Hillel and Jesus–and even Joḥanan ben Zakkai and Mark–is the improvement in the historical critical method. Most important is the world-wide recognition that sociology is essential in historical reconstruction. The sensitivity to anthropological and social phenomena found in the works of Max Weber[12] and Emile Durkheim[13] have opened our eyes to what had been before us for almost 2,000 years.[14] Weber's model of the charismatic has profoundly shaped our understanding of the Moreh has-Ṣedek and Jesus of Nazareth.[15] Durkheim's concept of purity has helped alert us to the social crises caused by the heightened demands for purification and extended limits of danger that are so obvious from the time of the writing of the *Temple Scroll* up until the time of the Great Revolt of 66 to 70 CE. Mary Douglas has developed related anthropological and sociological thoughts in a significant way.[16]

---

[10] See E. M. Meyers and J.F. Strange, *Archaeology: The Rabbis & Early Christianity* (Nashville: Abingdon, 1981) 24, 48-49, N. Avigad, *Discovering Jerusalem* (Nashville, New York: Nelson, 1983), and esp. the following: *The New Encyclopedia of Archaeological Excavations in the Holy Land*, 4 vols., ed. E. Stern, et al. (New York: Simon & Schuster, 1993). For a critique of this major reference work see Charlesworth's contribution in the Hengel Festschrift, ed. P. Schäfer, in press.

[11] See A. Negev, ed., *The Archaeological Encyclopedia of the Holy Land* (New York, London: Prentice Hall, 1986, 1990 [3rd ed.]) and Charlesworth, *Jesus Within Judaism: New Light from Exciting Archaeological Discoveries* (ABRL 1; New York, London: Doubleday, 1988) 103-30.

[12] H.H. Garth and C.W. Mills, editors and translators, *From Max Weber: Essays in Sociology* (New York: Oxford, 1946, 1958) see esp. "The Sociology of Charismatic Authority," on 245-52. M. Weber, *The Sociology of Religion*, trans. E. Fischoff (Boston: Beacon, 1963). M. Weber, *The Theory of Social and Economic Organization*, edited and translated by A.M. Henderson and T. Parsons (New York: Free Press, 1947, 1964). See the series titled Max Weber Gesamtausgabe, edited by H. Baier, et al., and published by J.C.B. Mohr (Paul Siebeck).

[13] See esp. E. Durkheim, *The Elementary Forms of the Religious Life*, trans. J.W. Swain (New York: Free Press, 1915, 1965).

[14] A good survey is now published by B. Holmberg and titled *Sociology and the New Testament* (Minneapolis: Fortress, 1990). For a sophisticated application of sociological insights into non-Palestinian settings, see W.A. Meeks, *The First Urban Christians: The Social World of the Apostle Paul* (New Haven: Yale, London: Yale, 1983). Of course, it is obvious from the phenomenal archaeological discoveries of pre-70 life in Judaea that the first urban Christians lived in Jerusalem.

[15] See esp. M. Hengel, *The Charismatic Leader and His Followers*, trans. J.C.G. Greig (Edinburgh: Clark, 1981) esp. 18; H.C. Kee, *Christian Origins in Sociological Perspective* (Philadelphia: Westminster, 1980) 54-73; and Charlesworth, "The Righteous Teacher and the Historical Jesus: A Study of the Self-Understandings of Two Jewish Charismatics," *Perspectives on Christology*, ed. W. Weaver (Nashville: Exodus, 1989) 73-94; and S. Talmon, "The Emergence of Jewish Sectarianism in the Early Second Temple Period," in *King, Cult and Calendar: Collected Essays* (Jerusalem: Magnes, 1986) 165-201 [heavily influenced by Weber].

[16] Fruitful in developing a sociologically informed re-creation of life in Jerusalem when the Temple was the focal point of purity and danger are the sociological insights published by M. Douglas in *Purity and Danger* (London, Boston: ARK, 1966, 1984).

The documentary evidence has forced us to recognize that we can no longer assume, or claim, that many Palestinian Jews were looking for the coming of the Messiah.[17] It is impossible today to offer the advice of H. B. Swete, who was the Regius Professor of Divinity and Fellow of Gonville and Caius College, Cambridge: "At Jerusalem all Jews thought of David as their father, and of Messiah as the Son of David in a special sense... ."[18] That sweeping claim misrepresents what we now know about pre-70 Jewish thought in Jerusalem and in ancient Palestine. In fact, if the Jewish and early Pseudepigrapha are a valid source of religious thought before 70 CE, then since most of them do not mention the Messiah we should conclude that it is at least conceivable that most Jews in Jerusalem were not looking for the coming of a Messiah. Moreover, since many of the pseudepigrapha that do mention the Messiah make no clear link between him and David, we may also imagine that many messianic Jews believed that the Messiah was not to come from the seed of David; he may come in a mysterious way known only to God.[19] We know about only three messianic Jewish groups that antedate 70 C.E.: the group founded by the Moreh haṣ-Ṣedek (which began around the middle of the second century BCE), the group who used the psalmbook called the *Psalms of Solomon* (which dates from the second half of the first century BCE and was centered in Jerusalem), and the Palestinian Jesus Movement (which began in the first half of the first century CE, was centered in Galilee, and then apparently moved to Jerusalem). Hence, the study of Christian Origins needs to be purged from the possible distortions of reading back into pre-70 Palestinian Judaism the messianic fervor found in the earliest kerygma of the New Testament. Even titles, or terms, which the New Testament authors assumed to be messianic may not have had messianic denotations during the time of Hillel and Jesus. The present paper helps to illustrate this point by looking at Mark 10:46-52, "The Healing of the Blind Bartimaeus."

Translation and Philological Observations

My translation of Mark 10:46-52 is as follows:

[17] See esp. the studies by L. Schiffman and S. Talmon in Charlesworth, ed., *The Messiah* (Minneapolis: Fortress, 1992).

[18] H.B. Swete, *The Gospel According to St Mark* (London: Macmillan and Co., 1920 [3rd ed.]) 243.

[19] See Charlesworth, "The Concept of the Messiah in the Pseudepigrapha," in *ANRW* II.19.1 (1979) 188-218, and Charlesworth in *The Messiah*, 16-24.

And they came to Jericho[20], and when he, his disciples, and a large crowd were leaving Jericho,[21] Bartimaeus, the Son of Timaeus,[22] a blind beggar, sat beside the road.[23] And hearing that (the commotion concerned) Jesus of Nazareth,[24] he began to cry out and say, "O[25] Son of David, Jesus, have mercy on me." And many rebuked him (urging him) to be silent. But he cried out more (vociferously): "Son of David, have mercy on me." And stopping, Jesus said, "Call him." And they called the blind man, saying to him, "Take heart, arise, he calls you." Then[26] throwing off his mantle, as he sprang up[27] he came to Jesus. And answering him,[28] Jesus said, "What do you want me to do for you?" And[29] the blind man said to him, "Rabboni, to see again.[30] And Jesus said to him, "Go, your faith has saved you."[32] And immediately he saw again and followed him on the way.

[20] This opening phrase is omitted by Vaticanus.

[21] The maverick text of Codex Bezae and some other witnesses substitute for this phrase "there with"; perhaps some scribes considered the phrase redundant.

[22] Why does the Greek have the unusual order "the Son of Timaeus, Bartimaeus"? Is emphasis placed on "the Son of Timaeus"? If so, does that indicate that this unknown person was prominent in or around Jericho or in the Markan community?

[23] For valuable insights on the variants and the uniqueness of *prosaites*, see B.M. Metzger, *A Textual Commentary on the Greek New Testament* (New York: United Bible Societies, 1971]) 108. This important information unfortunately is not found in the fourth edition (1994) of this valuable book.

[24] Why is this noun articular? It cannot be unnatural in Greek; no Greek scribe omits it. Many witnesses change the noun to an adjective. Apparently Codexes B and D, and others, found an articular noun awkward.

[25] Some early and important witnesses change the vocative υιε to the nominative H'σαϛ here and in v. 48 minuscule number 28 shows a later propensity: κυριε υιος.

[26] The connective is the mild adversative δε.

[27] Note the lack of a connective before "springing up"; the asyndetic contiguity seems to denote that Bartimaeus was casting off his mantle as he was springing up.

[28] This is a well-known Semitism; Bartimaeus has not asked Jesus anything.

[29] Greek δε.

[30] Gk. ἀναβλέψω; apparently we are being told that Bartimaeus has not been blind from birth (as is the case with ἄνθρωπον τυφλὸν ἐκ γενετῆς in Jn 9:1). A strictly philological approach to New Testament Greek can be misleading; the literary and social context of a pericope is obviously a key to unlocking the intended meaning. The Gk. ἀναβλέψω does mean "receive sight again." The Gk. βλέψω, "to see" (perhaps "to see" for the first time), colors the narrative of Jn 9 (esp. in vss. 15, 19, 21, 25 in which it appears) even though ἀναβλέψω is used in v. 11 (and it does not mean only "receive sight again" but also "obtain sight," and in a Johannine sense "to look up" to the ἄνω (the framework of John's narrative is cosmic: ἄνω and κατω). The author of John, unlike the author of Mark (or his source), is playing with the spiritual meaning of "seeing"; he and his community were apparently found of *double entendre* (as was the author of the *Odes of Solomon* and the Semitic sources antedating Jn).

[31] The noun is articular, but it is common for the noun Ιησους to take an article (631 times out of 990). Mark has only three anathrous uses of this noun in the nominative (1:9; 10:47; 16:6).

[32] This statement by Jesus is indeed odd in Mark; Bartimaeus has not expressed faith in Jesus. Perhaps one could find faith in "have mercy on me"; but, in contrast to a somewhat parallel account in Mt 9:27-31 something like the following is missing: "... and Jesus said to them [there are two blind men in this account], 'Do you believe that I have power to do this?' They said to him, 'Yes, Lord'" (Mt 9:28). On the concept of πιστις in Mark see A. Pilgaard, "Troens betydning i Markusevangeliets underfortaellinger," in *Nytestamentlige Studier*, ed. S. Pedersen (Teologiske Studier 4; Aarhus: Aros, 1976) 34-72; esp. see 52-55.

This pericope elicits numerous questions. In the order in which they are elicited by the text, here are the most impressive ones:

Why Jericho?[33]

Does the ὄχλος ("crowd, mob") function narratively like the Greek chorus?[34] If so, surely this is a Marcan creation.

What is the meaning of the Semitisms: Bartimaeus, son of Timaeus, "began to cry out and say," Jesus son of David, Rabbouni (changed by some Greek scribes to κυριε ραββι)[35] "stopping said" (v. 49)?

Is it significant that Bartimaeus was a "blind beggar"?

Is "Jesus" a title? And why is it found only in the first cry from Bartimaeus?

Is "Son of David" a title? What does it mean? Are the variants to it significant? Why is it found only here in Mark?

Is ἐλέησόν με a formula shaped by Jesus' earliest followers? What is the meaning of Bartimaeus' cry?

Why is the cry "Son of David" repeated?

Who are the "many" and why do they rebuke him?

Is this an example of the Markan secrecy motif?[36]

Is "Θάρσει, ἔγειρε, φωνεῖ σε " formulaic?

---

[33] I agree with E. Best that Mark has probably added this element. It is at the beginning of the pericope, clarifies both setting and movement towards Jerusalem, and–in the words of Best, "10.46-52 takes us from the discipleship section where discipleship is related to the cross of Jesus to the story of the cross itself (11.1ff) by means of a disciple who is prepared to go the way of the cross with Jesus" (134). I am also persuaded that much of 10:46-52 is pre-Markan; Best is also convinced of pre-Markan traditions (see 134-45). Best, *Following Jesus: Discipleship in the Gospel of Mark* (Journal for the Study of the New Testament Supplement Series 4; Sheffield: University of Sheffield, 1981). W. Marxsen stressed the pre-Markan source, which included the setting (Jericho) and the name of Bartimaeus, but (as one would expect and correctly I think) pointed to Markan redaction in 46a (entry into Jericho). See Marxsen, *Mark the Evangelist*, trans. J. Boyce, et al. (Nashville, New York: Abingdon, 1969) 73-74. I therefore disagree with H. Räisänen, who thinks that "Jericho" is part of the tradition and is not redactional to Mark. See Räisänen, *The Messianic Secret in Mark*, trans. C. Tuckett (Edinburgh: T.& T. Clark, 1990) 232.

[34] Our historical research also needs to be deepened by the sociological insight that the crowd is the most dangerous of all sociological groups. See esp. G. Le Bon, *The Crowd* (New York: Viking Press, 1960 [first published in 1895]).

[35] Ραββουνι appears only here in Mark.

[36] The so-called messianic secret did not originate with Mark. It is grounded in the Jewish traditions that the Messiah will be announced by God alone, and in his own time and way (see esp. PssSol and 4Ezra). The doublet in Matthew to the Bartimaeus pericope contains an exhortation to silence placed on the lips of Jesus and not paralleled in Mark: "And Jesus sternly charged them (the two blind men) saying, 'See that no one knows (it)'" (Mt 9:30). As Räisänen pointed out in *The Messianic Secret in Mark* (44) Wrede also did not claim–despite many contentions to the contrary–that Mark originated the messianic secret.

If Bartimaeus could not see, how could he spring up and come to Jesus? Did he know where to go because of Jesus' voice? The story is ambiguous here; is that intentional (and if so, by whom–Mark?)?

Is there a clash between "Son of David" and "Rabbouni"?[37]

How is the man healed? Why is it not described (cf. Mk 8:22-26)?

Does not σέσωκέν ("has saved") denote that in its present form this story is shapted by the Christian kerygma and about faith?

Do the words "and *followed* him on *the way*" reflect a theological motif,[38] and is there then a link between vv. 46 and 52?

Does the appearance of εὐθὺς (v. 52) not betray the editorial reworking of Mark?

All these questions, and those that spin off from them, cannot be explored, let alone answered, in one essay. These questions help us see the dynamics of the pericope, as our focus becomes centered on the questions involved in trying to ascertain the original historical setting and the tradition that Mark inherited; that is, what did the historical Bartimaeus think about Jesus? Assuming some accuracy in transmission, what did he mean when he hailed Jesus as "Son of David"? This cry is found not only in Mark, but also in each verse parallel to Mark 10:47 in Luke 18:38, and in Matthew's doublet–Mt 9:27 and Mt 20:31.

Son of David: The Messiah

The questions listed above focus our attention on Baritmaeus' outcry to Jesus, specifically his exhortation, "Son of David." It appears twice in the pericope. The customary exegetical approach to this passage indicates that the cry, "Son of David," acknowledges the messiahship of Jesus.[39] Convinced of Markan redaction, Rudolf Bultmann concluded that the pericope was created and "a late formulation."[40] Ezra P. Gould, in the ICC commentary on Mark, was convinced that "*Son of David* is a distinctly Messianic title, ..." He claimed that this

---

[37] The alteration to κυριε ραββι is clearly secondary, because of the replacement of the unfamiliar ραββουνι with the confessional and familiar, and the secondary nature of Codex D and many Old Latin manuscripts.

[38] See Best, *Following Jesus*, and P.J. Achtemeier, "'And He Followed Him': Miracles and Discipleship in Mark 10:46-52," *Semeia* 11 (1978) 115-45. The words in Mark may indicate that Bartimaeus joined the crowd going up to Jerusalem for the annual Passover pilgrimage.

[39] D. and P. Miller rightly see that the evangelist was intertwining "Solomon, Daniel and Jeremiah motifs," and that "Mark's new midrashic construction looks to both the David and Solomon traditions," but they fail to dig into the meaning of Bartimaeus' cry and simply assume it is "messianic." D. and P. Miller, *The Gospel of Mark as Midrash on Earlier Jewish and New Testament Literature* (Studies in the Bible and Early Christianity 21; Lewiston, New York: Edwin Mellen Press, 1990) 261-65. But see also Duling (note 94) and Achtemeier (note 101).

[40] R. Bultmann also contended that it "is hardly possible to believe that there is an original, conventionally narrated miracle story at the basis of this passage." *History of the Synoptic Tradition*, trans. J. Marsh (New York, London: Harper, 1963 [revised ed.]) 213.

messianic cry "reflects the sentiment of the multitude, who mean to make this a triumphal progress to Jerusalem, though as yet they are preserving a policy of silence."[41]

Even though Mark places Jesus' triumphal entry into Jerusalem immediately after the Bartimaeus pericope, Gould's exegesis is remarkable. He contends that Bartimaeus' cry clarifies the sentiment of the crowd. However, they are explicitly said to urge him to be silent, and these words appear in the pericope after he salutes Jesus as "Son of David." C.S. Mann, without exploring the possibilities in the words "Son of David," concludes that the "phrase is broadly 'messianic,' with nationalist hope and centered on a Davidic king (cf. *Pss Sol* 17:21 or in the DSS 4Q *Patriarchal Blessings* 1:34) with some reference back to the Old Testament (cf. Ps 110:1-5, Jer 23:5-6, Ezek 34:23-24)."[42]

Obviously, "Son of David" is clearly a messianic title in many Jewish compositions, and the passages Mann cites are well known and obviously important. The question, however, concerns the meaning of "Son of David" in Mark 10; and for my present research, primarily in the putative original historical setting and to a lesser extent in the present narrative context. That this term, or title, has obtained messianic overtones, or explicit messianic content, by the beginning of the first century CE in some documents does not mean that one does not need to explore its intended meaning in other writings.

Other scholars continue to perpetuate the contention, which was never fully researched, that Bartimaeus calls on Jesus as the Messiah.[43] Hugh Anderson, for example, notes that "Jesus, Son of David" does not appear elsewhere in Mark, and that "Son of David" is "here simply a messianic title."[44] He offers the opinion that "Mark may have seen a connexion between the designation Son of David here and the messianic fervour of the people on the entry into Jerusalem in 11:9-11."[45] Anderson may correctly have explained Markan redaction and theology, but an attempt to understand the theology of Mark must not mislead us from searching for the meaning of Batimaeus' cry in pre-Marcan tradition. Perhaps, also there is the possibility that Mark did not understand this dimension of the traditions he obviously received. I have no doubt that the pericope did not originate with him, as the doublet in Matthew (20:29-34, 9:27-31) and the traditional elements,

[41] E.P. Gould, *Gospel According to Mark* (ICC; Edinburgh: T. & T. Clark, 1897) 204.

[42] Mann, *Mark* (Anchor Bible; Garden City, New York: Doubleday, 1986) 422.

[43] J.D. Kingsbury, intent only on explaining Mark's christology, is led to argue that for Mark "Jesus wields his Davidic authority in order to have mercy on one who is afflicted (10:47-48, 52), to heal and in this fashion to 'save'" (106-07). Far more insightful is Kingsbury's study of the context of the Markan narrative: "The pericope on the triumphal entry (11:1-10) follows immediately that on the healing of Bartimaeus. Mark prepares for the triumphal entry by having Bartimaeus, his sight restored, join the throng accompanying Jesus to Jerusalem (10:32, 46, 52; 11:1)" (107). *The Christology of Mark's Gospel* (Philadelphia: Fortress, 1983).

[44] H. Anderson, *The Gospel of Mark* (London: Oliphants, 1976) 258.

[45] Anderson, *Mark*, 259.

especially the Semitisms, suggest.[46] Since the evangelist Mark must translate
Bartimaeus–a Semitic name that means "Son of Timaeus"–as "the son of Timaeus,
Bartimaeus" there can be virtually no doubt that the some of the tradition here goes
back to an Aramaic tradition, and perhaps source.[47]

Bartimaeus wants Jesus to heal him; he replies to Jesus' question, "What do
you want me to do for you?" (Τί σοι θέλεις ποιήσω) with the words "Rabbi, let
me see again" (Ραββουνι, ἵνα ἀναβλέψω). It is not wise to suggest that he thought
Jesus was the Messiah, despite the opinio of so many commentators. There is *no
early tradition that depicts the Messiah as a healer* or attributes to him the
function of healing (see the addendum) confused kerygmata with Jewish theology
and Jewish descriptions of the glorious messianic age, when humans will enjoy
bliss and be freed from all illnesses and the fear of death,[48] with messianology
(Jewish reflections on the Messiah).

Is it possible that Bartimaeus' "Son of David" denoted Solomon, David's
son through Bathsheba, and the third king of Israel? Why have commentators not
asked what is intended by tradition or redaction by "Son of David" in Mark 10?
Clearly, any study of the traditions describing Jesus' miraculous deeds must
include an examination of the cosmology, demonology, medicine, and magical
deeds and beliefs of Jews living in ancient Palestine before 70 CE.[49] And, as we
shall see, they are frequently associated with the "Son of David"–that is, Solomon.

Son of David: Royal Genealogy

Perhaps in the putative historical setting, pre-Marcan tradition, or even in the
Marcan narrative Bartimaeus was not confessing Jesus as the Messiah, but only
acknowledging–or portrayed as recognizing–that Jesus was of Davidic descent or
according him honor and respect.[50] The rejoinder that Davidids were not known
to exist in first-century Judaea is now disproved by the recovery in 1971 of an

---

[46] Matthew and the communities of the Palestinian Jesus Movement can–and did–add Semitism
to the Jesus traditions, but I am not convinced that Mark does not add Semitisms. I am more persuaded
that the Latinisms are from him or his own community.

[47] With E. Schweizer I wish to point out that 10:46 suggests that "the story was first told in
Aramaic, and then was taken over by a Greek-speaking church which added the translation of the foreign-
sounding name." Schweizer, *The Good News According to Mark*, trans. D.H. Madvig (Atlanta: John
Knox Press, 1970) 224.

[48] For some reflections on the messianic age and the utopian place of the Blessed Ones (two
traditions which must not be confused, even though the former coalesced with the latter), see
Charlesworth, "Greek, Persian, Roman, Syrian and Egyptian Influences in Early Jewish Theology: A
Study of the History of the Rechabites," in *Hellenica et Judaica: Hommage à Valentin Nikiprowetzky*,
ed. A Caquot, et al. (Leuven: Peeters, 1986) 219-43.

[49] M. Smith concluded that Jesus probably "did use magical methods," and that the New
Testament stories "have usually been shaped by knowledge of magical practices." Smith, *Jesus the
Magician* (Cambridge, London, New York: Harper & Row, 1978, 1981) 152.

[50] See the comments by Cranfield, *Mark*, 345.

ossuary from the environs of Jerusalem. The inscription refers to "belonging to those from the house of David" (שלבית דוד), and it dates from the first half of the first century BCE.[51] Families of Davidic descent existed (or were assumed to exist) in Jerusalem before the destruction of the Temple, since on the 20th of Tammuz "the family of David" brought to the Temple altar the wood- offering of the priests (see m.Taanith 4.5 and t.Taanith 3.5).

Son of David, Jesus: Joshua Ben Perahyah

Did Bartimaeus employ a title–"Jesus," or "Joshua"–when he called out Υἱὲ Δαυὶδ 'Ιησοῦ, ἐλέησόν με? An alleged healer named Joshua ben Perahyah (a *zuggot* with Nittai of Arbela and נשיא הסנהדרין) lived during the latter half of the second century BCE and the beginning of the first century BCE,[52] studied in Jerusalem under Yose ben Joezer of Zeredah and Yose ben Johanan, and is quoted in Pirke Aboth 1.6.[53] In rabbinic traditions he is not described as a healer.[54] It is possible that traditions about his healing powers were edited out of Jewish traditions by the compilers of the Mishnah, since they are recognized as deleting or ignoring traditions once regnant in pre-70 Judaism,[55] and they polemized against traditions that "Jesus" was a healer.[56]

---

[51] See D. Flusser's insights in *Jesus' Jewishness*, ed. Charlesworth (New York: Crossroad, 1991) 157-59 and Plate 19.

[52] See Josephus, *Ant* 13.376-83, *War* 1.90-98; b.Sota 47b; b.San 107b, j.Hag 2.2. In rabbinic traditions he is said to have fled to Alexandria to escape the persecutions of Pharisees by Alexander Yannai (Jannaeus). See A. Hyman, *Toldoth Tannaim Ve'Amoraim*, 3 vols. (Jerusalem: Machon Pri Ha'aretz, 1987) vol. 2, 647-48, and M. Margalioth, ed., *Encyclopedia of Talmudic and Geonic Literature*, 2 vols. (Jerusalem, 1987) vol. 2, cols. 471-72 [Hebrew]. Also see the important article by M.D. Herr, "Joshua ben Perahyah," in *Encyclopaedia Judaica* 10 (1971) 284-85. At the beginning of this century rabbinic experts sometimes placed the persecution of Joshua ben Perahyah during the time of John Hyrcanus. See J.Z. Lauterbach, "Joshua b. Perahyah," in *The Jewish Encyclopedia* 7 (1094) 295 and J. Krengel, "Josua ben Perachja," in *Jüdisches Lexikon* 3 (1929) cols. 362-63. Dated, but still valuable, is L. Blau, *Das altjüdische Zauberwesen* (Berlin: Lamm, 1914) esp. see 34-37. A reliable and succinct account of Joshua ben Perahya' persecution by Jannaeus is by J. Klausner in A. Schalit, *The Hellenistic Age* (The World History of the Jewish People 1.6; Jerusalem: Massada, 1972) 233-34, 244-45.

[53] m.Abot 1.4, "Joshua b. Perahyah said: Provide thyself with a teacher and get thee a fellow[-disciple]; and when thou judgest any man incline the balance in his favour." Danby, *The Mishnah* (Oxford: OUP, 1933, rep. many times) 447. For the Hebrew and another translation see m.Abot 1.6 in S.R. Hirsch, *Chapters of the Fathers*, trans. G. Hirschler (Jerusalem: Feldheim Publishers, 1989 [2d. ed.]).

[54] See the judicious discussions of him by M. Hengel in *Judaism and Hellenism*, 2 vols., trans. J. Bowden (Philadelphia: Fortress, 1974) vol. 1, 52, 80-82; vol. 2, 112.

[55] See notably J. Neusner, *Introduction to Rabbinic Literature* (ABRL; New York: Doubleday, 1994) and H.L. Strack and G. Stemberger, *Introduction to the Talmud and Midrash*, trans. M. Bockmuehl (Minneapolis: Fortress Press, 1992).

[56] See esp. t.Hullin 2 (also Strack-Billerbeck 1.36-37). C.K. Barrett rightly points to such passages to illustrate the claim that rabbinic scribes often polemized against the name of "Jesus" and forbid it "as a means of healing" (69). See Barrett, *The Gospel of John & Judaism*, trans. D.M. Smith

This "Jesus"[57]–that is Joshua ben Perahyah–is called "the healer" (אסיא) in Aramaic incantation texts.[58] At the outset, we should be dubious that magical charms, and indications that Joshua ben Perahyah performed exorcisms,[59] help us understand the words ascribed to Bartimaeus.   Perhaps all Bartimaeus acknowledged was Jesus' name, which was not a title.

Do the incantation texts indicate that Jews in the environs of Jerusalem, in Jericho in particular, revered Joshua ben Perahyah as a healer, who worked in and around Jerusalem? Did they accord him supernatural powers, such as exorcisms, and was he considered one who was apocalyptically inspired or influenced?[60] If so, then it is easy to see why, in Rabbinics,[61] he was thought to be associated with Jesus of Nazareth. If this association was possible in later times, in the Talmudim, then it is not inconceivable in the first century, perhaps even by a blind man in Jericho. These speculations need further refining and in-depth exploration. It is not impossible that a Bartimaeus called out to Jesus and associated him with a certain renowned healer who bore the same name; but, what is not impossible is far from what looms probable from careful historical scrutiny.

Son of David: Solomon

Is it conceivable that Bartimaeus, whether in historical or narrative context, was heralding Jesus of Nazareth as a Solomonic figure; that is, one who possessed

(Philadelphia: Fortress, (1975) 68-69, 90. The compilers of the haggadah about Joshua ben Perahyah in the Babylonian Talmud (Sot 47a) confused chronology and placed Jesus (probably of Nazareth) under the tutelage of Joshua ben Perahyah, who found him guilty of sin.

[57] Joshua ben Perahyah is probably "Rab Jesus bar Perahia" mentioned in CBS (= Catalogue of Babylonian Section in the University of Pennsylvania) 16086 (= No. 32 in Montgomery). For the standard text of the incantation texts see J.A. Montgomery, *Aramaic Incantation Texts from Nippur* (University of Pennsylvania; The Museum Publications of the Babylonian Section 3; Philadelphia: University Museum, 1913). [Henceforth, abbreviated as Montgomery, *Texts*].

[58] CBS 2922 = No. 17 in Montgomery and No. 13 in Isbell. See J.A. Montgomery, *Texts*; C.D. Isbell, *Corpus of the Aramaic Incantation Bowls* (SBL Dissertation Series 17; Missoula, Mont.: Scholars, 1975). [Henceforth, abbreviated as Isbell, *Corpus*]. Montgomery No. 17 is the most important incantation text for understanding the tradition that Joshua ben Perahyah was a renowned healer (see line 12: אסיא דיחושא בן פרוחיה. The noun אסיא probably means "the healer" (as Montgomery translated it [*Texts*, 191]) and not "savior" (as Isbell translated it [49]). The Aramaic אסיא derives from the verb אסי, which means "to be well," and the noun denotes "healer," "physician" or "surgeon." This term, איסא, has loomed large, as scholars know, in the discussion of the etymology of the "Essenes," who were accorded healing powers. For "savior" I would expect פריקא, which means "redeemer" in Jewish Aramaic (cf. Christian Syriac, פריקא = "Savior," "Deliverer"). For other texts referring to Joshua ben Perahyah, see also Montgomery No. 8 = Isbell No. 12, Montgomery 9 = Isbell No. 15, and Montgomery No. 32 (not in Isbell, *Corpus*).

[59] CBS 16086 = No. 32 in Montgomery (not in Isbell, *Corpus*).

[60] See CBS 16086 = No. 32 in Montgomery, esp. lines 7-8 (not in Isbell, *Corpus*).

[61] See y.Talmud Hagiga 2.2, San 6.8; b.Talmud Sanh 107b = Sota 47a.

the healing powers of Solomon?[62] Surely there is no reason to belabor the obvious that long before the time of Jesus, Solomon was considered a wise man, and that thus to him were attributed numerous writings in Israel's Wisdom Literature, namely Proverbs, Song of Songs, and the Wisdom of Solomon.

He was also considered an exorcist, and this tradition is well attested, especially in the magical incantation bowls from Nippur,[63] and in the *Testament of Solomon*.[64] The 40 bowls found at Nippur, which contain incantations, date from about 600 CE, or earlier.[65] In Nippur Incantation CBS 9012 (= Montgomery 34) we find the following tradition (lines 7-8):

> Charmed and sealed is all sickness (כולה בישותא) that is in the body of (בפגרה) Mihr-hormizd bar Mâmî, in his house,[66] his wife, and his sons, and his daughters ... and by the seal of King Solomon Son of David (ובעיזקתה דשלימון מלכא בר דויד).[67]

Two ideas in this incantation are extremely important for our present research, focused on Bartimaeus' exhortation to Jesus of Nazareth.

First, bodily sicknesses are protected (perhaps cured) by Solomon. The noun בישותא means "wickedness," but when combined with פגר, "body," and seen in light of the cognate noun, ביש, which means "bad," or "sick,"[68] it denotes

---

[62] C.C. McCown earlier in this century argued that "scores of amulets and incantations from all ages witness to a living faith in Solomon as a great magician who had power over demons and disease" (6). Our task will be to discern if "all ages" might include first-century Jericho. See McCown, "The Christian Tradition as to the Magical Wisdom of Solomon," *JPOS* 2 (1922) 1-24. See G. Salzberger, *Die Salomo-sage in der semitische Literatur* (Berlin, 1907), especially his discussion of Solomon's lordship over the demons on 92-129.

[63] In the late sixties L. Fisher urged scholars to pay attention to the incantation bowls in the attempt to understand more fully the range of meanings in "Son of David." See his "Can This be the Son of David?" in *Jesus and the Historian*, ed. F.T. Trotter (Philadelphia: Westminster, 1968) 82-97.

[64] See E. Lövestam, "Jésus Fils de David chez les Synoptiques," *StudTheol* 28 (1974) 97-109. I am grateful to D. Duling for drawing my attention to this article; see Duling's important study titled "Solomon, Exorcism, and the Son of David," *HTR* 68 (1975) 235-52. Also, see Duling, "Solomon, Testament of," *ABD* (1992) 6.117-19.

[65] C.H. Gordon dated them to shortly before or after 600 C.E. Gordon, *Adventures in the Nearest East* (London: Phoenix, 1957) 161. G. Vermes, et al., report that upon "the basis of stratification, the bowls can be assigned to c. A.D. 300-600." See E. Schürer, *The History of the Jewish People in the Time of Jesus Christ*, ed. G. Vermes, et al. (Edinburgh: Clark, 1986) vol. 3.1, 353.

[66] The fear of demons entering a house and killing or causing sickness to those in it was a real fear for all who believed, with the author of the Testament of Solomon, that there were demons who did such things. According to TSol 7:5, Lix Tetrax states, "I slither in under the corners of houses during the night or day." The corners of houses is where magical incantation bowls, turned upside down to entrap demons, were placed; see Montgomery, *Texts*, 40-42. Montgomery draws attention to an inscription that announces the demons are bound and sealed "in each one of the four corners of the house," and concludes that "we have to do with a species of sympathetic magic, the inverted bowls symbolizing and effecting the repression and suppression of the evil spirits" (42). The incantation bowls, the Testament of Solomon, and the New Testament pericopes present evidence of a wide-spread and ancient fear of demons causing illness.

[67] Translation mine. For text see Montgomery, *Texts*, 231.

[68] See Midrash Rabbah to Ecclesiastes 4.6 and the Palestinian Talmud of Baba M'tsi'a I, 60c.

"sickness." The context of this incantation is to appeal to Solomon to heal, or protect from sickness, those mentioned. Other Aramaic incantations indicate that we are confronted in No. 34, lines 7-8, with ancient (most likely pre-Christian) formulae.[69]

Second, Solomon receives a title: "Son of David" (בר דוד). It is possible to translate "the seal of King Solomon Son of David" as follows: "the seal of Solomon, the King, Son of David."[70] Here, "Son of David" is most likely a title. It appears repeatedly also in the Testament of Solomon; note Solomon's command to Asmodeus: "I am Solomon, Son of David" (5:10).

Solomon's powers as a healer and exorcist were well known.[71] There is no reason to doubt that Solomon was known as a healer, as well as a wise man, in pre-70 Palestinian Judaism. This conclusion seems valid even though he is not described in early hellenistic texts as a "healer," and even though we do not possess unedited Jewish pre-70 texts in which he is heralded as an "exorcist." His exorcisms are, however, narratively described in the *Testament of Solomon*.[72] Sickness and illness is caused by demons, and the demons are controlled by Solomon.[73] Note the following excerpts, highlighting Solomon's powers over demons who cause sickness. Ornias, who causes a boy to grow thin (and be sick), who strangles humans, and causes great pain (2:2), is controlled by Solomon (7:1-2). Onoskelis who strangles men is commanded and controlled by Solomon (4:1-12). A headless demon, named "Murder," who attacks ten-day-old infants, "inflames the limbs, inflicts the feet and produces festering sores" (9:6) is ordered by Solomon (9:7). A demon, named "The Lion-Shaped Demon," who prevents people from recovering from a disease (11:2), is sentenced and controlled by Solomon. A demon, who is a three-headed dragon and *blinds* children (τυπηλω τα παιδια)[74] in the womb (12:2) and who causes deafness and dumbness, is sealed and commanded by Solomon (12:4-5). A demon named Obyzouth, the one who

---

[69] See Isbell No. 48 (= Gordon B), according to which demons are sealed, and humans protected, "with the signet-ring of King Solomon the son of David, who worked spells on male demons and female liliths" (for text and translation see Isbell, 110). Also see Isbell No. 50 (= Gordon E), according to this text a household is sealed "with the signet-ring of King Solomon the son of David, ... Blessed art Thou, YHWH, God of Israel" (for text and translation see Isbell, 114). For Gordon B and E, see Gordon, "Aramaic Magical Bowls in the Istanbul and Baghdad Museums," *Archiv Orientální* 6 (1934) 319-34, 466-74.

[70] See TSol 3:3, "Solomon the King summons you."

[71] L. Ginzberg rightly points out that in ancient lore Jews celebrated Solomon for ruling over all creatures, including demons and spirits. See Ginzberg, *The Legends of the Jews* (Philadelphia: Jewish Publication Society, 1968) esp. vol. 4, 142-44 and vol. 6, 289. See the legends represented in "Solomon," *Legends*, vol. 4, 125-76.

[72] I am indebted to D. Duling and his work on the TSol in *OTP* 1.

[73] TSol prologue, TSol 12:4-5, 13:7, 15:24, esp. 18:41. Ironically a demon named Lix Tetrax, who causes problems relating to fire, is also a healer of "the day-and-a-half fever" (7:6-7).

[74] For the Greek see C.C. McCown, *The Testament of Solomon* (Untersuchungen zum Neuen Testament 9; Leipzig: Hinrichs; New York: Stechert, 1922).

causes eye injuries (οπητηαλμων αδικια 13:4), is controlled by Solomon (13:7).[75]

The most important passage for our purposes of understanding if Solomon was perceived only as an exorcist or was also conceived as one who could heal a person, especially one who was blind like Bartimaeus, is the *Testament of Solomon*, chapter 18. Here is an epitome of this section with a focus only on the illnesses caused by the demons:

demon's name	physical sickness it causes
Ruax	headaches
Barsafael	pains on the sides of heads
Artosael	eye damages (ὁπητηαλμους ἀδικω σπηοδρα)
Oropel	sore throats
Kairoxanondalon	ear obstructions
Sphendonael	tumors
Sphandor	weakened shoulders, deadened hand nerves and paralyzed limbs
Belbel	perverted hearts and minds
Kourtael	attacks on bowels
Metathiax	kidney pains
Phobothel	loosening of tendons
Leroel	chills, shiverings, sore throats
Soubelti	shivering and numbness
Katrax	incurable fevers
Ieropa	stomach convulsions
Mardero	incurable fevers
Rhyx Nathotho	problems with knees
Rhyx Alath	croup in infants
Rhyx Audameoth	heart pain
Rhyx Manthado	kidney pains
Rhyx Aktonme	rib pains
Rhyx Anatreth	gas and burning in the bowels
Rhyx, Enautha	making off with minds and hearts
Rhyx Axesbuth	diarrhea and hemorrhoids
Rhyx Hapax	insomnia
Rhyx Anoster	hysteria and bladder pains
Rhyx Physikoreth	long-term illnesses
Rhyx Aleureth	difficulties with swallowing
Rhyx Ichthuon	detached tendons

[75] Solomon controls a lecherous spirit by "the sign of the cross" (17:4); in its present form this passage is Christian, and it is not easy to discern Jewish traditions behind it.

Rhyx Achoneoth	sore throats and tonsillitis
Rhyx Phtheneoth	"the evil eye"[76]
Rhyx Mianeth	rotting flesh

The list impressively illustrates the healing powers attributed by Jews to Solomon. Most importantly, all these demons, and therefore the sicknesses reputedly caused by them, are controlled by none other than the Son of David, Solomon. The purpose of listing and describing the demons and the sicknesses is to clarify that Solomon controls what ails humans (18:41-42). Indeed, the *Testament of Solomon* was written to inform "the sons of Israel" of the power of demons and the means by which they are controlled (15:14). In twentieth-century language that seems to mean that the author of this pseudepigraphon wants his readers to know that the origins of sicknesses are known by the wise Solomon, who comprehends the means for healing each sickness. While Solomon is not hailed as a "healer," it is unrepresentative of the language and world view of the traditions in the *Testament of Solomon* to conclude that he was only an exorcist and not a healer. It is thus conceivable–indeed probable–that *Solomon was considered* to be not only an exorcist but also *a healer*.

In tracing the early legends about Solomon as a healer we need to remember that he was not celebrated as an exorcist or healer by many pre-70 Jews who wrote other apocryphal passages that revered him;[77] it is obvious, for example, that the authors of the *Psalms of Solomon* did not laud Solomon as a healer. Furthermore, in its final form the *Testament of Solomon* is too late and too heavily redacted by one or more post-first-century Christians to be used as if it were a first-century Jewish scroll. This pseudepigraphon may, however, be used with judicious evaluations of early and later strata to approximate Solomonic legends in Judaea and Jericho in the first half of the first century CE. The *Psalms of Solomon* are not a major impediment in this process; they may be inspired by distinctly other Solomonic traditions–especially the lore that Solomon composed 1005 songs (1 Kings 4:32)–and they in no way should be judged to have absorbed most of the vast Solomonic lore shared by many Jews in and around Jericho during the time of Hillel and Jesus.

It would be unwise, therefore, to ignore the early traditions preserved in the *Testament of Solomon*. Although in its present form it is probably a third-century writing, perhaps from Alexandria, the traditions preserved in it in many passages obviously antedate the origins of Christianity and help us obtain some insights into the fears, fantasies, and faith of many average Jews in the early first century. D. Duling correctly points out that Solomon, according to Theodoret (c. 393-c.466),

[76] I include this notation for inclusiveness and because it is impossible to exclude the effect of magic (the evil eye) on physical maladies.
[77] Sir 47:13, 23; 2 Mac 2:8, 9, 10, 12; 1 Ezra 1:3, 5; 5:33, 35; 4 Ezra 7:108; 10:46; 4 Mac 18:16; SibOr 11:80-103.

was considered "the source of all medical knowledge";[78] even earlier traditions, preserved in the *Testament of Solomon*, reveal the popular celebration of Solomon as the one who knew how to control diseases (*OTP* 1.956).

The Jewish Aramaic incantation texts, even though they are also late, are an independent witness to the lore of the ancients; they help us perceive what may well have been the original meaning of Baritmaeus' words. An important parallel to Jesus' healing of Bartimaeus is found in the Mandaic incantation texts, but they are far too late to help us considerably.[79] Jesus heals Bartimaeus without touching him and by merely speaking. Words are accorded magical powers in many cultures, especially those which are considered by sociologists and anthropologists to be "primitive". In the Mandaic incantation texts we find a formula, the angels are exhorted to heal by words: "... you are a healer (אסיא) who heals (דמאסיא) maladies by the word (במללא)."[80]

The Greek Magical Papyri conceivably also confirm an earlier date for the traditions that Solomon controls demons who cause sicknesses. Papyrus IV, which dates from the fourth century CE, contains a charm that is attributed to Solomon.[81] However, it is too late and too ambiguous to be of significant help in understanding Bartimaeus' cry addressed to Jesus.

There should be no doubt, as we shall see, that Solomon was accorded magical powers long before the dates given to the incantation texts. The early date of this idea seems confirmed by the *Apocalypse of Adam*, which contains traditions from the early centuries CE.[82] This pseudepigraphon, in 7:13, refers to Solomon and his army of demons. This idea is very close to many passages in the *Testament of Solomon*.

The pre-70 Jewish pseudepigraphon titled *Pseudo-Philo* also reflects the early tradition that Solomon was an exorcist and controlled evil spirits who cause injury and sickness. Note the words attributed to David, who has exorcised Saul; the words are directed to an evil spirit and the reference is to David's son, Solomon:

> But let the new womb from which I was born rebuke you, from which after a time one
> born from my loins will rule over you. (*LAB* 60:3; *OTP* 2.373 [Harrington])

[78] Theodoret, *Quaestiones in II Reg., Qu. X*; cf. Migne, *PG* 80.676AB.

[79] According to E.M. Yamauchi, the earliest texts are from around 400 CE (No. 22), the religious texts postdate the eighth century, and the magical bowls are from about 600. See his *Mandaic Incantation Texts* (American Oriental Series 49; New Haven: American Oriental Society, 1967) 2.

[80] See 7.22-24, 8.43-45, 18c.2-5, 19.15-16, 26.16. For texts and translations, see Yamauchi, *Mandaic Incantation Texts*.

[81] For the text see K. Preisendanz, *Papyri Graecae Magicae: Die Griechischen Zauberpapyri*, 2 vols., ed. A. Henrichs (Stuttgart: Teubner, 1973-1974) vol. 1, 102-104. For the English translation by W.C. Grese, see *The Greek Magical Papyri in Translation*, ed. H.D. Betz (Chicago, London: University of Chicago Press, 1986) 55-56.

[82] See G. MacRae's comments in *OTP*. 1.708.

The proof that by the first century CE Solomon was considered an exorcist and one who could control diseases, because he understood all wisdom, is found in the Wisdom of Solomon and Josephus. Comprehending the Solomonic traditions in the works already cited awakens perceptions of the possible wide-range of Solomonic lore behind such comments as the one in the Wisdom of Solomon 7:20-21. This passage states that Solomon knew "what is secret and what is manifest" (ησσα τε εστιν κρυπτα και εμφανη), especially the use of the varieties of plants and the (healing) powers of roots (φυτων και δυναμεις ριζων). These words are intended to be those of Solomon himself (see WisSol 17:1-14, 8:17-19:18). As B. M. Nolan stated, "The mantle of exorcist, and therefore healer, fell on Solomon, as Wisdom 7:20 indicates."[83] L. Hogan demonstrates that "the knowledge of healing arts is given as part of the contents of wisdom for which Solomon prayed."[84]

Josephus throws some light on first-century Solomonic traditions, especially the assumption that Solomon was an exorcist and healer.[85] The most important passages are in *Antiquities*, book 8, which records some of the Jewish lore associated with Solomon. According to Josephus, Solomon mastered every form of nature and demonstrated (επεδειχατω) "the most complete knowledge" of their peculiarities (ιδιωματων)" (*Ant* 8. 44). God taught (μαθειν) Solomon the art to be used against demons (δαιμονων), which was for "the aid and healing of humans" (ὀφελειαν και θεραπειαν τοις ἀνθρωποις; *Ant* 8. 45).[86] The common Jew apparently believed that Solomon knew the incantations by which diseases (τα νοσηματα; *Ant* 8.45) are relieved. He bequeathed to others "cures" (ἡ θεραπεια; *Ant*8.46), which were effective in the time of and in the presence of Vespasian and his sons. This passage does not call Solomon "a healer," but it clearly reveals that Solomon, according to first-century Jews, was the one who was given wisdom

---

[83] B.M. Nolan, *The Royal Son of God* (Orbis Biblicus et Orientalis 23; Göttingen: Vandenhoeck & Ruprecht, 1979) 166.

[84] L.P. Hogan, *Healing in the Second Temple Period* (Novum Testamentum et Orbis Antiquus 21; Freiburg: Universitätsverlag Freiburg Schweiz, Göttingen: Vandenhoeck & Ruprecht, 1992) 53, also see 226-27. Hogan rightly points to other ancient texts, which are too late for our present purposes; see Targum Sheni to Esther, Origen's *Comm. on Mt.*, Sermon 33.110, the Nag Hammadi "Testimony of Truth" 9.3, and the Paris Magic Papyrus (PGM 3007). Also, see D.J. Halperin's "The Book of Remedies, the Canonization of the Solomonic Writings and the Riddle of Pseudo-Eusebius," *JQR* 72 (1982) 269-92.

[85] G. Vermes rightly states that in first-century Palestinian culture "the devil was believed to be at the basis of sickness as well as sin." On the one hand, we must not strive to insist that a text refers only to exorcism and not to healing. See Vermes, *Jesus the Jew: A Historian's Reading of the Gospels* (London: Collins, 1973, repr. 1981) 61. On the other hand, it is obvious that in the New Testament there is some distinction made between exorcism and healing; as J.M. Robinson pointed out, "the hostile opposition which characterized the exorcism narratives is largely lacking from the miracle stories which are not specifically exorcisms." See Robinson, *The Problem of History in Mark* (Philadelphia: Fortress, 1982) 88-89.

[86] For the Greek text see J.St.J. Thackeray and R. Marcus, *Josephus* (LCL 5; Cambridge: Harvard; London: Heinemann, 1977) 594.

regarding healing. It is not difficult to indwell the ethos of Jericho, about the time of the incident described by Josephus, and to contemplate that a blind man, in such an affluent environment,[87] could call out to Jesus, "Son of David," and be thinking about the healing powers of Solomon.

Church historians have left us some additional data to digest. It is possible that the early Jerusalem Christians preserved some of the popular legends that evolved under the aegis of Solomon as the one who knew all wisdom and who controlled demons and thus cured diseases. They apparently revered in Jerusalem a cave in which "Solomon tortured the demons."[88] The anonymous pilgrim from Bordeaux, about 333 CE, referred to this *crepta ubi Salomon daemones torquebat*, and where Solomon's thaumaturgical powers were heralded.[89] This interesting data is rather late, although the healing pools of Bethsaida (or Beth Hesda ["House of Mercy"] clearly contain Herodian and Hasmonean constructions. All this data needs to be assessed and discussed before we can utilize it to understand the extent of the myth that Solomon controlled demons and diseases and was revered as healer in first-century Judaea.[90]

We should pause and reflect on the observation that Solomon is not unambiguously portrayed as a healer in the New Testament. Despite the proceeding exegesis of Wisdom of Solomon 7, there is no pellucid reference to Solomon as a healer in pre-70 Jewish pseudepigrapha, the Old Testament Apocrypha, or Philo. Should we conclude, therefore, that prior to 70 CE Solomon was portrayed only as a wise man?

Such a conclusion would be both foolish and myopic. A key to an appreciation of *the early nature of traditions* appearing in post-70 documents may be found in passages where "Son of David" is mentioned. As C. Burger, in *Jesus als Davidssohn*,[91] demonstrated, the application of the title "Son of David" to Jesus appears almost always within stories of healing. And as U. Mauser demonstrates,

---

[87] Jericho was world renowned for its verdancy; its palm and balsam groves were famous. Mark Anthony gave them to Cleopatra. See Strabo 16.2.41; Dioscorides, *De materia medica* 1.19.1; Diodorus Siculus 2.48. I am indebted here to E. Nitzer, "The Hasmonean and Herodian Winter Palaces at Jericho," *IEJ* 25 (1975) 89-100; and to D.A. Fiensy, *The Social History of Palestine in the Herodian Period* (Studies in the Bible and Early Christianity 20; Lewiston, New York: Edwin Mellen, 1991) 25-28.

[88] See B. Bagatti, "I Giudeo-cristiani e l'anello di Salomone," *RSR* 60 (1972) 151-60. See also Origen, *PG* 13.1757.

[89] See Bagatti, *The Church from the Circumcision*, trans. E. Hoade (Studium Biblicum Franciscanum 2; Jerusalem: Franciscan Printing Press, 1971, 1984) 136. Also see E. Hoade, *Guide to the Holy Land* (Jerusalem: Franciscan Printing Press, 1984) 212-13. These books, and many works on archaeology of the "Holy Land" need to be read critically.

[90] In the New Testament, of course, Solomon is portrayed as a wise man (Mt 12:42), a wealthy person (Mt 6:29), and his name was commemorated in the Temple, in the portico to the east (Jn 1:23).

[91] C. Burger, *Jesus als Davidssohn: Eine traditionsgeschichtliche Untersuchung* (FRLANT 98; Göttingen: Vandenhoeck & Ruprecht, 1970) esp. see 170.

in his *The Peace of the Gospel,*[92] seven sections in Matthew contain the title "Son of David," and six of these are healing stories (9:27-31; 12:22-24; 15:21-28; 20:29-34; 21:1-11; and 21:14-16). Why is Jesus hailed as the "Son of David"; that is, as one who heals? In assuming that this is a messianic title we become blind to possible Solomonic meanings.

This possibility increases perhaps by an examination of Matthew 12:22-23, which is independent of and not paralleled in Mark. According to Matthew 12 Jesus heals a man possessed of a demon; he is blind and dumb. When it is obvious that the demoniac is healed, all in the crowd (παντες οι οχλοι) exclaim, "Can (μητι) this be the Son of David?" The Greek particle μητι may indicate that a negative answer is expected, or it may imply that those in the crowd do not know what is the full content of the title. Matthew's text will not allow us to conclude that the crowd clearly thought Jesus was to be seen in terms of Solomon; but it may indicate that "the Son of David" denoted a healer, one who could exorcise a blind man and enable him to see. Apparently this concept was shared by first-century Palestinian Jews.

Perhaps the meaning of Matthew 21 will shine some light that will illuminate our search. Jesus' triumphal entry into Jerusalem was of special importance to Matthew. The traditions he preserves are of great significance for us, since the crowds (οχλοι) shout, "Hosanna to the Son of David!" (Mt 21:9).[93] Jesus allegedly heals the blind and the lame in the Temple, and then children cry out, "Hosanna to the Son of David!" (Mt 21:15). If the Messiah was not thought to heal, then what are the meanings of these exclamations?[94]

More questions are raised by our observations. The claim that Jesus was of the house of David was an early aspect of the kerygma and liturgy, as the pre-Pauline tradition in Romans 1:3-4 clarifies; but then we are led to the most important observation, as Burger stated, "dass sich im gesamten Stoff der

---

[92] U. Mauser, *The Peace of the Gospel* (Louisville: Westminster/Knox, 1992) 50-53. I appreciate Professor Mauser discussing these traditions with me; he is convinced that many of the "Son of David" passages in Mt have a basis in traditions about healing in pre-70 Palestine.

[93] The author (or authors) of the Gospel of John shifted the shout "Son of David!" to "the King of Israel" (Jn 12:13). As many specialists on the GosJn have pointed out, "Israel," in contrast to *Ioudaioi,* is positive, signifying (as it does in the Old Testament Apocrypha and Pseudepigrapha) the faithful ones of Yahweh. See esp. the following: S. Pancaro, "The Relationship of the Church to Israel in the Gospel of John," *NTS* 21 (1974-1975) 396-405; W. Meeks, "Am I a Jew?–Johannine Christianity and Judaism," in *Christianity, Judaism, and Other Greco-Roman Cults,* ed. J. Neusner (Leiden: Brill, 1975) 163-86; M. Lowe, "Who were the *Ioudaioi*?" *Novum Testamentum* 18 (1976) 101-30; D.J.A. Hickling, "Attitudes to Judaism in the Fourth Gospel," *L'Évangile de Jean,* ed. M. de Jonge (Gembloux: Leuven University Press, 1977) 347-54; U. C. von Wahlde, "The Johannine 'Jews': A Critical Survey," *NTS* 28 (1982) 33-60; R.A. Culpepper, "The Gospel of John and the Jews," *Review and Expositor* 2 (1987) 272-88.

[94] Duling points out that "the *title* Son of David is found only in the synoptic gospels and is associated primarily with a figure who is so addressed by people in need of exorcism or healing." *(HTR* 68 [1975] 235). I read Duling's paper after completing the present research, and I find much in his article that is informative and corroborative.

Evangelien keine Überlieferung zum Thema Davidssohn findet, die mit einiger Sicherheit auf Jesus selbst zurückgeführt werden könnte."[95] And so, we ask with more insight, if none of the Son of David traditions can be traced with assurance back to Jesus himself, then what are the reasons Jesus' followers claimed that he was the "Son of David."[96] Obviously, different Jews, representing the various groups within the Judaism of Jesus' day, would have felt free to express, perhaps narratively, their own perceptions. Paul is our first witness, and he indicates that he inherited the title "Son of David."[97] Obviously some of Jesus' followers (not necessarily disciples) understood "Son of David" to be a messianic title, but others most likely meant by it that he was Solomon *redivivus*. I have no doubt that other Jews, learned as well as the 'am ha-aretz, who used the title were not clear what it connoted or denoted. What Jesus may have understood by the title–if he ever used it–and what the Evangelist Mark intended, is another separate question.[98]

Summary

In summary, what did Bartimaeus mean when he called out to Jesus, Υὶè Δαυὶδ 'Ιησοῦ, ἐλέησόν? If this episode reflects an historical event, perhaps in Jericho, whether in actuality or in verisimilitude through Mark's narrative, then there are several possible ways of discerning an answer. The first is that we will never know and every attempt will be frustrated by the inability of discussing the claim directly with Bartimaeus and the complexity, incompleteness, redactional nature, and lateness of our sources.

Second, it is possible, but unlikely, that Bartimaeus was hailing Jesus as the Messiah. He clearly wanted to be healed, but we have no evidence that the Messiah was perceived as a healer in Palestine before 70 CE. Yet, this option is the one almost always chosen by the commentators on Mark 10. My own reading

---

[95] Burger, *Jesus als Davidssohn*, 165.

[96] M. de Jonge rightly points out that in "Mark we certainly do not find a clear connection between Jesus and Solomon as exorcist." He offers the opinion that Jesus was seen as David's Son because of the links between Jesus as prophet, teacher, exorcist, and healer and David as prophet and exorcist. See de Jonge, "Jesus, Son of David and Son of God," in *Intertextuality in Biblical Writings* (Kampen, 1989) 95-104; esp. see 100-101.

[97] I am indebted to Bent Noach for many insights; especially now I think of his "TESTE PAULO: Paul as the Principal Witness to Jesus and Primitive Christianity," in *Die Paulinische Literatur und Theologie: Anlässlich der 50. jährigen Gründungs-Feier der Universität von Aarhus*, ed. S. Pedersen (Teologiske Studier 7; Aarhus: Forlaget Aros, 1980) 9-28; esp. 22-23.

[98] B. Chilton is convinced that Jesus "embraced the characterization 'David's son', with its overtones of Solomonic wisdom and especially of exorcistic and therapeutic skill" (88). If that is historically accurate other problems are raised; for example, why did Jesus put stress only on proclaiming the dawning of God's Rule, and why was he embarrassed and disappointed at the crowds who came to him only to be healed? See Chilton, "Jesus *ben David*: Reflections on the *Davidssohnfrage*," *JSNT* 14 (1982) 88-112.

of the traditions about "the Son of David" force me to reject this option for the Bartimaeus pericope.

Third, Bartimaeus' call Υἱὲ Δαυὶδ may simply acknowledge Jesus' royal genealogy. This possibility can no longer be dismissed since we know about Davidids living in Jerusalem during the time of the alleged encounter between Bartimaeus and Jesus. Two observations militate against opting for this solution to the question what Bartimaeus may have meant by the words Υἱὲ Δαυὶδ. First, critical scholarship has raised serious questions about Jesus' Davidic lineage. Where we find it in the New Testament and related literatures it appears linked with the confession that Jesus is the Messiah and therefore must be of Davidic descent.[99] Secondly (and most importantly), this option is insensitive to the narrative in which the words, which may well be an invocation, are couched. That is, Bartimaeus wants to be healed, and any solution to the question of what he meant by Υἱὲ Δαυὶδ should attend to the relation between his plea and his need for healing. We receive the tradition in narrative form and narrative exegesis must not be ignored. The result moves us away from assuming Bartimaeus was thinking about Jesus' lineage.

Fourth, attention must be turned not only to the words, Υἱὲ Δαυὶδ, his sickness and to see again. Does he simply call out Jesus' name, or is it a title? We have no criteria or philological key by which to discern the one from the other. If Ἰησοῦ is a title, and if it is associated with a known healer, then it is conceivable that Bartimaeus is linking Jesus with the famous magician and healer named Joshua ben Perahyah, who lived in Jerusalem and was famous not only for his healings but also for his altercation with Alexander Jannaeus in the first third of the first century BCE. This possibility appears remote to me; and it certainly does not help us understand the most problematic words, namely Υἱὲ Δαυὶδ.

Fifth, by attending to the full narrative–the call Υἱὲ Δαυὶδ Ἰησοῦ, ἐλέησόν με and the healing of Bartimaeus' blindness–we are confronted with the most probable answer. Taken literally "son of David" would be Solomon. I am persuaded that the most probable explanation of the meaning of Bartimaeus' Υἱὲ Δαυὶδ is some Solomonic denotation.

We possess traditions that may well derive from the first century CE. in which Solomon is hailed as an exorcist who controls demons and the sickness, including blindness, they cause. This final option is conceivable, and to me fully convincing. The most probable conclusion to our research is that Bartimaeus called to Jesus and hailed him as one who like Solomon possessed miraculous powers of healing.

We have not endeavored to discern whether this conclusion leads us to a pre-70 historical context or to a narrative context. Before concluding, we may

---

[99] See the informed discussion in R.E. Brown, *The Birth of the Messiah* (Garden City, New York: Doubleday, 1977) 66-70.

speculate on the possibility that behind this gospel pericope there is some historicity. Mark certainly is inheriting Jewish traditions, and he does not seem to be interested in Jesus as a type of Solomon. Hence, it seems likely that he inherited the tradition about Bartimaeus. There is no evidence in the pericope to suggest that these traditions originated in the kerygma or didache of the Palestinian Jesus Movement, and there is considerable data to indicate that these traditions originated before 70 CE, or the time of Mark. It is conceivable, therefore, that there is some history behind the story.

Conclusion

It is evident that Mark 10:46-52 elicits many questions from the exegete. If the Messiah was not perceived as a healer and would not perform healing functions,[100] then it is improbable that Bartimaeus, who wanted to regain his sight, is to be perceived as one who hailed Jesus as the Messiah.[101] If the traditions about Solomon as an exorcist and healer mirror an almost lost aspect of pre-70 Jewish lore that he–the wisest of humans–controlled demons who caused illnesses, understood the art of healing, and was accorded the powers to heal, and if these traditions can be traced back to Jericho and date from the time of Jesus, then it seems to follow that Bartimaeus, according to the Markan narrative, was certainly thinking of Jesus as a healer, after the order of Solomon.[102] It is, furthermore, conceivable that Bartimaeus, or a redactor of the story, may have linked traditions in the Solomonic cycle with the traditions about the healer, Joshua Ben Perahyah, who was hailed as a great healer in Judaea. In any case it is no longer possible, in light of the vast amount of archaeological and literary data from pre-70 Judaism to conclude that "Son of David" in Mark 10 is "simply a messianic title, ..."[103]

---

[100] One of the problems in discerning the extent and purpose of the alleged Signs Source behind the GosJn is the recognition that in a Palestinian Jewish environment it would not follow that Jesus must be the Messiah because he performed miraculous deeds, including healing miracles. See R.T. Fortna, *The Gospel of Signs* (SNTS Monograph Series 11; Cambridge: CUP, 1970) esp. 230-34.

[101] Having completed this essay I decided to check on the secondary sources. I was pleased to find the following comments by P.J. Achtemeier, who is convinced (as I am) that "Son of David" in the Bartimaeus pericope does not mean the "Messiah." Note his insights: "Bartimaeus calls upon Jesus as Son of David to heal him, yet healing was not associated with David, either as historical figure or as one to come. There is, however, a strong later Jewish tradition which saw in Solomon, David's son and successor on the throne of Israel, the originator of the magical arts, and as a result many of the magical traditions which filled the Hellenistic world to overflowing were assigned to him" (p 57). Achtemeier, *Mark* (Proclamation Commentaries; Philadelphia: Fortress, 1986, 1989).

[102] For important probes into so-called medical knowledge in the first century CE and the place of magic in the hellenistic world, but with virtually no reflections on the place of Solomon, see the following: H. Flashar, ed., *Antike Medizin* (Wege der Forschung 221; Darmstadt: Wissenschaftliche Buchgesellschaft, 1971); R. Heiligenthal, *Werke als Zeichen* (WUNT 2.9; Tübingen: Mohr (Siebeck), 1983); H.C. Kee, *Miracle in the Early Christian World* (New Haven, London: Yale, 1983).

[103] D.E. Nineham, *The Gospel of St Mark* (Harmondsworth: Penguin Books, 1963) 286.

Mark's purpose in narrating this story is not clear. If he conceived of Bartimaeus' exhortation as a messianic confession then his handling of it contrasts markedly with his *Tendenzen* and penchant for the so-called Messianic Secret. If Mark the Evangelist expected his readers to comprehend "Son of David" as a messianic title, and that was the intention of Baritmaeus and the crowd, then it is odd that Mark did not portray Jesus silencing them. I have little doubt that one of the reasons Mark narrated this tradition is because of his apocalyptic eschatology; in the End-of-time God will come, אלהים הוא יבוא; then "the blind man's eyes shall be opened" (אז תפקחנה עיני עורים; Isa 35:4-5). Perhaps the link between Mark 10 and Isa 35:4 is obvious because of the concept of how God shall "save" (ישע in Isa 35:4 and σωζω in Mk 10:52). Perhaps it was Mark, or an early Christian, that brought out this link with scripture, since Jesus' injunction–"Go your way; your faith has made you well"–seems out of context with the simple story told and is in line with Markan theology. As Anderson points out, "For Mark the emphasis in the story is not on the *healing* as such (no action or healing word of Jesus is mentioned) but on the response of faith to God's call in Jesus ... through blind eyes are opened and true fellowship becomes possible."[104] This exegesis is sound, and it is confirmed by the way Mark has ended the story: "And immediately (ευθυς he received his sight and followed (ηκολουθει) him on the way (εν τη οδω)." It should be obvious that these terms reveal the hand of the early Christian community and probably of the redactor Mark.

The most important result of our present research is that we have become, once again, aware of the truncated and distortionistic view caused by a purely christocentric (or messianic) approach to traditions preserved in the New Testament. We dare not assume that what would become messianic symbols, terms, and titles possessed such meaning before the middle of the first century CE. By struggling with issues arising out of Mark's account of Bartimaeus' exhortation we are pulled beneath the kerygmatic context of the Markan text. Imaginatively, yet guided by remnants of pre-70 Palestinian traditions (in Mark especially), we enter the hellenistic world that antedates the Markan text of approximately 70 CE. It is obvious that these pre-70 traditions reveal a Bartimaeus who was not hailing Jesus as Messiah. He most likely believed that Jesus possessed the miraculous healing powers of Solomon.

Our research has helped clarify the complexity of the hellenistic world which obviously included erudite as well as uneducated Jews whether they lived in Jericho, Alexandria, or elsewhere. The insights obtained in these forays into pre-70 Palestinian Jewish lore help improve our exegesis of New Testament texts. Some "Son of David" passages are messianic, but others certainly reflect the Solomonic mythology of Jews contemporaneous with Hillel and Jesus. Behind the

---

[104] Anderson, *Mark*, 259.

Markan text we hear a Bartimaeus call on Jesus, who as Solomon, the Son of David, was reputed to have powers for healing.

Addendum: Does *On Resurrection* (4Q521) Depict a Messiah Who Heals?

The preceding research is based on the conclusion that no Jewish document that antedates 70 CE depicts a messiah who heals. This conclusion is now challenged by a Qumran text that has been published recently.[105] It is titled *On Resurrection* and was found in Cave IV (4Q521). The text does contend that "his messiah ... will heal the wounded, ..." So excerpted the Qumran fragment seems to suggest that the Messiah will be one who heals.

The problem with such an interpretation, however, is evident when one studies the text. The excerpt just quoted is not all the text says, and the abbreviated portion excerted misrepresents the full meaning of the document.[106] It is far from clear that any action is attributed to the Messiah in this text. The Hebrew for "his messiah" (למשיחו) receives the action; the noun is not a *nomen regens*. Unfortunately the words which preceded "[he]aven and earth will obey his messiah" (line 1) are lost.

The pertinent passage of 4Q521 (Frag. 2 ii) is as follows:

> ... [he]aven and earth will obey his messiah, (2) [and all th]at is in them will not turn away from the commandments of holy ones. (3) You who seek the Lord, stregthen yourselves in his service. (4) Is it not in this that you–all who hope in their hearts–will find the Lord? (5) For the Lord will seek out the pious ones and call the righteous ones by name, (6) and his spirit will hover over the poor ones and he will renew the faithful ones by his might. (7) For he will glorify the pious ones on the throne of an eternal kingdom, (8) releasing captives, giving sight to the blind ones and raising up those who are pro[strate]. (9) For[e]ver I shall cleave [to those who] hope, and in his kindness [...] (10) And the fru[it of a] good [wor]k will not be held back for anyone, (11) and the glorious things that have not occurred the Lord will do as he s[aid], (12) for he will heal the wounded, give life to the dead and preach good news to the poor ones, (13) and he will [sat]isfy the [weak ones] and lead those who have been cast out and enrich the hungry ones, (14) [...] and all of them [...] .

The bracketed ellipses [...] do not denote that I have omitted something from the text. They indicate that the leather has a hole (*lacuna*) or is defective at that particular spot.

Two observations indicate that this text does not portray the Messiah as one who heals. First, the subject (*nomen regens*) in the context contiguous with the

---

[105] G. Stanton, persuaded that God's agent is usually the one who preaches good news, concludes that "in line 12 at least, it is the Messiah who has the task of 'healing the wounded, giving life to the dead, and preaching good news to the poor'" (186). Stanton, *Gospel Truth: New Light on Jesus and the Gospels* (Valley Forge: Trinity Press, 1995).

[106] For photographs of the scroll, the Hebrew text, and critical discussion see E. Puech, "Une apocalypse messianique (4Q521)," *Revue de Qumran* 60 (1992) 475-519 with three plates.

reference to healing is not the Messsiah but the Lord.[107] Note the two passages that
are pertinent: "For the Lord (אדני) will seek out the pious ones and ... he will
glorify the pious ones ... giving sight to the blind ones," "... the Lord (אדני) will do
as he s[aid], for he will heal the wounded, ..." The actor is thus the Lord (and the
author uses the biblical terminology; there is no mention of אל).[108]

Second, the document is based on scripture and echoes it; that is, the pretext
of this intertextual document is clearly Psalm 146, especially verse 8: "the Lord
(יהוה) is the one giving sight to the blind ones, the Lord (יהוה) is the one raising up
those who are prostrate." The Hebrew here is identical, except for the plene
writing and the repetition of "the Lord."

What then is the importance of "his Messiah"? This Qumran scroll is clearly
messianic; it contains the Hebrew noun for Messiah (למשיחו).[109] The Messiah is
certainly a cosmic figure; heaven and earth will obey him. The Lord (אדני),
however, is the actor. The Lord will perform these acts when the Messiah comes.
The document does not state that the Lord will preform the acts specified through
"his Messiah"; and if that is the implication of the full document, then the author
has still stressed that the actor is certainly God.[110] In my judgment, Psalm 146
helps the exegete keep in focus the awesome *actions of YHWH*.

In conclusion, the newly published evidence from the Qumran caves does
not undermine the perception previously articulated; that is, there is not one pre-70
Jewish writing that depicts the Messsiah as one who will come and heal the sick
or give sight to the blind. The dominant biblical and parabiblical theme is the
same: God–almost always as the Lord (Yahweh)–is the one who heals (and no
other), as we know from the TANAKH (or Old Testament), especially Numbers
12:13, Deuteronomy 32:39, 2 Kings 20:8, 2 Chronicles 30:20, Psalms 6:2, 30:2 [cf.

---

[107] As J.J. Collins states, "... the Qumran text goes on to say that God will release captives, give
sight to the blind, etc. just as he does in the psalm. Again at vs. (*sic*) 12, it is God who will heal the
wounded, give life to the dead and preach good news to the poor." Collins, *The Scepter and the Star: The
Messiahs of the Dead Sea Scrolls and Other Ancient Literature* (Anchor Bible Reference Library; New
York: Doubleday, 1995) 117-18.

[108] Collins points out that the Lord is usually the one who raises the dead (cf. 18 Benedictions).
The Scepter, 118.

[109] As both Stanton and Collins emphasize, it is odd that the Lord is portrayed as one who
preaches good news to the poor. Surely the idea has evolved from Isaiah 61:1. Stanton, *Gospel Truth?*,
186; Collins, *The Scepter*, 118.

[110] Collins, I am persuaded, leans in that direction: "... it is likely that God acts through the
agency of a prophetic messiah in line 12." *The Scepter*, 118. The syntax is important; Collins did not
state that the messiah acts as God's agent, but that "God acts" through his messiah. The theological and
ideological link with the messianology of the *Psalms of Solomon* 17 and 18 is apparent. The author of
these psalms also stresses that the Messiah belongs to the Lord and that God, not the messiah, is their
king: φΗчϬϭϳ ϭΉϳͼ ͼdͼϭϭϭͼͶ ϭ'ͼϭϭ ͼϭϳ ͼϭϭ ϭ΅ͼϭͼ φͼϭ ͼͶϭ (18:1).

146:8], Jeremiah 17:14, 30:17, and from the apocryphal books, notably Wisdom 16:12[111] and Sirach 38:9.

This conclusion is confirmed now by the Qumran liturgy for healing (11Q11 = 11QPsAp[a]).[112] According to this scroll, "Yahweh will smite" the demon causing sickness and will affect healing, apparently sometimes directly and sometimes through his archangel Raphael, which is a paronomasia meaning etymologically "God heals."

These Qumran apocryphal psalms also seem to suggest that Solomon exorcized demons by invoking the name of YHWH (see 11Q11 Ps II col. 1, line 2). Hence, I am persuaded that Bartimaeus was not saluting Jesus as "the Messiah," but he may have been thinking about him in terms of Solomonic lore with the exhortation: "Son of David, Jesus, have mercy on me."

---

[111] Note the evidence of post-exilic Jewish theology in the targumic circumlocution: "but it was your word, O Lord, that heals all people." NRSV.

[112] See the bibliography, introduction, text, and translation by J.A. Sanders in the PTSDSS Project.

Rationale and Agenda for a Psychological-Critical Approach to the Bible and Its Interpretation[1]

Wayne G. Rollins
Assumption College

The psychological and psychoanalytical analyses of human experience have proven their worth in the area of religion and enable one to detect multidimensional aspects of the biblical message . . . . The aid that can come from this approach to . . . [the historical-critical] method cannot be underestimated.

Joseph A. Fitzmyer, S.J.[2]

If Rudolf Bultmann has . . . shown that they [Biblically-grounded theologians] cannot get along without philosophy, then the same is certainly also true for psychology.

Joachim Scharfenberg[3]

---

[1] Although the present article does not comport with the main thrust of John Priest's historical-exegetical work, it echoes one of his main interests, namely the relevance of the text for the experience of the reader. When we were colleagues at the Hartford Seminary Foundation, Priest contributed an article on "Myth and Dream in Hebrew Scripture" to a volume edited by Joseph Campbell, joining forces with psycho-literary critics Alan Watts, David Miller, Norman O. Brown, Rollo May, and Richard Underwood (*Myths, Dreams, and Religion* [New York: E. P. Dutton, 1970] 48-67). Though Priest insists on the difference between a Biblical and a contemporary psychological approach to myth and dream (p. 64), he nonetheless seems to hold in characteristic fashion that Biblical myth and dream have psycho-spiritual relevance in cultivating an "openness to the whole of reality without which . . . [a person] forever fails to be who he [or she] truly is" (pp. 66-67). The present paper was presented in its initial form to the Psychology and Biblical Studies Group at the SBL annual meeting, November 22, 1993, Washington, D. C., adapted from manuscript materials for the author's book, *The Bible in Psychological Perspective*, to be published by Fortress Press. The opening section is an amplified version of pp. 10 -14 of my article, "Psychology, Hermeneutics, and the Bible," *Jung and the Interpretation of the Bible* (ed. David L. Miller; New York: Continuum, 1995) 9-39.

[2] J. A. Fitzmyer, S. J., *Scripture, The Soul of Theology* (New York: Paulist, 1994) 51-52.

[3] J. Scharfenberg, *Sigmund Freud and His Critique of Religion* (Philadelphia: Fortress, 1988) 2.

I. Rationale

In the Fall of 1913 Carl Jung wrote to the newly inaugurated *Psychoanalytic Review*, congratulating the editors for their plans to "unite in their journal the contributions of . . . specialists in various fields." Jung counseled, "we need not only the work of medical psychologists, but also that of philologists, historians, archaeologists, mythologists, folklore students, ethnologists, philosophers, . . . pedagogues, . . . biologists" and "theologians."[4] Eighty years later the field of biblical studies returned the compliment in the 1993 inaugural issue of *Biblical Interpretation: A Journal of Contemporary Approaches* announcing the "need for the field of biblical studies to become more public and more pluralistic," inviting the submission of "articles that discuss specific biblical texts in the light of fresh insights that derive from the diversity of relevant disciplines," including sociology, anthropology, archaeology, philosophy, history, linguistics, literary theory, and psychology.[5]

In the eight intervening decades, "psychology" did not always enjoy a favorable press in biblical circles, popular or scholarly. Jung noted a certain, "wrinkling of the nose" among some clergy at the mention of the word.[6] As late as the 1970's Robin Scroggs reports how a discussion of psychological hermeneutics with an older European New Testament scholar ended with the comment, "Bultmann taught us years ago to be suspicious of psychology."[7] Gerd Theissen reports the same experience in the ironic opening line of his *Psychological Aspects of Pauline Theology*: "Every exegete has learned that psychological exegesis is poor exegesis."[8]

The antipathy to "psychology" that obtained in biblical scholarly circles for the first three-quarters of the twentieth century can be traced, in part, to late nineteenth-century reactions to the "psychological interpretation of the person of Jesus" that had been undertaken by Karl Hase (1829), Christian Hermann Weisse (1838), and Heinrich Julius Holtzmann (1863), who, among others, insisted that a valid historical reconstruction of the life of Jesus must include a "psychological analysis" of his developing messianic self-consciousness. The most enduring blows against these developmental psychological reconstructions came from Wilhelm Wrede and Albert Schweitzer. Wrede denounced the methodology of D. F. Strauss as a psychologizing depiction of the life of Jesus that cannot be supported from the text of Mark's Gospel: "The study of the life of Jesus

---

[4]C. G. Jung, *C. G. Jung Letters, I* (Bollingen Series; ed. G. Adler and A. Jaffé; Princeton: Princeton University Press, 1973) 29-30.

[5]J. C. Exum and M. G. Brett. "Editorial Statement," *Bib Int* 1 (1993) i.

[6]C. G. Jung, *C. G. Jung Letters, II* (Bollingen Series; ed. G. Adler and A. Jaffé; Princeton: Princeton University Press, 1975) 85.

[7]R.Scroggs, "Psychology as a Tool to Interpret the Text: Emerging Trends in Biblical Thought," *Christian Century* (March 24, 1982) 335.

[8]G.Theissen, *Psychological Aspects of Pauline Theology* (Philadelphia: Fortress, 1987) 1.

suffers from psychological conjecture, and this is a kind of historical guesswork."[9] Albert Schweitzer, in 1901, denounced them as a "patchwork of opinions" produced by "mediocre minds" who "with much else that is modern . . . transferred to him [Jesus] our modern psychology, without always recognizing clearly that it is not applicable to him and necessarily belittles him."[10] Schweitzer reinforced his attack on "psychology" in 1913 with the publication of *The Psychiatric Study of Jesus: Exposition and Criticism*, in which he took objection to four medical treatises that concluded on the basis of psychopathological analysis of the Gospel records that Jesus of Nazareth was "mentally diseased," a conclusion that Schweitzer thought, both on medical and historical-critical grounds, should "be rated as exactly zero."[11]

The result within the guild of biblical scholarship was a virtual blackout on things psychological for the better part of a century, from the early 1900's to the 1970's, particularly in the field of New Testament studies.[12] One does pick up occasional favorable signals toward psychology from members of the History of Religions school, Hermann Gunkel (1888), Johannes Weiss (1913), and Wilhelm Bousset (1913),[13] who from time to time employ psychological categories to explain biblical phenomena, but with little effect on the broader guild of scholarship. Vincent Taylor's *The Person of Christ in New Testament Teaching* (1959) surprisingly includes a chapter on "Christology and Psychology," urging attention to the research of "Freud and Jung into the nature of the unconscious."[14] H. Wheeler Robinson (1946) unapologetically appropriates "modern psychology" to illumine Old Testament prophecy in his essay on "The Psychology of Inspiration" in *Inspiration and Revelation in the Old Testament* [15] and Martin Buss anticipates his later work on "The Social Psychology of Prophecy" in his

---

[9] W. G. Kümmel, *The New Testament: The History of the Investigation of Its Problems* (Nashville: Abingdon, 1972) 284-285, citing Wrede's *Das Messiasgeheimnis in den Evangelien* (1901).

[10] *The New Testament: The History of the Investigation of Its Problems*, 93-95, 149, 152, 237, citing Schweitzer's, *Skizze des Lebens Jesu*. (1901).

[11] A. Schweitzer, *The Psychiatric Study of Jesus* (Boston: Beacon Press, 1948 [1913]) 7, 74.

[12] The antipathy to psychology is evidenced in Werner Kümmel's survey of New Testament scholarship, *The New Testament:The History of the Investigation of its Problems* (1972), which omits reference to works on "biblical psychology," e.g Franz Delitzsch's *A System of Biblical Psychology* (1861), M. Scott Fletcher's *The Psychology of the New Testament* (1912), and William Sanday's *Personality in Christ and in Ourselves* (1911). All references to "psychology" in Kümmel are pejorative, often linked with the dangers of idealistic philosophy and a "spiritualizing" interpretation of history. For example, he speaks of nineteenth century attempts to study the history of Jesus as being "encumbered from the beginning with a psychologically oriented understanding of Jesus" in a way that "dominated and interfered with research for almost four decades" (quotation from p. 152; see also pp. 95, 103, 149, 223, 237, 239, 285, 288). But see one positive note on p. 280, with regard to the work of Johannes Weiss.

[13] Cf. Theissen, on Gunkel, 268, and on Bousset, 16. On J. Weiss cf. Kümmel, 280.

[14] (New York: St. Martin's, 1959) 282.

[15] Oxford: Clarendon, 1946. Robinson uses the term "psychology" in the classical post-Reformation sense as a branch of anthropology that seeks to identify the biblical understanding of the origin, nature, and destiny of the human "psyche" (173-187).

1965 article on "Self-Theory and Theology."[16] But not until 1969, with Frederick
C. Grant's essay on "Psychological Study of the Bible" in the Goodenough
Festschrift, do we hear a clear call from a mainline scholar for the dismantling of
the wall that had divided psychology and biblical studies for the better part of the
century. Grant wrote in prophetic words, albeit largely ignored by the biblical
guild of the time, "that "Dr. Goodenough pointed out the value and importance,
even the necessity, of the psychological interpretation of the Bible. This is a new
kind of biblical criticism. The earlier disciplines are all necessary and important,
. . . but psychological criticism opens up a wholly new and vast, far-reaching scene
. . . . Beyond the historical and exegetical interpretation of the Bible lies the whole
new field of depth psychology and psychoanalysis."[17]

Two factors account for the change in attitude toward psychology among
biblical scholars echoed in Grant's essay. The first is the seismic paradigmatic
shift that develops in biblical scholarship in the late 1960's and early 1970's, when
the realization grows that the classical disciplines of historical and literary
criticism no longer prove sufficient in themselves for the increasingly complex and
multi-faceted task of Biblical interpretation as conceived at the end of the twentieth
century. Walter Wink's hyperbolic announcement in 1973 that "historical biblical
criticism is bankrupt" marks the divide[18] and signals the beginning of an
unprecedented proliferation of critical strategies to offset the shortcoming of
historical-literary criticism, from structuralist, rhetorical, and social scientific
criticism, to feminist, ideological, narrative, deconstructionist, materialist,
audience, and reader-response criticisms. Included in these new strategies is
psychological criticism, as indicated in the inclusion in 1991, for the first time in
its history, of a research unit on "Psychology and Biblical Studies" in the annual
program of the Society of Biblical Literature. More recently, Joseph A. Fitzmyer,
S. J., comments on the inclusion of section 1.D.3 on "Psychological and
Psychoanalytic Approaches" in the 1993 Pontifical Biblical Commission
document, "The Interpretation of the Bible in the Church":[19]

> The psychological and psychoanalytical analyses of human experience have proven their
> worth in the area of religion and enable one to detect multidimensional aspects of the
> biblical message. In particular, this approach has been invaluable in the analytical
> explanation of biblical symbols, cultic rituals, sacrifice, legal prohibitions, and biblical
> tabus. Yet once again, there is no one psychological or psychoanalytic exegesis that can

---

[16] *JR* 45 (1965) 46-53; and *Prophecy: Essays Presented to Georg Fohrer on His Sixty-fifth Birthday* (ed. J. A. Emerton; Berlin: Walter de Gruyter, 1980) 1-11.
[17] F. C. Grant, "Psychological Study of the Bible," *Religions in Antiquity: Essays in Memory of Erwin Ramsdell Goodenough* (ed. Jacob Neusner; Leiden: Brill, 1968) 112-113.
[18] W. Wink, *The Bible in Human Transformation: Toward a New Paradigm for Biblical Study* (Philadelphia: Fortress, 1973) 1.
[19] Pontifical Biblical Commission, *The Interpretation of the Bible in the Church* (Vatican City: Libreria Editrice Vaticana, 1993).

substitute for the properly oriented historical-critical method, whereas the aid that can come from this approach to that method cannot be underestimated.[20]

A second factor accounting for the glacial shift in attitude toward psychology among biblical scholars is the unassailably monumental achievement of Sigmund Freud (1856-1939) and Carl Jung (1875-1961) in initiating an entire culture in the art of thinking "psychologically" about itself, its traditions, texts, and institutions. *Freud's legacy* for biblical hermeneutics is the psychoanalytic groundwork and method he provides for attending to psychodynamic factors in biblical texts, characters, stories, mythic narratives, and religious practice , as well as in biblical interpreters. Freud's approach was at first adopted by analysts and theologians, and in time by Bible scholars. Robin Scroggs' article on "The Heuristic Value of a Psychoanalytic Model in the Interpretation of Pauline Theology" appeared in *Zygon* in 1978. Scroggs writes, "I believe that Paul shares with the psychoanalytic vision the same deep insights into human reality and dynamic, despite the apparent enormity separating the language systems. . . . Freud himself suggested that Paul made an important step toward bringing the repressed to consciousness. I believe this is true far beyond what Freud believed . . . ."[21] (142-3). Other biblical scholars who have utilized Freudian models for biblical interpretation in the past two decades include David Halperin,[22] Dan Merkur,[23] Stephen Moore,[24] Ilona Rashkow,[25] Gerd Theissen,[26] Mary Ann Tolbert,[27] and Wilhelm Wuellner.[28]

Jung's contribution to the rapprochement of biblical studies and psychology contrasts with Freud's in several ways. To be sure, Jung stands in Freud's debt. He wrote to physician Edith Schröder in April 1957, "Without Freud's 'psychoanalysis' I wouldn't have had a clue."[29] But as is commonly known, he departed from Freud on matters of fundamental significance that have implications for the application of psychology to biblical hermeneutics. First, Jung views the unconscious not as a repository of repressed material, as Freud does, but as a

---

[20] Joseph A. Fitzmyer, S. J. Scripture, *The Soul of Theology*. (New York: Paulist, 1994) 51-52.

[21] *Zygon* 13 (1978) 142-3.

[22] D. J. Halperin, *Seeking Ezekiel: Text and Psychology* (University Park, PA: Pennsylvania State University Press, 1993).

[23] D. Merkur, "The Visionary Practices of Jewish Apocalyptic" *The Psychoanalytic Study of Society* (ed. L. B. Boyer and S. A. Grolnick; 121-148; Hillsdale, NJ: Analytic Press, 1988).

[24] S. D. Moore, "Psychoanalytic Criticism," *The Bible, Literary Theory, and Cultural Criticism: A Roadmap to Contemporary Biblical Criticism* (ed. S. D. Moore and G. Phillips; New Haven: Yale University Press, 1993).

[25] I. N. Rashkow, *The Phallacy of Genesis: A Feminist-Psychoanalytic Approach* (Literary Currents in Biblical Interpretation; Louisville, KY: Westminster/ John Knox Press, 1993).

[26] G. Theissen, *Psychological Aspects of Pauline Theology* (Trans.J. P. Galvin; Philadelphia: Fortress, 1987).

[27] M. A. Tolbert, "Prodigal Son: An Essay in Literary Criticism from a Psychoanalytic Perspective," *Semeia* 9 (1977) 1-20.

[28] W. H.Wuellner and R. C. Leslie, *The Surprising Gospel: Intriguing Psychological Insights from the New Testament* (Nashville: Abingdon, 1984).

[29] Jung, *Letters, II* , 359.

creative psychic matrix out of which images, visions, ideas, and dreams (including some biblical materials) can emerge that are compensatory to consciousness in the service of an individuation process both individual and collective in scope. Second, Jung sees religion and all of its expressions and artifacts not simply as pathological, but as aboriginally and potentiably therapeutic and transformative. Third, and above all for our present purposes, Jung's life and work attest to dependence on, investment in, and commitment to the Bible, its world-picture and world-view, its archetypal images and symbols, and its interpretation in the modern world to a degree unparalleled in the life and work of any twentieth-century psychologist.[30] Freud might have developed his biblical "work" had time not run out.[31] But from beginning to end, Jung's life and work provide a basis for the development of a rationale, methodology, and agenda for the application of psychological insight to the history, text, and interpretation of the Bible.

Jung's influence is evidenced in the work of a number of psychologists and theologians who have applied Jung's thought to biblical interpretation: Eugen Drewermann and his monumental work, *Tiefenpsychologie und Exegese*,[32] which Ulrich Luz in his 1990 Sprunt Lectures characterized as "the most exciting event in the field of hermeneutics in the last decade";[33] David Cox's trail-breaking study in 1959, relating Paul's concept of "justification by faith" to the concept of individuation;[34] Edward Edinger's *The Bible and the Psyche*,[35] Peter Homans' extensive work on Jungian hermeneutics;[36] the work of Elizabeth Boyden Howes and Sheila Moon of The Guild for Psychological Studies significant for Walter

---

[30] See the present author's article, "Psychology, Hermeneutics, and the Bible," which spells out the role of the Bible in Jung's life and work.

[31] Beyond Freud's psychological writings on biblical themes, e.g.*Moses and Monotheism*, is a long-lasting interest in the Bible, along with his well-known fascination with Michelangelo's "Moses" in Rome. Freud reports that an "early preoccupation with the biblical stories, when I had scarcely learned the art of reading, defined in an enduring fashion the direction of my interest" (cf. Scharfenberg, *Sigmund Freud and His Critique of Religion* , 27). According to one commentator, Freud had planned to use *Moses and Monotheism* as the first in a series of works applying psychoanalytic theory to the entire Bible (H. L. Philp, *Freud and Religious Belief* [New York: Pitman Publishing Corp., 1956] 92).

[32] E.Drewermann, *Tiefenpsychologie und Exegese: Die Wahrheit der Formen: Traum, Mythos, Märchen, Sage, und Legende, Vol. 1; Tiefenpsychologie und Exegese: Die Wahrheit der Werke und der Worte: Wunder, Vision, Weissagung, Apokalypse, Geschichte, Gleichnis* , Vol. 2. (Olten/Freiburg: Walter, 1984).

[33] U. Luz, *Matthew in History: Interpretation, Influence, and Effects* (Minneapolis: Fortress, 1994) 9. He cites K. Berger, *Hermeneutik des Neuen Testaments* (Gütersloh: G. Mohn, 1988), 132, that Drewermann's works "really challenge an exegesis that . . . has rendered our religious experiences homeless."

[34] D. Cox, *Jung and St. Paul: A Study of the Doctrine of Justification by Faith and its Relation to the Concept of Individuation* (New York: Association Press, 1959).

[35] E. Edinger, *The Bible and the Psyche: Individuation Symbolism in the Old Testament* (Toronto: Inner City Books, 1986).

[36] E. g., "Psychology and Hermeneutics: Jung's Contribution." *Zygon* 4 (1969) and *Jung in Context: Modernity and the Making of a Psychology* (Chicago: University of Chicago Press, 1979).

Wink;[37] and the wide range of research reflected in the work of Morton Kelsey,[38] John Sanford,[39] David L. Miller,[40] Antonio Moreno,[41] Murray Stein,[42] Trevor Watt,[43] and Heinz Westman,[44] to which list must be added a growing number of *biblical scholars*, e.g. Schuyler Brown,[45] Adela Yarbro Collins,[46] James Goss,[47] Maria Kassel,[48] D. Andrew Kille,[49] Diarmuid McGann,[50] Gerd Theissen,[51] Michael Willett Newheart,[52] Walter Wink,[53] Wilhelm Wuellner,[54] and my own exploratory work on *Jung and the Bible*.[55]

[37] W. Wink, *Transforming Bible Study* (Nashville: Abingdon, 1980). See the dedication to Elizabeth Boyden Howes and the reference to the Guild for Psychological Studies in the "Acknowledgements," 5, 7.

[38] E.g., *Dreams: The Dark Speech of the Spirit* (New York: Doubleday, 1968) and *Christianity as Psychology: The Healing Power of the Christian Message* (Minneapolis: Augsburg, 1986) from among an extensive list of publications. Kelsey and John Sanford are the preeminent interpreters of Jungian thought for laity and clergy on the American scene.

[39] Four representative works from Sanford's extensive bibliography are *The Kingdom Within* (Philadelphia: Lippincott, 1970); *The Man Who Wrestled with God: Light from the Old Testament on the Psychology of Individuation* (King of Prussia, PA: Religious Publishing Co., 1974; Ramsey, NJ: Paulist Press, 1981); *Mystical Christianity: A Psychological Commentary on the Gospel of John* (New York: Crossroad, 1993); *King Saul, The Tragic Hero: A Study in Individuation* (New York: Paulist, 1985).

[40] D. L. Miller, ed., *Jung and the Interpretation of the Bible* (New York: Continuum, 1995).

[41] A. Moreno, *Jung, Gods, and Modern Man* (Notre Dame, IN: University of Notre Dame Press, 1970).

[42] M. Stein, *Jung's Treatment of Christianity: The Psychotherapy of a Religious Tradition* (Peru, IL: Chiron Publications, 1985); Stein and R. Moore, eds. *Jung's Challenge to Contemporary Religion* (Wilmette, IL: Chiron, 1987).

[43] T. Watt, "Joseph's Dreams," *Jung and the Interpretation of the Bible*, 55-70.

[44] H. Westman, *The Springs of Creativity: The Bible and the Creative Process of the Psyche* (Peru, IL: Chiron Publications, 1961); *The Structure of Biblical Myths: The Ontogenesis of the Psyche* (Dallas, TX: Spring Publications, 1983).

[45] S. Brown, "The Beloved Disciple: A Jungian View," *The Conversation Continues: Studies in Paul and John in Honor of J. Louis Martyn* (ed. R. T. Fortna and B. R. Gaventa; Nashville: Abingdon, 1990) 388-99.

[46] A. Y. Collins, *Crisis and Catharsis: The Power of the Apocalypse* (Philadelphia: Westminster, 1984).

[47] L. H. Martin and J. Goss, eds., *Essays on Jung and the Study of Religion* (Lanham, MD: University Press of America, 1985).

[48] M. Kassel, *Biblische Urbilder Tiefenpsychologische Auslegung nach C. G. Jung*, Vol. 147 (Munich: Pfeiffer-Werkbücher, 1982).

[49] D. A. Kille, "Jacob -- A Study in Individuation," *Jung and the Interpretation of the Bible*, 40-54.

[50] D. McGann, *Journeying Within Transcendence: A Jungian Perspective on the Gospel of John* (New York: Paulist, 1988).

[51] G. Theissen, *Psychological Aspects of Pauline Theology* (Philadelphia: Fortress, 1987).

[52] M. W. Newheart, "Johannine Symbolism," *Jung and the Interpretation of the Bible*, 71-91.

[53] W. Wink, "On Wrestling with God: Using Psychological Insights in Biblical Study," *Religion in Life* 47 (1978) 136-47.

[54] W. H. Wuellner and R. C. Leslie, *The Surprising Gospel: Intriguing Psychological Insights from the New Testament* (Nashville: Abingdon, 1984).

[55] Atlanta: John Knox Press, 1983.

One should add that the battery of critical strategies that have developed in biblical studies since the 70's (e.g. structural, rhetorical, narrative, and reader-response criticism, along with feminist, ideological, deconstructionist, canonical, and social criticism) have occasionally employed psychological models and tapped the vast repertory of psychological and psychoanalytic assumptions that established residence in Western culture as a whole, just as they have adopted assumptions, methodologies, and models that have become common cultural property from the fields of anthropology, sociology, philosophy, linguistics, and literary theory. But as Daniel and Aline Patte point out with respect to their research in "structural exegesis," although their goal has been to explore the "subconscious framework" of the "semantic universe" within which "the user of these systems of signs lives and thinks," they make "no pretense" of offering "an objective description of the manner in which aspects of the meaning of a narrative are produced and apprehended by the human mind; it is simply a *representation* of these phenomena".[56] As the Patte volume seems to imply, the task of describing the manner in which meaning is produced and apprehended by the mind constitutes the agenda for a discrete sub-discipline dedicated to a psychological-critical approach.

II. Agenda

What then is the nature and agenda of a psychological-critical approach to scripture? I would like to submit a thesis: *The goal of a psychological-critical approach is to examine texts (including their origination, authorship, and modes of expression, their construction, transmission, translation, reading, and interpretation, their transposition into kindred and alien art forms, and the history of their personal and cultural effect) as expressions of the structure, processes, and habits of the human psyche, both in individual and collective manifestations, past and present.*

Fleshing out this thesis in terms of a specific research agenda suggests five fruitful areas of inquiry and exploration: (1) *Forschungsgeschichte*, or history of research in the field of biblical psychology; (2) the development of a psychological theory and model as presuppositional for psychological criticism; (3) the contribution of psychological-criticism to biblical exegesis; (4) the contribution of psychological-criticism to biblical hermeneutics,and (5) the contribution of psychological criticism to *Wirkungsgeschichte*, or the "history of [biblical] effects."

1. *Forschungsgeschichte*. One suspects that when F. C. Grant issued his call for a "psychological study of the Bible," he was unaware of a discipline of "biblical psychology" that had been alive and well in the eighteenth, nineteenth,

---

[56]D. and A. Patte, *Structural Exegesis: From Theory to Practice* (Minneapolis: Fortress, 1978) 7, 12.

and twentieth centuries. When Franz Delitzsch, the eminent Hebrew scholar at the University of Leipzig, published the second edition of his *System der Biblischen Psychologie* in 1861, he acknowledged that he stood on the shoulders of three earlier works on "biblical psychology," written between 1769 and 1848 by Magnus Roos, J. T. Beck, and J. G. F. Haussmann.[57] Their work in turn, according to Delitzsch, was rooted in a "biblical psychology" that traces back to the *Peri psychês kai sômatos ê noos* of Melito of Sardis (d. ca. CE 190), to Tertullian's (CE 160-225) *De Testimonio Animae*, *De Anima*, and *Apologeticum*, and to the writings of Augustine (CE 354-430), who is often called the "father of modern psychology"[58] or "the first modern psychologist."[59] The "psychologies" of these early church writers were forged out of the dialogue between the Bible and classical Aristotelian, Platonic, and Stoic philosophy on the question of the nature, origin, destiny and "powers" of the soul, as evidenced in a third-century tractate of Tertullian, a sixth-century treatise of Cassiodorus, and a sixteenth-century commentary of Philipp Melanchton, all of whom adopted the title of Aristotle's *De Anima* (Greek: *Peri psychês*) for their biblically-oriented discourses on the *psyche* or soul.[60]

The agenda of a psychological-critical *Forschungsgeschichte* would include, (i) in the first instance, a historical review of the twenty centuries of what Delitzsch called "biblical psychology" and which he characterized, not inappropriately, as "one of the oldest sciences of the church."[61] (ii) A second item on the historical agenda would be revisiting those late nineteenth- to mid-twentieth-century works that applied psychological theory to biblical interpretation and were routinely ignored by mainline biblical scholarship, as demonstrated in Werner Kümmel's 1972 survey of New Testament scholarship, which mentions neither their names nor their works, resorting simply to conventional caveats against "psychologizing." A sample list would include the treatments of biblical psychology by Roos, Beck, Haussmann, and Delitzsch, cited above, along with works such as George Waller's, *The Biblical View of the Soul* (1904), W. Sanday's, *Personality in Christ and in Ourselves* (1911), M. Scott Fletcher's 1912 volume on *The Psychology of the New Testament*, Granville Stanley Hall's *Jesus, the Christ, in the Light of Psychology* (1917), as well as Freud's *Moses and Monotheism* (1939), Jung's *Answer to Job* (1952), and Theodor Reik's "Psychoanalytic Studies of Biblical Exegesis" (1951) and *Mystery on the Mountain: The Drama of the Sinai Revelation* (1959). (iii) A third historical task

---

[57] M. F, Roos, *Fundamenta Psychologiae ex sacra Scriptura collecta* (1769); J. G. F. Haussmann, *Die biblische Lehre vom Mensche* (1848); J. T. Beck, *Umriss der biblischen Seelenlehre* (Stuttgart: Belser, 1843). Delitzsch also refers to the work of F. A. Carus, *Psychology of the Hebrews* (1809) and G. F. Seiler, *Animadversiones ad psychologiam sacram* (1778-1787).

[58] D. F. Stramara, O.S.B., "The Use of Psychology According to Vatican II." *The Pecos Benedictine* (March, 1990) 2-3.

[59] H. Misiak and V.S. Sexton, *History of Psychology* (New York: Grune & Stratton, 1966) 8.

[60] Delitzsch, 2-5.

[61] Delitzsch, 3.

would be the exploration of the theological/ philosophical origins of the term
"psychology," which first appeared in its Latin form, *psichologia*, in the writings
of Marco Marulic *circa* 1524, and was first used in the title of an academic lecture
by Philipp Melanchton, Luther's protégé, *circa* 1530. The fruit of such research,
pointing to the historic ties between theology and psychology, might provide the
basis, in the present climate of ferment within both disciplines, for further
discussion between the two as they explore the degree to which the human
psyche/soul is conceived as the central concern of both, with the possible
recognition that the common "applied" task of both is the *cura animarum*, the care
and cure of the *psyche*.

2. *Psychological Theory* . A daunting but necessary assignment for
psychological criticism will be working toward a coherent theoretical
psychological base for a psychological-critical approach to the text. In his article
on "Psychological Interpretation" in the 1990 British publication, *A Dictionary of
Biblical Interpretation*, David Miell cites five weaknesses in the turn of the century
psychological approaches to scripture that soured mainline biblical scholarship
toward such approaches. First, these approaches lacked a systematic and coherent
set of well-articulated theories; second, they focused on abnormalities, e.g. the
personality of Job, the Messianic consciousness of Jesus, or the conversion of Paul;
third, they assumed, naively, that the psychological data supplied in Scripture was
historically reliable, not being privy to the results of historical criticism in biblical
scholarly circles; fourth, they were guilty of "psychologism," i.e. arbitrary and
speculative application of psychological theory to biblical interpretation; and fifth,
they were insufficiently aware of problems of cultural distance and of
reductionism.[62]   Although current psychological criticism would no longer be
susceptible to some of the faults Miell cites, it must still be consciously respectful
of the problems of cultural distance,[63] of reductionism, of "psychologizing," and
above all, of the need to attempt a systematic and coherent theoretical
psychological basis, as well as to attempt to advance a working model of the
human psyche whose habits psychological criticism would be enlisted to observe.

The danger of psychologizing has been addressed by Walter Wink,[64] and the
problem of reductionism was cited by Carl Jung as early as his 1922 essay "On the
Relation of Analytical Psychology to Poetry," speaking of the failed attempts at
psychological reductionism in art, literature, and religion. Jung writes that

[62] D. Miell, "Psychological Interpretation," *A Dictionary of Biblical Interpretation* (ed. R. J.
Coggins and J. L. Houlden; Philadelphia: Trinity Press International ,1990) 571-72.
[63] K. Berger, *Historische Psychologie des Neuen Testaments* (Stuttgart: Verlag Katholisches
Bibelwerk GmbH, 1991) expresses concern over the problem of historical distance and attempts to
construct an historical psychology of the New Testament with no presumptions about the applicability
of a first-century psychology to twentieth-century experience and perception.
[64] W. Wink, "The Dangers of Psychologizing in the Use of Psychoanalytic Insights in Biblical
Studies," paper delivered to the AAR-SBL Annual Meeting, Washington, D.C., 1974. . Also, "On
Psychologizing," *Transforming Bible Study: A Leader's Guide* (2nd rev. ed.; Nashville: Abingdon,
1989) 163-165.

> in the realm of religion . . . a psychological approach is permissible only in regard to the
> emotions and symbols which constitute the phenomenology of religion, but which do not
> touch upon its essential nature. If the essence of religion and art could be explained, then
> both of them would become mere subdivisions of psychology.

He adds, "If a work of art is explained in the same way as a neurosis, then either the work of art is a neurosis or a neurosis is a work of art." He concludes with the observation that "psychology has only a modest contribution to make toward a deeper understanding of the phenomena of life and is no nearer than its sister sciences to absolute knowledge."[65]

The problem of attempting a systematic theoretical psychological basis as well as advancing a working model of the human psyche is especially difficult in view of the fact that until recently, few mainline psychologists, aside from psychotherapists, have been willing to speak of the *psyche* as an object susceptible to empirical examination or description. To undertake such a task for the psychological criticism of Scripture would require rejoining the efforts of Aristotle, Tertullian, and Augustine, as well as of Jung and Freud, in the labor of constructing a unified model of the psychic structure, habits, and functions of human beings, toward the end of observing their influence and effect at work in the production, content, and interpretation of texts. The task of constructing such a model of the psyche is daunting, as Tertullian reminds us in his *De Anima*, citing the monition of Heraclitus, " You will never explore the furthest reaches of the soul, no matter how many roads you travel" (2,6). But the attempt must and is being made, as is evident not only in the Freudian and Jungian traditions, but also in recent philosophical psychological works by William Barrett in *Death of the Soul: From Descartes to the Computer* (1986)[66] and Richard Swinburne in his Gifford lectures, *The Evolution of the Soul* (1986),[67] as well as in contemporary psychophysiology as cited in a recent report on current thinking in the field of neuropsychology:

> As neurologists, psychologists and biologists have zeroed in more and more precisely
> on the physical causes of mental disorders, they have found themselves addressing a
> much deeper mystery, a set of interrelated conundrums probably as old as humanity:
> What, precisely, is the mind, the elusive entity where intelligence, decision making,
> perception, awareness and sense of self reside? Where is it located? How does it work?
> Does it arise form purely physical processes . . . ? Or is it something beyond the merely
> physical–something ethereal that might be close to the spiritual concept of the soul? [68]

---

[65] C. G. Jung, *The Collected Works of C. G. Jung*, Vol. XV (Bollingen Series; ed. G. Adler, *et al.*; Princeton: Princeton University, 1953-78) pars. 98-100.

[66] New York: Doubleday, 1986.

[67] Oxford: Clarendon, 1986.

[68] M. D. Lemonick, , J. M. Nash, A. Park, and J. Willwerth, "In Search of the Mind: Glimpses of the Brain," *Time* 146 (1995) 44.

3. *Exegesis*. One of the primary contributions of a psychological critical approach to exegesis resides in its vision of the text as a "psychic event." That is, *it views the text   not only as the product of historical, social, and literary processes, but as the product of a psychic process or processes in which the nature and habits of the human psyche, both in its conscious and unconscious fields of operation, are at work in the authors of the text, their communities, and historical settings, as well as in those of the readers and interpreters*. Exegesis undertaken from such a psychological-critical perspective has focused, to date, on four aspects of the "world of the text"[69]: (a) biblical symbols and archetypal images; (b) psychodynamic factors at work in biblical narrative and discourse; (c) biblical personality portraits; and (d) the psychological description and analysis of biblical religious phenomena. In addition (e) psychological criticism will train its eye on the "world behind the text," inquiring into the unconscious factors at work in the history of the text, its authors, and the community in which the text has been emerged.

a) Work done to date on a psycho-critical approach to *biblical symbols and archetypal images* includes E. R. Goodenough's ground-breaking work on *Jewish Symbols in the Greco-Roman Period* (1953-1968),[70] Patrick Henry's essay on "Water, Bread, Wine" (1979),[71] Michael Willett Newheart's essay on "Johannine Symbolism," Schuyler Brown's essay on "The Myth of Sophia" (1995),[72] and the prodigious work of Eugen Drewermann on "depth psychology and exegesis."

A psychological-critical approach to symbol will not only examine the catalytic effect that symbols can occasion in the human intellect, conscience, and will; it will also explore the psychological hypothesis that access to the value that certain symbols and archetypal images exercise in ancient texts and authors depends in part on a comparative symbology. Such a comparative symbology is predicated on the assumption of a "collective unconscious" that informs the constancy of value that is often mediated by a given symbol (e.g. water, light, bread, wine, serpent, fire) in various cultural settings. Walter Wink speaks to this point in observing that archetypal images appear

> so frequently in widely scattered mythic traditions that we are justified in regarding ... [them] as a standard component in spiritual development. The very pervasiveness of such stories ... is evidence that we are dealing with something fundamental to the

---

[69]The phrases, "the world of the text," along with "the world behind the text" and "the world in front of the text," capture the distinctive differences between exegesis, historical-archeological-cultural criticism, and hermeneutics respectively, and they have been adopted by a number of specialists in biblical interpretation, e.g. S. M. Schneiders, *The Revelatory Text: Interpreting the New Testament as Sacred Scripture* (San Francisco: Harper San Francisco, 1991) and W. R. Tate, *Biblical Interpretation: An Integrated Approach* (Peaabody, MA: Hendrickson, 1991).

[70]New York: Pantheon, 1953-68. Vol. 4 provides Goodenough's psychological presuppositions on the nature of symbols and their interpretation.

[71]"Water, Bread, Wine: Patterns in Religion," *New Directions in New Testament Study*, (Philadelphia: Westminster, 1979) 203-224.

[72]In *Jung and the Interpretation of the Bible*, 71-91 and 92-101.

spiritual journey itself, and not merely with etiological legends invented to " explain the origin of things."[73]

This observation suggests that one of the tasks for psychological criticism is to expand the existing collection of comparative archeological, linguistic, and historical data that biblical scholars have gathered in lexicons and handbooks, with the addition of comparative mythological and symbolic data recorded in statuary, paintings, texts, and inscriptions, collected by anthropologists, mythologists, and historians of religion, toward the end of extending our understanding and expectation of the range of potentiable values a given image found in the Bible but occurring in other religious and cultural settings can register in the human psyche. As John Dominic Crossan suggested some years ago, "The full study of a biblical text . . . will demand in the future as much use, for example of James Pritchard's magisterial *Ancient Near Eastern Texts and Pictures* as of Stith Thompson's equally magisterial *Motif-Index of Folk-Literature.*"[74]

b) To examine *psycho-dynamic factors at work in biblical texts* is to observe the way in which biblical narratives or discursive scenarios seem to exhibit established models of the nature, habits, procedures, and developmental patterns of the human psyche (e.g. the patterns of repression, projection, sublimation, transference, extraversion, introversion, rationalization, defense mechanism, or on a larger scale, patterns of individuation or other models of psychological ontogeny). Examples of this approach are to be found in the work of Francoise Dolto and Gérard Séverin, *The Jesus of Psychoanalysis: A Freudian Interpretation of the Gospel* (1979),[75] Dorothy Zeligs, *Moses: A Psychodynamic Study* (1986),[76] and most recently, D. Andrew Kille's masterful analysis of the Jacob saga in "Jacob–A Study in Individuation"(1995).[77]

c) Recent psychological-critical studies of *biblical personality portraits* have yielded promising psychological and even psychoanalytic observations. Though a psychoanalysis of biblical figures in the strictest sense is theoretically ruled out given the absence of the analysand, a number of recent studies have suggested that psychoanalytic observations in the hands of seasoned analysts can provide meaningful and compelling insight into the psychodynamic factors at work in the character construct of certain biblical personality portraits. Though early psycho-critical analyses of biblical figures focused on Jesus of Nazareth,[78] later

[73] W. Wink, "On Wrestling with God," 142.

[74] "Perspectives and Methods in Contemporary Biblical Criticism," *Biblical Research* 22 (1977) 45.

[75] New York: Doubleday, 1979. The treatment of the story of the Wedding at Cana (John 2: 1-12) is an especially rewarding example of this approach.

[76] New York: Human Sciences Press, 1986.

[77] In *Jung and the Interpretation of the Bible*, 40-54.

[78] Cf. H. Van de Kemp, "Psychologies of Jesus," *Psychology and Theology in Western Thought, 1672-1965: A Historical and Annotated Bibliography* (Bibliographies in the History of Psychology and Psychiatry; Millwood, New York: Kraus International Publications, 1984) 69-73.

studies approached the biblical portrait of Judas,[79] King Saul,[80] Paul, and Ezekiel,[82] fulfilling as it were an observation of Bernhard Anderson in his classic *Understanding the Old Testament*, that "Ezekiel *himself* was an unusual person whose psychic peculiarities make a fascinating psychological study."[83]

d) *The psychological description and analysis of biblical religious phenomena* constitutes a fifth major area of research for a psychological-critical agenda. The task will involve amplifying the work of sociologists, literary critics, theologians, and anthropologists with the insights of psychoanalysis, as well as of social, cognitive, behavioral, and developmental psychology, to explore the phenomena of inspiration, conversion, glossolalia, visions, *enthousiasmos*, demon possession, biblical dreams, ritual practices (footwashing, eucharist, burnt offering, purification rites), and psycho-spiritual experiential phenomena, e.g. sin, guilt, grace, forgiveness, salvation, redemption, and rebirth. Robin Scroggs writes that "salvation means changes, changes in how we think, in how we feel, in how we act. And that means, or so it seems to me, that psychological intuitions and, perhaps, even explicitly psychological models and terminology can give us insight into what these changes are . . . . " [84] Groundwork has been laid in this field by two journals in particular, *The Journal of Psychology and Theology* and *The Journal of Psychology and Christianity*, along with a range of studies on topics of perennial interest, e.g. conversion, mysticism, glossolalia, and dreams.

e) A presupposition of a psycho-critical exegesis is that the text emerges from conscious and unconscious depths in the author, the author's personal history, the author's communal history, and the history of the species, albeit realities to which the text itself rarely makes conscious reference. Understanding the text from a psycho-critical perspective would urge the unconcealing of these conscious and unconscious factors. Carl Jung alludes to such dimensions of the text in speaking of the unconscious substratum of the text's pre-Christian or pre-Israelite consciousness. He writes, "Everything has its history, everything has 'grown,' and Christianity, which is supposed to have appeared suddenly as a unique revelation from heaven, undoubtedly also has its history. . . . It is exactly as if we had built a cathedral over a pagan temple and no longer knew that it is still there underneath."[85] One of the tasks of psycho-critical exegesis is to make way for such

[79] A. Nicole, *Judas the Betrayer: A Psychological Study of Judas Iscariot* (Grand Rapids, MI: Baker Book House, 1924/1957).

[80] J. A. Sanford, *King Saul, The Tragic Hero: A Study in Individuation* (New York: Paulist, 1985).

[81] T. Callan, *Psychological Perspectives on the Life of Paul: An Application of the Methodology of Gerd Theissen* (Studies in the Bible and Early Christianity 22; Lewiston: Edwin Mellen, 1990).

[82] D. Halperin, *Seeking Ezekiel* .

[83] B. W. Anderson, *Understanding the Old Testament* (4th ed; Englewood Cliffs, NJ: Prentice-Hall, 1986) 429.

[84] "Psychology as a Tool," 336.

[85] C. G. Jung, *Psychological Reflections: A New Anthology of His Writings, 1905-1961*, (Bollingen Series, 31; ed. J. Jacobi and R. F. C. Hull; Princeton: Princeton University Press, 1953) 342;

facts in the mind of the exegete in order to expand the horizons of exegetical expectations of the text.

4. *Hermeneutics*. The focus of hermeneutics is the "world in front of the text," approaching it with a three-fold question: "What is it for a text to occasion meaning?" "What is it to read and understand texts?" and "What is it to interpret texts?"[86] Psychological criticism focuses on each of these questions with the presupposition that all three activities involve psychic factors, both conscious and unconscious, at work in texts, in readers, and in the interpretive performances of texts.

a.) *Texts*. A psycho-critical hermeneutic will approach texts with at least two concerns, "how texts effect meaning" and "how texts can mask the specialized interests of their authors."

Paul Ricoeur addresses the first of these with his interest in the creative and productive power of symbol, metaphor, and narrative[87] and in the "surplus" of meaning, or in Wolfgang Iser's perspective, "open spaces" that verbal images produce, rarely if ever conveying a single or univocal meaning. A psycho-critical hermeneutic will ponder the plenitude of meaning in biblical language with an eye to conscious and unconscious associations imported into the text by the author and to the psychological process by which they are triggered in the reader by the text.[88]

Carl Jung's theory of archetypal imagery as compensatory to consciousness and as native to the collective unconscious of both author and reader is helpful in comprehending the catalytic effect a biblical text can exercise on a reader, activating conscience, will, affect, conation, and imagination, and often propelling the reader into a course of creative, moral, or on occasion, even destructive action. The task of psychological-critical research is to note such "events" and to develop strategies for their analysis in the attempt to identify what in the text has catalytic force and what in the reader is susceptible to textual overtures.[89]

---

from multigraphed copies of Jung's Basel Seminar, 1934.

[86] This definition amplifies that of A. C.Thiselton, *New Horizons in Hermeneutics: The Theory and Practice of Transforming Bible Reading* (Grand Rapids, MI: Zondervan, 1992), 1: "What it is to read, to interpret, or to understand texts."

[87] Thiselton on Ricoeur, 14.

[88] S. Moore reminds us via Jacques Derrida and Jacques Lacan of Freud's observation that "the unconscious is itself irreducibly 'literary' in its workings," which leads to the consideration of the shaping of literary genres as a function of the unconscious. S. D. Moore, "Deconstructive Criticism: The Gospel of the Mark," *Mark & Method: New Approaches in Biblical Studies* (ed. J. C. Anderson and S. D. Moore; Minneapolis: Fortress, 1992) 98.

[89] Cf. chapter IV, "Biblical Symbols: The Vocabulary of the Soul," and chapter V, "Biblical Archetypes and the Story of the Self" in the author's *Jung and the Bible* (Atlanta: John Knox, 1983) 56-92.

Similarly, psychological criticism will want to explore the psychological dimensions of Hans Georg Gadamer's fruitful suggestion that texts can transform and enlarge the horizon of readers,[90] and of Gerd Theissen's observations on the cognitive restructuring or revisioning of reality occasioned by the biblical text.[91]

Another focus of a psycho-critical hermeneutic would be rooted in the Freudian-grounded "hermeneutics of suspicion" introduced by Ricoeur, with its insistence that "the human mind can deceive itself in varieties of ways, often in the interest of individual or of social power."[92] Joining forces with ideological criticism, along with Latin American, African-American, and feminist critiques, it would examine the degree to which the biblical text can covertly serve specialized, and often self-serving, interests of its authors (and interpreters).

b.) *The Reader*. As an addendum to "reader response criticism,"[93] with its analysis of the role of the reader in the "creation" or "production" of meaning, a psycho-critical approach to the reader would reassess Schleiermacher's contrast "between the grammatical and psychological axes of hermeneutics," noting the collaboration of objective criticism, on the one hand, and a "feminine" creative, intuitive response, on the other, in arriving at an understanding of the text.[94]

It would also inquire into the "psychological type" or mind set of the reader insofar as it affects interpretation. Cedric Johnson did ground-breaking work in this area, in *The Psychology of Biblical Interpretation*,[95] exploring the degree to which the presuppositions of biblical scholars affect the results of exegesis. Jung introduced a four-fold typology of thinking, feeling, sensing, and intuitive types, coming to grips with the fact that the hermeneutical event engages not only the intellectual function of the psyche, but the conative, intuitive, moral, spiritual, sensuous, and affective functions as well, suggesting that the meaning of a text may be opaque to a reader unless he or she adopts a mode of apprehension commensurate to the "type" of intention being conveyed. "Thinking," for example, will assist a reader in solving biblical riddles and unravelling rabbinic arguments in Paul's epistles but will not exploit the dimensions of meaning that the "sense" function taps in reading the Song of Solomon or the story of the Gadarene demoniac shrieking among the tombs. Likewise without the "feeling" function, the words of the Deuteronomic law code or Isaiah's "Holy, Holy, Holy" leave the reader untouched by the moral imperative of the text. Such an approach also

---

[90] Thiselton on Gadamer, pp. 7-10.

[91] Cf. Theissen's chapter 3, "The Cognitive Approach: Religion as Construction of an Interpreted World," *Psychological Aspects of Pauline Theology*, 29-39.

[92] Thiselton on Ricoeur, Freud, Marx, and Nietzsche, 14.

[93] Cf. excellent introductions to the application of Reader Response criticism to New Testament interpretation in E. V. McKnight, "Reader-Response Criticism," *To Each Its Own Meaning: An Introduction to Biblical Criticisms and Their Application* (ed. S. L. McKenzie and S. R. Haynes; Louisville, KY: Westminster/John Knox, 1993) 197-220; and R. M. Fowler, "Reader-Response Criticism: Figuring Mark's Reader," *Mark and Method*, 50-83.

[94] Thiselton 24, 558-562.

[95] Grand Rapids: Zondervan, 1983.

revives psychological interest in the rabbinic and medieval modes of biblical interpretation, the literal, allegorical, moral, and tropological, as "psychologically sound" strategies for appropriating the multiple, metarational meanings of the text. Along with analysis of various socio-cultural interpretive styles, from Asian to African-American and feminist interpretations, consideration will have to be given not only to the extent that specialized approaches skew the text, but also to the extent to which such approaches catalyze meanings resident in the text to which other approaches are impervious.

c.) *Textual performance.* A third hermeneutical interest of psychological criticism is the mode of "performance" by which the meaning that is "heard" in the text is conveyed. Tzvetan Todorov speaks of an "input text" of the author and the "output text" of the interpreter.[96] Traditionally, we are inclined to expect the form of interpretation to be literal and even rational, as the text is assumed to be. But as Frances Young has observed, the "actualization of textual meaning" is analogous to the "performance of music and art" [97] and in fact has, throughout the history of Judaeo-Christianity, been mediated through both. The psychological justification for amplifying the meaning of the text in non-verbal, imaginative, artistic, liturgical forms, is that the text contains and occasions unconscious meanings resident in the author and the author's tradition and potential in the reader and his or her community, that can be lured out through modes of interpretation other than rational, verbal discourse. Jung once commented, "Often the hands know how to solve a riddle with which the intellect has wrestled in vain."[98] The method of smoking out these largely unconscious factors in text and reader is suggested by the psychoanalytic strategies of free association (Freud) and the techniques of "amplification" and "active imagination" (Jung), which, in essence, have been operative within the Judaeo-Christian tradition for centuries in sermons, midrashic commentary, Bible study groups, preaching, teaching, and the artistic elaboration of the meaning of the text in miracle plays, liturgies, cantatas, soup kitchens, stained glass windows, paintings, and statuary that have been seized upon by the psyche as ways of amplifying and reimaging the meaning of the text.[99] This same process is at work in the biblical text itself as is visible in the prodigious production of myth, legend, psalm, religious tale, parable, hymn, and apocalypse in response to "texts," oral or written, received by the biblical authors. Three millenia of biblical interpretation provide a vast data base for psychological criticism to observe the way in which texts have been "performanced" in the

---

[96] T. Todorov, *Symbolism and Interpretation* (Ithaca: Cornell University Press, 1982); cited by Thiselton, 22.

[97] F. Young, *The Art of Performance: Towards a Theology of Holy Scripture* (London: Darton, Longman, and Todd, 1990); cited in Thiselton, 3.

[98] *Collected Works*, Vol. 8, par. 180.

[99] Wink, in *Transforming Bible Study: A Leader's Guide*, provides models of "active imagination" in biblical interpretation, as do also the Ignatian Exercises and *lectio divina* in their amplifications of the meaning of the text for the life of the reading community.

communities and the dimensions of the text that have been generated or "unconcealed" in the process, as well as to document the resourcefulness of the psyche in amplifying the proleptic power of biblical images and symbols, personally and collectively.

5. *Wirkungsgeschichte.* Borrowing a phrase from Gadamer, a sixth task on the psychological-critical agenda is the study of the "history of effects" of the biblical text at the psycho-spiritual level, individually and corporately, pathogenically and therapeutically.[100] In his article "The Study of Religion and the Study of the Bible," Wilfred Cantwell Smith issues a similar call, envisioning a new generation of biblical scholars specially bred to study what he calls the *Nachleben* or "continuing history" of the text, identifying the forces, for good and for ill, that Scripture has unleashed in its historical wake. To date, the research on the *pathogenic effect of the biblical text* is barely begun, though work has been done on the biblical roots of racial prejudice, violence, and anti-Semitism, and on the origins of child abuse.[101] The *therapeutic effect* of the Bible, however, has been amply noted, by the kerygmatic proclamations of religious institutions, by psychologists like Jung, who maintained that "religions are psychotherapeutic systems in the truest sense of the word" whose literature provides a description of the individuation process "with an exactness that far surpasses our feeble efforts," and also by the work of pastoral counselors Donald Capps,[102] Wayne Oates,[103] and Carroll A. Wise,[104] who have written on the role of the Bible in psychiatry and pastoral counseling.

In conclusion, we note that Carl Jung in his autobiography, *Memories, Dreams, Reflections,* advanced the conviction that the goal of humanity, which includes the world of critical scholarship, is "to create more and more consciousness."[105] Psychological criticism would contribute to that assignment, in the train of the promethean achievements of historical and literary criticism and in the company of the host of critical disciplines that have been spawned regularly over the past two decades, all in evidence of the seemingly endless virtuosity of the human psyche. As Gerd Theissen has observed with respect to New Testament scholarship:

---

[100] Cf. Luz, *Matthew in History*, 3.

[101] E.g., D. Capps, *The Child's Song: The Religious Abuse of Children* (Westminster/ John Knox, 1995); P. Greven, *Spare the Child: The Religious Roots of Punishment and the Psychological Impact of Physical Abuse* (New York: Knopf, 1991); A. Vergote, *Guilt and Desire: Religious Attitudes and Their Pathological Derivatives* (New Haven: Yale University Press, 1988); J. G. Williams, *The Bible, Violence, and the Sacred: Liberation from the Myth of Sanctioned Violence* (Valley Forge, PA: Trinity Press International, 1995).

[102] D. Capps, *Biblical Approaches to Pastoral Counseling* (Philadelphia: Westminster, 1981).

[103] W. E. Oates, *The Bible in Pastoral Care* (Philadelphia: Westminster, 1953).

[104] C. A. Wise, *Psychiatry and the Bible* (New York: Harper & Row, 1956).

[105] (New York: Pantheon, 1963) 326.

We do not yet grasp what historical forces brought forth and determined early Christianity. But beside and within this external history there is an inner history . . . . Anyone who thinks that this religion can be illumined historically and factually without psychological reflection is just as much in error as one who pretends that everything about this religion can be said in this fashion.[106]

---

[106] Theissen, *Psychological Aspects of Pauline Theology*, 398.

Philantropia in Philo's Writings: Some Observations[1]

Peder Borgen
University of Trondheim

In Jewish sources the words φιλανθρωπία and φιλάνθρωπος occur in the apocryphal writings of the Septuagint, in the Aristeas Letter, in Josephus', and in Philo's writings.[2] In the New Testament one or the other word is found in Acts 27:3; 28:2; and Titus 3:4. Josephus employs the terms quite extensively, and in Philo the words are used spottily in various treatises and appear in a concentrated manner in the section Περὶ φιλανθρωπίας in the treatise *On the Virtues (Virt.)* 51-174. Philo makes the transition between the preceding treatise, *On the Special Laws (Spec.)*, Book 4, and *Virt.* in this way: "The subject of justice and all the relevant points which the occasion requires have already been discussed, and I will take courage next in the sequence" (*Virt.* 1). The next virtue,

---

[1] It was my privilege to be a research fellow at Drew University, Madison, New Jersey from 1953 to 1956. During those years the University's Graduate School was founded. Those were stimulating and rewarding years due to an outstanding faculty as well as due to the inspiring intellectual and personal fellowship which flourished among the graduate students in residence. John Priest ranked high among these, with his keen mind, his ability to raise basic and critical questions, his sense of humor and his openness and concern for his fellow students, overseas students included. Since then we have recalled these good memories when we have met at conferences and symposia. Moreover, I have benefitted from his outstanding scholarship in Jewish studies as well as in his other areas of research. I am happy to have been given this opportunity to express my appreciation by contributing this essay to the *Festschrift* in his honor.

[2] U. Luck, "φιλανθρωπία κτλ," *TWNT*, 9 (1970) 109-10.

love of human beings, φιλανθρωπία, is introduced in § 51: "The next subject to be examined is φιλανθρωπία, the virtue closest akin to piety, its sister and twin."[3] The virtue repentance follows in § 175: "Our most holy Moses, who loves virtue and goodness and loves in particular human beings (φιλάνθρωπος) . . . offers to the repentant . . . the high rewards of membership in the best of commonwealths . . ." Finally nobility is introduced in § 187: "Thus those who hymn nobility of birth . . ." Of the 227 paragraphs in *Virt.*, courage receives 50 paragraphs; love of human beings, φιλανθρωπία, 123; repentance, 11; and nobility, 40 paragraphs. Thus the section on φιλανθρωπία receives the most comprehensive treatment. Philo here gives a characterization of Moses and several of his laws in Exodus, Leviticus, Numbers, and Deuteronomy to illustrate the subject matter.

Introduction

In the present study Philo's usage will be discussed, and material from other sources, Jewish or Greek, will be utilized to throw light upon Philo's usage. The essay "Philo's Ethical Theory" by D. Winston may serve as a convenient point of departure. He writes about Middle Stoa: "It was only the Middle Stoa, in the writings of Panaetius and Antiochus, through a fusion of the Stoic notion of *oikeioisis* and the Peripatetic doctrine of *oikeiotes*, that an all-embracing doctrine of human unity took shape."[4] He maintains that Philo's thoughts on *philanthropia* are based on the idea of human's kinship with God and correspondingly on a universalistic concept of humanity: "'All we men,' writes Philo, 'are kinsmen and brothers, being related by the possession of an ancient kinship, since we receive the lot of the rational nature from one mother' (*Questions and Answers on Genesis (QG)* 2:60; cf. *On the Decalogue (Dec.)* 41; *The Worse Attacks the Better (Det.)* 164; *Spec.* 4:14)."[5] Winston concludes his discussion of Philo's ideal of *philanthropia* by considering its implications for the biblical doctrine of election, and he states that Philo, at every possible opportunity, emphasizes the universal aspects of Jewish particularism.[6]

Against this background the following points serve as hypotheses for the present study:

1. In Philo's use of *philanthropia* two frames of references are seen: a) To Philo the most important thought-categories are: God, Moses, God's people, proselytes and settlers, irrational animals, and plants; b) There is an interplay and

---

[3] In this transitional statement Philo may be referring to a section on "piety." If so, that section is now lost. See L. Cohn, et al. (eds. trans.), *Philo von Alexandria. Die Werke in deutscher Übersetzung*, 2 (Berlin 1962, 1. ed. Breslau, 1910) 315. In this essay the English translation of Philo's writings are in general drawn from F. H. Colson and G. H. Whitaker (eds. trans.), *Philo with an English Translation (Loeb)*, 1-10 (Cambridge, Mass., 1929-62) and R. Marcus (trans.), *Philo. Supplement* 1: *Questions and Answers on Genesis*; 2: *Questions and Answers on Exodus (Loeb)* (Cambridge, Mass., 1953).

[4] D. Winston,"Philo's Ethical Theory," in *ANRW* II:21:1 (Berlin, 1984) 392.

[5] Winston, 393; cf. F. Geiger, *Philon von Alexandreia als sozialer Denker* (Stuttgart, 1932) 7-9.

[6] D. Winston, "Philo's Ethical Theory," 398.

partly a tension between this frame of reference and the thought-categories of God, human beings, animals, and plants. In Philo's works the Greek concepts of the virtues, in casu *philanthropia*, have been made to interpret aspects of the laws of Moses, and thereby of the Jewish religion.

2. Several concerns are at work in Philo's presentation of *philanthropia*: there are apologetic, systematic, and theological motifs.

3. Although the distinction is drawn between God's people and others, and between humans and animals, the concept of *philanthropia* may mean a reaching out across the boundaries, although without these boundaries being obliterated.

4. In Philo's writings the concept of *philanthropia* in some contexts means benevolence, but it has often the broader meaning of fellowship-feeling and related attitudes.

5. Although central aspects of the concept are associated with the nature of God and with the picture of kings, there is also seen an influence from the understanding of humanity, as for example human qualities in contrast to those of the beasts. A universalistic perspective is in Philo's writings tied to the notion of the people of God being the center of humankind.

God – Moses – The People

Philanthropia characterizes God's relationship to human beings. This is seen:

a) when he revealed himself to Abraham, the Sage, who, as a proselyte, migrated from astrology and the Chaldean creed that the world itself was god, *On Abraham (Abr.)* 77-84: When it is said in Gen 12:7 that "God was seen (ὤφθη) by Abraham," it meant that God was not manifested (ἐμφανής) to him before, but that he, in his love for human beings and when the soul came into his presence, came and revealed his nature, so far as the beholder's power of sight would allow. As a result his name was changed from Abram to Abraham (Gen 17:5).[7]

b) when he, the King of kings, dwells in the soul as a palace-temple to show goodness to "our race," *On the Cherubim (Cher.)* 98-100: In Num 28:2 God gives regulations to Moses and the people about "bounties, and gifts and fruits which you shall observe and offer to me at my feasts." When Philo elaborates upon the word "feasts", he offers sharp criticism of the festal assemblies among the different nations, whether Greek or barbarian. As a contrast to the external temples, he speaks of the soul as a house of God: "What house shall be prepared for God the King of kings, the Lord of all, who in his tender mercy (δι' ἡμερότητα) and love of human beings (φιλανθρωπίαν) has deigned to come from the boundaries of heaven to the utmost ends of the earth, to show his goodness (ἐπ' εὐεργεσία) to

---

[7]This view that God's *philanthropia* brings about the initial revelation of God to a proselyte and the change in the person's situation and identity is an interesting parallel to the use of the term in Titus 3:3-7.

our race (τοῦ γένους ἡμῶν)?" (*Cher.* 99). The answer is: the soul that is fitted to receive him.[8]

c) when, in *Virt.* 77, God's love of humanity is in particular directed to the twelve tribes. Here it is told that Moses offered his benedictions to the tribes of the nation (Deut 33), and Philo adds his own comment: One ought to believe that these benedictions will be fulfilled, because Moses who gave them was beloved of God, the lover of human beings (φιλάνθρωπος) and those for whom he asked held the highest rank in the army led by the maker and Father of all.

d) when God's love meets the needs of human beings (corresponding to the behavior of an ideal king), *On Noah's Work as Planter (Plant.)* 90-92: When Jacob said "And the Lord shall be to me for God" (Gen 28:21), it meant that God as a king in his love for human beings makes it his delight to supply what is lacking (τὸ ἐνδεές) in each one.

e) when specific needs, such as hunger, are met by God, *On the Life of Moses (Mos.)* 1:191-208: Philo paraphrases and elaborates upon the giving of the manna, Exod 16, and writes in § 198 that God was moved by the clemency and love to human beings that belongs to his nature (διὰ τὴν σύμφυτον ἐπιείκειαν καὶ φιλανθρωπίαν) and took pity on them and healed their sufferings.

f) when the angels, as the "words" of God, οἱ τοῦ θεοῦ λόγοι, descend as helpers, *Somn.* 1:146-47: Here Philo internalizes the biblical story about Jacob's ladder, Gen 28, to mean the "logoi" that ascend and descend between the heavenly mind and the earthly sense-perception. They descend out of love for human beings and compassion (διὰ φιλανθρωπίαν καὶ ἔλεον) for our race (τοῦ γένους ἡμῶν), to be helpers and comrades, in order that with the healing of their breath they may quicken into new life in the soul.

The background for the use of *philanthropia* in these passages is the fact that already in Greek usage the term characterized the attitudes and behavior of the gods (for example Hermes, Eros, and Demeter) towards human beings (Aristophanes, *Peace*, 392-93; Plato, *Symposium*, 189C; Plutarch, *Moralia* 758AB; Apollonius of Tyana, *Epistle* 75:55K).[9] When Philo in *Cher.* 98-100 and *Plant.* 90-92 pictures God as king and tells that as king he acts in his love of human beings, he had as background Hellenistic ideas of kingship. Philo himself provides examples of this use when he in *On the Embassy to Gaius (Legat.)* 67 and 73 tells about the *philanthropia* of the emperor Gaius Caligula and in *Legat.* 158 of the emperor Augustus.[10]

---

[8] Cf. the similar thought in *Virt.* 188.

[9] See J. Schmidt, "Philanthropos (φιλάνθρωπος), Götterbeiname," in *Pauly-Wissowa*, 19A (1938) col. 2125; R. Hirzel, *Plutarch* (Leipzig, 1912) 23-24; U. Luck, "φιλανθρωπία κτλ," 107-08; R. le Déaut, "Φιλανθρωπία dans la Littérature Grecque jusqu'au Nouveau Testament (Tite III, 4)," *Mélanges Eugène Tisserant,* 1: *Écriture Sainte - Ancien Orient,* (Rome, 1964) 256-60; H. D. Betz (ed.), *Plutarch's Ethical Writings and Early Christian Literature* (Leiden, 1978) 480-91.

[10] See further U. Luck, "φιλανθρωπία κτλ," 108-10; R. le Déaut, "Φιλανθρωπία, 264, 267-68; B. Due, *The Cyropaedia. Xenophon's Aims and Method* (Aarhus, 1989) 163-70.

Picturing Moses as the paradigm of φιλανθρωπία, Philo first refers to his two treatises on the life of Moses in which he sets forth the actions that Moses performed from his earliest years to old age for the care for each single person and for them all, *Virt.* 52. Then Philo illustrates Moses' royal and paradigmatic role further by reporting on biblical events related to the end of his life, such as the appointment of his successor, Joshua (Num 27:16-23; Deut 33:7, 23), his hymnic song to God (Deut 32:1-43), and the benedictions offered on the twelve tribes (Deut 32), *Virt.* 55-79. Moses should give the election of his successor to God alone, especially since the person appointed would preside over the nation that is a suppliant of him who truly exists and is the most populous of all the nations upon earth (*Virt.* 64).

Philo characterizes Moses' unselfish and pious way of selecting his successor, as "proof of the love of man and faithfulness which he showed to his whole tribe (δεῖγμα τῆς πρὸς ἅπαν τὸ ὁμόφυλον αὐτοῦ φολανθρωπίας καὶ πίστεως; *Virt.* 66).[11] Philo concludes his characterization of Moses as a paradigm in this way: "We have stated the proofs of the legislator's *philanthropia* and fellowship-feeling (τὰ δείγματα τῆς τοῦ νομοθέτου φιλανθρωπίας καὶ κοινωνίας) . . . , a quality which he possessed through a happy gift of natural goodness, and also as the outcome of the lessons which he learnt from the holy oracles (*Virt.* 80)." Thus Moses loved virtue, goodness, and humanity (*Virt.* 175).[12] It is worth noticing that Moses is not called the sage and the wise man (ὁ σόφος) in this section of *On the Virtues*, although that often is the case elsewhere in Philo's writings.[13]

Going one step further, Philo in different ways states that God's people, with their laws and worship, are the center of the world. In *Spec.* 2:166-67 he relates this idea to *philanthropia* without explicitly using this word itself. When other peoples went wrong and worshiped many gods, the error that the rest committed was corrected by the nation of Jews (τὸ ᾽Ιουδαίων ἔθνος), who chose to worship and serve the Uncreated and Eternal. This nation uses its prayers and festivals and first-fruit offerings as a means of supplication for the human race in general, and this demonstrates that the Jews do not have dislike of humankind (ἀπανθρωπία).

Philo can furthermore use the term *philanthropia* to characterize non-Jews. The Emperor Gaius Caligula's performance in the initial stage of his reign receives such a positive evaluation: "For as they [the multitude] had hoped that kindness and love for men (χρηστότητα γὰρ καὶ φιλανθρωπίαν) were established in his soul . . ." *(Legat.)* 73). The Emperor Augustus was fair in his treatment of the Jews.

---

[11] The idea of Moses' unselfishness when selecting his successor is also found in rabbinic writings. See *Sifre Num*, 138; *Midrash Shir* 1:10b-11a: Moses, being a truly pious man, thought when he saw his end approach, not of himself, but of the welfare of the community, for whom he implored a good and worthy leader.

[12] See further on Moses in M. van Veldhuizen, "Moses, a Model of Hellenistic Philanthropia," in *Reformed Review*, 38 (1985) 215-24.

[13] *Leg. all.* 2:87,93; 3:45,131,140f.,144,147; *Spec.* 2:194; 4:69,143,157,175, etc.

When the doles in Rome were distributed on the Sabbath, he ordered the dispensers to reserve for the Jews till the morrow the charity (φιλανθρώπια)" (*Legat.* 158).

Seemingly Philo goes even further, when relating the concept to human beings in general. In *Virt.* 81 he writes that, before dealing with *philanthropia* in relationship to animals, he will begin with humans. As it turns out, in *Virt.* 82 and subsequent paragraphs, the boundary between God's people and others is still basic since "the men" consist of the members of the same nation οἱ ὁμοεθνεῖς, incomers (proselytes), οἱ ἐπηλύται, and settlers, μέτοικοι (*Virt.* 102-05). Philo's characterization of οἱ ἐπηλύται, incomers, shows that proselytes are meant: "abandoning their kinsfolk by blood, their country, their customs and the temple and images of their gods, . . . they have taken the journey to a better home . . . to the worship of the one and truly existing God" (*Virt.* 102). The acceptance of proselytes by the Jews is also seen by Josephus as a proof of their love for humanity and their magnanimity (*Against Apion* [*Ag.Ap.*]) 2:261). As for the settlers, they are, according to Philo, foreigners who, being unable to live in their own land, live in an alien state (*Virt.* 105).

In *Virt.* 106-08 Philo refers to a named non-Jewish people, the Egyptians. He quotes Deut 23:7, "you shall not abhor an Egyptian because you were a sojourner in Egypt" (*Virt.* 106), and in § 108 he paraphrases Deut 23:8, "The children of the third generation that are born to them may enter the assembly of the Lord" in this way: "And if any of them should wish to pass over into the community of the Jews, they must . . . be so far favored that the third generation is invited to the congregation (εἰς ἐκκλησίαν)." It is evident that Philo does not only refer to the laws of Moses as such, but that he also applies Deut 23:8 to the concrete Jewish community in his own time, since he writes "into the community of the Jews (πρὸς τὴν Ἰουδαίων πολιτείαν)." As for the relation to other non-Jews, Philo deals with them in specific situations, such as enemies in wartime (*Virt.* 109-15, based on Deut 20:10-13). Philo here probably had mainly non-Jewish enemies in mind. Analogous application of *philanthropia* to the treatment of enemies is found in Xenophon, *Cyropaedia* VII:5. 73 and in Plutarch's *Lives*, *Cleomenes* 30:1; *Alexander* 44:3.[14]

In what ways are then non-Jews in general included in the practice of *philanthropia* by Jews? In the section on *philanthropia,* Philo writes that "we should do no wrongs to men of other nations (οἱ ἑτεροεθνεῖς), if we can accuse them of nothing save difference of race (τὸ ἀλλογενές)" (*Virt.* 147). In the treatise *On Joseph* Philo states that a guiding principle for Joseph, as viceroy of Egypt, was "the natural *philanthropia* (ἡ φυσικὴ φιλανθρωπία)" that he felt to all, and particularly to those of his blood (*On Joseph* [*Jos.*] 240). When in *QG* 3:62 it is said that Abraham, according to Gen 17:27, circumcised persons of foreign birth,

---

[14] See H. Martin, Jr., "The Concept of *philanthropia* in Plutarch's *Lives*," *American Journal of Philology*, 82, (1961) 171 and 174.

Philo generalizes it to mean that the Sage is helpful and philanthropic (Marcus: φιλάνθρωπος). He saves and calls to himself also those of foreign birth and of different opinions (Marcus: ἑτεροδόξους), giving them of his own goods with patience and ascetic continence. Philo may here say that the Sage (i.e. the proper Jew) shares circumcision with non-Jews to make them to become proselytes, or he may think of the spreading of the practice of circumcision even among some non-Jews.[15]

When Philo in *Virt.* 125-60 moves on to animals and plants, he holds to the proper meaning of φιλανθρωπία as love toward humans, and does not identify Moses' regulations for man's treatment of animals (§§ 125-47) or man's handling of plants (§§ 148-60) as in themselves *philanthropia*. But human attitudes towards animals and plants should be of the same kind as the attitude of *philanthropia* in relationships among people, such as the attitudes of moderation and gentleness (ἐπιεικὲς καὶ ἥμερον, *Virt.* 125), etc. The interplay between human beings and animals is in *Virt.* 140 characterized in this way:

> Moses rising to a further height extended the duty of fair treatment (τὸ ἐπιεικές) even to irrational animals, so that by practicing on creatures of dissimilar kind we may show love to humans (φολανθρωπία), abstaining from strokes and counter-strokes to vex each other, and not hoarding our personal good things as treasures, but throwing them into the common stock for all in every place, as for kinsmen and brothers by nature.

It should be noted here that Josephus as well as Plutarch can apply the term *philanthropia* to man's proper behavior to animals, Josephus, *Ag.Ap.* 2:213 and Plutarch, *Cato Maior* 5:5; *De sollertia animalium* 6:964A, and 13:970A.

Motifs

Philo defends his people against charges of misanthropy. The background was the widespread tensions between Jewish communities and some of the non-Jews.[16] Already the Egyptian priest Manetho (c. 300 BCE) criticized the Laws of Moses. According to Manetho Osarsiph (= Moses) ordained that the Jews "should have no connection with any save members of their own confederacy" (Josephus, *Ag. Ap.* 1:239).[17] Also Hecataeus of Abdera (c. 300 BCE), who in general had a sympathetic attitude towards the Jews, states that "as a result of their own expulsion from Egypt he [Moses] introduced an unsocial and intolerant mode of life (διὰ γὰρ τὴν ἰδίαν ξενηλασίαν ἀπάνθρωπόν τινα καὶ μισόξενον βίον εἰσηγήσατο)."[18] Apollonius Molon (first century BCE) charged the Jews with

---

[15] See A. Mendelson, *Philo's Jewish Identity* (Atlanta, 1988).

[16] For the following, see P. Borgen, "Philo and the Jews in Alexandria," in P. Bilde et al. (eds.), *Ethnicity in Hellenistic Egypt* (Aarhus, 1992) 125-27; A. Mendelson, *Jewish Identity.*

[17] See M. Stern (ed.), *Greek and Latin Authors on Jews and* Judaism, 1 (Jerusalem, 1976) 78-83, quoting Josephus, *Ag.Ap.* 1:228-52.

[18] M. Stern (ed.), *Greek and Latin Authors,* 1.26 and 28.

xenophobia and exclusiveness. He reviled the Jews as atheists and misanthropes (ὡς ἀθέους καὶ μισανθρώπους).[19] Similarly Diodorus Siculus (first century BCE), writes: "[The Jews] alone of all nations avoided dealings with any other people and looked upon them as their enemies . . . They made their hatred of mankind into a tradition, and on this account had introduced utterly outlandish laws . . ."[20] According to Tacitus (c. 56-120 CE) hate and enmity towards other people are the counterpart to the strong solidarity that the Jews display towards one another: "toward every other people they feel only hate and enmity (*sed adversus omnes alios hostile odium*).[21] "They sit apart at meals and they sleep apart, and . . . they abstain from intercourse with foreign women".[22]

Both Philo and Josephus defend the Jews against such criticism, and they do it not by evading Jewish particularism but by stressing philanthropic aspects of the Jews as expressed in their specific laws and their role as God's people. Referring to the unjust attacks rendered against the lawgiver, Moses, by Apollonius Molon, Lysimachus, and others, Josephus gives a brief account of the Jewish constitution. In this way he will make apparent that the Jews possess a code designed to promote piety (πρὸς εὐσέβειαν), fellowship (πρὸς κοινωνίαν), and love of humankind within the world at large (πρὸς τὴν καθόλου φιλανθρωπίαν), besides justice, hardihood, and contempt of death (*Ag.Ap.* 2:145-46). In contrast to the Spartans, who expelled foreigners, the Jews showed love to people (φιλανθρωπία) and magnaminity by welcoming others who wish to share their own customs (*Ag.Ap.* 2:261). Philo also relates the attitude of *philanthropia* to the proselytes, but instead of characterizing proselytism in general, as Josephus does, he, as shown above, characterizes the attitudes and actions of the Jews towards those who have become proselytes. Towards the proselytes the commandment of neighbourly love, Lev 19:33-34, applies: "He [Moses] commands the members of the nation to love the proselytes . . . as themselves both in body and soul" (*Virt.* 103).[23]

As a refutation of charges of misanthropy, Philo maintains that the Jewish nation and their laws even go beyond the normal meaning of *philanthropia* by acting correspondingly even to creatures of dissimilar kind, to animals, and that through the instruction of the laws the Jews learn gentle behavior:

---

[19] M. Stern (ed.), *Greek and Latin Authors,* 1.154-55, citing Josephus, *AgAp* 2:145-48.

[20] M. Stern (ed.), *Greek and Latin Authors,* 1.183, with reference to *Bibliotheca Historia,* Fragments of Book 34, 1:1-2.

[21] M. Stern (ed.), *Greek and Latin Authors on Jews and Judaism,* 2 (Jerusalem, 1984) 19.

[22] M. Stern (ed.), *Greek and Latin Authors,* 2.26.

[23] I. Heinemann,"Humanitas," in Pauly Wissowa, *RE,* Suppl. 5, (1931) col. 308, rightly states that Philo does not refer to the commandment on the love of neighbor as found in Lev 19:18. A. Nissen, *Gott und der Nächste im antiken Judentum. Untersuchungen zum Dobbelgebot der Liebe* (Tübingen, 1974) 478, makes the general statement that "der Gedanke einer *Liebe* zum mitmenschen bei ihm nirgendwo begegnet; er scheint ihm so fremd und fern zu sein, dass er auch das biblische Gebot der Nächstenliebe weder zitiert noch paraphrasiert, weder auf es anspielt noch es auswertet." Nissen has here overlooked that Philo draws on the commandment of neighborly love as it is rendered in Lev 19:33-34.

... let those clever libellers continue, if they can, to accuse the nation of misanthropy and charge the laws with enjoining unsociable and unfriendly practices, when these laws so clearly extend their compassion to flocks and herds, and our people through the instruction of the law learn from their earliest years to correct any wilfulness of souls in gentle behavior" (*Virt.* 141).

Even in the exclusive role of the Jews, understood as those who worship the true God, Philo argued that the Jews manifest care for all humankind:

> . . . it astonishes me to see that some people venture to accuse of inhumanity (ἀπανθρωπία) the nation which has shown so profound a sense of fellowship and good will to all men everywhere, by using its prayers and festivals and first fruit offerings as mean of supplication for the human race in general (ὑπὲρ τοῦ κοινοῦ γένους τῶν ἀνθρώπων) and of making its homage to the truly existent God in the name of those who have evaded the service which it was their duty to give, as well as of itself (*Spec.* 2:167).

Thus the particularistic and special worship of God by the Jews was by Philo interpreted as universal in its outreach, and in principle the duty of all people.

In his organization of the material Philo follows a systematic perspective. Thus the book *On the Virtues* is part of Philo's comprehensive series of treatises called *The Exposition of the Laws of Moses*.[24] The extant treatises of this *Exposition* are: *On the Creation of the World; On Abraham; On Joseph; On the Decalogue; On the Special Laws; On the Virtues; On Rewards and Punishment.* In this exegetical work, Philo paraphrases and expands or abbreviates the biblical text. The systematic outline of this body of writings is given by Philo in *Pream.* 1-3:

> The oracles delivered through the prophet Moses are of three kinds. The first deals with the creation of the world, the second with history and the third with legislation. The story of the creation is told throughout with an excellence worthy of the divine subject, beginning with the genesis of Heaven and ending with the framing of humans . . . The historical part is a record of good and bad lives and of the sentence passed in each generation on both, rewards in one case, punishment in the other. The legislative part has two divisions, one in which the subject matter is more general, the other consisting of the ordinances of specific laws. . . further the virtues which he assigned to peace and war, have been discussed as fully as was needful in the preceding treatises, and I now proceed in due course to the rewards and punishments which the good and bad have respectively to expect.

Within this systematic outline the discussion of the virtues that Moses assigned to peace and war is found in *Spec.* 4:133-238, where the virtue justice is discussed, and then in *Virt.* where the virtues of courage, *philanthropia*, repentance, and nobility follow.[25]

---

[24] See P. Borgen, "Philo of Alexandria," in M. Stone (ed.), *Jewish Writings of the Second Temple Period, CRINT*, 2:2 (Assen, 1984) 233-41; P. Borgen, *Philo, John and Paul* (Atlanta, 1987) 18-29.

[25] Concerning the research on Philo's *De Virtutibus,* see E. Hilgert, E.,"A Review of Previous Research on Philo's *De Virtutibus*, in *SBL 1991 Seminar Papers*, (Atlanta, 1991) 103-15.

The virtues are common to all commandments, and do not fit in with any one particular commandment in the Decalogue (*Spec.* 4:133-35). Philo knows the list of the so-called four cardinal virtues: wisdom, temperance, justice, and courage, φρόνησις, σωφροσύνη, ἀνδρεία, δικαιοσύνη (*The Allegorical Laws [Leg. all.]* 1:63)[26] but, as can be seen from the last section of *Spec.* together with the treatise *Virt.*, he operates with several virtues beyond these four. One such additional virtue is *philanthropia*, a virtue which in Philo's time already had increased its importance in the Hellenistic world.[27] This virtue, together with the other virtues, binds all commandments together (*Spec.* 4:133-35).

A theological motif is present when Philo uses *philanthropia* to characterize God, whom he also understands to be the source of *philanthropia* on the human level. Thus in *Virt.* 51 Philo stresses that *philanthropia* is the virtue closest akin to piety (εὐσεβεία), its sister and twin. Elsewhere he states that the one who is pious is also one who loves all people (*Abr.* 208). Accordingly he criticises those who divides the two:

> Now we have known some who . . . turning their backs upon all other concerns devoted their personal life wholly to the service of God. Others, conceiving the idea that there is no good outside doing justice to people have no heart for anything but companionship with people . . . These may be justly be called lovers of human beings, the former sort lovers of God. Both come but halfway in virtue; they only have it whole who win honour in both departments . . . (*Dec.* 108-10).

As shown above, the concept of *philanthropia* is, in Hellenistic, sources often seen as an attribute of gods, as Philo correspondingly applies the concept to God. Philo characterizes the dual perspective of divine and human *philanthropia* as *imitatio Dei*. In *Virt.* this idea is made explicit in §§ 168-69, with primary reference to the ideal behavior of rich and prominent persons:

> Especially does he give this lesson as most suitable to the rational nature that a person should imitate God (μιμεῖσθαι θεόν) as much as may be and leave nothing undone that may promote such likeness (ἐξομοίωσιν), as is possible.[28]

Here Jewish and Greek ideas are fused together to characterize the life based on the Laws of Moses. The concept of *imitatio Dei* is found in several Jewish sources: in *Mekilta*, Beshallah 3 on Exod 15:2; *b. Shabbat* 133b; *b. Sotah* 14a. According to Mekilta, Abba Saul interpreted Exod 15:2 in this way:"I will imitate Him [God]. As He is merciful and gracious, be you also merciful and gracious." As for the idea of being like God (*Virt.* 168), Philo knows that the idea was Platonic, since he cites Plato, *Theaetetus* 176AB:"we ought to fly away from earth to heaven as quickly as we can; and to fly away is to become like (ὁμοίωσις) God,

---

[26]Concerning other Jewish uses of the Platonic/Stoic cardinal virtues, see Wis 8:7; 4 *Macc.* 1:2-4.

[27] See D. Winston, "Philo's Ethical Theory," 394; R. Hirzel, *Plutarch*, 24-25.

[28] See further D. Winston, "Philo's Ethical Theory," 398, with reference also to *Spec.* 4:73; cf. *Spec.* 1:294; *Congr.* 171

as far as possible. And to become like Him is to become holy, just, and wise" (*On Flight and Finding* [*Fug.*] 63). The idea of ascent to heaven, which is exploited by Philo in *Fug.* 62-63, is not utilized by him in *Virt.* 168-69, but to both Plato and Philo to imitate and become like God means living a virtuous life.

Interpersonal Relationships - Benevolence

According to H. Bolkenstein the term φιλανθρωπία in Philo essentially means benevolence, i.e. care for the poor. Thus in general Philo understands the concept in what Bolkenstein calls its oriental usage.[29] According to him *philanthropia* in *Virt.* largely refers to commandments and rules in favour of the poor: §§ 82-87: not to exact interest on loans; # 88: wages of the poor are to be paid on the same day; § 89: the creditor is not to enter the debtor's house to seize a pledge; §§ 90-94: the gleaning of the harvest is to be left to the poor; §§ 121-24: the treatment of servants and slaves.[30]

Bolkenstein's view is one-sided, however, when he stresses so much the aspect of benevolent favours towards the poor. Some of the references he makes to *Virt.* do not deal only with the poor. For example, the theme in *Virt.* 82-87 is that one shall not exact interests on loans to brothers, including anyone of the same citizenship or nation. Although the prohibition is of special importance to the poor, it has a broader address as well. For example, according to § 89 the debtor may or may not have money to pay back a pledge or a surety. Similarly, hospitality has a broader connotation than benevolent help to the poor. Drawing on Gen 18 Philo explains that Abraham showed his *philanthropia* by being hospitable to three travellers, and Philo makes the following generalization, which does not focus on the poor: "For in the Sage's house no one is slow in showing *philanthropia*; but women and men, slaves and free, are full of zeal to do service to their guests" (*Abr.* 109).[31] It may be added that in Acts 28:2 hospitality and *philanthropia* were more of a benevolent act, since the Maltesians showed hospitality to the shipwrecked ones. Thus, a broader and more balanced understanding of the concept *philanthropia* than that suggested by Bolkenstein is needed in order to do justice to Philo's varied application of the term. To Philo it covered aspects of fellowship feelings and corresponding behavior, and not primarily benevolence to the poor.

There are even paragraphs in which the concept of *philanthropia* is not primarily seen as the proper behavior with an emphasis on the others to whom the virtue is addressed. Instead it may be is used to characterize the acting person himself or herself. Moses "perhaps loved her [*philanthropia*] more than anyone else has done, since he knew that she was a high road leading to holiness . . ."

[29] H. Bolkenstein, *Wohltätigkeit und Armenpflege im vorchristlichen Altertum*, (Groningen, 1967) 426-28.

[30] Bolkenstein., 427 n 1.

[31] Concerning the relationship between *philanthropia* and hospitality in Greek sources, see U. Luck, "φιλανθρωπία κτλ," 107-08

(*Virt.* 51). He set before his subjects his own life as a model. As mentioned above, Philo tells that at the end of his life Moses did not choose anyone from his own family as his successor. He entreated God and asked him to find the man, and he blended his thankfulness to God with his affection to the nation. Here the term φιλανθρωπία, love for people, is used together with πίστις, faithfulness, and κοινωνία, fellowship feeling, primarily to characterize Moses himself (*Virt.* 51-80).

In a corresponding way Philo may focus attention upon the attitude and practice of the persons themselves, those who display *philanthropia*. Thus, in *Virt.* 95, he says that according to the laws of Moses they are not to regard the firstborn of oxen and sheep and goats as their personal property, but as first fruit. In this way they honour God and demonstrate that they do not take all things as their personal gain. As a result they may have the ornament of those queens of the virtues, piety and *philanthropia*. Similarly, Moses in his laws did not give full liberty to food and drink, but bridled them with ordinances most conducive to self-restraint and love of humankind (πρὸς ἐγκράτειαν καὶ πρὸς φιλανθρωπίαν) and most of all to piety (πρὸς εὐσέβειαν) (*Spec.* 4:97).[32]

This combination of piety, self-restraint, and *philanthropia* makes it understandable that Philo maintains that Moses, with all the injunctions in *Virt.* 51-160 tamed and softened the minds of the citizens of his commonwealth and set them out of the reach of pride and arrogance (§§ 161-74). Thus,

> he who has been carefully taught that his vigour and robustness is a gift of God, will take account of his own natural weakness, the weakness which was his before he enjoyed the gift of God, and will thrust aside the spirit of lofty arrogance and give thanks to Him who brought about the happy change (§ 165).

Robustness

Although the concept of *philanthropia* has to do with the feeling of fellowship and mercy, Philo makes clear that this is only one attitude among several, since this virtue belongs together with other virtues, such as justice and courage. Moreover, Philo's particularism and corresponding restrictions at times modify *philanthropia* to a large extent. For example, although board and hospitality are usually given to neighbors, the first fruits must be kept out of the hands of a dweller near the priest, because there is a danger that the consecrated meats may be profaned through an untimely generosity (*philanthropia*). Otherwise order will be destroyed (*Spec.* 1:120). As for the treatment of settlers, *philanthropia* means that they are allowed to stay in a country not their own on the

---

[32] In the picture of Cyrus as an ideal king, Xenophon pictures him as one who in his life displayed self-restraint, love of (other) human beings and piety. As Moses is pictured as a model king by Philo, Cyrus is seen as a model king by Xenophon. See B. Due, *The Cyropaedia,* 147-84.

condition that they pay some honour to the people who have accepted them (*Virt.* 105).

Philo demonstrates a restrictive attitude when he writes: "But while the law stands pre-eminently in enjoining fellowship (κοινωνία) and love of people (φιλανθρωπία), it preserves the high position and dignity of both virtues by not allowing anyone whose state is incurable, to take refuge with them . . . (*Spec.* 1:324). An elaborate exposition follows in *Spec.* 1:325-45, in which Philo explains that those who are to be kept away are sexual deviates (Deut 23:1-2), polytheists, and others. In conclusion Philo indicates clearly that he has his own contemporary situation in mind, since he characterizes the positive and contrasting group as "we, the pupils and disciples of Moses" (*Spec.* 1:345).

In some of the Greek sources the concept of love of humankind, φιλανθρωπία, is modified by particularistic virtues. Thus, Isocrates (436-338 BCE) in *To Nicocles* 2:15 associates it with "love for the city," φιλόπολις.[33] Correspondingly, Moses' φιλανθρωπία is focused upon his patriotic love for his people, τὸ φιλοεθνὲς πάθος (*Virt.* 69). Also Plutarch has a particularistic use of the concept of *philanthropia*, since he identifies it with Greeks and with Hellenic civilization, laws, and way of life (*Pyrrh.* 3-4; *Phil.* 8:1-3, etc.).[34] The difference between Philo and Plutarch concerning *philanthropia* is that Philo basically applies it to the Jewish people, whereas Plutarch applies it to the Hellenic civilization as it was practised by the Greek people and by other persons and peoples.[35]

The Question of Anthropology

The question of the universalistic concept of humankind needs be touched upon once more, however, since Philo, besides thinking in terms of God, the people, and others also uses the broader categories of human beings, animals, and plants:

[Moses] did not set up consideration and gentleness as fundamental to the relation of humans to their fellows only, but poured it out richly with lavish hands on animals of irrational nature and the various kinds of cultivated trees (*Virt.* 81; cf. 125, 140 and 148).

How can Philo combine such univeralistic categories with his focus on God's love towards the Jewish people and the mutual love of persons within this one nation? Greek usage at times limits the application of *philanthropia* to the

---

[33] See R. le Déaut, "Φιλανθρωπία," 267-68.

[34] See H. Martin, Jr."The Concept of *philanthropia,* 167-68.

[35] ibid., 168 notices that since *philanthropia* may be identified with civilized way of life as such, then bathing and anointing of one's body can be called *philanthropia* (Plutarch *Lyc.* 16:12). This is what civilized persons do. Philo has a similar statement in *Migr.* 217: "... merchants and traders for the sake of trifling profits cross the sea ... letting stand in their way ... neither the daily intercourse with friends ... nor the enjoyment of our fatherland and of all the gracious amenities of civic life" (πατρίδος καὶ πολιτικῶν φιλανθρωπιῶν ἀπόλαυσιν).

polis, the people, or Hellenic civilization, while in Greek philosophical traditions the universalistic application of *philanthropia* might be derived from the idea of the kinship among all human beings.[36] A Jewish understanding was that one regarded the Jewish people of God to be the center of humankind. They were the true humans: "Yet out of the whole human race He chose as of special merit and judged worthy of pre-eminence over all, those who are in true sense men, and called them to the service of Himself . . ." (Philo, *Spec.* 1:303). As already stated above, the Jewish nation has received the gift of priesthood and prophecy on behalf of all humankind (*Abr.* 98). It is consecrated to offer prayers on behalf of the human race, and their worship is on behalf of all (*Mos.* 1:149; *Spec.* 2:167). So also the high priest of the Jews makes prayers and gives thanks not only on behalf of the whole human race, but also for nature (*Spec.* 1:97). The Jewish nation is to the whole inhabited world what the priest is to the *polis* (*Spec.* 2:163).

From the people of God the impact of *philanthropia* is to be spread to all. Cautiously Philo indicates that the whole human race ought to follow the Mosaic legislation. He hints at this perspective in *Virt.* 119:

> This (τοῦτο) is what our most holy prophet through all his regulations especially desires to create, unanimity, neighbourliness, fellowship, reciprocity of feeling, whereby houses and cities and nations and countries and the whole human race may advance to supreme happiness.

This is a generalizing elaboration of the preceding paragraphs, 116-18, where Philo has interpreted Exod 23:5 about protecting and restoring animals to enemies and thereby bringing about reconciliation and ending a feud among the persons involved.

Philo expresses his own personal hope for reconciliation and peace in the following way:

> Hitherto indeed, these things live only in our prayers, but they will, I am convinced, become facts beyond all dispute, if God, even as He gives us the yearly fruits, grants that the virtues should bear abundantly. And may some share in them be given to us, who from well-nigh our earliest days have carried with us the yearning to possess them (*Virt.* 120).

Summary

1. The hypothesis given at the beginning of this essay has been confirmed in the present analysis: Philo's concept of *philanthropia* is rooted in ideas about God, Moses, and God's people. In this way the Greek concepts of the virtues have been made to interpret the laws of Moses and to serve Jewish religious categories.

---

[36] R. le Déaut, "Φιλανθρωπία," 280-81, with references to Aristotle, *Nicomachean Ethics* 1155a.20; Stoa, I. von Arnim (coll.), *Stoicorum veterum fragmenta*, 1 (Leipzig, 1904) 262. See especially D. Winston, "Philo's Ethical Theory," 392.

2. In Greek usage the application of *philanthropia* may be restricted to love of the polis, the people, or Hellenic civilization. In Greek philosophic traditions, however, the universalistic application of *philanthropia* might be derived from the idea of the kinship among all human beings. In a Jewish understanding the application of the concept of *philanthropia* to the particular people of God was central. The universalistic aspect then was understood to mean that this Jewish people of God with its laws and worship was the center of humankind. They were the true humans. From the people of God the influence of *philanthropia* is to be spread to all. Philo specifies persons and groups such as proselytes, settlers, and Egyptians.

3. *Philanthropia* characterizes God's relationship to human beings. The background for the use of *philanthropia* in these passages is the fact that already in Greek usage the term characterized the attitudes and behavior of the gods. When God is pictured as a king who acts in his love of human beings, then the background is the Hellenistic ideal of kingship.

4. Having pictured Moses as the paradigm of φιλανθρωπία, Philo gives in *Virt.* a survey of his laws and regulations that fit this model.

5. When Philo in *Virt. 125-60* moves on to animals and plants, he holds to the proper meaning of φιλανθρωπία, as love to persons, and does not identify Moses' regulations for human treatment of animals or handling of plants as in themselves *philanthropia*. But the human attitude towards animals and plants should be one of moderation and gentleness, etc. By practising on creatures of dissimilar kind one may learn to show love to all persons.

6. The laws of Moses instruct the conquerors to treat enemies with generosity and mercy, *philanthropia*. The same attitude is advocated by Xenophon in *Cyropaedia* and by Plutarch in his *Lives*.

7. Several motifs are seen to be at work in Philo's interpretations, such as:
   •an apologetic motif, where Philo defends the Jews against charges of misanthropy;
   •a systematic motif, where it can be seen that Philo deals with *philanthropia* within the large scheme of his "Exposition of the laws of Moses." The virtues are common to all commandments and bind them together.
   •a theological motif, when Philo uses *philanthropia* to characterize God, whom he also understands to be the source of *philanthropia* on the human level. It is the virtue closest akin to piety (εὐσεβεία), its sister and twin.
   •a drive for fusing Jewish and Greek ideas together. For example, Philo combines the Jewish concept of *imitatio Dei* and the Platonic idea that the human goal is to be like God.

8. Bolkenstein interpreted *philanthropia* in Philo's writings mainly as benevolence to the poor. A broader and more balanced understanding of the concept is needed in order to do justice to Philo's varied application of the term.

In Philo's writings it covers also aspects of fellowship feelings and proper behavior in cases where the recipients are not poor or in need of mercy.

9. There are paragraphs in which the concept of *philanthropia* is not primarily seen as the proper behavior to others, but is used to characterize the acting person himself, his self-restraint and his veneration of God.

10. Philo makes clear that love of humankind, *philanthropia,* does not lead to softness. This virtue is only one among several. It belongs together with other virtues, such as justice and courage. Moreover, Philo's particularism brings several restrictions in the application of *philanthropia.*

In conclusion: Philo's varied usages of the concept of *philanthropia* should be seen against 2 the background of the varied usages in Greek sources. In different ways both general and particularistic applications of the concept are present in both areas. This approach seems to be more adequate than measuring Philo's interpretations and applications primarily against the background of universalistic ideas about the unity of humankind found in some developments of Greek philosophy.

Humanitas in the Greco-Roman Papyri

Eldon Jay Epp
Case Western Reserve University

W hile searching the Greco-Roman papyri[1] for very specific evidence regarding the speed and efficiency of the informal mail service in an effort to discover something new about how quickly New Testament manuscripts may have moved in early Christian antiquity,[2] I encountered much more than I had bargained for in terms of information about human life and day-to-day living in that period. Whereas I was looking for largely impersonal, technical details of the sending and receipt of letters, as well as any intellectual content that might inform us about the circulation, use, and critique of ancient literary works, what faced me time and again was real life–*humanitas*–or those qualities of human

---

[1] Papyri are cited below in accordance with J. F. Oates, R. S. Bagnall, W. H. Willis, and K. A. Worp, *Checklist of Editions of Greek and Latin Papyri, Ostraca and Tablets* (4th ed.; Bulletin of the American Society of Papyrologists: Supplements 7; Atlanta, GA: Scholars Press, 1992), where abbreviations and publication information can be found. LCL refers to the Loeb Classical Library, specifically to *Select Papyri* (3 vols.; Cambridge, MA: Harvard University Press, 1932-41), vols. 1-2 ed. by A. S. Hunt and C. C. Edgar and vol. 3 ed. by D. L. Page.

Papyrus documents are fully or extensively quoted in this paper whenever feasible so that the full flavor of the original communication can be appreciated.

It should be noted that, in Egypt, terms of family relationship ("father," "mother," "sister," and "brother") are not always to be taken literally, but can be used as expressions of respect and affection. "Sister" can and often does mean "wife"; in addition, brother and sister marriages were common.

[2] "New Testament Papyrus Manuscripts and Letter Carrying in Greco-Roman Times," *The Future of Early Christianity: Essays in Honor of Helmut Koester* (ed. B. A. Pearson; Minneapolis, MN: Fortress, 1991) 35-56. A number of the examples in the present article were used there to illustrate the social context.

nature, character, and feeling that distinguish civilized human beings from the uncivilized and from beasts.   Indeed, the whole spectrum of the human predicament is laid bare as the papyri disclose the full range of human endeavor and human emotion.   Naturally, the papyri of a private nature evince these human feelings with a special poignancy; and very quickly a modern reader peering into very personal matters–at times with the near embarrassment of violating rights of privacy–realizes that little has changed in the interpersonal relationships and the human emotions and feelings that accompany both the great and the small crises of life then and now.   Yet, this so often is what makes the study of antiquity so rewarding–to observe the continuity (and even the constancy) of *humanitas* from age to age.

Please Write! The Importance of Written Communication in Antiquity

Though personal letter-writing in our day has given way almost entirely to the telephone and to facsimile transmission and electronic mail, it is appropriate to begin by pointing to the significance, in antiquity, of receiving or not receiving letters. Since communication over any distance was confined to a messenger's transmittal of either oral or written material, the receipt of some word from a family member or from a relative or associate assumed a heightened importance. For example, a slave to the Strategus of a nome in Upper Egypt writes to her master, "I beg you, my lord, if it seems good to you, to send us a letter also, since we die if we do not see you daily. Would that we could fly to you and come and greet you. . . . So be good to us and send us a message" (2nd century CE; *PGiss* 17–tr. Winter;[3] cf. LCL 1.115). Or from Misenum, a port near Naples, a marine writes to his father in Philadelphia in the Fayyum:

> Apion to Epimachus, his father and lord, very many greetings. . . . I thank the lord
> Serapis that when I was in danger at sea he straightaway saved me. On arriving
> at Misenum I received from Caesar three gold pieces for traveling expenses. And
> it is well with me. Now I ask you, my lord and father, write me a little letter,
> telling me first of your welfare, secondly of my brother's and sister's, and
> enabling me thirdly to make obeisance before your hand[writing], because you
> educated me well and I hope thereby to have quick advancement, if the gods so
> will. . . (2nd century CE; *BGU* 423; LCL 1.112).

The son, newly settled at his naval assignment, thinks of home--of the welfare of his father, brother, and sister–and even a "little letter" written in his father's own hand would bring to him all the warmth of home and hearth.

---

[3] This is the translation of J. G. Winter, *Life and Letters in the Papyri* (Jerome Lectures; Ann Arbor, MI: University of Michigan Press, 1933) 130. [Further notes of "tr. Winter" refer to this volume.] LCL (in 1932) adopted an alternative translation that makes the request to the master "send for us" rather than "send [a letter] to us."

Indeed, failure to write becomes a common complaint. For example, a father addresses his son, Dionysotheon: "Having had the luck to find someone going up to you I felt obliged to address you. I am much surprised, my son, that to date I have received from you no news of your welfare. . . . Reply to me promptly, for I am quite distressed at having no letter from you" (3rd/4th century CE; *POxy* I.123; LCL 1.159); a son writes to his mother: "How many letters have I sent you and not one have you written me in reply, though so many people have sailed down!" (2nd century CE; LCL 1.121); and a pregnant woman scolds her family in Karanis: "You have not even thought fit to write me one letter" (ca. 200 CE; *PMich* VIII.508). Concern is intense when an associate in Alexandria does not hear from Leon, the toparch, in Philadelphia: "When I wrote you many letters and no sound was uttered to me from you, being the more anxious because until now I have heard nothing concerning you, I consulted the god frequently; but when Protolaus brought word to us about you, I was most delighted" (12 January 229 BCE; *PYale* I.42).

Hopeful recipients are also creative in their efforts to elicit letters: "I sent you papyrus so that you might be able to write me concerning your health" (early 2nd century CE; *PMich* VII.481); or hyperbolic: "For I have already used up a papyrus roll in writing to you, and I received barely one letter from you. . . ." (2nd century CE; *PMich* VIII.496); or they appeal to lack of love, as in these three letters: "I want you to know that . . . you have sent me no word from the day that I came to Alexandria. If then you love me, do not neglect to write to me" (3rd century CE; *PMich* VIII.513); a soldier in far-off Bostra in Arabia writes to his father in Karanis: "If, then, you love me, you will straightway take pains to write to me concerning your health. . . (19/20 February 107 CE; *PMich* VIII.466); and a certain Ptolemaeus writes to a respected friend (in a papyrus letter hard to decipher): ". . . Please write to me constantly in order that I may know in this way that you love me, since by your not writing to me it will be a sign showing that you have forgotten me . . ." (2nd century CE; *PMert* I.22). Again, a daughter, Plutogenia, writes from Alexandria to her mother in Philadelphia in severe language: "It is already eight months since I came to Alexandria, and not even one letter have you written to me. Again then you do not regard me as your daughter but as your enemy" (ca. 296 CE; *PMich* III.221). Obviously, there was a larger problem here than mere delinquency in letter writing (cf. the fuller context below). As a further example, a son away for schooling sends a scolding but plaintive letter to his father:

> To my lord and father Arion from Thonis greeting. . . . Look you, this is my fifth letter to you, and you have not written to me except only once, not even a word about your welfare, nor come to see me; though you promised me saying, "I am coming," you have not come to find out whether the teacher is looking after me or not. He himself is inquiring about you almost every day, saying, "Is he not coming yet?" And I just say "Yes." Endeavor then to come to me quickly in

order that he may teach me as he is eager to do. If you had come up with me, I should have been taught long ago. And when you come, remember what I have often written you about. . . . [postscript–between the lines] Remember our pigeons (early 3rd century CE; LCL 1.133).

Similarly, a mother (who happens to be a Christian) writes to her son (referring to herself):

. . . Your mother Cophaena is ill, look you, thirteen months, and you had not the good grace even to write me a letter, since you yourself know that I have dealt more kindly with you than my other children [?], and you had not the grace, on hearing that I am ill, you had not the grace to send me at once anything at all. . . . I pray for your welfare for many years (4th/5th century CE; *BGU* 948–tr. Winter, 154-55).

Finally, "And do not hesitate to write letters," a man addresses his brother, who resided in Karanis (in the Fayyum), "since I rejoiced exceedingly, as if you had come. From the day that you sent me the letter I have been saved" (23 August 133 CE; *PMich* VIII.482). The letter goes on, incidentally, to report that "Peteeus, who is writing this letter for me, salutes you repeatedly as well as your wife and your daughter and Bassus your horse" (!).

Already in these few excerpts we see *humanitas* as it extends from pathos (in its Greek sense of "suffering") all the way to humor. As we examine additional letters and other relevant documents in the vast corpus of more than 40,000 papyrus texts[4], the whole range of human experiences, actions, and feelings unfolds before us.

Life Begins: Birth, Adoption, Exposure

Births represent happy family events–at least most of the time. In upper class families, births were frequently registered: ". . . We register our son, Didymus, as having been born in the 16th year of Antoninus Caesar the lord, and as being four years old in the present 19th year. We enter the notice of the birth" (156 CE; *PGen* I.33--tr. Winter 52-53). Births were also reported to relatives, as did this soldier in writing to his mother in Karanis about the arrival of his child [portions of a lengthy letter]:

Saturnalus to Aphrodous his mother, very many greetings. Before all things I pray for your health and prosperity. I wish you to know that I sent you three letters this month. I have received in full the monthly allowances which you sent me by Julius and a basket of olives by the lad of Julius. I wish you to know that another male child has been born to me, whose name, the gods willing, is Agathos Daimon. If I find an opportunity of

---

[4] According to a report by W. H. Willis, "The New Compact Disk of Documentary Papyri," *Proceedings of the 20th International Congress of Papyrologists, Copenhagen, 23-29 August, 1992* (ed. A. Bülow-Jacobsen; Copenhagen: Museum Tusculanum Press, University of Copenhagen, 1994) 628-31, the Duke Data Bank of Documentary Papyri contains (ca. 1994) 41,000 texts in some 4.4 million words.

putting my plan into effect, I am coming to you with letters [i.e., he has a commission for carrying letters]. . . . I was afraid to come just now because they say, "The prefect is on the route," lest he take the letters from me and send me back to the troops, and I incur the expense in vain. . . . If you wish to see me a little, I wish it greatly and I pray daily to the gods that they may quickly give me a good chance to come. . . . Gemella salutes you all, as do Didumarin and the newly-born Agathos Daimon and Epictetos . . .. I pray for health to you all (1st/2nd century; *PMich* III.203).

Nannies were needed and offers of employment extended:

Valeria and Thermouthas both to Thermoution their "sister," greeting. As I asked you when I was on the point of sailing down, regarding the child of Thermouthas, take and rear it, and you will be happy if you do. With reference to the two houses, you will find joy and pleasure. Receive/accept five staters. If you consent to rear [the child], you will receive a greater rate [than is usual] since it is free-born; and you will find your own pleasure and parents [i.e., you will be like a daughter] if you do it. Sail down in the boat in order that you may return with us together with the child. Bring from my mother five staters if you come down so that we may return, or take what you wish. I am asking you to sail down that you may prosper, for a free-born child is one thing, a slave child another. Farewell. The year 8 of Trajan our lord (105 CE; *PMich* III.202–tr. slightly modified.)

A wet nurse might be employed:

. . . Didyma agrees to nurse and suckle, outside of her own home in the city, with her own milk pure and untainted, for a period of 16 months . . . the foundling infant slave child . . . which Isidora has given out to her, receiving from her, Isidora, as wages for milk and nursing 10 silver drachmae and 2 cotylae of oil every month. So long as she is duly paid she shall take proper care both of herself and of the child, not injuring her milk nor sleeping with a man nor becoming pregnant nor suckling another child. . . . Didyma shall visit Isidora every month regularly on four separate days bringing the child to be inspected by her. . . . [signed] I, Isidora agree on the above terms. . . . I, Didyma, agree on the above terms (13 BCE; *BGU* 1107; LCL 1.16).

And toys were sent to little children: "Diogenis to her brother Alexander, greeting. . . . Many salutations to the little Theon. Eight toys have been brought for him by the lady to whom you told me to give your salutations, and these I have forwarded to you" (3rd century CE [?]; *PSI* 1080; LCL 1.132). On another occasion, however, an excuse was offered for not sending gifts:

Troilos to his sister [wife?] Mazatis, greeting. Before everything I pray that you prosper, and the child also, bless him. I wanted to send the child a few gifts, and the post left and the camels had gone unexpectedly. Please sister, hasten the making of my tunic, so that when I come to you after the feast I may find it finished. . . (3rd century CE [?]; *PFuad* I.6).

On the other hand–and most unhappily–children, usually female, might be exposed, as one husband advised his wife in a letter:

> Hilarion to Alis, his sister [i.e., wife], very many greetings. . . . Know that I am still in Alexandria. And do not worry if they all come back and I remain in Alexandria. I ask and beg you to take good care of our baby son, and as soon as I receive payment I will send it up to you. If you are delivered of child [before I get home], if it is a boy keep it, if a girl discard [expose] it. You have sent me word, "Don't forget me." How can I forget you? I beg you not to worry. The 29th year of Caesar [i.e., Augustus], Pauni 23 (17 June 1 BCE; *POxy* IV.744–tr. N. Lewis;[5] cf. LCL 1.295)

Egyptians, whose religion precluded child exposure, often rescued discarded babies, and the law permitted their adoption. Such children often received names appropriate to the situation, such as Kopreus (and its variants), which means "off the dunghill."[6] This is illustrated in another papyrus that tells of a boy who was rescued from exposure on a dunghill and became the object of a lawsuit, for--after being entrusted to a nurse--the rescuer felt the boy was being neglected and took him from the nurse, who, however, surreptitiously took him back; then the rescuer sued to have the boy returned to him, but the judge awarded him to the nurse (49 CE; *POxy* I.37).

Children were adopted under more routine circumstances, as documented in this rather straightforward agreement:

> We agree, Heracles and his wife Isarion, on our side, that we have surrendered to you, Horion, for adoption our son Patermouthis, about two years old, and I, Horion, on my side, that I hold him as my own son as regards the maintenance of the rights appertaining to him from the succession to my inheritance; and it shall not be lawful for me to send him away or to reduce him to slavery, because he is well born and the son of well born, free parents. . . . I, Aurelius Horion . . . wrote for him, since he is illiterate (355 CE; *POxy* IX.1206–tr. Winter, 58; cf. LCL 1.10).

We learn more, however, about some of the reasons why children were given up for adoption from this much later papyrus agreement:

> . . . Aurelius Herais, daughter of John and Susanna, . . . to [. . .], son of Menas, and Mixima your wife, . . . greeting. [. . .] years ago, more or less, my husband died, and I was left toiling and suffering hardship for my daughter by him, in order to provide for her the necessary sustenance; and now, not having the means to maintain her . . . , she being 9 years old, more or less, I have asked you . . . to receive her from me as your daughter, and I acknowledge that I have handed her over to you from now for all succeeding time as your legal daughter, so that you shall supply her needs and fill the place of parents to daughter, and I have no power henceforth to take her away from you. . . (554 CE; *POxy* XVI.1895; LCL 1.11).

Giving up a "child" in another context is more tragic; a woman whose own mother gave her to prostitution was murdered; appearing in Hermopolis at the trial of the alleged murderer, Diodemos, the mother makes a request:

---

[5] N. Lewis, *Life in Egypt under Roman Rule* (Oxford: Clarendon Press, 1983; repr. 1994) 54.
[6] *Life in Egypt*, 54.

> It was for this reason that I gave my daughter to the pimp, that I might be supported. Since then my daughter having died I am deprived of means of support; for this reason I ask that I be given a modest woman's portion for my support.

The court's judgment was that:

> Theodora, the poor and elderly mother of the dead woman, who because of her constant poverty deprived her own daughter of modesty, and through which she also killed her, will inherit a tenth part of the belongings of Diodemos, the laws suggesting this to me and magnanimity supporting the power of the laws (late 4th century CE; *BGU* IV.1024).[7]

Anxiety Is a Two-way Street: Children and Family Away from Home

The fortunate preservation of a small family archive of seven letters provides more insights into the situation of a Greek family in Gerzah (ancient Philadelphia) than can normally be expected, for the various letters permit us to grasp the character and moods of the various family members–a husband and father, his wife, his daughter, his mother-in-law, and his brother. Paniskos, the husband, had gone to Upper Egypt and writes from Koptos to his wife, Ploutogenia:

> Paniskos, to my wife Ploutogenia, mother of my daughter, very many greetings. First of all I pray daily for your good health in the presence of all the gods. . . . We are in Koptos near your sister and her children, so that you may not be grieved about coming to Koptos; for your kinsfolk are here. And just as you desire above all to greet her with many greetings, so she prays daily to the gods desiring to greet you along with your mother. So when you have received this letter of mine make your preparations in order that you may come at once if I send for you. And when you come, bring ten shearings of wool, six jars of olives, four jars of liquid honey, and my shield, the new one only, and my helmut. Bring also my lances. Bring also the fittings of the tent. . . . Bring all our clothes when you come. When you come, bring your gold ornaments, but do not wear them on the boat. I salute my lady daughter Heliodora (296 CE; *PMich* III.214).[8]

So the cast of characters, except for Aion the brother at home, is introduced in this first letter. But Paniskos's next letter is occasioned by his wife's failure to come, though his hopes are still high:

> Paniskos to his wife and his daughter, many greetings. Before all else I pray before the lord god that I may receive you and my daughter in good health. Already I have written you a second letter that you might come to me, and you have not come. If, then, you do not wish to come, write me a reply. Bring my shield, the new one, and my helmut and my five lances and the fittings of the tent. . . . I send many salutations to my daughter

---

[7] Tr. by R. Bagnall, *Egypt in Late Antiquity* (Princeton, NJ: Princeton University Press, 1993) 196-98.

[8] Published by J. G. Winter, "The Family Letters of Paniskos," *Journal of Egyptian Archaeology* 13 (1927) 59-74, but revised for the official publication in Winter's *Michigan Papyri, Vol. III, Papyri in the University of Michigan Collection: Miscellaneous Papyri* (Ann Arbor, MI: University of Michigan Press, 1936) 275-98. The sequence of letters is that determined by Winter.

and to your mother and those who love us, by name. I pray for your welfare (296 CE;
PMich III.216)

Still Ploutogenia does not come, and her apparent visit to her mother–rather than
to him–elicits a sharp reproof and rather direct remarks from Paniskos about the
independent willfulness of both his wife and his own mother. One could easily add
exclamation points to several of the sentences!

> Paniskos to Ploutogenia his wife, greeting. I enjoined you when I left that you should
> not go off to your home, and yet you went. If you wish anything you do it, without
> taking account of me. But I know that my mother does these things. See, I have sent
> you three letters and you have not written me even one. If you do not wish to come up
> to me, no one compels you. These letters I have written to you because your sister
> compels me here to write. But since you find it impossible to write about this, then write
> other things about yourself. I have heard other things which do not concern you. Send
> me my helmut and my shield and my five lances and my breastplate and my belt. I
> salute your mother Heliodora. The letter carrier said to me when he came to me: "When
> I was on the point of departing I said to your wife and her mother, 'Give me a letter to
> take to Paniskos,' and they did not give it." I have sent you one talent by Antoninus
> from Psinestes. I pray for your welfare (296 CE; *PMich* III.217).

We now learn that his daughter was named for her maternal grandmother, and
Paniskos recites compounded evidence that Ploutogenia neither wishes to come to
him nor even to write him, including an unusual and incriminating citation of the
letter-carrier's report. Nevertheless, Paniskos sends money for her use.

The tone of the fourth letter is much softer and includes the possibility of his
return home, and his daughter remains much on his mind:

> Paniskos to his wife, many greetings. I send many salutations to Heliodora, my
> daughter. And do you attend to her. I wish to see if you have need of anything. I wrote
> to Aion [i.e., to supply your wants], and if you happen to go off to Heliopolis send [word
> to him] for the things you need. And I sent fleeces for yourself in order that if you want
> anything you may [sell them and] spend the money for yourself. And attend to your
> cattle, and as for the three *holokottina* [gold coins], make anklets of them for my
> daughter, and make ready the materials of your *chiton* [garment] and your *himation*
> [outer garment]. And if the god wills and I come, I will send Achaos there [i.e., to
> inform you]. . . . I pray for your health. I send many salutations to your mother. . . (296
> CE; *PMich* III.218).

Another letter, from Paniskos to his brother Aion (in Karanis), is badly
damaged, but it clearly reveals Paniskos's recurring concern for his daughter:

> Paniskos to Aion, his brother, many greetings. Before all else I pray before the lord god
> to receive you in good health. I wish you to know that, god willing, we are in good
> health. And I enjoin you in my behalf, brother, attend to my daughter; and if she has
> need of anything give it to her. Impose your commands on her gently even if she
> contradicts you; write in reply to me and gladden me if she does well and attends her
> flocks (296 CE; *PMich* III.219).

There were at least three additional letters that have been lost; the sixth and final extant letter from Paniskos (296 CE; *PMich* III.220) was still written from the Koptos area and obviously has been dictated to a scribe, for Ploutogenia's name is misspelled ("Protogenia")–hardly likely to be done by the husband himself. The letter adds little to our story since it treats some matters of business, though there are the customary salutations: "I salute you, Heliodora my daughter, and all our kinsfolk."

The remaining item in the archive is a letter from Ploutogenia to her mother Heliodora, though it defies chronological placement in the sequence of Paniskos's experiences in the preceding letters. Since there are no greetings to a daughter, it might possibly predate Ploutogenia's marriage to Paniskos,[9] but there is no way of knowing. It is written by Ploutogenia after she has been away from home for eight months–in Alexandria:

> Plutogenia to my mother, many greetings. First of all I pray before the lord god for your good health. It is already eight months since I came to Alexandria, and not even one letter have you written to me. Again then you do not regard me as your daughter but as your enemy. . . . Attend to the irrigation wheel and to your cattle. . . . And if your daughter intends to marry, write to me and I come. I salute you together with your children. I salute also by name those who love us. I pray for your continued health (ca. 296 CE; *PMich* III.221)

What kind of family do Paniskos and Ploutogenia represent at the very end of the third century in Egypt? The references to gold jewelry and coins and to other funds, as well as to flocks and to cattle twice, suggest a family of some prosperity and independence.[10] Was Paniskos a soldier in Upper Egypt? Why then, as J. G. Winter asks, would he have left so much of his armor and other equipment at home? Or could he have been a merchant in the armor trade?[11] Though much of the family's situation cannot be known, we do gain a fascinating picture of personal feelings and of interpersonal relationships in a family group around 300 CE that had been separated by distance.

Other families find themselves in various circumstances with a range of joys and concerns–including interpersonal problems. A son can chastise his father, as in this tantruming letter found at Oxyrhynchus–in poor handwriting and atrocious

---

[9] Winter, "Family Letters," 73, though he drops this possibility in the 1936 publication (p. 297; see preceding note).

[10] Winter, "Family Letters," 69, 74. The formulaic use twice of "the lord god" (in 216 and 219), following an earlier use of "all the gods" (214), might suggest (1) that the family may have been Christian and (2) either that Paniskos may have converted to Christianity between letters–highly doubtful–or that the first letter (214) may have been written during the Diocletian persecution and employed nonincriminating language, with Paniskos reverting to the Christian formula after the danger was over–also doubtful. Winter originally (1927, pp. 62-63) speculated along these lines, but none of this appears in his 1936 publication.

[11] See Winter, "Family Letters," 59-60, and his reference to *PGiss* 47, attesting to armor trade in Koptos at the time of Trajan (p. 59 n. 2).

grammar and spelling–though when the last lines are reached his letter seems to be good natured and written out of serious concern:

> Theon to Theon his father, greeting. You did a fine thing; you didn't take me with you to the city. If you do not wish to take me with you to Alexandria, I'll not write you a letter or talk to you or wish you good health. What's more, if you go to Alexandria, I won't take a hand from you or greet you again. So if you do not wish to take me with you, that's that! . . . But you did a fine thing; you sent me presents, big ones, [bean] pods! . . . But send for me, I beg you. If you do not send, I won't eat, won't drink! There! I pray for your good health (January, 2nd or 3rd century CE; *POxy* I.119–tr. Winter, 60).

More complex is the situation involving a mother and her two sons. In this case, as happens on occasion, two letters are found on the same sheet; one son (probably in Alexandria) writes both, with only the first intended for the ears of the mother--who probably could not read herself--and the second for his brother, who resided with or near her, but apparently not entirely in happiness:

> Sempronius to Saturnila his mother and lady, very many greetings. . . . I have sent you so many letters and you have written me none in return, although so many people have sailed down. Please, my lady, write me without fail about your well-being in order that I may be less troubled. For your well-being must always be my prayer. I salute Maximus and his wife and Saturnilus and Gemellus and Helene and her household. Tell her that I have received a letter from Sepronius from Cappadocia. . . . Do keep well for my sake, my lady, at all times.

The second letter, addressed to Maximus only, reprimands the brother and pleads for proper respect for the mother:

> Sempronius to Maximus his brother, very many greetings. . . . I learned that you are treating our revered mother harshly as if she were a slave. Please, dearest brother, do not distress her in anything. If any one of the brothers talks back to her, you ought to box their ears. . . . For we ought to reverence her who bore us as a god, especially when she is so good. This I have written to you, brother, since I know the sweetness of dear parents. Please write me about your health. Farewell, brother (2nd half of 2nd century CE; Preisigke-Bilabel, 6263; LCL 1.121–tr. Winter, 48-49).

We learn also that a father's clout–whether political or otherwise–can effect his son's transfer from a military legion to the cavalry:

> Pausanias to his brother Heraclides greeting. I think our brother Sarapammon has informed you of the reason why I went down to Alexandria, and I have written you before about my boy Pausanias taking service in a legion. As however he wished no longer to serve in a legion but in a squadron, I was obliged on learning of this to go and see him, although I did not want to. So after many entreaties from his mother and sister to transfer him to Koptos, I went down to Alexandria and used many ways and means until at last he was transferred to the squadron at Koptos. . . . I beg you, brother, to write to me about your being all well, as I heard at Antinoopolis that there has been plague in your neighborhood. So do not neglect to write, that I may feel more cheerful about you.

Many salutations to my lady mother and my sister and our children, whom the evil eye shall not harm. Pausanias salutes you. I pray for the health of you and all your household (3rd century CE; *POxy* XIV.1666; LCL 1.149).

Another soldier, Terentianus, in the course of a lengthy letter written (in Latin) from the area of Alexandria to his father, Tiberianus, in Karanis says, "Moreover, I ask and beg you, father, to reply to me immediately about your health, that you are well [?]. I am worried about trouble at home [?] if you do not write back" (early 2nd century CE; *PMich* VIII.468). Actually, we have ten letters from Terentianus to his father (part of an archive found under the stairway of a house) and an eleventh to his sister, Tasoucharion, in which Terentianus shows his concern for her health in an interesting way: "I sent you papyrus so that you might be able to write me concerning your health" (*PMich* VIII.481).

Still another soldier, sending a lengthy list of wants (Send me! Send me!), castigates both of his parents for neglect:

To . . . my dearest mother, hearty greetings! Before all I pray that you and all your household are well. When you receive my letter, kindly send me 200 drachmae. When Geminus came to me I had only twenty staters; now I haven't one, because I got a mule car and I've spent all the money on it. I write this to you that you may know. Send me a thick woollen cloak and a purse, and a pair of leggings and a pair of leather cloaks, some olive-oil and the wash-basin of which you spoke and a pair of pillows. In addition, then, mother, send my monthly allowance in all haste. You said to me when I came to see you, "Before you reach your camp, I'll send one of your brothers to you," and you sent me nothing, but left me as I was, with nothing at all. . . , no money, nor anything–you left me as I was, like a dog; and my father came to me and gave me not a farthing, nor a purse nor anything. But they are all jeering at me, saying, "His father's a soldier and has given him nothing." He said, "If I go home, I'll send you everything": you sent me nothing. Why so? Valerius's mother sent him a pair of belts and a jar of olive-oil and a basket of meat, and clothing and 200 drachmae. So I beg you, mother, send me the things; do not leave me as I am. But I went and borrowed money from a comrade and from my adjutant. . . . When you receive my letter, kindly send me the things in all haste (3rd century CE; *BGU* 814).[12]

Fragments of writing on the margin show an additional "Send me." ("Why so? asks the young soldier; today the response might be "Tough love.")

A young man finds it necessary to defend himself against some (unknown) complaints by his (illiterate–or perhaps Egyptian-speaking) mother and sister while at the same time lodging a complaint himself that they have not inquired about his illness:[13]

---

[12] I use the tr. of W. G. Waddell, *The Lighter Side of the Papyri* (Low Fell, UK: C. F. Cutter, 1932) 6-7.

[13] The direct address to the person who was to read this letter to the recipients is unparalleled, according to the editor, A. Bülow-Jacobsen, *Papyri Graecae Hauniensis* (Bonn: Rudolf Habelt, 1981) 12-17.

You who are reading this letter, whoever you are, make an effort and translate to the
women what is written in this letter and tell them: Ptolemaios to his mother Zosime and
his sister Rhodous, greetings. You blame me through letters and through people as if I
had done wrong, so I swear by all the gods that I have done nothing of what has been
said except only about the donkey of Karas. You seem to be lying in wait for me and if
you are angry because I did not send you anything though I had heard, the reason is that
I was kicked by a horse and was in danger of losing my foot or even my life. I blame
you because you did not inquire about me, neither by words nor by letters (2nd century
CE; *PHaun* 14).

From other papyri in the famous Zenon archives–nearly two thousand papers
from 260-240 BCE of a certain Zenon, the manager of the 6,800-acre Philadelphia
estate of Apolonius, the finance minister under Ptolemy II–we already know the
addressee and the other characters in a letter written in early March, 257 BCE. It
is addressed to Zenon by Simale, who had indentured her son, Herophantos, into
the service of Apolonius about a year earlier and had received an appropriate
payment (one mina). Olympichos, Herophantos's supervisor, is known from three
other Zenon papyri, though his exact supervisory role is not known:[14]

Simale, mother of Herophantos, to Zenon, greeting. Since I heard that my boy had been
quite badly treated, I came to you; and when I came, I desired to complain to you about
these matters. When Olympichos hindered me from seeing you, I got admission to the
boy as best I could, and although I laughed heartily at him, I found him lying ill; and the
first sight of him was enough to grieve me. But when Olympichos joined us, he said that
he would beat him until he wore him out–or he had done so, since he was nearly that
already [?]. Properly, therefore, I beg and beseech you to bring about a change in these
matters and to report to Apollonios in what manner my boy has been constantly insulted
by Olympichos, as if he, indeed, were to blame for his sickness. I also [wish to point
out?] that I have received nothing for a year now except the mina and three artabs of
wheat since the month Dystros, when Herophantos came to you. The boy himself tells
me of the good will of Apollonios and yourself which you have constantly shown toward
him. I ask you, therefore, and beg that, if Apollonios has given orders to pay him
anything, his wages be paid to me. Be assured that as soon as the god frees him [of his
sickness], I will bring him back to you in order that I may see you regarding other
matters. The rest please learn from the man who brings you the letter. For he is not a
stranger to us. Goodbye (*PCol* III.6)

Members of other families away from home send and receive plaintive
letters. A daughter away needs the thoughts and affection of her father:

Serenilla to Socrates her father, heartiest greetings. Before all I pray for your good
health and make supplication for you daily to the lord Serapis and the other gods who
share his temple. I want you to know that I am all alone. Keep always in your mind,
"My daughter is in Alexandria," so that I may know that I have a father, and others may
not look on me as having no parents. Give the bearer of this letter a reply about your

[14] For discussion of all these matters, see W. L. Westermann and E. S. Hasenoehrl, *Zenon Papyri:
Business Papers of the Third Century B. C. Dealing with Palestine and Egypt* (Columbia Papyri: Greek
Series 3; Zenon Papyri,1; New York: Columbia University Press, 1934) 1.35-39.

health. Greetings to my mother and brothers, to Sempronius and his household (2nd/3rd century; *BGU* 385).

Then a certain Ptolema, in an unskilled hand with numerous spelling errors, writes two letters on a single papyrus sheet from Alexandria back home to two other female household members; the second letter reads:

Ftolema [= Ptolema] to Heros her sister, greetings. I am sorry, sister, that I did not see you when I was setting out for Alexandria. Since I have nothing just now, send what I wrote you about, sandals and five pairs of loaves. Get these from the food supply. Greet your sister-in-law and your husband and your brother-in-law. Farewell (1st/2nd century CE; *PMich*, inv. 4203).[15]

A plea for some basics: shoes and bread!

A son away at school reassures his father: "Now do not be uneasy, father, about my studies; I am working hard and taking relaxation; I shall do well" (3rd century CE; *POxy* X.1296; LCL 1.137). Another son sends a sharp, yet presumably good-natured retort to his father's questioning of his moral behavior in Alexandria:

To my dear father Origenes, I, Trophimus, send many greetings . . .. You wrote me in your letter that I am boasting in the presence of Diodorus because I sent you money; but I do not boast idly; I did send [it] by Philoxenus. . . . If it seems good to you, send me a jar of oil. You wrote to me: "You are staying in Alexandria with your paramour." Write me, who is my paramour? I pray for your welfare (3rd or 4th century CE; *POxy* VIII.1160–tr. Winter, 61-62).

And Trapbos, a young man apparently working away from home, writes urgently for his father to come to his rescue:

Trapbos to Herakles his father, very many greetings. Before all else I pray for your health. I have caused unpleasantness for my overseers, and I want to get away from them. If you can come, come at once. For if I do not get away from them, then they will give me a flogging every day. Give salutations to all in the house (127 CE; *PMich* III.204).

In another case, through a public document at Hermopolis, parents cut their son adrift:

Since our son Castor, along with others in riotous living, has squandered all his own property and now has laid hands on ours and desires to scatter it, on that account we are taking precautions lest he should deal despitefully with us, or do anything else amiss–we beg, therefore, that a proclamation be set up that no one should [any longer lend him money] (1st/2nd century CE; *PFlor* 99).[16]

[15] Published by J. Whitehorne, "Two Michigan Papyri," *Aegyptus* 71 (1991) 17-23.
[16] For this tr., see G. Milligan, *Selections from the Greek Papyri* (Cambridge: Cambridge University Press, 1910) 71-72.

Finally, the famous letter–because it parallels the Parable of the Prodigal Son in Luke 15:11-32–from a penitent son, Antonius Longus, to Nilous, his mother in Karanis, deserves quotation, at least in part:

> I was ashamed to come to Karanis, because I go about in filth. I wrote to you that I am naked. I beg you, mother, be reconciled to me. Well, I know what I have brought on myself. I have received a fitting lesson. I know that I have sinned" (2nd century CE; *BGU* 846; LCL 1.120).

Relationships Formed and Broken: Marriage and Divorce

Marriage contracts lack nothing in their details (and this one is too long to quote in full):

> For good fortune.   Aurelia Thaesis daughter of Eudaemon and of Herais, of Oxyrhynchus, acting with Aurelius Theon also called Nepotianus and however he is styled, has given her daughter Aurelia Tausiris in marriage to Aurelius Arsinous son of Tryphon and of Demetria, of the said city, as husband, to whom the said giver brings as the dowry of her said daughter the bride in common gold on the Oxyrhynchite standard a necklace of the kind called *maniaces* with a stone, weighing without the stone 13 quarters [here follows a list of three pieces of jewelry and four items of clothing]. . . . And questioned concerning the aforesaid dowry by the giver of the bride, Aurelia Thaesis, the bridegroom Aurelius Arsinous acknowledged that he had received the full number at the aforesaid weight and valuation. Wherefore let the parties to the marriage live together blamelessly, observing the duties of marriage, and let the bridegroom supply his wife with all things necessary in proportion to his means. But if–which heaven forbid–owing to disagreement a separation takes place between the parties, the bridegroom shall restore to the giver of the bride, if still alive, or, if not, to the bride, the aforesaid dowry in full within sixty days from the date of the demand. . . . If at the time of the separation the bride is pregnant, the bridegroom shall give her for the expenses of her confinement 40 drachmae. . . . This contract is valid, being written in duplicate so that each party may have a copy . . . , and to each other's questions whether this is done rightly and fairly they have given their assent. . . . [signed] I Aurelia Thaesis, have given my daughter in marriage to the above-mentioned Arsinous and have presented to him the aforesaid dowry as stated, and in answer to the formal question I have given my consent. I, Aurelius Theon also called Nepotianus, acted with her and wrote on her behalf, as she is illiterate. I, Aurelius Arsinous, have received the aforesaid dowry, and if–which heaven forbid–a separation takes place, I will restore it as stated above, and in answer to the formal question I have given my consent (260 CE; *POxy* X.1273; LCL 1.5).

Wedding invitations were delivered locally, usually a day ahead: "Theon son of Origenes invites you to the wedding of his sister tomorrow, Tubi 9, at the 8th hour" (Oxyrhynchus, 4th century CE; *POxy* XII.1487; LCL 1.174; cf. *PFuad* 7 [2nd century CE]), and "Herais invites you to the marriage of her children, at home, tomorrow, the 5th, starting at the 9th hour" [= 3 p.m.] (3rd century CE; *POxy* I.111)–in this case the wedding of a brother and sister, which was common in

Egypt until forbidden by a Roman imperial edict in 295 CE.[17]   Sometimes, however, a wedding invitation elicited regrets, as in the following letter, which–incidentally– must have come from an affluent family:

> Apollonios and Sarapias to Dionysia, greeting. You filled us with joy in announcing the good news of the wedding of your fine Sarapion, and we should have come straightaway on that day, most longed-for by us, to attend upon him and share your joy, but on account of the annual assizes and because we are recovering from illness we could not come. Roses are not yet in full bloom here–in fact they are scarce–and from all the nurseries and all the garland-weavers we could just barely get together the 1,000 that we sent you with Sarapas, even with picking the ones that ought not to have been picked till tomorrow. We had all the narcissi you wanted, so instead of the 2,000 you asked for we sent 4,000. We wish you did not think us so petty as to make fun of us by writing that you have sent the money [for the flowers], when we too regard your children as our own and esteem and love them more than our own, and so we are as happy as you and their father (2nd century CE; *POxy* XLVI.3313).[18]

Wedding gifts were sent: "Isidoras to Chenanoubis best greetings. Before all I pray you are well. Look, we gave instruction to my father about you so that he might bring them to you with him to your daughter's wedding, bringing what we intend to give her. See that you do not, therefore, do otherwise and cause us grief" (Fayum, 1st half of 2nd century CE; *PYale* 78). On another occasion a gift was given merely to maintain propriety, as indicated in this postscript to a letter from a mother to her son: "At your wedding the wife of my brother Discas brought me 100 drachmae; and now that her son Nilus is about to marry, it is right that we should make a return gift, even if we have grievances against them still pending" (2nd century CE; *PFlor* III.332).

A prospective mother-in-law requires tactful and careful treatment:

> To my most honorable Nonna, [from] Papais, greeting. Before all I salute you and the mistress, my bride. I explained to your goodness already through the reader Serenus that you should take pains to arrange a house for me–only near to your own dwelling. For it is fitting that we should not be separated from one another. For next to God I respect you as my mother and my sister and you mean everything to me, if only my bride is in good health. But if you do not like to do this and feel troubled by remaining in the immediate neighborhood of your house, let me know, so that I may write to my brother Cronius and he may get ready for me the [alternate ?] house . . . or I may get the house. . . . When I come I am also bringing the sandals of P[. . .]ia; and if you have thought of anything useful for the wedding, write to me so that I may bring it with me when I come; for there is no dissension [?] between her and the bride. I pray for your lasting health (4th century CE; *PAnt* II.93).

---

[17] See the discussion in N. Lewis, *Life in Egypt,* 43-44. Sibling marriages had an economic advantage: keeping two shares of an estate entirely within the family (p. 44).

[18] Cf. N. Lewis, *Life in Egypt,* 80.

As the earlier marriage contract implied, estrangement may occur and may not always be rectified–with divorce as the result:

> Soulis, grave-digger, of the toparchy of Kusis, to Senpsais daughter of Psais and of Tees, grave-digger, of the same toparchy, greeting. Since through some evil spirit it has come about that we have separated from each other in respect of our common wedded life, I, the aforesaid Soul, herewith acknowledge that before sending her away I have received in full all the objects given to her by me in any manner whatsoever and that I will not hereafter take proceedings against her about cohabitation or wedding-gift, but that she is free to depart and marry whom she chooses; and I, the aforesaid Senpsais, acknowledge that I have received in full from him, the aforesaid Soul, all that was given to him by way of dowry . . . ; and we will not henceforth take proceedings against each other about any matter at all of any kind, written or unwritten, because the separation is absolute (305-6 CE; *PGrenf* II.76; LCL 1.8).

Life Goes On: Love and Loneliness, Conflict and Reconciliation

Husbands and wives may experience differences and the papyrus letters reveal the intense feelings involved. One husband seeks reconciliation with his wife, who has left him, and misses her deeply, as indicated in an impassioned though uneducated and therefore at points obscure communication. Though we possess only the husband's response, his wife seems to have run off with a man named or nick-named "Bobtail" (*Kolobos*), and strong emotion is conveyed in striking ways:

> Serenus to Isidora, his sister and wife, very many greetings. Before all else I pray that you are well, and every morning and evening I do obeisance in your name before [the goddess] Thoëris, who loves you. I want you to know that ever since you left me I have been in mourning, weeping at night and lamenting by day. After I bathed with you on Phaophi [=month] 12th I had neither bath nor oil-rub till Hathyr 12th [=the next month], when I received from you a letter that can shatter a rock, so much did your words upset me. I wrote you back on the instant, and sent it on the 12th with your letter enclosed. You say in your letter, "Kolobos has made me into a prostitute," but he told me, "Your wife sends you this message: '[Remind him] it was he himself who sold my necklace, and it was he himself who put me on the boat.'" You're just saying that so people won't believe my rebuttal. But look, I keep writing you and writing you. Are you coming [back] or not coming? Tell me that (2nd century CE; *POxy* III.528; LCL 1.125).[19]

Not only has he responded on the very day of receipt but has returned her letter as well--perhaps so that his wife can reread the letter that has so disturbed him and be brought to her senses.

When the situation is reversed–a husband who is away but does not return as expected–both affection and anger emerge in the same letter:

> Isias to her brother [as often, doubtless = husband] Hephaestion, greeting. If you are well and other things are going right, it would accord with the prayer which I make

[19] For this tr., see N. Lewis, *Life in Egypt,* 56.

continually to the gods. I myself and the child and all the household are in good health and think of you always. When I received your letter from Horus, in which you announce that you are in detention in the Serapeum at Memphis,[20] for the news that you are well I straightway thanked the gods, but about your not coming home, when all the others who had been secluded there have come, I am ill-pleased, because after having piloted myself and your child through such bad times and been driven to every extremity owing to the price of corn I thought that now at least, with you at home, I should enjoy some respite, whereas you have not even thought of coming home nor given any regard to our circumstances, remembering how I was in want of everything while you were still here, not to mention this long lapse of time and these critical days, during which you have sent us nothing. As, moreover, Horus who delivered the letter has brought news of your having been released from detention, I am thoroughly displeased. Notwithstanding, as your mother is also annoyed, for her sake as well as for mine please return to the city, if nothing more pressing holds you back. You will do me a favor by taking care of your bodily health. Goodbye (168 BCE; *PLond* 42; LCL 1.97).

The Family Celebrates: Parties and Pleasure

Social events require invitations to dinner: "To my lord Macarius from Gennadius, adjutant. Deign to gladden the birthday festival of my son Gennadius by dining with us on the 16th at the 7th hour" (5th century CE; *POxy* IX.1214).[21] They also require food: "Greetings to Horion. Send me tomorrow, the 14th, a tasty fish. For you know that it is my official birthday. The 13th" (2nd century CE; *PPrinc* III.165), and "For dinner on the 5th, a Canopic [town in lower Egypt] liver; for dinner on the 6th, 10 oysters, 1 lettuce; for dinner on the 7th, 2 small loaves, 1 fattened bird from the water, 2 snipe [or vegetables ?]" (1 CE; *POxy* IV.738). Finally, they require entertainment:

> Silvanos son of Ammonios, Hermopolite, business manager, to Ploution son of Tapous and Dioskoros son of Hadrianos, both from Alabastrine, greeting. I have agreed with you for me to perform on the flute, together with my entire company, in the aforesaid village for 8 days from the 24th of the next month Epeiph, for a wage each day of . . . drachmas of silver." (late 2nd century CE; *PCol* VIII.226).

Failure to attend a party–here a birthday celebration–could elicit a rather sarcastic response:

> Flavius Herculanus to the sweetest and most honored Aplonarion, very many greetings. . . . I was exceedingly grieved that you did not come for my boy's birthday, both you and your husband, for you could have enjoyed yourself for many days along with him. But

---

[20] Presumably the cloistering was in obedience to the perceived will of the god Serapis, and "the recluse was 'possessed' by the god, whether for a short period or for many years" (LCL 1, p. 283 n. b).

[21] For a discussion of dinner and wedding invitations, see J. F. Oates, A. E, Samuel, and C. B. Welles, *Yale Papyri in the Beinecke Rare Book and Manuscript Library* (ASP 2; New Haven, CT/Toronto: American Society of Papyrologists, 1967) 260-64; and J. F. Gilliam, "Invitations to the Kline of Sarapis," *Collectanea Papyrologica: Texts Published in Honor of H. C. Youtie* (ed. A. E. Hanson; Papyrologische Texte und Abhandlungen, 19; Bonn: R. Habelt, 1976) 315-24.

doubtless you had more important business; that is why you disdained us." (3rd century CE; *POxy* XIV.1676).

It may be, also, that the family home needs redecoration:

> Capito to his dear friend Teres, many greetings. .... With regard to the dining room (for I will do nothing but what you require) I have of course had everything put in hand–in fact, rather more. For I greatly value and cherish your friendship, and everything that you enjoined on me in your first letter you will find accomplished. . . . And the plasterers have done everything in bright colors and are still at it. With regard to the terrace portico, as you are intending to redecorate it, write me what you want done, what you mean to have there, whether the siege of Troy or some other subject. The space demands something of the kind. Farewell (1st century CE; *PBerl* 11662).[22]

Incidentally, if needed, a mouse-catcher could be hired: "Horus to his esteemed Apion, greeting. Regarding Lampon, the mouse-catcher, I paid him for you as earnest money 8 drachmae in order that he may catch the mice while they are with young. Please send me the money. . . . Goodbye" (late 1st century CE; *POxy* II.299).

The Bigger World out There: Work, Health, Security

Agriculture has its ups and downs. A school exercise on a wooden tablet from 4th century Roman Egypt provides ten lines of verse that its latest editor has entitled, "The Happy Farmer." It was found in a Delta region known for animal husbandry, and each line ends with a crudely-drawn cross–certifying an attempt at poetry:
Great is the farmer. A list of his noble virtues.

> Grant me to speak and I will address [them] in my verses.
> Well provided is the farmer even if he sows the land all by himself,
> enjoying sweet toils in the country,
> taming the ox with the yoke and setting it there to plow,
> in the dark night taking care of the fodder,
> during the days as well practicing his trade.
> Even when the farmer cannot find sufficiency,
> ever devoting his care, with joy, to farming,
> he has the fruit of toils upon toils.[23]

Both animals and farm workers were to be kept busy:

---

[22] No. 34 in B. Olsson, *Papyrusbriefe aus der frühesten Römerzeit* (Uppsala: Almqvist & Wiksells, 1925) 99-103; tr. taken from D. Brooke, *ed., Private Letters Pagan and Christian* (New York: Dutton, 1930) 66.

[23] Staatsbibliothek Preussischer Kulturbesitz, Berlin, MS graec. qu. 36; see R. Cribiore, "The Happy Farmer: A Student Composition from Roman Egypt," *Greek, Roman, and Byzantine Studies* 33 (1992) 247-63.

> Isidorus to his brother Aurelius, many greetings. . . . As to the bulls, make them work, don't allow them to be entirely idle. Carry all the branches into the road and have them tied together by threes and dragged along. You will find this of service. Don't make over anything to their masters. I shall perhaps give him nothing. I am causing them much trouble [?]. Don't allow the carpenters to be altogether idle; worry them. I pray for your health (3rd century CE; *POxy* I.121).

But on occasion someone takes more than is properly due him and is reprimanded with sarcasm and threats:

> Apollonios to Phanias. You acted splendidly, going to Theadelphia and getting 2 art. of wheat from Sakaon instead of one! One is due to you from the account of the month of Thoth, but you, you went and got 2 art. instead of one. In the past too you went to Taurinou and got 2 art. instead of one through Sakaon. Well, return to Sakaon the artaba of wheat you gratuitously got from him, or else you will have cause to feel sorry (no date; *PSakaon* 55).

Then, too, debts could be hard to collect: "Let me tell you that you owe me seven years' rents and revenues, so unless you send remittances you know the risk you run" (late 3rd century CE; *PTebt* II.424).

But life has its more serious downsides. Inflation, for example, is no modern development: from the Hermopolite nome in the 3rd century comes the complaint that ". . . it is inexpedient to buy. We have not even found here a cloak for Eupsephia, for everything has risen in price. . ." (*PRyl* II.244); and, for reasons not fully understood, severe economic losses compelled a Karanis man to resign from a guild: "To Thrax, the president, and to the fellow guildsmen, from Epiodoros. Since I am impoverished and unable to act as patron of the club, I ask that you accept my resignation. Farewell" (184 CE; *PMich* IX.575). Moreover, disasters occur, not only on the farm: "Write to me about any matter that you choose. We heard that mice have eaten up the crop. Pray come to us and buy wheat here. . ." (late 2nd century CE; *PTebt* I.56; LCL 1.102), but also in town: ". . . They brought your letter about what is happening in the village by reason of the break in the dam" (2nd century CE; *PMich* VIII.488; cf. the plague in *POxy* XIV.1666, quoted above). And illness is frequent, prompting this urgent request: "Apion to Didymus, greeting. Put off everything, and immediately on receipt of this letter of mine come to me, since your sister is sick" (3rd century CE; *PTebt* II.421). A woman concerned about her mother's health writes:

> Apollonous to Thermouthas her mother, many greetings. Before all things we pray that you are in good health, along with Apollonarion. I want you to know that I heard from those who have come to me that you have been ill; but I was glad to hear that you have gotten better. I ask you earnestly and beg you, take care of yourself and also of the little girl, so that you may get through the winter, so that we may find you in good health. We are also all well (ca. 100 CE; *PCol* VIII.215).

In a reverse situation, a mother writes to her grown son who, she is told, has a sore foot from a splinter and can only walk slowly: "Do not then forget, my child, to write me regarding your health, for you know the anxiety [of a mother] for a child" (3rd century CE ; *BGU* 380–tr. G. Milligan[24]).

Framed in a surprisingly philosophical analysis by a man in some unknown distress comes this impassioned plea for help:

> Hermias to his sister, greeting. What remains to write to you about I do not know, for I have told you of everything till I am tired, and yet you pay no attention. When a man finds himself in adversity he ought to give way and not fight stubbornly against fate. We fail to realize the inferiority and wretchedness to which we are born. Well, so far nothing at all has been done; make it your business to send some one to me . . . to stay with me until I know the position of my affairs. Am I to be distracted and oppressed until Heaven takes pity on me? . . . See that matters are properly conducted on your own part or our disasters will be complete. We are resolved not to continue in misfortune[?].
>
> Farewell; I wish you all prosperity (4th century CE; *POxy* I.120).

On the reverse side, he pleads again: "Whatever you do, do not fail me in my trouble. . . . Can time accomplish everything after all?"

Another unknown calamity prompts a defiant threat even to the gods:

> To Stephanus from Hephaestion. On the receipt of the letter of my son Theon put off everything and come at once to the homestead because of what has happened to me. If you take no heed, as the gods have not spared me, so will I not spare the gods. Goodbye (3rd century CE; *POxy* VII.1065).

Reports of thefts and robberies were common:[25] "On the 6th of the present month . . . a brood-sow about to litter, tawny-colored, worth 12 drachmae, was thievishly stolen from me in the village by certain individuals" (34 CE; *PRyl* II.134); "Chaeremon son of Moschas, who was formerly a brewer on the estate, not content with heaping insults on my dependents, caught Artemidorus, now my brewer, and gave him many blows all over his body, and robbed him of a female donkey, a sack full of *cnecus* (safflower), 40 silver drachmae, and clothes" (38 CE; *PRyl* II.145); or, "Heraïs, wife of Heraclas, . . . having entered the house which I possess in the village seized my daughter, gave her numerous blows all over her body, tore her purple tunic, and carried off 100 drachmae from the money of the gymnasiarch which I administer" (40 CE; *PRyl* II.151). Assaults for other reasons were also common, as this document from the Aurelius Isidorus archive at Karanis illustrates:

---

[24]G. Milligan, ed., *Selections from the Greek Papyri* (Cambridge: Cambridge University Press, 1910) 104-5.

[25]For a general discussion of crime and its control, see R. Alston, "Violence and Social Control in Roman Egypt," *Proceedings of the 20th International Congress of Papyrologists, Copenhagen, 23-29 August, 1992* (ed. Adam Bülow-Jacobsen; Copenhagen: Museum Tusculanum Press, University of Copenhagen, 1994) 517-21.

> . . . The cattle of Pamounis and Harpalus damaged the planting which I have and what
> is more [their cow] grazed in the same place so thoroughly that my husbandry has
> become useless. I caught the cow and was leading it up to the village when they met me
> in the fields with a big club, threw me to the ground, rained blows upon me and took
> away the cow–as indeed the (marks of) the blows all over me show–and if I had not
> chanced to obtain help from the deacon Antoninus and the monk Isaac, who happened
> by, they would quickly have finished me off completely (June 324 CE; *PColl.Youtie*
> II.77).

Incidentally, how were individuals identified in Greco-Roman Egypt? Lacking fingerprint and photographic technologies, physical characteristics or marks were utilized: ". . . Sarapas, about 21 years old with a scar on his forehead on the right" (88/89 CE; *PMich* IX.545); "Philoxena. . . , whose vision suffers from cataracts, with a mole on the right side of her nose and a scar on her [. . .] brow," followed by the description of another person in the same document: ". . . 22 years old, of medium height, honey-complexioned, with a long face, a straight nose, a white spot on the right eye" (9 February 44 CE; *PColl.Youtie* 19); and ". . . Tapekusis, daughter of Horos, the son of Katoites, about 45 years old with a scar on her upper lip to the left" (120 CE; *PMich* III.188). A young boy, a slave, is described (along with three others) in more detail: "Okaimos, about 7, round face, nose flat, grey eyes, fiery complexion, long straight hair, scar on forehead above the right eyebrow, circumcised" (12 May 257 BCE; *C.Pap.Jud* I.4). People without distinguishing marks are so noted: ". . . Hero, about 50 years old, unmarked. . ." (164 CE; *PMert* III.105).

There was also prejudice. In a document addressed to "King Ptolemy," a petitioner in a property dispute refers to the defendant as "holding me in contempt because I am an Egyptian" (246-221 BCE; *PYale* 46). Also, in the course of a brief business letter from the Arsinoite nome discussing wages and harvest comes the assertion, "For all Egyptians are dull" (Greek = lacking common sense, tact; stupid, "blockheads") (250-300 CE; *PUps.Frid* 10; cf. *SB* V.7529 for a parallel characterization). Similarly, in a crudely written letter, a worker (probably an Arab, since camels and Syria are mentioned) complains to the famous Zenon that he has not received wages due him:

> Well, they treated me with scorn because I am a "barbarian." I beg you therefore, if it
> seems good to you, to give them orders that I am to obtain what is owing and that in
> future they pay me in full, in order that I may not perish of hunger because I do not know
> how to act like a Greek. You, therefore, kindly cause a change in attitude toward me (ca.
> 256/255 BCE; *PCol* IV.66 = *PCol.Zen* II.66).

Prejudice directed toward another group emerges through a clear sentence in an otherwise damaged and obscure papyrus letter: "You know that they loathe the Jews"–possibly the earliest known expression of anti-Jewish feeling in daily life in Hellenistic Egypt (1st half of 1st century BCE; *C.Pap.Jud* I.141).[26] Finally, a letter giving advice to a man in financial difficulty tells him how to deal with his creditor: "Entreat him every day; perhaps he may take pity on you. If not, like everybody else, beware you too of the Jews" (41 CE; *BGU* 1079; LCL 1.107).

Life Ends: Wills, Death, and Burial

Following all the exigencies of family and social life comes death. Like all wills, those written in Greco-Roman times–often lengthy and detailed documents–were prepared in anticipation of death:

> The 19th year of the Emperor Caesar Titus Aelius Hadrianus Antoninus Augustus Pius, the 30th of the month Germaniceus, at Oxyrhynchus in the Thebaid; for good fortune. This is the will made in the street [= public notary] by me Acusilaus son of Dius son of Dionysius also called Acusilaus and of Dionysia daughter of Theon, of the city of Oxyrhynchus, being sensible and in my right mind. So long as I survive I am to have power over my property, to make whatever disposition I choose and to alter and revoke the present will, and whatever disposition I make shall be valid. But if I die leaving the present will, I set free . . . my slaves Psenamounis . . . and Hermas and Apollonous . . . and her daughter Diogenis and another slave of mine called Diogenis. I bequeath to my wife. . . , being well disposed and showing all faithfulness towards me, whatever I may leave in the way of furniture utensils, objects of gold, clothing, ornaments, wheat, pulse, crops, all my household stock, and debts owed to me, recorded and unrecorded. I leave my son Dius . . . [etc., etc.].
> My wife, and after her death my son Dius, shall give to my slaves and freedmen for a feast which they shall hold beside my tomb every year on my birthday 100 silver drachmae wherewith to furnish it. . . . This will is valid. I, the aforesaid Acusilaus son of Dius, have made this will, the whole body of which is in my own writing, with all the above provisions. I am 48 years of age, with a scar on the right foot, and my seal is an image of Thonis (156-165 CE; *POxy* III.494).

When death comes, it is reported, but there is no *humanitas* in a legal death notice:

> To [name missing], Komogrammateus of Psenuris, from Papontos, son of Paseis son of Papontos, his mother being from Apia, from the village of Psenuris. My son Papeeus, whose mother is [name missing], a minor, registered in the aforesaid village, died in the month of Epeiph of the present 10th year of Hadrian Caesar the lord. Therefore I make this report that he may be entered in the register of those who have died (126 CE; *PMich* IX.538).

Pathos, however, can be conveyed through a mere half dozen words on a wooden mummy label from our period: "Psais, son of Psais, grandson of Pianes, lived 6

---

[26]See the discussion in V. A. Tcherikover and A. Fuks, *Corpus Papyrorum Judaicarum* (3 vols.; Cambridge, MA: Harvard University Press, 1957-64) 1.256.

years. Farewell" (*Mich* inv. 4534 [10]).[27] An attempt at consolation was made by a woman after the death of Eumoerus:

> Irene to Taonnophris and Philo, be of good cheer! I was as much grieved and shed as many tears over Eumoerus as I shed for Didymas, and I did everything that was fitting, and so did all my friends. . . . But still there is nothing one can do in the face of such trouble. So I leave you to comfort yourselves. Goodbye (2nd century CE; *POxy* I.115).

Another such attempt, filled with clichés of the time, may not have been much more successful:

> Mnesthianus to Apollonianus and Spartiate, be brave! The gods are witness and when I learned about my lord your son I was grieved and I lamented as I would my own child. He was a person to be cherished. . . . Well, bear it nobly, for this rests with the gods. . . . I too have had a loss, a houseborn slave worth 2 talents. I pray that you fare well . . . in the benevolence of all the gods (14 December 235 CE; *PSI* 1248).

Another death notification, lacking the beginning, was motivated by self-protection:

> . . . as he was pasturing his sheep. As I was unable to carry his body, not without difficulty, or to ascertain his cause of death (for I do not know how he passed away) without official certification, I submit this report to you to safeguard myself regarding this matter and so that you may take cognizance. Farewell (8 January 317 CE; *PTheon* 57 = *PSakaon* 50 [reedited]).

Greed, however, may have motivated this request found in the archive of Tiberianus in Karanis: "You wrote me, saying that Gaius has sold something. I therefore ask you, brother, to find out what he has sold, and write to me. And about Sextus, I heard that he passed away. So learn who his heir is and when the will is to be opened" (early 2nd century CE; *PMich* VIII.475); and certainly greed dominated another case involving two brothers of the deceased:

> Melas . . . to Sarapion and Silvanus . . . greeting. I have sent you by the grave-digger the body of your brother Phibion and have paid him the fee for transporting the body, being 340 drachmae of the old coinage. And I am much surprised that you departed for no good reason without taking the body of your brother, but collected all that he possessed and so departed. And from this I see that you did not come up for the sake of the dead, but for the sake of his effects. Now take care to have ready the sum spent. The expenses are: [here follows a lengthy list comprising 17 lines]. . . total 520 drachmae. You will therefore make every effort to serve the person who will bring the body by providing loaves and wine and oil and whatever you can, in order that he may testify to me. . . .
> I pray for your health (3rd/4th century CE; *PGrenf* II.77; LCL 1.157).

---

[27]Published in A. E. Hanson, eds, *Collectanea Papyrologica: Texts Published in Honor of H. C. Youtie* (Papyrologische Texte und Abhandlungen 20; Bonn: Rudolf Habelt, 1976) 651.

Humanitas reappears, however, when a woman must be notified of her sister's death and it falls to her Christian niece to break the news:

> Madam and dearest aunt, Tare, your sister Allous's daughter, greets you in the Lord. Before all things I pray God that my letter finds you in good health and happy. That is my prayer. I have to tell you that since Easter my mother, your sister, has died. When I had a mother, she was an entire kindred to me. Since she is dead, I am alone, with no one belonging to me, in a strange land. Dear aunt, remember me, as if my mother herself asked you, and if the opportunity should offer, send someone to me. Greet all our family. May God keep you in good health many happy years, madam (5th century CE; *PBour* 25).[28]

Conclusion

Most researchers explore and scrutinize the ancient papyri for "serious" purposes, that is, to discover something about Egypt in Late Antiquity in terms of its history; or its politics, government, demography, and military forces; or its economy, production, agriculture, and transportation; or its literacy, education, and culture; or its laws, courts, and justice; or–yes–its people and day-to-day life. Yet, this last category has been too much neglected–with the notable exception of scholars like Naphtali Lewis and, currently, Roger Bagnall.[29] Yet, the ostensibly less "serious" purpose pursued in the present paper on ancient papyri may also be judged worthwhile if, as R. G. Collingwood argued long ago, "history is for self-knowledge."

For example, in my own field–manuscript studies of the New Testament– "serious" questions include: How did papyrus function as writing material? How expensive was it? How durable was it? How well and how fast did papyrus letters and manuscripts travel in antiquity? What is the comparative quality of the biblical text transmitted by the papyri? How long were papyrus manuscripts used in church settings before they were discarded? To be sure, as our earliest extant manuscripts, the New Testament papyri are of the highest significance in understanding the transmission of the New Testament text. And, by focusing on questions such as these, we may well advance "knowledge" in the areas specified, but what have we missed in the process? If history is for "self-knowledge," how is the "self" nourished by pursuing these cold, stark issues in rather impersonal, detached ways? On the other hand, how moving, how poignant, how contemporary are the papyrus letters and documents when we permit them to speak for themselves on the living and lively issues that we, like their writers and recipients of long ago, face day by day. Though many other papyri preserve classical texts, like Homer and Euripides, from which we have long gained insight

---

[28] Tr. from D. Brooke, ed., *Private,* 134.

[29] N. Lewis, *Life in Egypt under Roman Rule* (Oxford: Clarendon Press, 1983) and *Greeks in Ptolemaic Egypt: Case Studies in the Social History of the Hellenistic World* (Oxford: Clarendon Press, 1986); R. S. Bagnall, *Egypt in Late Antiquity* (Princeton, NJ: Princeton University Press, 1993).

into human nature, the letters and documents we have sampled here are "down to earth"–from real people of all social strata and various vocations and circumstances of life. And somehow, through these humble private letters and mundane public records on papyrus, our lives are linked with theirs in a continuity of despair and joy, of exasperation and affection, of greed and generosity, of illness and health, and of adversity and good fortune–all components of our common *humanitas.*[*]

*.The friendship that John and I have shared over these past thirty years was forged out of controversy--someone else's, not ours! Our paths joined briefly more than thirty years ago, during the hectic process by which the National Association of Biblical Instructors evolved into the American Academy of Religion. The AAR became a legal entity in 1964; in 1965, John Priest was Secretary and Acting Treasurer of AAR, and I was a member of its National Executive Council and also President of the Pacific Coast Section.

The controversy erupted in 1965, when John was nominated for the presidency and I for the vice presidency (to succeed to the presidency in 1967). But it was not to be. A floor fight developed and--to preserve the fledgling organization--both John and I withdrew. A new presidential nomination was proposed, with John becoming the vice presidential nominee, to assume the presidency in 1967--which he did, serving with distinction both as president and later as executive director.

Subsequently, each of us has followed his own career path--similar in several ways, though far removed geographically. Borne out of that experience, it is my pleasure, then, to dedicate this essay on *humanitas* in recognition of what so well characterizes this exemplary person: his own genuine humanity.

Insects in Classical
And Early Christian Literature

Robert M. Grant
University of Chicago

But between us and the Insects, namely nine-tenths of the living, there grins a prohibitive fracture
empathy cannot transgress:
(What Saint made a friend of a roach or
preached to an ant-hill?)[1]

Why Insects ?

Pliny the Elder apologizes for discussing insects at all.

> I feel sure that some will be disgusted at the animals I shall treat of, although Virgil did not disdain to speak quite unnecessarily of ants and weevils (*Georgics* 1.185-86), and of 'sleeping places heaped up by cockroaches that avoid the light' (4.243). Nor did Homer disdain among the battles of the gods to tell of the greed of the fly (*Iliad* 17.570), nor did Nature disdain to create them because she creates man.[2]

---

[1] W. H. Auden, *Epistle to* a *Godson and Other Poems*, 32 (my thanks to Nathan Scott for the reference). From *Collected Poems of W. H. Auden* by W. H. Auden. Copyright (e) 1972 by The Estate of W. H. Auden. Reprinted by permission of Random House, Inc.

[2] Pliny, *Natural History* 29.28; cf. Aristotle, *Parts of Animals* 645a6-23.

Inspired by his examples we proceed, illustrating close ties between entomological and theological, biblical and humane, for our old friend and colleague John Priest.

Considerate Bedbugs

Just as we look to the apocryphal *Acts of Paul* for a baptized animal, so we look to the *Acts of John* for considerate insects that respond to the orders of the apostle at an inn.[3] "I tell you, bugs," says the apostle, "behave yourselves one and all; you must leave your home for tonight and be quiet in one place." The author of the *Acts* reports that "we saw a mass of bugs collected by the door of the room we had taken." In the morning John addressed the bugs again. "Since you have behaved yourselves and listened to my counsel, go back to your own place." The bugs came running from the door towards the bed, climbed up the legs, and disappeared into the joints. (John obviously lacked concern for future hotel guests.)[4]

John's considerate companion was the *koris* or *cimex lectularius*, familiar in the world of Aristophanes as well as in hotels.[5] In his admirable study of hotels, restaurants, and cabarets, Kleberg refers to Aristophanes, to the "Augustan" *Life of Hadrian* (16.4, translated by D. Magie, LCL):

> I don't want to be a Florus,
> Stroll about among the taverns,
> Lurk about among the cook-shops,
> And endure the round fat insects,

and to Pliny's *Natural History* 9.154:

> Even the creatures found in inns in summertime, that plague us with a quick jump or hide chiefly in the hair, live in the sea and are often drawn out of the water clustering around the bait.[6]

In addition, Petronius tells of a slave in an inn holding his breath against the bugs in the bedding.[7] Artemidorus notes that bedbugs in dreams are symbols of cares and anxieties: "For bedbugs, like anxieties, keep people awake at night." [8] In

---

[3] *Acta Iohannis* 60-61, pp. 180-81 Bonnet.

[4] For a commentary see E. Junod and J. D. Kaestli, *Acta Iohannis* (*Corpus Christianorum: Series Apocryphorum* 2, Turnhout: Brepols, 1983), 527-41. The parallels cited are not close.

[5] Aristophanes, *Clouds* 634, 699, 710, 725; *Frogs* 115 (in hotels).

[6] See T. Kleberg, *Hotels, restaurants et cabarets dans l'antiquité romaine* (Uppsala: Almqvist & Wiksells, 1957) 93, 113.

[7] Petronius, *Satyricon* 98. His word *sciniphes* = Greek *skniphes* or *sknipes*. For *sknipes* in a tree cf. Plutarch, *Table-Talk* 2.3, 636D (translated in LCL 8, 1969, as "bark beetles"), surely not what Petronius means.

[8] Artemidorus, *Oneirocritica* 3.8, cited by P. Cox Miller, *Dreams in Late Antiquity* (Princeton University Press, 1994), 86-87.

addition, they point to impending disgust and distress for one's relatives, especially female.

Greek writers tell us that flies as well as bedbugs can exhibit religious sentiment. Pausanias reports that sacrifices to Zeus at Olympia drove flies out, but Aelian is more thoughtful. The flies of Olympia at the time of the feast make peace, so to speak, with visitors and the local inhabitants. In spite of the quantity of sacrifices, of blood shed, and of meat hung up, the flies voluntarily disappear and cross to the opposite bank of the Alphas. Afterwards "the flies come back, like exiles allowed to return by a decree."[9]

A much later account of St. Leutfred (he died in 738) is straightforward. One hot day he was troubled by flies and could get no rest, but when he folded his hands over his eyes and prayed all the flies disappeared, never to enter the house again."[10]

Bugs in Conflicts over Providence: Pro

When Stoics and others defended the providential arrangement of the world, they had to take insects into account and thus led the way to apologetic entomology. The optimistic Stoic Chrysippus defended bedbugs as really "useful for waking us up," as well as mice for "making us attentive about putting things away carefully,"[11] not to mention cocks, that (like mice) wake us up and pluck out scorpions and arouse us for battle.[12] They can all be fitted into the providential scheme.

The Stoic view appears again in the list of the workings of divine providence by the Christian Clement of Rome. Providence provides for "the smallest animals to come together in concord and peace."[13] Waszink notes many patristic parallels, especially from Jerome and Augustine.[14] The statements imply that these animals

[9] Pausanias, *Geography* 5.14.1; Aelian, *Nature of Animals* 5.17, cf. 11.8. I owe these references to E. Junod and J. D. Kaestli (n. 4 above) on *Acta Johannis* 60-61.

[10] E. C. Brewer, *Dictionary of Miracles* (Philadelphia: Lippincott, c. 1884), 364. H. Thurston and D. Attwater, *Butler's Lives of the Saints* 2 (New York: P. J. Kenedy, 1956), 610, say his life "deserves little confidence." The text is printed in B. Krusch and W. Levison, *Passiones vitaeque sanctorum* (*Monumenta Germaniae historica, Scriptores rerum Merovinqiorum* 7, Hannover/Leipzig: Hahn, 1919) 1-18 (c. 18, p. 15, 18-24).

[11] *Stoicorum Veterum Fragmenta* [SVF] II 1163 = Plutarch *Stoic Self-Contradictions* 1044D (Aristeas, however, is unenthusiastic about mice, 163-64). Not fleas, in spite of A. Terian, *Philonis Alexandrini De Animalibus* (Chico, CA: Scholars Press, 1981), 51 n.187; perhaps cheese (*ibid.*).

[12] SVF III 705 = Plutarch, *Stoic Self-Contradictions* 1049A (LCL 13.2) 1976, 538-39, with notes by H. Cherniss.

[13] 1 Clement 20.10; cf. Cicero, *Nature of the Gods* 2.123: spiders, mussels, crabs *quasi societatem coit; pisciculi parvi, sic dissimillimis bestialize communiter cibus quaeritur* (cf. A. S. Pease, *M. Tulli Ciceronis De Natura Deorum Libri III* 2 [Cambridge MA: Harvard University Press, 1958], 862-63). J. J. Thierry (*Vigiliae Christianae* 14 [1960] 235-44) notes that the subject is food and rightly criticizes those who find sex in *syneleuseis*

[14] J. H. Waszink, *Tertulliani De Anima* (Amsterdam: Muelenhoff, 1947) 188-89.

have moral goals and therefore reason. Beyond this, *Genesis Rabbah* quotes "the rabbis" as saying that

> Even things that you regard as completely superfluous to the creation of the
> world, for instance fleas, gnats, and flies, also fall into the classification of
> things that were part of the creation of the world.[15]

Significantly, Basil of Caesarea concludes a brief discussion of the wonders of insects with the statement, Peripatetic in origin, that "God created nothing unnecessary or lacking anything that is necessary."[16]

Bugs in Conflicts Over Providence: Con

Criticism of providence because of insects, on the other hand, appears in Porphyry's treatise *On Abstinence* (ultimately from the Academic philosopher Carneades).

> If God prepared the animals for human use, what use can we make of flies, mosquitoes,
> bats, cantharides, scorpions, vipers, some of which are ugly to view and foul to touch and
> unbearable to smell and make horrible and unattractive sounds, while others are deadly
> to those who encounter them?[17]

The dualist theologian Marcion and his followers went farther by assigning inconvenient insects to an inferior Creator. Tertullian addresses Marcion thus:

> You deride the more minute animals, [but] imitate if you can the buildings of the bee,
> the stables of the ant, the nets of the spider, the threads of the silkworm; check if you can
> those beasts of your bed and rug, the cantharides' poisons, the house fly's sting, the
> gnat's buzzing and sting.[18]

H. J. Schoeps correlated Marcion's complaints with his well-known abomination of women and sex, and urged psychoanalysts to be analytic enough to investigate him: "His vermin-phobia is in fact worthy of a psychiatric investigation.'"[19] I agree that his expressions about women sound shrill, but the complaints about bugs are merely conventional, coming from predecessors among the Academics. Philo of Alexandria discusses three kinds of insects (spider, bee,

---

[15] *Genesis Rabbah* I (tr. J. Neusner, Atlanta: Scholars Press, 1985) 104, from Parashah 10.

[16] Basil, *Hexaemeron* 8.7, p. 470 (Giet). Giet refers to Aristotle. *Parts of Animals* 661b23.

[17] Porphyry, *Abstinence* 3.20, p. 210, 10-15; based on Plutarch; cf. H. Cherniss, *Plutarch's Moralia* 13 (Cambridge, MA: Harvard University Press, 1976) 503; J.S. Reid, *M. Tulli Ciceronis Academica* (London: Macmillan, 1885) 318.

[18] Tertullian, *Against Marcion* 1.14.1; cf. *Soul* 10.5, trans. Waszink, *De Anima*, 187; A. Harnack, *Marcion: das Evangelium* vom *fremden Gott* (Texte und Untersuchungen 45, 1924) 270*.

[19] Schoeps, *Aus frühchristlicher Zeit* (Tubing en: Mohr, 1950) 257n2.

and ant) in his treatise *On Animals* and supplies Academic criticisms of them plus his own Stoic counter-arguments.[20]

A similar approach was related to the fact that in Genesis 1:31 God declares that his creation is "very good," in spite of the insects presumably present in it. Theophilus gave one solution to the implicit problem by claiming that since human beings were masters of all the animals, when they fell their slaves fell too.[21] Augustine's explanation is more subtle. He argued that the "natural power" of insemination from decaying matter (spontaneous generation) produced the wonders of minute insects like flies and ants. This aspect of the divine plan was present in the creation from the beginning, although not worked out until later.[22] The discussion and debate were inconclusive.

The *Clementine Homilies* and *Recognitions* face another kind of question: why the elephant's great bulk is carried on four legs, while the tiny mosquito or gnat has six. "Clement" sagely replies that the time is not right for an answer.[23] The atmosphere was that of "learned folklore," as Marrou remarked on Augustine's notes on curiosities.[24]

Biblical Bugs: Pro

Some insects lead exemplary lives. The Solomon of Proverbs could say, "Go to the ant, thou sluggard" (6:611). Here the Septuagint adds the bee as a model, following ordinary Hellenistic ideas about model insects.[25] Ants are among the "smallest on earth yet wise beyond the wisest;" they "have no strength yet prepare their store of food in the summer" (30:24-25). Search 11:3 tells us that while the bee is small, as winged creatures go, its product is very sweet.

Insects have a very minor role in the second-century *Physiologus*. Only the admirable ant appears in the oldest version (though the bee is added in the "Byzantine redaction"). Information comes from animal lore like Aelian's, combined with Proverbs 6:6 for the ant and Sirach 11:3-4 for the bee. *Physiologus* 12 discusses the ant:

> When the ant walks in line, each carries a seed in its mouth, and the empty ones do not
> ask for some[26] but go away and collect for themselves. When they store the grain in the

[20]Terian, *Philonis Alexandrini*: pro (and con) spider, 17-19 (77-78); bee, 20-21, 61, 65 (77-78); ant 42 (91-92). See S.O. Dickerman, "Some Stock Illustrations of Animal Intelligence in Greek Psychology," *Transactions and Proceedings of the American Philological Association* 42 (1911), 123-30

[21]Theophilus, *To Autolycus* 2.17

[22]Augustine, *Genesis to the Letter* 3.14.22 (PL 34.288-89); for spontaneous generation cf. Origin, *Homilies on Luke* 14, p.101 Rauer; *Against Celsus* 4.57. On Augustine, P. De Vooght, "La notion philosophique du miracle chez saint Augustin dans le 'De Trinitate' et le 'De Genesi ad litteram'," *Recherches de théologie ancienne et* médiévale 10 (1938), 317-43; also 11 (1939), 5-16; 197-222.

[23]*Clementine Homilies* 1.10 = *Recognitions* 1.9.

[24] H. I. Marrou, *Saint Augustin et la fin de la culture antique* (Paris: Boccard, repr. 1983) 136-41.

[25]Cf. Dickerman, "Some Stock Illustrations," 123-30 (usually ant, bee, spider).

[26]Cf. Matt 25:8

ground they divide the seeds in two so that when winter comes they will not sprout again
and cause starvation. At harvest the ant goes to a field and climbs on the sheaf and takes
the seed, but first smells the stem of the sheaf to know if it is barley or wheat (it eats only
this).

Even later, Jerome states in his *Life of Malchion* that this monk was greatly
edified by ants he saw working together in the desert.[27]

Biblical Bugs: Con

Like Marcion and us, the ancient Hebrews found flies annoying, alive or
dead. ("Dead flies make the perfumer's sweet ointment turn rancid and ferment."[28])
The dog-fly (*kynomuia*) was a plague against Egypt (Exodus 8:20-32).[29]
Baalzebub, the name of a Philistine god at Ekron (2 Kings 1:2, etc.), means "lord
of flies" in Hebrew, while in the synoptic gospels Beezeboul is prince of demons.
William Golding followed tradition when he identified the two deities in his novel
Lord of the Flies. Origin points out how minute it is but how unpleasant its sting.[30]

Leviticus 11:22-23 lists four kinds of locusts (grasshoppers?) that can be
eaten, including the "desert locusts" that John the Baptist presumably consumed
in the desert. He combined them with wild honey (Mark 1:6; Matt 3:4) since the
ancients did not possess sugar as such. Some of his critics supposed that he did not
eat or drink at all but was a demoniac (Matt 11:18), but Luke (7:33) more
accurately reports that he ate no bread and drank no wine. Origin, relying on
Proverbs 30:27, says locusts have no king.[31]

Moths, of course, produced nothing but trouble since they were so damaging
to clothes. Job mentions them four times (4:19; 27:18,20; 32:22) and uses the
word "moth-eaten" in 13:28. Moths appear three times in Isaiah (33:1; 50:9; 51:8),
once in Micah (7:4), once in Hosea (5:12). They are also found in Psalm 39:11,
Proverbs 14:30 and 25:20, and Sirach 19:3 and 42:13. They obviously consume
"treasure" on earth, though not in heaven (Matt 6:19-20 = Luke 12:33). James 5:2
is even more explicit about their destructiveness: "Your riches have rotted and
your garments are moth-eaten" (the same word as in Job).

Do Bugs Think?

Graeco-Roman scientists and philosophers often observed selected animals,
including a few insects, or repeated stories about them, classified them, and
inquired whether their behavior was rational or instinctive. Animal rationality, if
it existed, had implications for human nature and its rank in the operation of the

---

[27] Jerome, *Life of Malchion* 7, PL 23,59C.
[28] Eccl 10:1.
[29] Cf. Aelian 4.51, 6.37.
[30] Origen, *Exodus Homilies* 4.6, p.178 Baehrens.
[31] Origen, *Exodus*, p.179

universe (providential or not) and for the related topic of "animal rights."[32] (No one thought there were insect rights, however.)

The anti-Christian author Celsus uses stock examples of the rationality of ants and bees as he reworks a study like that by Philo.[33] Bees are rational, Celsus claims, because they have a leader, attendants and servants, undertake wars and conquests, kill the losers, have cities and suburbs, pass work from one to the next, and drive out and punish drones. Ants save for the winter, help others, have graveyards, and discuss routes with one another. (According to Cicero, the Academic philosophers argued that they have sensus, mens, ratio, and memoria.[34]) Origen replies with the traditional claim that their activities are instinctive, not rational. To be sure, he has to admit that according to Proverbs 24:59-60 ants are included among the "wiser than the wise" (though they have no strength, they prepare their food in summer), but he insists that the text has a hidden meaning, presumably because no one can be wiser than the wise.

The marvels of creation (in an Aristotelian-Stoic mode) win out in Basil of Caesarea, who discusses the wonders of bees at length in his homilies on the *Hexaemeron*, treating them among the birds created on the fifth day. Bees are not rational but they share a common life and common work and are governed by a non-hereditary, non-elective king.

They instinctively prepare wax and honey and make hexagonal cells for the honeycomb to protect the honey.[35] In his commentary on Isaiah, Basil states that flies are born out of manure, but then so does Aristotle,[36] whom he follows for nearly all his information about insects, not using him directly[37] but relying on an epitome close to the one by Aristophanes of Byzantium, which Lambros printed in the *Supplementum Aristotelicum*.[38]

---

[32] On ants cf. P. Rech and E. Stemplinger, "Ameise," *Reallexikon für Antike und Christentum* 1 (1950), 375-77; on flies, A. Hermann, "Fledge (Mucke)," *Reallexikon* 7 (1969), 1110-24.

[33] Origen, *Against Celsus* 4.74-87, with the notes of H. Chadwick, *Origen Contra Celsum* (Cambridge: Cambridge University Press, 1953) 242-53.

[34] Cicero, *Nature of the Gods* 3.21, with Pease's note (n.13 above), 2.1009.

[35] *Homilies* 8.4; cf. S. Giet, *Basile de Césarée Homélies sur l'Hexaéméron* (Paris: Cerf, 1950) 446-52; Y. Courtney, *Saint Basile et l'hellénisme* (Paris: Firmin-Didot, 1934) 117-20.

[36] Isaiah 7:18-19 (PG 30,468B), cited by Hermann, "Fledge," 1120; cf. Aristotle, *History* 539a23; 551a4. All Basil's information about insects comes ultimately from Aristotle: Courtonne, *Saint Basile*, 188-20.

[37] J. Levie, "Les sources de la 7e et de la 8e homélies de saint Basile sur l'Hexaéméron," *Musée Belge* 19-24 (1920) 142, notes that Basil worked in "demi-lumière, source ordinaire des méprises."

[38] *Supplementum Aristotelicum* 1.1. *Excerptorum Constantini de natura animalium libri duo. Aristophanis Historiae animalium epitome*, ed. S. P. Lambros (Berlin: Reimer, 1895). Summaries of Aristotle on insects appear at pp.3, 1 and 32, 1. On the work cf. R. Pfeiffer, *History of Classical Scholarship* 1 (Oxford: Clarendon, 1968) 172-73.

Classical antiquity knew few moral tales about insects,[39] though Aesop tells of a flea that justified its habit of biting because of "the way we insects live" and Lucian has a very mildly amusing parody-encomium on the fly.[40]

Do Bugs Breathe?

Do insects breathe or not? Aristotle, *On Respiration,* argued that insects do not breathe because when centipedes are cut up the parts stay alive, and flies and bees can swim in liquid for a long time. (On the other hand, in his *History of Animals* he noted that all insects die if covered with oil, a point suggesting that they do breathe.)[41] At Alexandria the Christian Clement marshaled a supposedly scientific account of breathing (mostly that of insects) in order to attack the less complicated idea that God enjoys smelling the smoke of sacrifices. How could God breathe? Clement deals with respiration and nourishment systematically. First, plants are nourished from the density of the air,[42] while hibernating bears are nourished from the exhalation arising from their own bodies.[43] Demons ventilate internally (*diapneitai*);[44] fish inhale (impunity) through the dilation of their gills; [45] and insects circumspire (*peripneitai*) through pressure of membranes on the waist (entome);[46] finally there are creatures that inhale (*anapnei*) by rhythmic beats corresponding to the counter-dilation (*antidiastole*)[47] of the lungs against the chest. A little later, Clement notes that land animals and birds inhale as human beings do, though fish breathe the air infused into the water at the creation. Theophilus too had remarked on this infusion.[48]

A few years later Tertullian rejected the claim that insects live without breathing and have no lungs or windpipes. He claims that they may well have such organs, for though some philosophers deny that gnats, ants, and moths have them,

---

[39] A. Marx, *Griechische Märchen von dankbaren Tieren* (Stuttgart: Kohlhammer, 1889) 124.

[40] B. E. Perry, *Babrius and Phaedrus* (Cambridge MA: Harvard University Press, 1965) 477, #272.

[41] *Respiration* 471b23; 475a29; W.S. Hett, Aristotle *On the Soul Parva Naturalia On Breath* (LCL 14, 1957), 436,454; cf. *History* 487a30 (tr. A. L. Peck; LCL 9, 1965). Contrast *History* 605b20; Pliny holds that they do breathe (*Natural History* 11.5-8).

[42] His contemporary Marcus Aurelius noted (*Meditations* 6.16) that plants ventilate internally (*diapneitai*; *anapnein* is for animals).

[43] Clement, *Miscellanies* 7.31.4-5, 32.1-2.

[44] The comparison is to the passage of air through the arteries: F. J. A. Hort and J. B. Mayor, *Clement of Alexandria, Miscellanies, Book* V (London: Macmillan, 1902) 244, citing Michael Psellus (= *PG* 122.841) on the breathing of demons, as well as (p.243) Marcus Aurelius on life as *anathymiasis* from blood and *diapneusis* from air (*Meditations* 6.15).

[45] According to Aristotle, fish do not breathe (*Respiration* 479b13, followed by Basil, *Hexaemeron* 7.1) but Anaxagoras and Democritus (cited by Aristotle) and Pliny insist that they do breathe (*Natural History* 2.18).

[46] Aristotle explains buzzing in this way (*Respiration* 475a1).

[47] The word occurs in Galen, *Distinction of Pulses* 4.16 (Vol.8, p.760 Kuhn).

[48] Clement, *Miscellanies* 7.34.1 = *SVF* 2.721. Infused: Theophilus, *To Autolycus* 2.13.

they can't see the eyes, jaws, etc., of these insects, though they exist.[49] The ancients, of course, had no microscopes.

Basil of Caesarea also touches on the breathing of insects. The grasshopper makes a sound as it draws in air by the dilation of its thorax.[50] Such insects as bees and wasps, however, do not respire and have no lungs, but breathe air through their whole bodies (Clement's "circuminspire"). They perish when covered with oil but revive when vinegar is poured on them and their pores open.[51]

Scientific Entomology?

Harpaz cites two passages from the Talmud to show scientific concerns among the rabbis, one of whom, R. Simeon b. Halafta, was actually called "an experimenter." He was proving that Proverbs 30:27 is right: ants do not have a king. (But Proverbs is speaking of locusts.) The passkeys also show that such concerns were unusual.

He went out at the summer solstice and spread his coat over an ant hill. When one came out he marked it, and it immediately entered and informed the others that shadow had fallen, whereupon they all came forth (for ants shun the fierce heat of the sun and in summer only venture forth in the shade or in the dark). He then removed his coat and the sun beat down upon them. Thereupon they set upon this ant and killed it.   He then said: It is clear that they have no king, for otherwise they would surely have required to obtain royal sanction [for the execution of the delinquent ant].[52]

The other passage deals with ant control. How are they destroyed?

> R. Simeon b. Gamliel says: Soil is fetched from one hole and put into another, and they strangle each other. R. Yammer b. Shelemia said in the name of Abaye: That is effective only if they are situated on two sides of a river and if there is no bridge and not even a crossing plank and not even a rope to cross by. How far apart? Up to one parasang [about 4 miles].[53]

While these rabbis were keen and prattle observers of insect life, this is hardly "scientific" unworn, any more than among Greeks, Romans, or Christians in the late Roman empire. The classical tradition, along with Jews and Christians who lived in it, turned insects into moral examples. Their goodness or badness

---

[49] Tertullian, *Soul* 10.2, 4-5; cf. J.H. Waszink, *Tertullian De Anima* (Amsterdam: Muellenhoff, 1947) 186: "This primarily refers to Aristotle."

[50] Aristotle mentions the sound of the grasshopper (*Respiration* 475a8; *History* 535b7); cf. Pliny, *Natural History* 11.266.

[51] Basil, *Hexaemeron* 8.7, pp. 468-71; compare Clement, *Tutor* 2.66.2. Aristotle too says that insects die in oil (*Respiration* 605b20), as does the epitome by Aristophanes of Byzantium (see n.38), p.32, 2-3; nothing about vinegar.

[52] *Hullin* 57b, cited by I. Harpaz, "Early Entomology in the Middle East," *History of Entomology*, ed. R. F. Smith et al. (Palo Alto: Annual Reviews, 1973) 30-31.

[53] *Mo'ed Katan* 6b, cited by Harpaz, "Early Entomology," 35.

was paramount. It may be true that no saint had a roach for a friend, nor did any philosopher or rabbi. What mattered in such a relationship, as we saw it in the *Acts of John*, was the obedience of subhuman nature to the divine purpose. In a sense it is an extension of Mark 4:41: "Who is this that wind and sea obey him?"

Salus ex Libris:
Reflections on Augustine's *Confessions*

Lawrence S. Cunningham
The University of Notre Dame

T his paper begins, not with Augustine, but with one of his more assiduous readers, Dante Aligheri. In canto V of the *Inferno* Dante recounts one of the most touching and celebrated stories of the *Commedia*: the unhappy fate of the lovers, Paolo and Francesca who, inflamed by the reading of a chivalric tale of Lancelot, yielded to love only to be killed *in flagrante* by Francesca's husband. The story of that event, recounted with Dante's usual economy (it occupies only nine tercets), focusses on the power of the tale to change innocent readers into adulterers. It stands in the canto that deals with the sin of sexual lust. Unlike Don Quixote who was merely addled (and not permanently so) by an addiction to such romances, Paolo and Francesca, in Dante's telling, are eternally damned by their reading. The enormity of their fate is such that the poet himself is so overwhelmed with sadness at their end that he falls into a dead faint.

The Paolo and Francesca episode is so redolent with echoes of book VIII of Augustine's *Confessions* that one can quite easily view it as a kind of anti-type of the conversion scene in the garden of Augustine's friend. The general theme is obvious: through the chance reading of a book the young couple falls into sexual sin just as Augustine, already intellectually converted, overcomes his problems with sexual continence by the chance reading of Romans 13:13. The literary signal that Dante had Augustine in mind is, I think, found in the last two lines of Francesca's narrative:

> A pander was that book and he that wrote it/
> that day we read in it no further (Inf V.137).
> [*Galeotto fu il libro e chi lo scrisse/*
> *quel giorno piu non vi legemmo avante.*]

That couplet seems to echo a parallel line in *Confessions* VIII.8:

> "I had no wish to read more and no need to do so."
> [*Nec ultra volui legere et opus non erat.*][1]

My purpose in recalling this literary appropriation of Augustine by Dante is not to show that Dante knew the *Confessions* (which he undoubtedly did) but to point out Dante's recognition of the axial importance of reading as the occasion for conversion or aversion. Augustine's own account of his encounter with the codex of Romans in the garden of Alypius was a *topos* powerful enough for Dante to reverse its intentions for his own account of misplaced love.

It is also worth noting, in passing, that Augustine, in *The Confessions*, is remembering his past life ("roaming the spacious halls of memory" as he would phrase it in Book X) just as Francesca is tortured by the memory of her happier days before sin brought her and Paolo down. Before she begins her story she says: "There is no greater sorrow/than to remember happy times in misery" [*Nessun maggiore dolore/ che ricordarsi del tempo felice/nella miseria*] (Inf. V: 121-122).

It is, however, Augustine and his reflections on the power of books on which this paper wishes to attend. When we look closely at the garden scene in book VIII of the *Confessions* we find that the moment when Augustine took up and read (the *tolle et lege* of the children's chant) he did so in obedience to something else he had read (about the desert ascetic Antony) which prompted his action: "for I had heard the story of Antony and I remembered how he had happened to go into a church while the Gospel was being read and taken it as a counsel to himself.." (VIII.12). This was the remote preparation for Augustine's yielding to the suggestion of the unseen voices outside the garden walls.

We have, in short, in the garden scene, a reading inspired by a reading: Augustine recalls the example of Antony which he read about in Athanasius's life of the saint which leads him to pick up the codex of Romans. Furthermore, there is another doublet involving the *Life of Antony* and the Epistle to the Romans, recounted earlier in book VIII as a kind of prelude to Augustine's conversion incident. This earlier doublet involves Ponticianus who picks up by accident a codex of Romans which leads Augustine to speak of the life of Antony. Ponticianus, in turn, tells of friends at Trier who stumbled on the *Life of Antony* by

---

[1]All quotations from Augustine are from the Pine-Coffin translation of *The Confessions* (New York: Penguin, 1961); for the benefit of those who use other versions I will cite book and chapter in the text. Latin citations are from the text in the Loeb Classics (1912).

Athanasius. They were impressed enough to move towards a more ascetical life as *servi Dei*.

The garden scene in the *Confessions* has been the subject of intense literary scrutiny by more than a generation of scholars although I will taken as a given the basic historicity of the event no matter how embellished it might be at the hands of the master rhetorician.² For our purposes we may work backward to see the basic structure of the event of the reading episodes to which I alluded above:
1) In obedience to his memory of Antony's example of seeking counsel after an accidental hearing of the scriptures read in church
2) Augustine picks up the codex of Romans and turns accidentally to Rom 13:13 (VIII.13)
Just as earlier (VIII.6)
1) Ponticianus picks up a copy of Romans in the home of Alypius and, inspired by that chance gesture, listens to Augustine speak of Antony and then relates how
2) He stumbled on a copy of the *Life of Antony* while in the company of two friends (who, as a result of reading it entered into the monastic way) at the imperial city of Trier.

The doublet is one of reversal: In the case of Ponticianus it is the casual discovery of Romans that leads him to tell Augustine of the discovery of the work of Antony; in the case of Augustine, he remembers what he had heard of Antony and that triggers in him a desire to pick up Romans. In both cases, it is the Antony/Paul connection which is central.

There are any number of things in the *Life of Antony* that Augustine and his set might have found attractive: the *askesis* of the body as a prelude to the ascent of the soul to God; the theme of withdrawal from society in order to pursue ultimate ends; the naked encounter with the power of the Good in its struggles with evil; and so on. Indeed, one need not read to closely to find such Antonian elements praised in the *Confessions.*

More germane to our purposes, however, is Antony's understanding of the power of scripture as both an oracle of truth and as a goad to action. When Antony hears the reading of the gospel (Matt 19:21) about selling all for the following of Christ, Athanasius says that Antony "immediately" went out of the Lord's house to sell his ancestral patrimony holding back only that which was necessary for the sustenance of his sister (chap.2).³ Indeed, Athanasius continues, a second chance

²The pioneering work of P. Courcelle's *Recherches sur les confessions de Saint Augustin* (Paris, 1950) and a number of subsequent articles has been deftly summarized in J. J. O'Meara's *The Young Augustine* (London: Longmans, 1954), pp. 183-190. The standard contemporary commentary is *Confessions, By Augustine: Commentary: Books 8-13* Edited by J. J. O'Donnell. (Oxford: Clarendon, 1992).
³All quotations are from *Athanasius: The Life of Antony and The Letter To Marcellinus*, edited by R. C. Gregg. (New York: Paulist, 1980) with chapters cited in the text. Still useful for a consideration of the saint: L. Bouyer. *La Vie de S. Antoine* (Begrolles-en-Mauge: Bellefontaines, 1977).

hearing of the scriptural injunction about not having care for the morrow, induces
him to sell even those possessions in order to free his sister to found a *coenobium*
of women (chap.3).

While one might think, and at a superficial level, it is obvious, that Antony
was obedient to a quasi-divinatory gesture like the ancient *sortes virgilianae*, one
must also remember that, at least in Athansius's construal of the matter, Antony
had an adamantine conviction about the scriptures as an oracle of the truth of
divine revelation in general and as a source for a way of life in particular.

Examples of this conviction are not difficult to come by since they are
studded in the very narrative of *The Life of Antony*. Athanasius says quite simply
that Antony absorbed everything that he read from the scriptures so that "memory
took the place of books" (chap.3) and, further, when he instructed disciples later
in his life it was as a "teacher to many in the discipline he had learned from the
scriptures"(chap.46). Antony, in short, became an *icon* of the gospel: "For simply
by seeing his conduct, many aspired to become imitators of his life" (*ibid*).

There is a final point about *The Life of Antony* worth noting; indeed, I think
it crucial. In the last chapter of the book, Athanasius recommends his work to two
quite different classes of people. First, the book is seen as an *exemplum* for the
edification of those who have chosen the monastic path. In that sense, the book is
a portrait text for the monk to emulate. Secondly, however, Athanasius sees his
work as an instrument of conversion for the unbeliever still enthralled by pagan
learning: "And if need arises, read this to the pagans as well so that they may
understand by this means that Our Lord Jesus Christ is God and Son of God..." (
chap.94). In other words, Athanasius's purpose was both to hold up a model for the
monk and to provide occasion for the unbeliever to draw closer to Christ and be
converted to the ascetic life. Whether Augustine had this second purpose of
Athanasius in mind when he figures the life of Antony so prominently in the
Confessions would be hard to prove but not implausible.

One cannot help but wonder whether Augustine had both Athanasian
purposes in mind but especially the latter admonition in mind when he recalled, not
once but twice, the encounter with that book on the part of late Roman intellectuals
who were not then fully formed Christians. This possibility gains further
plausibility from the fact that even when Augustine reads the platonists he had a
deficient christology ("I thought of Christ my Lord as no more than a man of
extraordinary wisdom.."; VII.19) as did his friend, Alypius; his incipient faith
needed refinement. Athanasius, by contrast, wants people to read Antony's life in
order to learn that Christ is "God and Son of God." This was by no means an
incidental end for a bishop like Athanasius who had been so vigorous (and crucial)
in defense of the Orthodox faith against the Arians.

Augustine, then, reads Romans as a gestural *sortes* inspired by the example
of Antony who heard,by chance, the gospel pericope which was to give shape to
his future life. We should remember that this exercise is in direct conflict with

Augustine's dismissal of the practice of *sortes* that he described as part of his struggles against astrology when he was young. A wise doctor persuaded him that it was merely chance when a person "opened a book of poetry at random and, although the poet had been thinking, as he wrote, of some quite different matter, it often happened that the reader placed his finger on a verse which had a remarkable bearing on his problem" (IV.3). It would only be in book VI that Augustine would finally note his triumph over the lure of the astrologers with their "illusory claim to know the future and their insane and impious ritual" (VI.6).

Here again, we might note in passing, is a doublet concerning books: he rejects the *sortes* of the poets in Book IV only to utilize that same strategy with Romans in Book VIII. It is not clear, however, that Augustine, when he wrote those words in Book IV, had the reversal of the reading of Romans in mind. If he did it is one more example of the symmetrical polarities that one finds throughout the *Confessions*.

Let me mention another one. In an interesting article on the structure of *The Confessions* [4] Marjorie Suchocki makes the intelligent observation that Augustine's conversion can be seen as being symbolically framed between two trees: the pear tree of Book II and the Fig Tree of Book VIII; between the tree of sexual sin (the tree in the garden of Eden) and the tree of conversion (the cross). The analogy between the Edenic tree and the tree of Golgotha is, of course, a patristic commonplace but the force of Suchocki's argument derives from her understanding that the *moral* conversion of Augustine is symbolically framed between those two images: from his false sense that he was so autonomous that he could vandalize a pear tree "just for the hell of it" to his late understanding that his incontinence could be cured only by an act of faith in Christ which demanded an abandonment of that earlier attitude.

Augustine's conversion, however, followed a two tiered track. There was the more difficult mastery of the moral self and the somewhat easier (and prior) victory over his intellectual doubts. If the two trees symbolize the moral victory over incontinence, then two books frame the intellectual problem: The now lost *Hortensius* of Cicero and Paul's Letter to the Romans. Indeed, if we accept those two books as symbols (after the manner of the two trees) we have a shorthand description here of Augustine's intellectual worldview: the marriage of the classical and Christian tradition. Cicero is the launchpad whose trajectory will lead him to the books of the Neoplatonists just as his encounter with the scriptures will compel him, afterwards, to cry out to God: "Open to me the pages of your book" (XI.2) as he attempts to plumb the mysteries of Genesis.

Augustine was barely out of his teens when he read the *Hortensius*, a work, as he says, that "altered my outlook on life" (III.4). That Cicero's exhortation

---

[4]M. Suchocki. "The Symbolic Structure of Augustine's *Confessions*," *JAAR* 50 (1982), 365-378. For further analysis of this symmetry, see: K. Burke. *The Rhetoric of Religion: Studies in Logology* (Berkeley,CA: University of California Press, 1970), 93-117; L. Ferrari. "The Pear Theft in Augustine's *Confessions*," *Revue des Etudes Augustinennes* 16 (1970), 233-41.

(*protreptic*) to search for wisdom is not merely a rhetorical flourish is evident from Augustine's hearty recommendation and wide use of it in an earlier work which predates his writings of the *Confessions*: the *Contra Academicos*.[5]

Augustine is quite clear about the significance of the shift in his thinking that resulted from his encounter with this now lost work. The *Hortensius* let him see that it was possible to move away from the study of rhetoric as a mere instrumentality (To sharpen his tongue–*ad acuendam linguam*–is his pungent phrase) towards a form of study that would be a path towards wisdom and a way of life; study would now be the instrument towards a finality and not merely a device to make his way in the world.

We might better understand the significance of the encounter with the *Hortensius* by applying some distinctions that Augustine would later employ in his celebrated adumbration of the proper way to approach the scriptures in the *De Doctrina Christiana*. Augustine begins that work by saying that he will first discuss a way of discovery and then a way of teaching.[6] In both cases, he continues, the fundamental point is that one must distinguish, either in discovery or teaching, *use* and *enjoyment*. Enjoyment "makes us blessed" (I.3) and, ultimately, that which is to be enjoyed is "the single Trinity" which, technically, is not a "thing" but the "cause of all things" (I.5). It is crucial, then, not to confuse the utility of means with the ultimate desirability of ends; scripture was not to be read to exhibit rhetorical skills but to come to a direct knowledge of God, inchoately in this life, and eternally, in heaven.

When Augustine encounters the *Hortensius* he discovers a book which would provide him with a direction, i.e. a *use* which, though he did not know it at the time, would lead him to the *enjoyment* of the knowledge of God. That direction saved him from the false *use* of rhetoric which would have kept him trapped in his former way of life and incapable of *enjoyment* as he would later come to understand it. Indeed, it would be otiose to cite the number of times that Augustine feels compelled, in *The Confessions*, to deprecate the misuse of rhetoric for sophistic persuasion and/or profit based on that sophistry.

Using the *Hortensius* as the point of departure one can then trace his subsequent encounters with books as he slowly disentangles himself from the grip of manicheaen thought as well as the temptations of the then fashionable skepticism of the academics. Some books had a negative impact in the sense that they created enormous intellectual difficulties for him. When he read, at the age of twenty, Aristotle's *Categories* he found himself fruitlessly attempting to wrestle

---

[5]See: *Saint Augustine: Against the Academics*, edited by J. O'Meara. ACW 12 (Westminster, MD: Newman Press, 1950). In that work (I.4) Augustine urges the reading of the work as a way of getting his young pupils interested in philosophy.

[6]All citations will be to book and chapter from *Saint Augustine: On Christian Doctrine*, translated by D. W. Robertson, Jr. (Indianopolis,IN: The Library of Liberal Arts, 1958).

his then inadequate concept of God ("a bright unbounded body" IV.16) into those categories. But with what profit he asks? None was his answer (*ibid*).

The crucial encounter, described in VII.9, mediates between the lesson of the *Hortensius* (seek wisdom and seek it with love and not for ignoble ends) and the meeting of God's voice in *Romans* is of course, his study of "some of the books of the Platonists, translated from the Greek into Latin" (VII.9). It is from those books that Augustine saw his way out of the prisonhouse of manichaean materiality and its attendant dualism. He now began to understand both the role of the Word as creator and evil, not as something, but as privation. What was absent from those books was, of course, the name of Christ. Augustine, however, was finding that name by a parallel encounter which he narrates in tandem with these moments of intellectual discovery, namely, a renewed sense of the possibilities in the Christian scriptures coming to him as a result of listening to the bishop of Milan, Ambrose.

It is instructive to read the relevant chapters (9-21) of Book VII with one eye on the platonists and the other on Augustine's more confident use of, and appreciation for, scripture. He begins with a series of rhetorically charged observations about what he found/what he did not find as he read. VII.9 is illuminating in this regard because in a series of short bursts he tells us that he learned of the Word but not the Word made flesh; of the equality of the Word with the Father but not of the kenotic self-emptying of Phil 2:6; of the eternity of the Word but not of his death on the cross; and so on. Those antinomies, of course, are directed both at the anti-materialism of the manichees and, as it were, as a prelude to Augustine's later extended meditation on the *historicity* of Christian revelation in his massive meditation on the Two Cities. In the platonic corpus (as much of it as he had read) Augustine found a metaphysic; what he would find in scripture was economy, i.e. the Incarnation.

The juxtaposition of the writings of the platonists and the scriptures, however, did not only reveal doctrinal differences; they also highlighted matters of ethical urgency and doxological response. The scriptures, in short, nourished more than the intellect alone. The very goodness of creation triggers praise (VII.13) both of itself and in the heart of a person who perceives it as a good creation (*ibid*). Indeed, in VII.20, Augustine thanks God that he had encountered the works of the platonic school before he read the scriptures because they solved certain intellectual conundrums and, then, scripture rooted him in a orthodox relationship with God. Without that scriptural nourishment he might not have been able to distinguish *presumptio* from *confessio*. It was scripture, in short, that made Augustine, in the word of the old translator W. Watts, "tractable" in the hands of God.

It is at this point in the *Confessions* where Augustine makes another observation of how books lead to books; a link, I think, that must be seen as another thematic construct which so studs his work. At the end of his reflections on the *libri platonicorum* Augustine says of their impact: "I seized eagerly upon those venerable writings inspired by your Holy Spirit, *especially those of your Apostle Paul* " (VII.21; emphasis added). It was a renewed attempt to read Paul but, this time, the earlier problems disappeared as Augustine realized that what the platonists said was all there in Paul with this significant addition: "praise for your grace bestowed" (VII.21). Furthermore, as he adds, what a reading of scripture added was the power to make him a convert; grace added to conviction. It was in Paul that he found "the tears of confession" and the "salvation of your people" (*ibid*) .

In terms of symmetry, what is most interesting about this particular part of the *Confessions* is the parallel to the conversion scene (with its doublet): just as Augustine encounters the *Vita* of Anthony and is lead to Romans so, at an earlier monent, he reads the *libri platonicorum* and is, as he says, driven to Saint Paul.

We find, then, in Augustine's *Confessions* a kind of bibliographical symmetry in which books lead to books by a series of doublets.Behind the rhetorical strategy of symmetry, however, is Augustine's firm conviction that good books lead to truth; that they have power either in their use or, as a pointer, to enjoyment–which is the vision of God.

Dante perceived Augustine's strategy and used an antitype–the seductive power of the romance–to show the opposite: that books can also lead away from truth and, indeed, into damnation. While doing this, Dante, in a line, pays explicit tribute to the powers of Augustine's testimony.

We began with Dante but let us end with another reader of Augustine, a powerful woman who lived more than two centuries after his time: Saint Teresa of Avila (1515-1582). Teresa spent twenty years (1535-1555) at the convent of the Incarnation in Avila leading a rather conventional religious life. Towards the end of 1554 she underwent a profound conversion (she is a textbook example of William James's "twice born" religious figure) that led her back to the more eremitical roots of the Carmelites. That conversion, as well as her enduring friendship with Fray Juan de la Cruz (John of the Cross) would result in a great flourishing of Spanish mysticism whose echos are heard to this day.

Teresa's 1554 second conversion was more in the fashion of an illumination or intuition which provided a solution to an existential question that had tormented her into a state of near despair: the conflict between her deisre to be a person of prayer and the tortures she underwent as a result of a too scrupulous conscience. She found a sense of tranquillity by a twofold discovery, both of which coming to her in a quite accidental fashion.

First, she chanced upon a small figure of Christ in his sufferings (an *Ecce Homo* figure) which triggered in her an immense feeling for Christ and a concomitant sense that she need to trust in Christ and leave off her own strenuous efforts at concentrating on prayer and resisting with her own power, the temptations which came her way. Teresa's second discovery is best described in her own words taken from her autobiography:

It was at this time that I was given the *Confessions of Saint Augustine* and I think the Lord must have ordained this, for I did not ask for the book nor had I ever seen it...When I started to read the *Confessions* I seemed to see myself in them and I began to to commend myself to that glorious saint. When I got as far as his conversion and read how he heard that voice it seemed exactly as if the Lord were speaking in that way to me or so my heart felt...[7]

This, then, is the pathway of some books: from Paul's Letter to the Romans that led to the *Life of Antony*; from the Life of Antony that led to Paul's Letter to the Romans. That journey finds its chronicler in Augustine's account of the *Confessions*. The *Confessions*, in turn, provides both a warning for Dante and an occasion of grace for Teresa of Avila. I map this journey out not to pretend to comprehensiveness but to make the simple point that books not only matter but can be, as I have attempted to show, epiphanic occasions for the intrusion of grace.

How wise the injunction of Seneca: *Probatos itaque semper lege*—"Always [or perhaps: 'continuously'] read the classics." The advice is solid. John Priest has read and commented upon The Classic which is the Bible for most of his life. As one who shaped the Florida State University graduate program in Humanities he would also endorse, I believe, the continuous readings of those great works which were written as extended meditations on the Bible. I have attempted, modestly, to follow just one thin branch that ramifies out from the biblical milieu which John Priest knows so expertly. It is in that spirit that this modest meditation is offered in homage.

---

[7] *The Autobiography of Teresa of Avila*, translated by E. A. Peers. (Garden City,NY: Doubleday, 1991) 117-118. *The Confessions* had been translated and published in Spanish that year and dedicated to a friend of Teresa who may well have been the one who gave her the book. The critical edition of *Mi Vida* in translation with annotations is to be found in the first volume of *The Collected Works of Teresa of Avila*, edited by K. Kavanaugh and O. Rodriguez. (Washington,DC: Institute of Carmelite Studies, 1979).

Luther and Tillich:
A Consideration of Tillich's Dialectical Relationship with Luther and Lutheranism

John J. Carey
Agnes Scott College

B efore I turn to the substance of this essay, I want to pay a special tribute to my friend and former colleague John Priest. We were colleagues at Florida State University for 19 years (1967-1986). During that time, John served as Professor of Religion, Director of Graduate Studies in Religion, Director of the Graduate Program in Humanities, Executive Director of the American Academy of Religion, and Chair of the Religion Department (1978-1984). Not only his gifts as a biblical scholar but his broader interests and training in classical languages, textual studies, literary criticism, and intellectual history made him a special resource to those of us working in religious studies and humanities. At an earlier time he encouraged me to pursue work on Luther and Tillich, and it is a pleasure for me to submit the fruits of that on-going work as my contribution to this *Festschrift*.

In recent years, sparked by the observation of the five-hundredth anniversary of Luther's birth in 1983, there has been in academic circles considerable interest in analyzing Luther's intellectual and theological legacy to the twentieth century. In that spirit it is interesting to examine Luther's influence in Paul Tillich, a German-born, Lutheran-raised Protestant theologian who is widely considered as one of the three or four most influential Christian thinkers of the 20th century. It is both noteworthy and curious that among the voluminous secondary literature on

Tillich there has been relatively little work done on Tillich's debts to Luther.[1] Luther is, of course, famous as a church reformer, Bible translator, German nationalist, and as one who spawned a religious community that bears his name. In this essay I am more concerned to reflect on his theological work, both in method and substance, since it is his theological vision that helped to mold Paul Tillich. I should say at the outset that Tillich was a multi-faceted thinker who drew on many sources, and in probing his debts to Luther we do not come to the key that unlocks all of Tillich's theological system. To hold these two thinkers together is, however, an interesting exercise in intellectual history, and I think we will find that Luther is a richer influence on Tillich than has normally been acknowledged in Tillich scholarship. Let us begin this task by sharing some preliminary words about Tillich's life and career.[2]

I

Tillich was born August 20, 1886, in the village of Starzeddel in the district of Gubenme, Germany, which is now part of Poland. His father was a Lutheran pastor and diocesan superintendent of the Prussian Territorial Church. Tillich studied at the Humanistic Gymnasium in Konigsberg-Neumann and subsequently in Berlin. He began his theological studies at the University of Berlin in 1904 and read widely in philosophy as well as in theology. He attended lectures in theology

---

[1] Probably the best assessment of these two thinkers remains J. L. Adams' essay "Paul Tillich on Luther," in J. Pelikan, ed., *Interpreters of Luther* (Philadelpha: Fortress Press, 1968), 304-334. Interesting but more marginal for our purposes here is Wilhelm Pauck's essay, "Paul Tillich: Heir of the Nineteenth Century," in Pauck's volume *From Luther to Tillich: The Reformers and Their Heirs* (San Francisco: Harper and Row, 1984), 152-209. This book has several insightful chapters on Luther's faith, but the Tillich chapter does not directly compare Luther and Tillich. It is quite helpful, however, in analyzing Tillich's debts to Martin Kähler and to Herman Schafft (1883-1959) and to the moderate Lutheranism that they represented (see 157-168). Of broader interest but also more indirect for our purpose is G. A. Lindbeck, "An Assessment Reassessed: Paul Tillich on the Reformation," *Journal of Religion*, v. 63 (1983), 376-393. In this article, Lindbeck (himself a Lutheran) analyzes Tillich's stress on justification by faith (which he says is at the heart of Tillich's "Protestant Principle") and *sola gratis*, as the two key Reformation themes. He indicates, however, that Tillich is indebted to the early Luther and not the later Luther, that Tillich was shaped far more by Luther than Melanchlon, and that Tillich's later developed theology stays within the guidelines of the Augsburg Conference. A 16-page bibliography of secondary literature of Tillich from 1975-1982 prepared by Ellen J. Burns of the Fondran Library at Rice University surfaced several European articles dealing with some later Lutheran responses to challenges posed by Tillich but no articles directly comparing Luther and Tillich. A 1995 computer scan of three databases of secondary literature from 1983-1995 revealed no articles dealing directly with Tillich's debts to Luther.

[2] Tillich wrote two autobiographical reflections in his lifetime: the first in 1936 (shortly after his arrival in America), published as *On the Boundary* (New York: Charles Scribner's Sons) and the second in 1952, published as "Autobiographical Reflections" as an introduction to the volume edited by R. Bretall and C. Kegley, *The Theology of Paul Tillich* (New York: Macmillan). Fuller treatments of the relationship of his life and thought are found in Wilhelm and Marion Pauck, *Paul Tillich: His Life and Thought*, Vol. 1 (New York: Harper and Row, 1976), and in Carl Heinz Ratschow, *Paul Tillich* (The North American Paul Tillich Society, 1980). Numerous other secondary treatments of Tillich's thought are available.

at the University of Halle from 1905 to 1907, where he came under the influence of the distinguished German theologian Martin Kähler. In 1910 he received his Doctorate of Philosophy from the University of Breslau and in 1912 his Licentiate in Theology from the University of Halle. For each degree he wrote a dissertation dealing with aspects of Schelling's philosophy of religion. He was ordained a minister of the Evangelical Lutheran Church in Berlin on August 18, 1912, and spent the next two years as an assistant pastor in a working class section of Berlin. He served as a chaplain in the German army on the western front from 1914-1918 and received the Iron Cross for courageous service to the wounded and the dying.

After World War I, Tillich accepted an appointment as a Private Dozent in Theology at the University of Berlin and stayed there until 1924 when he was appointed as Associate Professor of Theology at Marburg. In 1925 he accepted an appointment as Professor of Philosophy at Dresden and remained there until 1929 when he accepted an appointment at the University of Frankfurt. While at Frankfurt, Tillich became engaged with other leading philosophers and social scientists in what was known as the "Frankfurt School"[3] and was quite active in the German political scene. From his time in Berlin until 1933 he was active with a small group of religious socialists as they tried to find a middle way between Christian political thought and the Socialists' critique of Western bourgeois culture.

Tillich was dismissed by the Nazis from his position at the University of Frankfurt on April 13, 1933, and in December of the same year he and his family came to America, where he began a second career at Union Theological Seminary in New York City. He stayed at Union until 1956, when upon his retirement he accepted an appointment at Harvard as a University Professor. He remained at Harvard until 1962, and following his second retirement, he moved to Chicago where he taught until his death in 1965.

In 1977, Dr. Thor Hall of the University of Tennessee at Chattanooga sent a questionnaire to 554 American theologians asking them whom they would regard as their "major mentor." Of the people who replied, 123 designated Tillich; he led over such other distinguished theologians as Thomas Aquinas (87), Karl Rahner (78), Karl Barth (76), and Saint Augustine (51). In America, at least, Tillich, therefore, appears to be the most influential Christina theologian of the twentieth century. If we can understand his relationship to Luther and Lutheranism, it would give us a good window from which to see Luther's legacy to the twentieth century.

---

[3] For detailed assessments of Tillich's relationship to the Frankfurt School see T. O'Keeffe, "Tillich and the Frankfurt School," and G. B. Hammond, "Tillich and the Frankfurt Debates about Patriarchy and the Family," in John J. Carey, ed., *Theonomy and Autonomy: Studies in Paul Tillich's Engagement with Modern Culture* (Macon, GA: Mercer University Press, 1984), 67-88, 89-110.

II

Tillich's Views on Luther and Lutheranism

As we turn to consider Tillich's views on Luther and Lutheranism, we should note initially that Tillich was not a Luther scholar in any technical sense. Tillich never published any technical article on any facet of Luther's theology. Tillich was a systematic and philosophical theologian, and he tended to appropriate contributions of previous thinkers creatively and adapt their insights into his own system of thought. This is not an uncommon practice with contemporary theologians, but we should be mindful of this tendency as we begin our consideration of Tillich's debts to Luther.

It is clear, however, that Tillich recognized that he himself had been deeply molded by the Lutheran tradition. In 1936 he wrote:

> I, myself, belong to Lutheranism by birth, education, religious experience, and theological reflection. I have never stood on the borders of Lutheranism and Calvinism. The substance of my religion is and remains Lutheranism ... not only my theological but also my philosophical thinking expresses the Lutheran experience.[4]

Secondly, Tillich's teachers were predominantly Lutherans: Martin Kähler, Ernst Troeltsch, and Adolf Von Harnack all stood in the Lutheran tradition, although they had their quarrels with the Evangelical Church of Prussia. Many of Tillich's formative philosophical mentors (Hegel, Kierkegaard, Schelling) were Lutherans and also lived in considerable tension with the Church. There was a sense, at least, in which Lutheranism was as natural to Tillich as the air he breathed. In his "Autobiographical Reflections," published in 1952, Tillich noted that even his romantic appreciation of nature came from his Lutheran roots.[5]

But what does it mean to stand in the Lutheran tradition? Tillich noted that this includes a consciousness of the corruptness of existence, a repudiation of every kind of social utopia, an awareness of the irrational and demonic nature of existence, and appreciation of the mystical element in religion and a rejection of puritanical legalism in private and corporate life.[6]

Those who know Tillich's thought well recognize how all of these themes continued to mold his personal as well as theological consciousness. These themes are perhaps best understood when contrasted with Roman Catholic, Reformed, or free church viewpoints, but more extended discussion of these comparisons is beyond the scope of this essay.

It is worth noting that Tillich's dialectical relationship with the Lutheran tradition was expressed after he came to America. Here he chose to affiliate with

---

[4] *The Interpretation of History,* New York: Scribners, 1936, 54.
[5] "Autobiographical Reflections, " 5; see note 2 above.
[6] *On the Boundary,* 74-75.

the Evangelical and Reformed Church, a predominantly German midwestern denomination made up of two streams of German immigrants. Tillich's close friends, Richard and Reinhold Niebuhr, both came out of the Evangelical and Reformed tradition, and, though it expressed a residue of Lutheranism, it also was distinct from the generally more conservative Lutheran bodies in America. (The Evangelical and Reformed Church in 1957 joined with the Congregational churches to form the United Church of Christ). Even though Tillich seldom functioned as a minister, he was ordained and granted ministerial standing in this communion.

How did Tillich understand Luther? Although, as we have noted, Tillich was not a historical theologian, he nevertheless treated Luther in his lectures on the history of Christian thought that he gave at Union Seminary in 1953-54.[7] Tillich was also quite interested in the phenomenon of Protestantism and discussed Luther in the course of various lectures on Protestantism (many of which were translated and edited by James Luther Adams and published in *The Protestant Era)*. In his lectures on Luther in *The History of Christian Thought*, Tillich observed:

> He is one of the few great prophets of the Christian Church and his greatness is overwhelming. .... He is responsible for the fact that a purified Christianity, a Christianity of the reformation, was able to establish itself on equal terms with the Roman tradition.[8]

Yet another interesting insight about Luther comes from Tillich's essay (1929) on "Protestantism as a Critical and Creative Principle."[9] In that essay Tillich contrasted "rational" and "prophetic" streams of thought in the Western intellectual tradition. The rational stream Tillich defined as critical humanistic, cultural, and scientific analysis; such reflection is, of course, essential to thought and culture and most of what we know as scholarship in the humanities and philosophical dialogue would be in this category. Prophetic criticism, however, is the kind of perception that goes beyond all intellectual and social forms to the realm of existence and spirit; it transcends all human works and achievements. It is the kind of insight and criticism that critiques human thought and institutions "through the unapproachable fire of the divine majesty." Tillich argued that this prophetic criticism has appeared only three times in the history of the Judao-Christian tradition: (1) prophets of the Hebrew Bible who stood against Hebrew nationalism, (2) in the Apostle Paul, who stood against the moralistic

---

[7] These lectures, recorded in shorthard by Peter H. John, were subsequently edited by Carl E. Braaten and published as *A History of Christian Thought* (New York: Harper and Row, 1968). All subsequent references to this text are to the Braaten edition. It should be noted, however, that Tillich never approved the publication of these lectures.

[8] 227.

[9] This essay, originally published in a volume edited by Tillich entitled *Protestantismus als Kritik und Gestaltung* (Darmstadt: Reichl, 1929), was translated by J. L. Adams and published in his edited volume of Tillich's early German writings entitled *Political Expectation* (New York: Harper and Row, 1971). See 10-39 of that volume, especially 10-18.

claims of a religion of law, and (3) in Luther, who stood against the hierarchy, power, and sacramental structure of the medieval church.

Tillich understood Luther as an exemplar of courage and heart. He was one who lived in a "boundary situation" in response to his conscience and held to the authority of scripture over against the claims of all religious institutions. As such, Tillich felt that Luther was a unique instrument of the power of God and one of the great benchmarks in the history of Christian thought. Tillich was aware, however, that Luther's greatness was limited by some of his personal traits, his temperament, the medieval ethos in which Luther lived, and the general acrimony of the sixteenth century. As far as Tillich was concerned, therefore, Luther has to be seen contextually and appropriated selectively in order to speak to the modern period.

When Karl Holl's famous book on Luther appeared in 1922, Tillich reviewed the volume and took issue with Holl's thesis that Luther belonged to the middle ages. Tillich said, by contrast, that Luther "belongs neither to the middle ages nor to the modern period, but to the great entirely unique period between 1250 and 1750 for which he represents the turning point and the high point."[10]

Our task in this essay, however, is not just to note Tillich's opinion of Luther or Lutheranism, but rather to trace Luther's influence on Tillich's thought. That is a difficult assignment because of the differences in temperament, orientation, and time between these two thinkers.

Differences in Luther and Tillich

Luther, reflecting the theological ethics of the sixteenth century, was also profoundly biblical in his world view and theological orientation. He wrote and interpreted the Bible before the advent of modern biblical criticism; he interpreted the "Old Testament" (particularly the Psalms) from a Christological viewpoint and in general was steeped in the Ptolemaic cosmos. Luther was also an activist in the political and ecclesiastical turmoils of his time; one reason why he never produced a systematic theology is that he was always engaged in responding to immediate issues of the times. This wide diversity within the corpus of Luther's writing helps to explain why so many people have found so many different things in his writings and why he lends himself to such widely diverse types of interpretation. We should also note that if Luther were to be on the scene today, he would definitely be a seminary man and a church man, and not a university man in the modern sense.

Tillich, by contrast, was not primarily a biblical exegete but a philosophical theologian. He was interested in philosophy in a way that Luther never was and also interested in broader dimensions of culture (art, philosophy, literature, science,

---

[10] See his essay, "Holl's Lutherbuch," in *Vossische Zeitung*, no. 381, *Literarissche Umschau*, no. 33, (1922) 1. This review is cited by J. L. Adams in his article "Paul Tillich on Luther," 332; see note 1.

and the social sciences) in a way that Luther was not. Tillich participated in the new world of North America in a way that Luther, of course, never did. He had to deal with the major threats to Western philosophy and religion posed by Marx and Freud, and all his life he struggled with the questions of doubt, skepticism, and cynicism that had grown out of the history, technology, and secularization of the twentieth century. One might say that Luther assumed what was for Tillich problematic: i. e., theistic faith, the authority of the Bible, and the biblical cosmology. Tillich also struggled with questions of Christianity's relationship to other world religions in a way that Luther never did. In the modern North American sense, Tillich would be a university man more naturally than a seminary man.

One way of sharpening these differences is to note that Luther's problems were not Tillich's and vice versa. Luther continually struggled with the question "How can I believe in a merciful God?" Tillich struggled with the question "How can one be a believer in the modern age?" and asked how we can break through the technical reasoning of the twentieth century to cope with the deeper realms of life and faith.

Although in this study we are primarily interested in Tillich's debts to Luther, it is only fair to point out initially that Tillich would reject Luther's view of biblical authority, Luther's method of biblical exegesis, Luther's view of the Jews, Luther's Christology, Luther's view of the church, Luther's political conservatism, Luther's view of church and state relations, Luther's attitude towards philosophy, and his attitude toward humanistic learning. For these reasons, I have sub-titled this essay "A Consideration of Tillich's Dialectical View of Luther and Lutheranism."

Our task of comparison is further complicated when we recognize that both theologians wrote voluminously, both were powerful and subtle in their thought, both dealt with complex issues, and there is not always a clear one-to-one relationship even when Tillich acknowledges debts to Luther. But the task of comparison is not impossible, and I now wish to consider four areas where I think there are genuine affinities between Luther and Tillich.

III

Theological Method

The issue of theological method needs to be discussed primarily because of the volume by Wayne G. Johnson entitled *Theological Method in Luther and Tillich*.[11] This book was Johnson's doctoral dissertation at the University of Iowa and argues the thesis that there is a general similarity between Luther's theological

---

[11] W. Johnson, *Theological Method in Luther and Tillich.* Washington, D. C.: University Press of America, 1981.

method and that of Tillich. It is an open question in Luther scholarship whether Luther in fact had a clearly defined theological method. Johnson argues, however, that the key for Luther as a theologian was his understanding of law and gospel. In Luther's lectures on Galatians in 1531, he asserted: "The knowledge of this topic, the distinction between law and gospel, is necessary to the highest degree; for it contains a summary of all Christian doctrine."[12] We need to examine in some detail what Luther meant by this relationship of law and gospel.

In brief, Luther understood the "law" to mean the commands of God, both those summarized in the Decalogue and Pentateuch, but also that natural law of God which Luther felt was broadly written on the minds of all persons everywhere. Luther believed that the law has a double use. The first use of the law is to restrain the wicked in the area of community life, and thereby provide a basis for a sound political order. (Luther called this the "civil" use of the law.) The civil law is expressed through legal structures and codes, and explains why Luther was such a political conservative. Political authority, which creates and interprets these laws, is therefore deemed by Luther to be part of the plan of God.

The second use of the law is what Luther called the "proper" use, or we might say the "theological" use. Law gives us a knowledge of our sins and shortcomings, and reveals to us that we are guilty before God. The law humbles us and brings us to the point of despair. As such, the law prepares us to hear the good news of the gospel.

Luther felt that if the law terrifies us, the gospel reassures us and gives us hope. The seriousness of our sin, once we grasp that, prepares us to understand the depth of God's goodness and mercy in the devine act of reconciliation. The law and gospel can sometimes be understood as God's "no" and God's "yes"; Luther's word about this has become a classic: "deeper than the no and above it the deep mysterious yes."

This distinction between "law" and "gospel" gave Luther some perspective on diversity of biblical writings and was the perspective from which he measured the authority and significance of different biblical writings. In a theological sense, this distinction sharpened for Luther the difference between sin and grace, between judgment and mercy; and between death and salvation. (It should be clear from this analysis that of all the viewpoints found in scripture, Luther was essentially a Paulinist in perspective and vocabulary.)[13]

Tillich took the problem of theological method more seriously than did Luther because he struggled with some ambiguities that Luther did not feel. Tillich was also more interested than Luther ever was in the philosophical issues related to the nature of theological language and religious knowledge. In a formal

---

[12] Cited by Johnson, *Theological Method*, 2.

[13] This distinction between law and gospel, and especially of the uses of the law, has generated much discussion in Luther scholarship. A special controversy is related to how much emphasis Luther felt should be placed on the "didactic" or third use of the law. See the discussion of this debate in Johnson, 7-8. Further discussion of this point, however, is beyond the scope of this essay.

sense, I would argue that Tillich is actually closer to Thomas Aquinas than to Luther in theological method. Tillich frequently argued that the concept of the *analogia entis* (the analogy of being) is the *sine qua non* of any kind of theological language. That is to say, Tillich insisted that unless we can assume there is some broad analogy between human life and the divine life, between human experience and the divine experience, it is not possible to say anything about the mystery or nature of the divine. That analogy, however, also led Tillich to feel that we can come at the theological task by first analyzing what it means to be human with the confidence that our understanding of the human situation has some affinity with the Divine. Tillich, therefore, began his famous "method of correlation" by asking first what are the basic questions and issues of human life and then followed that with answers that the Christian tradition has towards those questions. In his understanding of the human condition, Tillich actually drew most significantly from existentialist literature and interpreted our humanity around our concepts of fear, selfishness, striving, home and anxiety. A person who is most profoundly human, said Tillich, always recognizes the edges of despair. We might note in passing that Tillich thought that perception was true for all people, male and female, rich and poor, black and white, east and west, north and south.

What made Tillich a Christian theologian was his assertion that amid the complexities of brokenness, alienation, and estrangement there does appear the reality of "new being": reunion, reconciliation, newness of life. In his view, that message was exemplified in Jesus as the Christ, whom Tillich liked to call the paradigm of "New Being." Just as Jesus in the quality of his being rose above solitude and estrangement, so, Tillich argued, we also know the experience of new being through the grace of God.[14]

Now the question for us to ask is what evidence is there that Tillich's method of correlation in fact is similar to (or derives from) Luther's working hypothesis of law and gospel. I do not think that Johnson establishes this case in his book, and I note that never in Tillich's three volume *Systematic Theology* does he refer to Luther's law and gospel scheme. I do not, therefore, think that formal analysis of the starting point of Luther and Tillich can establish that here Tillich drew significantly from Luther.

There is another way, however, in which there is a distinctive affinity between Luther and Tillich in theological method. Both thinkers, for example, are persuaded that there is a power greater than humanity, which people do encounter in the course of their lifetimes. Both were therefore persuaded that theology is tied to human experience and that in our experience we can know the saving reality of God. Both Tillich and Luther, furthermore, believed that theology is "existential" (that is, it deals with profound issues of life) and that theological discourse finally revolves around matters of ultimate concern. I think therefore, that in the matter

---

[14] For a fuller description of how Tillich understood the designation of "New Being," see his sermon "The New Being," in *The New Being* (New York: Scribner's 1955), 15-24, and his discussion in *Systematic Theology,* Vol. II (Chicago: University of Chicago Press, 1957), 118-138.

of intensity and engagement, we see a distinct similarity between Luther and Tillich. There is no doubt that Luther was an exemplar for Tillich in this way, and that Tillich admired Luther's heart, courage, and passion. One of Luther's famous sayings was that "It is not by thinking or speculating that one becomes a theologian, but by living, dying, and being damned." Tillich, in his own way, understood this point of view and in this important way, he stood in the tradition of Martin Luther.

The Concept of God

In this area, Luther made one of the great breakthroughs in Christian theology by stressing the dynamic activities of God. Luther's understanding of God, of course, has to be seen in the broader context of the medieval church and against many of the assumptions of scholasticism. Luther believed that the Western church had developed a theology about the Divine that was too rational, too amenable to human description, too confined to theological prepositions and institutional definitions. Against that rational tradition, Luther argued that God is sheer will: God can do whatever God wants. God acts in everything and through everything. The theme of God's sovereignity is therefore one that scholars often attribute to Luther and Calvin. Luther made a major distinction, however, when he distinguished between God's *absolute* power and God's *ordered* power.

Luther understood that the basic human sense of God is discerned within the structures of creation. Through the structures of creation we receive identity and continuity. We discern rules of law that govern society, the seasons of nature, and the rhythms and rituals of birth and death. Against such order and predictability, however, Luther pointed to the absolute power of God, which he said is "like a threat to those ordering rules, like in an abyss in which they may be swallowed up at any moment."[15] There is, Luther insisted, mystery, darkness and paradox in the heart of God. God does "strange" work along with his proper work. This led Luther to feel that there is no final safety in rules and order, or in rational perceptions of the Divine; we need to recognize that we are human and not divine, and hence are limted in what we can perceive and understand.

Luther also spoke of the hidden and revealed qualities of God, which he called *Deus Absconditus* and *Deus Revelatus*. Luther scholars have debated at length how to understand this distinction, but on the whole it appears to me that the theme of God's hiddenness refers to the deep, mysterious, and ineffable qualities of God. There are dimensions of God we cannot know, as God works through nature, history, nations, great persons, and social movements.

---

[15] Luther elaborated on this point in many of his essays, but the most sustained theological argument is in his book *On the Bondage of the Will* (1524), written in response to Erasmus' tract *On the Freedom of the Will* that same year. See E. M. Plass, *What Luther Says: An Anthology,* St. Louis: Concordia Publishing House, 1959, Vol. II, 551.

Luther's awesome sense of the power of God likewise led him to repeatedly inveigh against idols. Luther insisted that "God alone is God" and alone worthy of our ultimate allegiance. Much of Luther's concern here was, of course, related to practices of the medieval church and claims made for the authority of Rome. In his own way, however, he thereby was a major figure in recovering and emphasizing the sovereignty of God.

The concept of God was likewise a rich area for Tillich (see his *Systematic Theology*, Volume 1) and was obviously an area in which he made a major contribution to twentieth-century theology. Tillich, however, drew on a wide variety of sources as he tried to understand the God problem. He was indebted to the German idealistic philosopher Fredrich Schelling, to the German mystic Jakob Boehme, and to George Hegel as he combined the categories of biblical faith with issues raised by Western philosophy. Tillich felt that one could grasp the mystery of the Divine through the Judaeo-Christian tradition and also through various philosophical systems. In his approach to "God language," Tillich was clearly concerned to move beyond the inadequate theistic understandings of God (i.e., God as a person or as a being) and to press for a larger and more comprehensive understandings of God. Tillich understood that the biblical concept of transcendence needed to be replaced with more adequate metaphors that can do justice to a scientific understanding of the universe. In his book, *The Courage To Be* (1954), Tillich developed a notion of the "God beyond God" and offered such suggestive metaphors as "God as Being Itself," God as the "ground of being," and God as the "power of being."[16]

An especially important insight in Tillich's concept of God is the idea of the demonic. Tillich insisted that the Divine contained within itself the element of non-being as well as being. This is a relative type of non-being as opposed to an absolute type of non-being, but is an insight through which Tillich thought one could understand the elements of mystery and depth in the Deity. There is an irrational dimension in the Divine. There is a structural character to evil. In an article written in 1948, which looked back on 22 years of his use of this concept, Tillich reflected on how the symbol of "the demonic" applied not only to the Divine but also to his understanding of history:

The third concept decisive for my interpretation of history is that of "the demonic." It is one of the forgotten concepts of the New Testament, which, in spite of its tremendous importance to Jesus and the apostles, has become obsolete in modern theology. . .The idea of the demonic is the mythical expression of a reality that was in the center of Luther's experience as it was in Paul's, namely, the structure, and therefore inescapable, power of evil. . .The powerful symbol of the demonic was everywhere accepted in the sense that we had used it, namely, as

---

[16] See *The Courage To Be*, (New Haven: Yale University Press, 1954) 156-190. Implications of these metaphors are also developed in *Systematic Theology*, Vol. I (Chicago: University of Chicago, 1951).

a "structure of evil" beyond the moral power of good will, producing social and individual tragedy precisely through the inseparate mixture of good and evil in every human act.[17]

To say this in a different way, the demonic is an inchoate tendency in the essense of God. Tillich felt, by the way, that his thought about the demonic as a component of the Divine was his major contribution to the God question in the twentieth century.

Where then are the parallels between Luther's understanding of God and Tillich's understanding of God? Tillich felt a clear affinity with Luther concerning the irrational, hidden, mysterious dimension of God. In his lectures on Luther, he stresses that Luther emphasized the *tremendum fascinosum* of the divine majesty, giving it depth, mystery, and a numinous quality. Tillich felt that Luther was one of the few theologians of Christiandom who understood the paradox of God and the limits of reason, and that Luther thereby safeguarded the prophetic tradition over against the rational humanists like Erasmus. It was for these reasons that Tillich claimed that "Luther's idea of God is one of the most powerful in the whole history of human and Christian thought."[18]

A related and likewise important debt is what Tillich drew from Luther's theme that "God alone is God." That same motif appears in Tillich as the concept of the "Protestant Principle," whereby he argues that Protestantism as a movement affirms the fundamental dictum that "God alone is God," and that no other person, object, or institution is worthy of our ultimate loyalty. In this way, Tillich felt that Protestantism is a corrective principle to Roman Catholic claims for the church, Orthodox claims for church councils, and Protestant fundamentalist claims for the unique authority of scripture. Protestantism, Tillich maintained, lives where this principle is vital and has no authenticity where the principle is weak.[19] I think this is a direct link between Luther and Tillich.

The Human Condition (The Doctrine of Man)

The third point of similarity between Luther and Tillich is in their understanding of the human situation. Both of them stand in the tradition of Paul and Augustine, which emphasizes the sinful state of humanity. In Luther's lectures on Galatians and Romans, he underscores that to be a human being is to be filled with pride, selfishness, disobedience, and concupisence. This latter trait is often understood as sexual desire but is more that that; it is an unlimited striving for sex, power, and knowledge. And Luther felt that concupisence is a cancer in the heart

---

[17] Paul Tillich, "Author's Introduction," in J. L. Adams, ed., *The Protestant Era* (Chicago: University of Chicago Press, 1948), xvi-xvii.

[18] *History of Christian Thought,* 247.

[19] See the various essays on Protestantism in *The Protestant Era,* 192-233.

of all people.[20] These marks of fallenness touch all elements of human life: our reason, our will, and our emotions. Our fallenness is so total that Luther felt that we in fact were enslaved by demonic forces. That enslavement leads us to unbelief, which Luther regarded as "the very essense of sin." It was this conviction about the total fallenness of the human condition that prompted Luther to break with Erasmus in their famous dispute over free will in 1524. Luther thought that Erasmus was "soft" on sin, in the sense that he believed that our reason was still free enough to make it possible for us to make free choices to cooperate with God.

It is well known, of course, that Luther thought that in spite of God's good news of redemption, that we remain in this totally sinful condition all of our lives. The famous Lutheran expression that we are *"simul justus et peccator"* (simultaneously justified and sinful) did not mean for Luther that we are 50% justified and 50% sinful. It meant rather that we are 100% justified and at the same time 100% sinful. This, of course, would be another example of Luther's sense of paradox in theology but Tillich regarded it as a profound insight. Luther knew in his own heart that there is a dark side to human nature and that nothing that we deem reprehensible of others is totally alien to ourselves. Luther interpreted Paul's famous discussion in Romans 7 ("the good I would do, I do not, and the very thing I would not do, that is what I do") as being a description of the Christian life. It is as though centuries before Freud, Luther understood something of the dark side of human nature and the mysterious domain of the unconscious.

Tillich, by contrast, developed a vocabulary different from Luther as he analyzed the human situation in Volume II of his *Systematic Theology.* His bottom line perspecitive, however, was very consistent with Luther. Though ideally we are created for fellowship with God, actually in our fallen human state we find ourselves estranged, alienated, racked by unbelief, driven by *hubris* (the drive to elevate ourselves to the form of the divine), and concupiscence. Tillich felt that Freud, with his sense of the libido, and Nietzsche, with his sense of the will to power, both had profound insights into what it is to be a human being.

Estrangement and alienation are realities that touch us collectively as well as individually. They are responsible for the experiences of loneliness, suffering, meaninglessness, anxiety, and despair that drive us compulsively. This condition, however, is too much for us, argued Tillich, and all persons seek some escape from it through legalism, asceticism, mysticism, and sacramentalism-- religious modes of "self salvation." But what we really need we cannot provide for ourselves. We yearn for renewal, reunion, and reconciliation with ourselves, our neighbors, and with God. That experience is what Tillich called "New Being."It is true that in Tillich's assessment of the human condition he draws heavily on existentialist literature, but his assumption is that only one who is radically honest about the

---

[20]This theological assessment, so critical for Luther, indicates that, like all of his sixteenth-century colleagues, he was not sensitive to the differences of gender. The same criticism can be directed at Tillich, four centuries later.

depth of despair in life can understand the meaning of grace and new being. The fact is that new being *does* occur, and we have a model for it in Jesus of Nazareth.

How then can we draw a line from Luther to Tillich concerning the human situation? We have to be cautious at this point; Luther was not the only one to depict the condition of fallen humanity in this way, and Tillich clearly draws on other people besides Luther to substantiate the condition of estrangement, alienation, and despair. Tillich also had the advantage of doing his theology after Freud, and he utilized Freudian insights about the unconscious in his analysis of the human situation. Both Luther and Tillich agreed, however, that only the person who knows sin can know grace. Both would agree that only the one who knows sin can know the meaning of forgiveness. Tillich, in his famous sermon "To Whom Much is Forgiven" in *The New Being*[21] maintained that the one who forgives little loves little. In his lectures on Luther in *A History of Christian Thought*, Tillich noted that Luther alone among the great reformers, "was a depth psychologist in the profoundest way without knowing the methodological research we know today. Luther saw those things in non-moralistic depths which were lost not only in Calvinist Christianity but to a great extent in Lutheranism as well."[22]

The Concept of Justification (How are we "restored" to God?)

All students of the Reformation know that this was one of Luther's breakthrough concepts. It was at the heart of his break with Rome. Luther thought that this idea was the heart, the touchstone, the measuring line of all doctrines. In the technical sense it is hard for Luther scholars to know when Luther first came upon this first insight. There are some hints in his lectures on the Psalms and also more extended discussions in his lectures on Romans, in the Galatians commentary of 1531, and other academic disputations. Luther's grasp of this concept may have been more rooted in Luther's own experience of dread and anxiety that in his disputes with other medieval theologians.

Briefly put, Luther --drawing heavily upon the apostle Paul--felt that our deliverance from sin is a free act of God. As fallen, sinful human beings, we claim no merit or worth; we deserve nothing more than condemnation; but we receive grace through faith. Luther in various ways thought that this came to us through the suffering of Christ, who through his own suffering made us more aware of our sin, but Luther was convinced that God has acted mysteriously in the event of Christ to restore all of humanity. We are "imputed righteous" (as it were) in spite of the fact that we remain sinful. The doctrine of justification is therefore related to a sense of the divine forgiveness and the mercy of God.

An important corollary to stress is that though Luther waxed eloquent on his forgiveness and restoration, he had little sense of sanctification or (as we might say) growth in the religious life. Here is where Luther differed profoundly from

[21] 3-14.
[22] 246.

Calvin, Thomas Aquinas, John Wesley, and even some of the Anabaptists. We are, in Luther's judgement, sinners and we remain sinners, but we rejoice that God claims us in spite of our sin, and we can live confidently with faith in Christ Jesus. That meant for Luther that though we know we are sinners, we should not be paralyzed by that awareness. Life in the world requires inevitable compromises between unpleasant alternatives and ambigious options. As some interpreters of Luther have said, his theology is as dangerous as it is profound!

Tillich stands very close to Luther on the matter of justification, but again uses a different vocabulary. Tillich talks about the grace that comes totally from the divine initiative. It is a grace that brings about a new creation, a new being; it is the power of transformation. Justification, Tillich noted, is both an act of God and a human experience; it is decisive for the whole Christian message as a salvation from despair about one's guilt.

In an attempt to make this idea more understandable to a twentieth century audience, Tillich likes to use the word "acceptance" which he drew from the terminology of psychotherapy. In one of his sermons entitled "You Are Accepted," he wrote:

> Grace strikes us when we are in great pain and restlessness. It strikes us when we walk through the dark valley of a meaningless and empty life. It strikes us when we feel that our separation is deeper than usual, because we have violated another life, a life which he loved, from which we were estranged. It strikes us when our disgust for our own being, our indifference, our weakness, our hostility, and our lack of direction and composure have become intolerable to us. It strikes us when year after year the longed for perfection of life does not appear, when the old compulsions reign within us as they have for decades, when despair destroys all joy and courage. Sometimes at that moment a wave of light breaks in to our darkness and it is as though a voice were saying: "You are accepted. *You are accepted*, accepted by that which is greater than you, and the name of which you do not know. Do not ask for the name now; perhaps you will find it later. Do not try to do anything now; perhaps later you will do much. Do not seek for anything; do not perform anything; do not intend anything. *Simply accept the fact that you are accepted!*" If that happens to us, we experience grace. After such an experience we may not be better than before, and we may not believe more than before. But everything is transformed. In that moment, grace conquers sin, and reconciliation bridges the gulf of estrangement. And nothing is demanded of this experience, no religious or moral or intellectual presupposition, nothing but *acceptance*. [23]

To summarize the similarities of language and concern about our being restored and forgiven by God: Luther is more Christ-centered and traditionally Pauline in his vocabulary. Tillich breaks from the conventional categories and uses psychological language to express this old truth in a new way. But in theological substance, he again stands very close to Luther.

---

[23] "You Are Accepted," in *The Shaking of the Foundations* (New York: Scribner's, 1953), 161-62.

IV

This study has been a modest analysis of Luther's influence upon a twentieth-century German-American theologian. Of course the influence of Luther goes in many ways through the centuries and is felt in intellectual history, politics, and culture as well as through theology. Yet by clarifying how Paul Tillich drew on Luther (remember that he called Luther "one of the few great prophets of the Christian Church") and noting how Tillich adapted Luther's ideas, we are reminded that whoever studies Luther deals not only with sixteenth-century history but also with continuing insights about God, life, death, and destiny.

I have also tried to clarify in this essay in what ways Tillich stood in the Lutheran tradition. Although Lutheran by birth and culture and influenced by Luther on several critical theological points, it is clear that Tillich was not a typical Lutheran confessional theologian. In some ways his differences with Luther were as profound as his debts. Though Luther was a giant over a 500-year span of Christian life and thought, Tillich was also keenly aware of how his ideas were molded by the parochial framework of history and culture of his time. Clearly Tillich never thought that Luther could simply be "reheated" and presented to the twentieth century as a viable theological voice. Luther's insights need re-formulation and adaptation to a new social, cultural, and political climate. Tillich is one model of how this might be done.

There is however, one more point emerging out of this study for contemporary Tillich scholarship. On the whole, recent Tillich scholarship has been much more interested in Tillich's contributions as a theologian of culture than in his work as a systematic theologian.[24] Scholars have tended therefore to probe his relationship to Schelling and Hegel far more than his relationship with Luther or any other major Christian thinker. I hope that this study makes clear, however, that whoever would wish to understand Tillich as a theologian needs to look not only to Hegel, Schelling, and Kierkegaard, but also in some special ways to Tillich's life-long engagement with the reformer of Wittenburg.

---

[24] See, for example, the various assessments of Tillich offered in my edited books *Kairos and Logos: Studies in The Roots and Implications of Tillich's Theology* (Macon, GA: Mercer University Press, 1984) and *Theonomy and Autonomy: Studies in Paul Tillich's Engagement with Modern Culture* (note 3).

Death-God-Comedy:
Moral Wisdom and Biblical Tradition

A. Roy Eckardt
University of Oxford

My association and friendship with John Priest go far back to halcyon days when the now-humongous American Academy of Religion was the then-humble National Association of Biblical Instructors, yet when every teacher of religion was nothing less than prophet (*nabi*)—provided she or he was a paid-up member of our organization. John Priest stands among my scholarly and humane heroes of those good years. I am blessed to have a part in this *Festschrift* in his honor. In accord with John's own specialty, I shall try to make my presentation wisdomly biblical—or at least not violative of a biblical stance.

This essay seeks to address the relation between the dominion of death (*mot*) and the biblical Lord of life (*haim*). Methodologically but also substantively speaking, I utilize the instrument of comedy construed as incongruity. To anticipate the argument—or perhaps better, the confession: If death is the ultimate comedy (incongruity) of life—*never* a "part" of life, *always* the contradictory of life—so too the divine salvation (the salvation *of* God, the God who *needs* saving, not the salvation of anyone else) entails a final incongruity as between finite reality and extrafinite love. However entrenched is "theodicy" as an effort to justify God in the presence of evil, the theodicean enterprise is to be rejected on principle. The ground for this repudiation is that human beings never "elect [themselves] into being" (H. Richard Niebuhr). The divine crime (God in the guise and role of Devil) is overcome only through the divine repentance, which makes possible the human forgiveness of God (a consummating incongruity).

251

Prologue

Before the blink of an eye the lowly hyphen is able to bind together entire universes of meaning/discourse: Death-God-Comedy. What could a poor philosopher ever do to match such marvelous effrontery?

Wendy Farley sums up the fate/future of human beings. We are "sojourners on the way to death."[1] Goethe once commented, "der Teufel, der ist alt." To conjoin these two recognitions is to bring to remembrance the singular scientific affirmation (*scientia*, knowledge) of the New Testament wherein death is counted amongst the demonic powers that dominate the present age (1 Cor 15:24-26). The Devil has been widely apprehended, not alone as tempting to human sin, but as coupled with death itself. In the Epistle to the Hebrews the Devil retains the very power of death (2:14). Satan even gets equated with death.[2] Speak of death, and the Devil is bound to appear.

Yet if Walter Wink's contrasting word is correct, that Satan has come to stand among "the unmentionables" of contemporary culture,[3] this brings together two conspicuous silences of our modern/postmodern world: We must not speak of the Devil. We must not speak of death.

Are we still permitted to speak of God? What does it mean to talk of God as intervention between death and comedy?

Should God be characterized as Lord of life, where does this leave God respecting the dominion of death? However, once death is apprehended as the final incongruity of life, and once comedy is identified with incongruity (a major interpretation, though alternate viewpoints vie for attention), an essential between death and comedy has begun to emerge.[4] Indeed the ultimate question of comedy

---

[1] W. Farley, *Tragic Vision and Divine Compassion: A Contemporary Theodicy* (Louisville: Westminster/John Knox Press, 1990), p. 37.

[2] J. B. Russell, *The Devil: Perceptions of Evil from Antiquity to Primitive Christianity* (Ithaca/London: Cornell Universty Press, 1987), p. 240; see also pp. 216, 256; *Satan: The Early Christian Tradition* (Ithaca/London: Cornell University Press, 1987), p. 119; and S. G. F. Brandon, *The Judgment of the Dead: The Idea of Life After Death in the Major Religions* (New York: Charles Scribner's Sons, 1967), p. 114. After the eleventh century, death and the Devil are usually portrayed separately (Jeffrey Burton Russell, *Lucifer: The Devil in the Middle Ages* [Ithaca/London: Cornell University Press, 1986], p. 210).

[3] W. Wink, *Unmasking the Powers: The Invisible Powers That Determine Human Existence* (Philadelphia: Fortress Press, 1986), p. 1.

[4] Philosophers who center attention upon the category of incongruity as crucial to comedy include Kant, Hegel, Schopenhauer, and Bergson. I tend to think of comedy as broader and deeper than humor, and certainly than the physiological act of laughter. For varied renderings of the nature of humor and comedy, consult my trilogy (*Sitting in the Earth and Laughing: A Handbook of Humor* [New Brunswick/London: Transaction/Rutgers University, 1992]; *How To Tell God From the Devil: On the Way to Comedy* [New Brunswick/London: Transaction/Rutgers University, 1995]; *On the Way To Death: Essays Toward a Comic Vision* [New Brunswick/London: Transaction/Rutgers University, 1996]) and my *The Comic and the Ethicist: A Kind of Team* (forthcoming). Also see Marcel Gutwirth, *Laughing Matter: An Essay on the Comic* (Ithaca/London: Cornell University Press, 1993), pp. 110-15, and John Morreall, ed. *The Philosophy of Laughter and Humor* (Albany: State University of New York Press, 1987).

is the question of death. Perhaps this is what brings so much pain to our comedians. Sören Kierkegaard stipulates that "the more one suffers, the more has one a sense for the comic."[5]

The Ugliest Customer

The anticipation of their death brings great suffering to human beings, quite independently of the act of dying itself. William Hazlitt called death "the ugly customer." He might better have said "ugliest," since death is the one annihilation that is certain, universal, and unexceptional, the one Absolute that suffuses finite existence. Ernest Becker observes that "of all things that move man one of the principal ones is his terror of death." For "underneath the most bland exterior lurks the universal anxiety, the 'worm at the core,'" that "layer of our true and basic animal anxieties, the terror that we carry around in our secret heart."[6] This terror encompasses not simply one's individual death but the deaths of loved ones and friends. Those deaths can be more terrible than the portent of one's own demise. Furthermore, why ought these other persons have to endure *my* death? Why must I be compelled to do such a thing to them? And why must they be forced to do the very same to me? These actions must themselves be numbered within the terrors of death. Death is the most radical, the most terrible of evils.

Beyond Theodicy

G. Tom Milazzo asks: "Why, in the presence of God, is there death?"[7]

The question of God is drawn into the question of the Devil (and hence into the question of death) in and through Jeffrey Burton Russell's unexceptionable finding, "the study of the Devil indicates that historically, he is a manifestation of the divine, a part of the deity. *Sine diabolo nullus Deus*. Yet, morally, his work is completely and utterly to be rejected."[8] ("Devil" may here announce itself as Thrust toward Malignity, with "God" as corresponding Thrust toward

---

[5] *Parables of Kierkegaard*, T. C. Oden, ed. (Princeton: Princeton University Press, 1978), p. 30. Cf. Alexander Walker on Robin Williams: Williams has "the feeling many comics have, that the worst is always certain . . . but maybe, if one's lucky, not just yet. Humour for him is a defence mechanism against a world he feels potentially hostile. For him, the best defence is attack—'Get the laugh' is his war-like command to himself. . ." ("Jet Stream Robin," in *High Life* [British Airways], April 1994: 84).

[6] *The Denial of Death* (New York: Free Press, 1973), pp. 11, 21, 57. It was William James who called death "the worm at the core" of human pretensions to happiness (*The Varieties of Religious Experience* [New York: Mentor, 1958], p. 121.) See also L. R. Bailey, Sr., *Biblical Perspectives on Death* (Philadelphia: Fortress Press, 1979); A. Roy Eckardt, "Death in the Judaic and Christian Traditions," in A. Mack, ed., *Death in American Experience* (New York: Schocken Books, 1973), pp. 123-48; N. Elias, *The Loneliness of the Dying*, trans. Edmund Jephcott (Oxford: Basil Blackwell, 1985); and S. B. Nuland, *How We Die* (New York: Alfred A. Knopf, 1994).

[7] *The Protest and the Silence: Suffering, Death, and Biblical Theology* (Minneapolis: Augsburg/Fortress Press, 1991), p. 52.

[8] *The Devil: Perceptions of Evil . . .*, pp. 31-32.

Righteousness.) Implied within Russell's finding is the end of theodicy. More exactly, any effort to justify radical evil may be viewed as a form of devilishness. It is entirely fitting that in Elie Wiesel's *The Trial of God (as it was held on February 25, 1649 in Shamgorod)*, the stranger who offers to serve as defense attorney for God should turn out to be the Devil.[9] A straightforward translation of Professor Russell's theological/moral finding will read: If we are ever going to reject radical evil we are compelled to punish God as Devil. Or, even stronger: Unless we reject God, in God's culpability for radical evil and suffering, we ally ourselves with the Devil, we become the Devil's silent mouthpiece.

However, to declare the Devil a manifestation of the divine is not without its compensations, of which two may be singled out.

1. The associating of death now with the Devil and now with God supports a judgment of moral bankruptcy upon any separation between the two sides, the divine and the diabolic. Indeed, within one application of Jungian thought, the Devil is approached via the symbol Shadow of God, the dark side of the God who is.[10] The nonseparation of God and Devil—cf. Isa 45:7: "I make weal and create woe"—stands in contrast, on the one hand, to a theological dualism that agrees to settle for Evil as boasting either deciduous or lasting sovereignty and, on the other hand, to a theological monism that tries to assimilate evil to nonbeing. The massive challenge to dualism is: What is to be the fate of goodness? And the terrible dilemma of monism is that radical evil stays rife. The troubles that assail dualism and monism can be offset but only via the admission of consanguinity as between God and Devil, an admission that, naturally, brings us much anguish. (The *easiness* of dualism and the *idealism* of monism continue to lurk as powerful tempters.)

2. The persuasion that the Devil's work may be said somehow to precede evils committed by humanity—a viewpoint attested to by Reinhold Niebuhr among others[11]—counteracts in a positive, morally valuable way the travesty of making

---

[9] *The Trial of God . . .*, a play in three acts, trans. Marion Wiesel (New York: Random House, 1979).

[10] J. B. Russell, *The Prince of Darkness: Radical Evil and the Power of Good in History* (Ithaca/London: Cornell University Press, 1992), pp. 245-48; cf. C. G. Jung, "Good and Evil in Analytical Psychology," in *Civilization in Transition, Collected Works* 10, trans. R. F. C. Hull (London: Routledge & Kegan Paul, 1964), pp. 456-68, and "The Shadow," in *Collected Works* 9 (1968), pp. 3-7, and "The Light With the Shadow," in *Collected Works* 10 (1968), pp. 218-26.

[11] R. Niebuhr, *The Nature and Destiny of Man* I (New York: Charles Scribner's Sons, 1941), pp. 180-81, 254. Niebuhr's exposition of the Devil and the issue of ultimate responsibility for moral evil is fully analyzed in Eckardt, *How To Tell God From the Devil*, chap. 6. See in this connection B. W. Anderson, *Creation versus Chaos: The Reinterpretation of Mythical Symbolism in the Bible* (Philadelphia: Fortress Press, 1987), pp. 164-70 and more generally chap. 5. Walter Wink writes: If the "first fall" is that of humankind, "the second fall is that of the angels: there is a rupture in the very spirituality of the universe (Gen 6:1-4). *Human sin cannot therefore account for all evil*" (*Engaging the Powers, op. cit.*, p. 77; my italics). This viewpoint is represented as well in C. G. Jung: If the Devil "fell away from God of his own free will," this helps establish "that evil was in the world before man, and therefore that man cannot be the sole author of it" (*Aion: Researches into the Phenomenology of the Self*, in *Collected Works* 9, II, [Princeton: Princeton University Press, 1968], p. 48).

humankind, and not God, the subject of rebuke for the horrors of this world, particularly the specter of death. (Who but the Devil could be diabolical enough to explain radical evil via human "sin" or "free will"?) It is as, *kivevachol* (so to speak), the Shadow of God—indeed as an instrument of God, God's (vocational) "fallen angel"[12] —that the Devil enters onto the cosmic/world stage. The classical tie of the Devil to Death thus gains a certain plausibility. Of course, this is not to exempt the human being from all moral liability. The biblical myth of the Fall, writes Reinhold Niebuhr, "seeks to do justice to both the universality of sin and self-regard and to the element of personal responsibility in each sinful act."[13] In a word, *humanity remains proximately blameworthy for evil, but never ultimately blameworthy*. Ultimate blameworthiness is the property of the Devil, which is to say of the Shadow of God, which is to say of God. Such appellations of the Devil as "Shadow of God" and "fallen angel" help sustain significant economies: a denial of sovereignty to the Evil One (against the predicament of metaphysical/religious dualism) and at the same time a refusal to exculpate God from sin (against the predicament of metaphysical/religious monism). For the *work* of the Devil/of God as Devil is, morally, to be "completely and utterly rejected" (Russell).

The two foregoing points suggest the query: *O felix culpa dei?* Yet there lingers as well the question: Did the Devil ask to exist?

Human Innocence and Divine Crime: the Triplets of History

The quality of innocence is bound to the truth that the creation has no say in its own appearance or primordial realization. As H. Richard Niebuhr declares, we humans "are 'thrown into existence,' fated to be. . . . [We] did not elect ourselves into being." This "self which lives in this body and this mind did not choose itself."[14] Innocence cannot mean the absence of all moral responsibility or of a sinful corruption of freedom, any more than innocence need imply that all suffering is perforce nonredemptive. Notwithstanding, it is with respect to innocence as *thrownness* that the inflicting of radical evil and suffering upon the human (and extrahuman) creation becomes classifiable as a crime.

Divinity, Humankind, Deviltry—strange triplets of the history of this world, triplets of the generations (*toldot*)—all bear within their varying morphologies of freedom the singular and shared mark of accountability (*Verantwortlichkeit*): three moral deciders, three fallen realities, three comic (incongruous) characters, three representations—in sharply varying measures—of life-and-death. One of the

---

[12] See Russell, *The Devil, op cit.*, pp. 227-28, 241-43, 252-53. Cf. Job 1:6ff; Eph 2:1-2; Rev 12:7-9. Consult also G. MacGregor, *Angels: Ministers of Grace* (New York: Paragon House, 1988), chap. 5 - "Satan: The Realm of Angels Gone Wrong."

[13] *The Self and the Dramas of History* (New York: Charles Scribner's Sons, 1955), p. 99.

[14] H. R. Niebuhr, *Faith on Earth: An Inquiry into the Structure of Human Faith*, ed. R. R. Niebuhr (New Haven/London: Yale University Press, 1989), p. 65.

players (Humanity) appears as peculiarly subject to death. But can the particularly devilish one of the triplet be turned and beamed toward the annihilation of himself—in order that, or at least with the consequence that, the third one of the triplet (Divinity) might live?   If at least two of the characters (Humankind, Deviltry) bring a modicum of innocence to their fallenness (they never asked to be), as at the same time they remain fallen and responsible amidst that very innocence (they consort with evil), the Eternal One marshals a certain innocence as well—the innocence of pristine Being. Nevertheless, there is a divine Fall. Indeed, the devil's evident thrownness into existence itself points, by contrast, to the divine Fall as Final Fall. For the blameworthiness of God persists as the only ultimate blameworthiness—quite unsoftened by any plea of existence-apart-from-volition.

Thus does a shadow (Shadow) continue to fall across the entire ontic creation. Transgressions have been committed and they will have to be paid for. The life journey of God moves into the future. That future is fraught with incalculable risk, the risk of nothing less than total condemnation.

The Tale of God's Salvation

Beyond the futility, even immorality, of theodicy *as idea* lies the potentiality of redemption *as act*.

There is no interest here in obviating, or even competing with, the active redemptions of humans (Yom Kippur, *bodhisattvas*,[15] the death of Jesus, etc., etc.). Yet such redemption remains futile, or at least extraneous, respecting the evil of the divine crime.

Is there a divine praxis that comprises a punitive program and self-atonement for God? That question is approachable via another one: How may God respond in action to the human denunciation of God?

We are not engaged in an exercise in comparative history or mythology. Since we have operated thus far out of a broadly biblical-Western tradition, we may remain with that *Anschauung*. There follows an elementary scenario, within but a single accounting of the divine redemption:

(a)   *Anger as the condition of prayer.*

> Reb Dovid Din was sought out in Jerusalem by a man who ranted and raved for hours. At last he said to him "Why are you so angry with God?"
>
> The question stunned the man, who had said nothing at all about God. The man then responded: "All my life I have been so afraid to express my anger to God that I have always directed my anger at people. Until this moment I did not understand this."
>
> Reb Dovid told the man to follow him to the site of the ruins of the Temple and express there every anger he felt toward God. For over an hour the man struck the *Kotel* [wall] with his fists and screamed his heart out. After that he began to cry and could not stop crying. Little by little his cries became sobs that turned to prayers.

[15] K. Armstrong, *A History of God* (London: Mandarin Books, 1994), pp. 101-04.

And that is how Reb Dovid taught this man to pray.[16]

(b) *A "boldness respecting heaven" (hutzpa k'lapei shamaya) and the rousing of God.* This praxis, constituent to the Jewish narrative tradition, extends as far back as the Abrahamic story. Chutzpa may be grasped, not as a dubious or illegitimate assertion of human willfulness or impudence, but as a rightful declaration of human dignity, grounded in and justified by the *imago dei* and for that matter the *imitatio dei*. From this standpoint, one or another refusal to judge God is not alone a matter of hidden self-hatred; it is also a form of *unfaithfulness* to God. Paradoxically, such a refusal betrays the very will of God, the God who is entirely prepared and entirely willing to be accountable, to be obligated. Thus is chutzpa seen to be a materially holy act.[17]

When Abraham asks, "Shall not the Judge of all the earth do what is just?" (Gen 18:25), he is no more than demanding that God do what God Godself maintains and reveals to be just. The righteousness that is prerequisite within, and constituent to, a manifesting of holiness (Isa 5:16) is hardly Abraham's invention.

Jon D. Levenson shows how by the time of the exile of the sixth century BCE, one major component (among many diverse components) of the spiritual life of Israel was concern over Yahweh as "a semiotiose deity," yet one who could nevertheless be summoned to respond to anguished cries from the cultic community.

> Awake! Do not cast us off forever!
> Why do you hide your face?
> Why do you forget our
> affliction and oppression (Ps 44:23-24).

God is "*reproached* for his failure, told that it is neither inevitable nor excusable."[18]

(c) *The God who weeps.* There must be shame and repentance for the divine crimes.

In "*Ani Maamin*," Elie Wiesel's poetic retelling of a Talmudic tale, no less noble a trio than Abraham, Isaac, and Jacob engage in remorseless intercessions and terrible denunciations of God for the radical suffering of God's people. There is inserted as well an echo of the Devil's own brand of theodicy:

---

[16] This is adapted from "Trying to Pray" in *Gabriel's Palace: Jewish Mystical Tales*, ed. and compiler Howard Schwartz (New York: Oxford University Press, 1993), p. 267,; original source, p. 355. For a Christian viewpoint, consult P. Wolff, *May I Hate God?* (New York: Paulist Press, 1979).

[17] Consult A. Laytner, *Arguing With God: A Jewish Tradition* (Northvale, NJ/London: Jason Aronson, 1990). For Christian support of this Jewish tradition, see D. J. Fasching, *Narrative Theology After Auschwitz: From Alienation to Ethics* (Minneapolis: Fortress Press, 1992) esp. chap. 3, and cf. B. C. Lane, "Hutzpa K'Lapei Shamaya: A Christian Response to the Jewish Tradition of Arguing With God," *Journal of Ecumenical Studies* 23 (1986): 567-86.

[18] Levenson, *Creation and the Persistence of Evil* (San Francisco: Harper & Row, 1988), pp. 50, 24. I offer a full exposition of Levenson's work in *How To Tell God From the Devil*, chap. 3.

> The Master of the World
> Disposes of the world.
> His creatures
> Do their creator's bidding,
> Accept his laws
> Without a question.

But, of moral necessity, there comes a Nevertheless: When Abraham snatches a little girl from before the machine guns and runs like the wind to save her, and she whispers to him weakly that she believes in him, "he does not, cannot, see that God for the first time, permits a tear to cloud his eyes." When Isaac beholds the mad Dayan singing "of his ancient and lost faith," of "love of God and love of man," of "the coming of the Messiah," Isaac too "does not, cannot, see that for second time a tear streams down God's sober countenance, a countenance more somber than before." And when Jacob finds a death camp inmate declaiming that the Haggadah lies, that God will not come, that the wish to be in Jerusalem will never be granted, but that he will continue to recite the Haggadah as if he believes in it, and still await the prophet Elijah as he did long ago, even though Elijah disappoint him, Jacob too "does not, cannot, see that God, surprised by his people, weeps for the third time—and this time without restraint, and with—yes—love. He weeps over his creation—and perhaps over much more than his creation."[19]   Why should the secret of the weeping of God—kept successively from each member of the trio—be said to extend "perhaps over much more than" the entire creation? Secrets tempt to the fabricating of added secrets, added midrashim. Perhaps the secret of the "more" here consists in the shedding of tears for the divine sin, for the pact with Satan (Job 2:6), for the terror of human death, for the suffering of *this* child, *this* woman, *this* man, *this* animal, *this* bird—of *every* child, *every* woman, *every* man, *every* animal, *every* bird. (No exceptions are allowed, for no creature has asked to exist.)

(d) *God's response to the human ethic of audacity: Prayer.* In the train of Jacques Ellul and others, Darrell J. Fasching puts forward an ethic of audacity/theology of chutzpa.[20] In the same vein, declares David Wolpe, God must act "to effect His own salvation."[21] To this end, God is found resorting to prayer.

> Said R. Yohanan in the name of R. Yosé, "How do we know that the Holy One, blessed be he, says prayers?"
> Since it is said, "Even them will I bring to my holy mountain and make them joyful in my house of prayer" (Isa 56:7).
> "Their house of prayer" is not stated, but rather, "my house of prayer."
> "On the basis of that usage we see that the Holy One, blessed be he, says prayers."

[19] Elie Wiesel, *"Ani Maamin": A Song Lost and Found Again*, trans. M. Wiesel (New York: Random House, 1973), pp. 17ff., 31, 33, 49, 55, 65, 67, 89-103.
[20] Fasching, *Narrative Theology After Auschwitz: From Alienation to Ethics* (Minneapolis: Fortress Press, 1992), pp. 156-57, 161.
[21] *The Healer of Shattered Hearts* (New York: Henry Holt, 1990), p. 13.

"What prayers does he say?"

Said R. Zutra bar Tobiah, "May it be my will that my mercy overcome my anger, and that my mercy prevail over my attributes, so that I may treat my children in accord with the trait of mercy and in their regard go beyond the strict measure of the law."[22]

(e) *The apodictic/moral command: Resurrection.* There must be retribution for the sin of God, for human and other suffering and death. The scales of righteousness have to be balanced. For one of many archetypes of justice, return may be made to Moses, patriarch and prophet:

"To annul the decree of death, Moses draws a magic circle around himself and hurls his prayers to the Heavens. God orders the Gates of Heaven shut but Moses' prayers batter against the gate and set all the angels atremble. To no avail." Having been told in no uncertain terms that he must die without ever passing over the River Jordan into the land of promise, Moses accuses God of making a fraud of God's own Torah, insisting that God incurs guilt b2y violating Deuteronomy 24:15. Among God's responses is an assurance that Moses will live and be rewarded in the World to Come (*olam ha-ba*). "But Moses clings to life. Defiantly, he takes up writing a Torah scroll and the Angel of Death fears to approach him to take his soul. When ordered to return a second time, the Angel of Death receives a beating from Moses' staff. Finally, God resolves to act and calms Moses' fears directly. *God Himself, not the Angel of Death nor human beings, will attend Moses' burial.* With sweet words God calls forth the soul, and *weeping*, gives Moses the kiss of death."[23]

Who is God, in an angelogical frame of reference? God is that Angel whose tears are *preceded* by the promise and warranty of resurrection. Resurrection is the escort beyond tragedy. As Wylie Sypher writes, tragedy is distinguished from comedy in this wise: The former's cycle is birth, struggle, death: the latter proclaims birth, struggle, death, resurrection.[24]

(f)   *Love as the shepherd of God.*

On Mount Moriah in Jerusalem there once lived two brothers. One had a wife and children: the other was unmarried. They all lived together. . . .

When it was harvest time, they reaped their grain and brought the sheaves to the threshing floor. There they divided the sheaves into two equal piles and went home.

That night the brother who had no family said to himself, "I am alone, but my brother has a wife and children to feed. Why should my portion be equal to his?"

So he rose from his bed and went to the threshing floor. He took some sheaves from his own pile and added them to his brother's.

---

[22] Babylonian Talmud *Berakot* 7A, XLIX, as cited in J. Neusner, *Telling Tales* (Louisville: Westminster/John Knox Press, 1993), pp. 134-35.

[23] Laytner, *op. cit.*, pp. 63, 65-66, my italics; for the biblical and rabbinic sources see Laytner notes, pp. 264-65.

[24] Cited in N. N. Holland, *Laughing: A Psychology of Humor* (Ithaca/London: Cornell University Press, 1982), p. 97.

That same night, the other brother said to his wife, It is not right that my brother
has the same number of sheaves as I. For I have a greater share of happiness since I have
a wife and clildren, but he is all alone."

So the brother and his wife went secretly to the threshing floor and put some of
their own sheaves on the single brother's pile.

The next morning the two brothers rose early and went to thresh their sheaves.
Both were astonished to find the piles still equal. That night they both went again to the
threshing floor and met each other there. When they realized why they were both there,
they embraced and kissed each other.

That is why God chose their field as the site of the Holy Temple, for it was there
that two brothers showed their great love for each other.

All this helps to explain how "on the day the Temple was destroyed, the Messiah was
born."[25]

The Divine Comedy

There can be no more radical or complete incongruity than the praxis of a
God of all eternity and all creation who bows before the demands and interests of
puny earthlings. God creates, God sins, God repents. And God will put Death to
death (Rev 20:14; 21:4). Indeed, "the only way God can win the human heart is by
freeing human beings from death. For only when the human heart is free from
death are humans free to love God."[26] Human thrownness will be justified. God
will step forth from the Shadow into God's own light. Once God is saved, God is
set free to save.   In the meanwhile, the reason is disclosed why it is on the Feast
of Purim that *The Trial of God (as it was held on February 25, 1649, in
Shamgorod)* must take place, for Purim means those two odd days of the year
when the mundane scene is orbited into hilarity and joy. And it is on Purim that a
kind of Hymn to the Hyphens can at last be sung: Death-God-Comedy. But equally
in the meanwhile, the solitary prayer of God, "may it be my will that my mercy
overcome my anger," finally gains a counterpart in the solitary (*einzeln*) prayer of
humankind, as given voice by a young man called Benjamin of the village of
Zemyock. Benjamin has just reached the terrifying conclusion that were God not
to be, Zemyock would become no more than an absurd fragment of the universe.
And so Benjamin prays: "If you do not exist, where does all the suffering go? It
goes for nothing. Oh, my God, it goes for nothing."[27]

I confess the foregoing line of reasoning in thanksgiving for, and in comic
laughter with, the contribution and career of our good colleague John Priest.

[25] E. Frankel, *The Classic Tales: 4,000 Years of Jewish Lore* (Northvale, NJ/London: Jason
Aronson, 1993), pp. 241-42, 338; sources, pp. 619, 623.
[26] G. T. Milazzo, *The Protest and the Silence: Suffering, Death, and Biblical Theology*
(Minneappolis: Augsburg Fortress, 1991), p. 159.
[27] A. Schwarz-Bart, *The Last of the Just*, trans. S. Becker (New York: Atheneum, 1961), p. 69.

Myth and Midrash

Christine Downing
San Diego State University

John Priest and I both did our graduate work at Drew University, and although I began my graduate studies after he had completed his, it has always felt as though we were fellow students, mostly I think because we were each fellow students and close friends of Richard Underwood's whose time at Drew overlapped both of ours. John's doctoral studies had focused on Hebrew Scriptures, mine emphasized the interconnections between religion and literature, religion and depth psychology. What we had in common was that we both loved stories, although back then the stories that interested me most were often different from those that attracted John. Since then I have come to appreciate more and more how deeply the stories that have always been most important to him, the stories told in the Hebrew Bible, inform my life.

I am inhabited by stories, stories of what might have happened and of what did, personal stories and age-old stories, Greek myths and Hebrew legends.

I was born in Germany in 1931 and my father was a Jew, at least in Hitler's eyes. His grandfather had been an assimilated secular Jew; his father had become an Anglican as a young man and married a Viennese Catholic. My father grew up in a Lutheran part of Germany, was baptized and confirmed as a Lutheran, and married a woman from a family that had been Lutheran since the sixteenth century. He has never thought of himself as Jewish.

Nevertheless, because he was a university professor, my father lost his job in 1933 when Hitter came to power, a few months before my brother was born. In November 1934, after fruitless attempts to find a position as a chemist in Germany, he came to America; by then my mother was already pregnant with their third child. Three months after my sister's birth, my mother and we three children joined my father in America. We arrived on the Fourth of July.

Given this background, it is probably not surprising that all my life I have been haunted by two shadow selves, two alternate lives I might easily have lived. One of these is the life that would have unfolded had my entire family stayed in Germany and eventually been sent to an extermination camp. The other is connected to the possibility that my gentile mother might have agreed to the urgings of both sets of her children's grandparents and decided not to follow my father to America. The force of these urgings is suggested by the fact that her father–and she was very much a father's daughter–never forgave her for choosing to go to America (as he'd almost not forgiven her for marrying a man he viewed as a Jew). After her departure he never had any further contact with her. As I imagine it, my parents would have been divorced, and my mother would have returned to the small town where her father was the headmaster of a boys' secondary school, and eventually she would have married the childhood sweetheart who, as she often tells us now, was still in love with her. I would have grown up absorbing the taken-for-granted anti-Semitism of that milieu and very likely the Nazi enthusiasms of my peers.

These two other selves have always been there for me, though obviously in the first few years in America there was more just a sense of "the girl I left behind in Germany," the girl who would go on with her/my life there, the girl who still saw her grandparents regularly, the girl who still spoke our mother tongue. Especially at first she, her life, felt even more real than the life of the one who had suddenly found herself uprooted. I can remember dreaming of her every night, keeping her alive.

Only gradually did she become two, as I only gradually discovered that I was partly Jewish by birth and that we had left Germany because of that, and as I only gradually learned how much the life of a German Jewish girl would differ from that of a gentile peer. My given name was Christine Rosenblatt–an obvious sign of this double destiny to those who could read such signs. But I can still remember vividly the occasion when I was ten years old when for the first time a stranger, hearing my name, let me know she assumed I was Jewish, and how disbelieving I was.

Since then they have always been there, these two other selves, haunting my dreams, shaping my feelings, affecting my decisions in ways only recognized retrospectively. I have come to sense how they have helped determine whom I've chosen as friends, how they've entered into my scholarly involvements with Buber and Freud (who are, in a sense, the Jewish grandfathers I never knew), how my most basic sense of what the world is like is due more to them than to anything I've experienced in my protected life here in America.

They have always been there, these two other selves, but as vague presences, never quite in focus, never directly engaged. But in September 1992 I took a trip back to Saxony, the homeland to which I'd never returned since we left when I was four, and since then I have known I need to get these shadow selves, these selves that still live in the shadows, in focus. I need to see them clearly–in order to see myself clearly.

I had at first imagined writing fictional accounts of these lives but came to realize I must rather imagine myself in the process of trying to get these figures into focus, much as I might try to pull back into consciousness an evanescent dream. I needed to address each (somewhat as in Gestalt therapy one might address a silent figure in the other chair) with my questions, my imaginings. For each "she" can tell her story only in dialogue with me, for in a sense she exists only in that dialogue, has no existence apart from our interaction.

But to engage her in dialogue I need to call her forth by name, and it seems obvious to me that neither would still be Christine Rosenblatt. The girl who went back to Zeitz with her mother would never have kept that Jewish last name. She would have been known by her mother's maiden name and then by the name of her mother's new husband. She would have become Christine Fischer Tollert. The girl who went to Terezin with her father and eventually to Auschwitz would not have stayed Christine. At first I thought she might have become known as Sara, the name the Nazis required all Jewish females to adopt. But then suddenly I *knew*–she would have been called Ruth.

My reading these last few years has taught me that actually, historically, ending up in an extermination camp was a much less likely possibility for me, a second degree *Mischling* according to the Nuremberg Laws, than I had previously always imagined. But nevertheless that was the alternate life that had always haunted me, because a part of me has always felt with respect to my Jewish ancestry, *whither thou goest, I will go.*

I know that, born of a non-Jewish mother and never inculcated in Jewish ritual, in Jewish eyes I am not a Jew at all. Yet, since I first became aware of my family history I have always felt a strong connection to my Jewish heritage–not to the religion.(I am a polytheist not a monotheist, a pagan not a Jew), but to the stories.

I have devoted much of my time in the last few decades to the stories of ancient Greece and to modern, especially feminist, rereadings of these stories. I have been particularly drawn to the story of Demeter and Persephone.[1] This story is in some ways a story about my relation to my mother and to my own motherhood and more deeply for me a story about the human relation to grief and rage, loss and death, and the underworld. And, thus, even this story is connected for me to Auschwitz and to all Auschwitz reveals about the cruelty and vulnerability of our human being-here.

But the Hebrew stories are mine, too. I keep returning to them, to Sara and Abraham, to Esau and Jacob, to Rachel and Leah, to Tamar, to Joseph–to Ruth.

---

[1] See my *The Long Journey Home,* Shambhala, 1994.

I remember being taught that in Greece the stories belonged to the poets, and that the poets kept the myths alive through their creative reworking of them. In Israel, by contrast, I was told, the stories belonged to the priests, who held that there was only one right way to tell them, the way enshrined in the canon. But, of course, this isn't true, at least not for Jews. Torah and midrash belong together. According to the sages there is always another interpretation, always another way of telling or understanding the tale, and all later commentary, not just the commentary of the Talmudic or medieval rabbis but our commentary too, is implicit in the revelation given at Sinai, as though already written in invisible ink. Midrash immerses us in a sea of quotations, allusions, elaborations, extrapolations, and plausible inventions that add ethical judgment, sociological density, and psychological motivation to biblical texts. To engage in midrash is to look at what's troubling in the canonical version, to note contradictions, missing details. Such fresh, passionate, playful rereadings of the Torah honor, challenge, and sometimes subvert the traditional tales.

My own sense of many of the biblical stories comes as much from Thomas Mann's midrashic versions in *Joseph and His Brothers* as from the Book of Genesis. But Mann never wrote about Ruth, and it is Ruth who has become focal for me. Ruth, whose connection to the Jewish story was peripheral, easily disowned, until she chose to make it central. It's her *choice* of a destiny that moves me—and also that she made her choice on the basis of her commitment to a woman. For even though in my own case the shadow self that might have gone to Auschwitz would have followed her father there, nevertheless part of the power of this story for me is the way in which it is a story about a woman's love for a woman. What pulls us *to* a story is not always what keeps us returning to it.

Of course, we return to it for many different reasons. I've been struck by how many contemporary women, particularly Jewish women, are pulled to reclaim this story as their own. As adults they discover depths and complexities in the story that they had not been aware of when they heard it as children.[2]

> When you pick up the Tanakh and read
> the Book of Ruth, it is a shock
> how little it resembles memory.
> It's concerned with inheritance,
> lands, men's names, how women
> must wiggle and wobble to live.
> Yet women have kept it dear
> for the beloved elder who
> cherished Ruth, more friend than
> daughter. Daughters leave. Ruth
> brought even the baby she made
> with Boaz home as a gift.

[2] See J. A. Katz and G. T. Reimer, eds., *Reading Ruth: Contemporary Women Reclaim a Sacred Story,* Ballantine, 1994. My own rereading has been very influenced by the many fine essays in this book.

Where you go, I will go too,
your people shall be my people,
I will be a Jew for you,
for what is yours I will love
as I love you, oh Naomi
my mother, my sister, my heart.[3]

The Book of Ruth reads like a folktale, like the legends in Genesis, and its focus on food and famine, on infertility and birth, suggest it might once (as part of a lost oral tradition) even have been connected to some old goddess tale. But as part of my own adult return to this text, I have learned that actually it is a sophisticated, deliberately anachronistic, composition probably written in the post-exilic period with clearly intended, pointedly meaningful, allusions to other biblical texts.

As my curiosity about Ruth led me to return to a text I may not have read since I was a child, I have been surprised to find how many parts of the story resonate with my own, but not in any neat parallel analogical way. These recognitions give me a sense of how a gifted novelist like Mann could enter into the received stories and then recreate them in a way that suggests he knows each character from within. Each scene, each figure, becomes vividly alive. Elimelech isn't like my father, but at a critical moment they made similar decisions. Seeing that connection makes my experience of the biblical story richer and helps me see that moment in my father's life more complexly. I catch glimpses of connections between my mother's story and Naomi's, and somehow I come to feel more compassion for both. I came to the Book of Ruth because of Ruth, but I find, as I have always found with Greek myths (and with dreams), that I need to pay attention to the associations stirred by each part of the tale.

The biblical story is set in the long ago time before the rise of the monarchy, "in the days when the chieftains ruled," but without the focus on violence and war found in the Book of Judges. The text is traditionally ascribed to Samuel, the prophet who anointed David king, and is customarily read at Shavuot. This festival which honors the giving of the Torah is celebrated on David's birth and death day. Indeed, the Book of Ruth, which relates the courtship of David's great grandparents, can be seen as itself a midrash on the giving of Torah, a midrash that implies that *chesed,* lovingkindness, not law, is the essence of Torah.

Many scholars believe the text was written to put forward a subtle but forceful challenge to the laws promulgated by Ezra calling upon Jews to divorce their foreign wives. I've long known about the changes introduced into Israelite life after the Exile but had not known that the Book of Ruth may have been written in protest against the new emphasis on untainted genealogy. Learning this, as I returned to the text deliberately open to connections between it and personal

---

[3] M. Piercy, "The Book of Ruth and Naomi," *Mars and Her Children,* Knopf, 1992. (included in Katz and Reimer, p. 159.)

experience, gave me a new sense of the *pain* this new law must have inflicted on the husbands and wives affected by it. Among the stories my mother still tells of those first years after Hitler came to power is what it was like for her, after my father had already left for America and we were waiting to join him, to be told (by the magistrate to whom she was required to report every day) that as a good German woman she should divorce her Jewish husband, stay in Germany, and have German babies. That her father, more gently, more lovingly, was giving her the same message cannot have made it easier. (She wasn't actually *forced* to divorce him, but later on in Germany many gentiles married to Jews had to choose between divorce and the camps.)

The Book of Ruth makes its point against the exclusion of the outsider quite dramatically: it tells us that King David is descended from a Moabite. This, of course, implies that the Messiah (who is to come from the House of David) participates in the same tainted genealogy. Ruth is not just a stranger but a Moabite, from the biblical perspective the most *other* other imaginable. According to the Torah, although descendants of Esau and even Egyptians may be granted entry into the covenant, Moabites and Ammonites (because they had refused bread and water to the Hebrews during their years of wandering between Egypt and Canaan) are forever to be excluded, and Jews are explicitly forbidden to marry Moabites. A midrash, attempting to reconcile Ruth's story with this prohibition, says that perhaps the Moabite *women* were blameless. Ruth's bringing Naomi the gleanings from the barley and wheat harvests is a tacit allusion to the ancient tale; she now gives what was once withheld.

When we hear that Ruth is a Moabite we are expected to remember not only this injunction but also the story of how Lot's daughters, believing that they and their father were the only humans left alive after the destruction of Sodom, got Lot drunk and had intercourse with him in the hope of thus preserving the human race. Both daughters got pregnant; one gave birth to Ammon, the other to Moab. There are obvious parallels to Ruth's more innocent, more decorous, lying at the feet of Boaz in the hope of preserving Elimelech's family line.

The story, however, begins not with Ruth but with Elimelech, a man who had brought his family to Moab from Bethlehem (the House of Bread) at a time of famine (as Jacob's family had once gone to Egypt.) His wife Naomi followed him, as Ruth later followed Naomi. Elimelech dies; the two sons marry moabite women and then the sons die. The place of refuge becomes a place of death. Some midrashim understand these deaths as punishment for Elimelech's leaving his own people at a time of famine and allowing his sons to marry Moabite women. They view Elimelech as rich and selfish, having the means for such a journey while others don't, fearful of their need (as the Moabites long ago seem to have been fearful that the Hebrews might "lick up all that is around us, as the ox licks up the grass of the field.")

I find myself silently protesting this harsh, judgmental view, and I wonder why. Then I realize: my father left Germany, *we* left, we were able to leave; my father was warned early and heeded the warning; he had skills that made it possible for him to find a position abroad and eventually the means to enable us to join him. Others stayed, didn't leave or couldn't, were deported, incarcerated, exterminated. Some few made a very different decision from my father's. Leo Baeck, for example, had the opportunity to go to America or Palestine but refused to leave his people. But I can't blame Elimelech or my father for going. I only wish everyone might have gone.

Elimelech disappears from the story early on and Naomi appears as the central figure. Although the book bears Ruth's name and for most readersRuth is probably the most important person in the story, the story is also Naomi's–she is there from the beginning to the end–and, of course, the story looks different if we focus on her role, try to imagine her perspective, her feelings. (Mann, I know, would have narrated this brilliantly.) Nor is this way of looking at the story foreign to the biblical text. To the chorus of Bethlehem women who greet Naomi upon her return and who give Ruth's child its name as they rejoice, "A son is born to Naomi," Naomi clearly is the more important figure.

Naomi enters the tale as Elimelech's wife, but after his death he becomes just her husband. Left alone, she moves to the center, but as someone (like Demeter) defined by her losses, as someone whom God has forgotten. Her name means "pleasant," but now bitterness is her lot. Bereft of husband and sons, she cannot bear to remain in Moab. When she hears that God has remembered his people in Judah, that the famine in Bethlehem has ended, she decides to return home. When she arrives back in Bethlehem, the women of the town, barely recognizing her, ask, "Can this be Naomi?" and she tells them, "Do not call me Naomi. Call me Mara (bitter)."

Naomi seems consumed by her emptiness, her barrenness. She has lost her identity; she is no longer a mother of sons. The theme of infertility looms large in the tale and seems to be all-important to Naomi. Neither Ruth nor the other daughter-in-law, Orpah. have had children. Naomi knows she is too old to bear more sons whom they might marry in accordance with the levirate law. This law calls upon the brother of a deceased husband to marry his brother's widow so that there might be a son to carry on the dead man's lineage. (Naomi's allusion to levirate marriage prepares for the role Boaz will play later in the tale.) Because she feels she has nothing left to offer them, Naomi tries, shortly after they have all set out for Judah together, to send Ruth and Orpah back to their *mothers'* houses. This striking locution serves to underline the emphasis on female experience in this singular text. It may also connote that Naomi is sending the two young women back to their own potential motherhood, an interpretation confirmed by her going on to voice a hope that they might yet find new husbands among their own people and bear them children.

The text leaves Naomi's motivation unclear and so the commentators wonder, does Naomi ask them to go back because, as Moabites, they are part of her problem, part of what she wants to leave behind, reminders of her loss, or because of her concern for them? On the one hand, although the narrator speaks of Orpah and Ruth as Naomi's "daughters-in-law," she herself addresses them more tenderly as "daughters." On the other, she is silent after Ruth's passionate declaration that she will not let Naomi go on alone. The text says simply "and the two went on," not even that they went on "together," and Naomi utters not a word of relief or gratitude. Naomi's telling the women who come forth to welcome her to Bethlehem her that she has come home empty, completely ignoring the presence of Ruth by her side, suggests how totally caught up she is in her own suffering.

And for this suffering she blames God. She feels that though God has remembered his people, as he once remembered Sarah in her barrenness, he has forgotten her. When Naomi speaks of her abandonment by God she, poignantly and pointedly, speaks of him as El Shaddai, the god associated in Genesis with the theme of being fruitful and multiplying, the god who promised Abraham that he would be the father of a multitude. Shaddai, she tells the Bethlehemite women, has made her lot bitter, has brought her back empty, has dealt harshly with her, has brought misfortune upon her. Like Job she seems to be asking, "And why? Of what am I guilty?"

Naomi is not Demeter; her rage and grief exist on a smaller, more human scale. But her tale, too, speaks to us of particularly female experiences of loss–the loss of a husband, of children, of one's own fertility–of the vulnerability of women for whom marriage and children, have been self-defining. In some ways Naomi's story is my mother's. She, too, followed her husband to a foreign land and raised her children there. For a long while her life was full, with children and then with grandchildren, with gardening and poetry, but now she sees it as empty, barren. She hasn't literally lost her husband or children; they are still alive and very much part of her life, but she has lost the sense that this is enough, that it is meaning-giving, life-giving. She hasn't literally gone back to live in her original homeland, but when she reflects back on what life seemed to promise her when she was young in Germany, what she is aware of is loss. She, too, would say: don't call my life pleasant, call it bitter. And there is no consoling her.

For me, as for most readers, Ruth is at the center of the story, though not, I've come to see, the figure in it to whom I feel closest. Her name in Hebrew means friendship, which may help us see that this is not another story about mother-daughter (or even sister-sister) love but about friendship between women, passionate, committed friendship. I see Ruth as a fiercely auto-nomos woman (evident not only when she chooses to go on with Naomi but perhaps even earlier when she chose to marry a foreigner, Naomi's Hebrew son, Mahlon) who has chosen her own destiny. Yet I am struck that *what* she chooses is not autonomy and separation but relationship. As Naomi seems to be defined by her losses, Ruth is defined by her choice: henceforward she is the woman who came back with Naomi.

Ruth is said to *cling* to Naomi, as the Bible calls upon a wife to cling to her husband and asks Israel to cling to God. The Bible also speaks of Jonathan clinging to David, Ruth's great grandson. Jonathan's "soul was knit with the soul of David." David, grieving over Jonathan's death, sang that Jonathan's love to him had been wonderful, "passing the love of women"; the women of Bethlehem, seeing Ruth's love for Naomi, say she is better to her than seven sons. It seems relevant somehow that the Bible's most moving account of a man's love for a man should be thus associated with this tale of a woman's love for a woman. I don't mean this is a lesbian story. I don' t think it is, but it is a story about love between women, and as a lesbian it is a story that inspires me. (I am always a little amused when Ruth's pledge to Naomi is made part of a heterosexual marriage ceremony without any apparent recognition of the original context in which these words were spoken.)

No doubt our response to Ruth's declaration is inevitably colored by our own experience. I have a friend who reads Ruth's pledge to Naomi and finds herself remembering with horror what it is like to have someone cling to you, make her life dependent on yours, go where you go with no direction of her own. This is her Ruth. It is not mine. To me the love that Ruth expresses in the first words we hear her speak, as well as in her words and actions throughout the rest of the story, is brave and free and generous.

Naomi chooses to return to Bethlehem, and all the connotations of *tsuvah*, of "return" as signifying a turning back to God, are implicit in her choice. But Ruth is "returning" to a place she's never been. Her "I will go" can be seen in counterpoint to Abraham's silently obedient response to God's call to him to "Go forth." Like Abraham, Ruth is setting out on a journey to an unknown place, but Ruth is not called by anything outside her own heart, and nothing is promised her. She sets forth without family, wealth, or servants. She is choosing Naomi, Naomi's people, Naomi's god.

Many of the traditional commentators, of course, emphasize Ruth's choice of Naomi's god, the Jewish God. There are midrashim that imagine an explicit conversion (even though there was, of course, no conversion ritual in the time of the Judges.) But it seems evident to me that Ruth is not so much choosing Naomi's god as choosing Naomi and all that this choice necessarily entails if made without reservation. She embraces Naomi's god not out of love of God but out of love of Naomi. Like Marge Piercy (in the poem quoted above), I hear Ruth saying: "I will be a Jew *for you.*" I also believe it is important to note that she is choosing the very god whom Naomi names as the source of her bitterness. She seems to be saying, your god will be my god no matter what pain and sorrow that commitment may include.

This is clearly why "Ruth" has appeared to me as the name of the shadow self that would have gone with my father to Terezin and Auschwitz. That Ruth is the part of me that would have followed my people to Auschwitz–out of a kind of loyalty to, identification with, a father, a people, not out of a religious commitment to the Hebrew God.

When the two women first find themselves back in Bethlehem, Naomi seems to be still lost in her grief, paralyzed. Ruth is the one to suggest that she glean in the fields of Boaz, Elimelech's well-to-do kinsman. When Boaz learns that the unfamiliar woman in his fields is the Moabite who came back with Naomi, he addresses Ruth as "daughter" and advises her to stay with (cling to) the other women, away from the young male reapers by whom he fears she might be molested. He lets her know that he knows her story, knows she has left father and mother and the land of her birth, knows how good she has been to Naomi. We may wonder then why all the initiative is left to the women, why Boaz had not himself spontaneously offered to help the two women, and why, once the barley and wheat harvests are over, he feels no concern for their continued well-being. We may also wonder why later Naomi couldn't directly raise with him the possibility of his marrying Ruth rather than rely on her rather uncertain scheme, though the biblical text never raises any questions about Boaz's good-heartedness.

Again, I think of a connection to my family history. When my father had gone ahead to America and my mother was left behind with two young children and another on the way and no income beyond the little her parents could spare, almost none of her neighbors or my father's former colleagues seemed to wonder how she was getting by. But twice a week Werner Heisenberg's wife would appear on her bicycle, its basket filled high with eggs and butter, freshly baked bread, and vegetables from her garden.

The text leaves room for much speculation about Boaz. It tells us so very little about him; it does not say whether he was a lifelong bachelor or a recent or longtime widower, whether he'd had children, or just how old he was. The midrashim picture him as old, old enough to be Ruth's father, perhaps to highlight the parallels between the story of Ruth and Boaz and the story of Tamar and Judah. Judah was Jacob's fourth son, the inheritor of the divine blessing that through Rebecca's trickery had gone to Jacob rather than Esau. Tamar, like Ruth, was a woman who inserted herself into Hebrew history. First married to Judah's eldest son Er, she was. after Er's early death, married in accordance with the levirate law to his second son Onan, who also died young. Fearful for the life of his third son, Judah told Tamar that she must remain a widow until Shelah grew up. But Tamar was determined to be part of Jacob's family. (Mann's version of this resolute and deeply thoughtful young woman is unforgettable) and so in disguise as a harlot she inveigled the unsuspecting Judah into having intercourse with her. When Judah learned the truth, and that Tamar was carrying his child (indeed, she turned out to be carrying twins), he acknowledged them as his own. The firstborn was Perez, Boaz's great-great-great-great-grandfather.

Unlike Tamar, Ruth did not herself dream up the plan which leads her to Boaz's threshing floor. Naomi, who by this point in the story seems to have begun moving beyond her grief, suggests to Ruth a plan reminiscent of Rebecca's cunning, reminiscent also of Lot's daughters' seduction of their father and Tamar's of Judah (also a father figure.) (A contemporary feminist midrash, acknowledging the riskiness of Naomi's scheme, pictures Naomi praying to God that her plan not put Ruth into a shameful compromising situation.[4]) So, as Naomi had directed, after Boaz had laid himself down for the night by his grainpile, Ruth stealthily approached and lay down at his feet. In the middle of the night Boaz awoke, saw her, and asked "Who are you?,"as Jacob had asked of the dark stranger with whom he wrestled through the night. And like Jacob, Boaz seems to ask in fear. One wonders if he perceives his unknown nocturnal visitor as a a phantom embodiment of his own lust. The scene is discreetly reported; it is never said that the two ended up making love. Boaz spreads his robe over Ruth; she lies at his feet until dawn but leaves before anyone might see a woman pass by and recognize her. Rabbinic midrashim tend to read the Book of Ruth as though it were a love story between Boaz and Ruth and to sexualize their encounter, at the same time denying that it was *really* sexual. The rabbis praise Boaz for struggling with his own lust and prevailing; they praise Ruth for denying her own desires and choosing an older man able to provide for her and Naomi. Even Naomi (who asks Ruth, "Who are you, daughter?" in a way that implies "who are you *now*?" when she returns home in the morning) seems a little worried about what might have happened and what the consequences will be.

Of course, it all works out well. The next day the nearer kinsman of whom Boaz had told Ruth chooses not to act as a redeemer and so Boaz may. But his marriage vows are surely not couched in the language of romantic love: "I am acquiring from Naomi all that belonged to Elimelech and all that belonged to Chilion and Mahlon. I am also acquiring Ruth the Moabite, the wife of Mahlon, as my wife so. . . that the name of the deceased may not disappear from among his kinsmen."[5] Boaz was not obligated by the laws of levirate marriage to marry Ruth; his agreeing to do so was a kind of metaphorical extension of those laws, a *chesed* version of a *mitzvot*. Unlike some other contemporary readers of the story, I do not see this marriage as simply an ugly example of "the traffic in women," as just another version of the old story of a young woman giving herself to an old man for food.[6] I note that in sending Ruth to Boaz, Naomi says she is hoping to help her find a home where she may be *happy* and that Boaz seems to be marrying Ruth not out of avarice or lust but because of his respect for her loyalty to Naomi. It is as though he loves her for her love of Naomi (as Ruth loved Naomi's God out of her love for Naomi.)

The elders of the community add their blessing after Boaz has spoken, by asking God to make the woman coming into his house "like Leah and Rachel."[7] This leads me to remember that, as far as I know, the only two women, other than Naomi and Ruth, whose conversation with one another is directly presented in a biblical text are Rachel and Leah. Among the most unforgettable passages in

[4] R. H. Sohn, "Verse by Verse," in Katz and Reimer, p. 24.
[5] Ruth 4: 9-10.
[6] See for example N. Rosen, "Dialogue on Devotion," in Katz and Reimer, p. 350.
[7] Ruth 4:12.

Joseph and His Brothers are those in which Mann presents the ambivalent and always competitive love for one another between these two sisters who shared a household lifelong–and a husband. Obviously there is a barely hidden sense in which Naomi and Ruth share a husband too: when Ruth gives birth to Boaz's son, the chorus of Bethlehem women announce that a son has been born to *Naomi*!

The elders' blessing was surely consciously meant only as an expression of their hope that the marriage of Boaz and Ruth would be a fruitful one. And, indeed, Ruth gives birth to a son Obed who becomes the progenitor of the House of David, as the children of Rachel and Leah became the forefathers of the twelve tribes of Israel.

After the marriage and the conception of this child, Boaz disappears from the story. As though to highlight the notion that Boaz enters the story only so that Ruth the Moabite and Tamar might be brought into the lineage that issues in David, a midrashic tradition claims that Obed was conceived on the night of the wedding, which was also, we are told, the last night of Boaz's life.[8]

As I read the story, Ruth marries Boaz so that the two women can stay together; the marriage is pragmatic not romantic, yet based on love, the women's love for one another. When Ruth gives birth to her child she seems happy to give him to Naomi to hold, to have Naomi become his foster mother, to allow the neighbor women to give him his name. It is as though having a son was never as important to her as she knew it was to Naomi. It is almost as if, with the birth of Obed, Naomi is given a second family, as Job is in the epilogue to his story. In a sense Ruth may be serving as a surrogate mother for Naomi, as Hagar did for Sarah, as Leah's and Rachel's handmaidens did for them, but the story suggests she chooses to do so, out of love, knowing (as Naomi's women friends also knew) that the child would renew Naomi's life and sustain her old age. I imagine the relationship between Naomi and Ruth as enriched by their sharing of Ruth's child, as I know my relationship with my mother was deepened and expanded when I brought my children to her and let her care for them.

Ruth's handing her son over to Naomi is but another expression of that same *chesed* that leads her to follow Naomi to Bethlehem. I find her extraordinary. and, although my closer study of her and her story only confirms my hunch that "Ruth" is the right name for that shadow self who would have ended up in an extermination camp, I do not imagine that I– whatever life I might have led, the one I've actually led here in America, the one I might have led as a German gentile girl exposed to all the pressures of my contemporaries' surrounding enthusiasm for Hitler, or the one I might have led in Hitler's camps–would ever have been so extraordinary, so bravely risk-taking, so loyal, so determined.

And so I have come to recognize that the figure in the tale with whom I actually most identify is Orpah, the other Moabite daughter-in-law. Initially Orpah too protests that she will return with Naomi, but as Naomi again asks the two

---

[8] Midrash Rabba, as cited by S. R. Torn, "Ruth Reconsidered," in Katz and Reimer, p. 339f.

young women to turn back and return to their mothers' houses, Orpah weeps and kisses Naomi good-bye. I agree with Cynthia Ozick that Orpah is never, never to be blamed for staying home, for making the more conventional, the ordinary choice.[9] She belongs to the story as much as Ruth, as Ruth's necessary foil, as Ismene (whom George Steiner called "the most beauteous measure of the ordinary"[10]) belongs in the story of Antigone. I have come to honor these women who choose the ordinary rather than the extraordinary, who choose survival. The life I've actually lived is more Orpah's than Ruth's, a safe and in many ways conventional life. I am aware of having consciously chosen such a life. I can even remember the moment of choosing. Shortly after the end of the Second World War when I had just graduated from college and was pregnant with my first child, I went back to Germany for the first time since I'd left when I was four. There I met a young German man, just a few years older than I, who had survived the camps. I remember asking him what. in the light of all that had happened, I should do with my life. "Live in a way that shows it is still possible to live an ordinary human life," he told me. And so I have tried to do.

What Orpah loses is the three thousand years of being part of the Jewish story, which is what I, in the life I've actually lived, have also lost. And yet in a sense both of us *are* part of the story.

---

[9]C. Ozick, "Ruth," *Metaphors and Memory,* Knopf, 1989 (incl. in Katz and Reimer, p. 224.)
[10]G. Steiner, *Antigones,* Oxford University Press, 1984, p. 121

Uniqueness and Universality in the Holocaust: Some Ethical Reflections

John T. Pawlikowski
Catholic Theological Union

My basic introduction to the complexities of the uniqueness/universality problematic relative to the Holocaust has come not merely through the reading of books. In large measure it has been fashioned by the discussions surrounding the development of the U.S. Holocaust Memorial Museum in Washington. Having been involved with committees mandated to determine the content of the Museum from the very inception of its planning. I know from personal experience how difficult and contentious the issues can become.

After some struggle the decision was made to include brief displays on the non-Jewish victims of the Nazis within the central thematic exhibit of the Museum. In the end the entire Council membership supported such inclusion, though this point of consensus was not achieved easily. Polish and Roma (Gypsy) victims are accorded the most space, but some mention is also made of the disabled, Russian prisoners of war, and homosexuals.

While many organizations dedicated to preserving the memory of non-Jewish victims consider their present depiction in the U.S. Holocaust Museum as inadequate, the very fact that they have been included as an integral part of the central Holocaust narrative represents a considerable advance in Holocaust interpretation. Only rarely do displays or publications on the Holocaust include material on their victimization. In part, this is due to the minimal number of documents, reliable secondary materials, and artifacts available to the research scholar and museum curator. This reality has certainly impeded more extensive presentation of non-Jewish victims in the Washington Museum. The situation is a bit better with respect to Poles, but generally speaking the state of research on non-Jewish victims is still in its early stages. This was clearly demonstrated in many of the presentations at the groundbreaking 1987 State Department Conference on non-Jewish victims co-sponsored by the U.S. Holocaust Memorial Council.[1] While the situation has improved somewhat since that time, the overall picture has not changed in any substantial way. And a further complication arises from the fact that some of the existing analysis is intermixed with polemical or political claims to the point where the research itself becomes compromised.

While the effort of the national Holocaust Museum to include the non-Jewish victims in its main narrative presentation is commendable, many basic issues remain unresolved. Fundamentally the Museum, while accurately portraying in brief fashion the scope of the Nazi attack on the various non-Jewish groups, leaves unanswered the root question of how their victimization relates to that of the Jews. Was the Holocaust primarily the result of classical antisemitism in modern guise or was it essentially the result of new realities made possible by advances in technology, science, and bureaucratic development with traditional antisemitism serving to generate popular support in the case of the Jewish victims? If the latter, then were the non-Jewish victims adjuncts to the annihilation of the Jews? Or is their victimization to be understood as intimately related to the basic processes that unleashed the Holocaust?

My principal argument in the following pages will be to show that there is a need for a basic paradigm shift in Holocaust interpretation, which moves our understanding of the event from a mere repetition of classical antisemitism to a distinctly modern phenomenon whose central intent went beyond making Europe (or even the world) *Judenrein*. In that context, while the annihilation of the Jews became all-consuming as an initial Nazi goal (and classical antisemitism undoubtedly influenced the designation of the Jews as the primary victims), there is now sufficient evidence to suggest that the Nazis intended to do much more.

The first victims chronologically were in fact the physically and mentally disabled. While the attack on the was suspended as a result of considerable public outcry, including protests from religious leaders, it is probable the Nazis would have tried to complete the elimination of all disabled once they had eliminated the Jews. And more and more evidence is emerging from both Jewish and non-Jewish scholars to suggest that the annihilation of the European Gypsy community was taking place simultaneously with that of the Jews even though it received far less publicity.

The Nazi attack on the Polish nation, which included an effort to wipe out all vestiges of Polish culture, was evidently much more than a mere effort to

---

[1]See M. Berenbaum (ed.), *A Mosaic of Victims: Non-Jews Persecuted and Murdered by the Nazis* (New York and London: New York University Press, 1990).

subdue militarily a neighboring state. Even when the Nazis had accomplished that task in a relatively short time despite determined Polish resistance, they committed military power and human resources to the Polish to subhuman status. Evidence has now surfaced in the form of remarks of Himmler and Hitler, to be cited subsequently, that gives credence to the view that the Nazis might well have attempted the total annihilation of the Poles (and perhaps other Slavic peoples) if they had been allowed to pursue their plans.

Clearly the Nazis regarded these attacks on the disabled, the Gypsies, gays and Poles as crucial to their overall plan for the emergence of a new humanity. And obviously these attacks were not motivated by antisemitism. This emerging evidence relative to non-Jewish victims reveals the need for new language to describe the relationship between Jewish and non-Jewish victims of the Nazis. Some of the more popular formulations such as "Jews were killed for who they were; others were killed for what they did" simply no longer meet the test of available data.

A word of dedication and appreciation is certainly due at this point to Professor John Priest whom this volume honors. As Executive Director of the American Academy of Religion Dr. Priest has made a place over the years for sessions dealing with the Holocaust, thereby helping to move Holocaust scholarship towards mainstream religious thought. He has always encouraged the challenging of established viewpoints. This article represents one such challenge which I and some other colleagues are beginning to raise. No better tribute could be offered to Professor Priest for his years of genuine leadership in religious studies than by dedicating one such critical inquiry to his name.

Victimization During the Holocaust

Since the development of scholarship on the Holocaust in the 1970s an intense discussion has ensued regarding its uniqueness. This debate has focused to some extent on the relationship between Jews and other Nazi victims, but even more on the comparability of the Holocaust to other examples of mass death and genocide, such as the slaughter of the Armenians in the early years of this century, the mass exterminations that took place in Cambodia under the Khmer Rouge, and the elimination of indigenous peoples and their cultural traditions in the Americas. Jewish scholars and activists in the main have argued for some measure of uniqueness for the Jewish experience. Some would maintain that any comparisons between the fate of the Jews under the Nazis and other instances of massive human brutality distort the magnitude of the crime against the Jews. Others, while recognizing the special character of the Nazi attack on the Jewish people, have searched for an authentic way to include the other Nazi victims within the general umbrella of human suffering during the period and have acknowledged the need for carefully-stated comparisons between the Jewish experience, and other genocides, if humankind is to retain an interest in studying the Holocaust.

Each of the scholars addressing the issue of universality have tended to give it his or her own particular interpretation. Michael Berenbaum, Director of the U.S. Holocaust Memorial Museum's Research Institute, has attempted to group the differing perspectives within two broad categories. The first of these he terms uniqueness by reason of *intention*. The second he calls uniqueness by reason of *results*.[2]

Those scholars locating the uniqueness of the Holocaust primarily in the intentionality of the perpetrators emphasize the central role of ideology and directed decision-making in the carrying out of the Nazi plan. On the other hand, those who favor the "results" perspective concentrate far more on the processes of human destruction designed by Hitler and his collaborators. For these scholars, how the annihilation took place assumes far greater importance than its philosophical or theological roots, which may always remain somewhat ambiguous.

One of the principal proponents of the *intentionality* view-point is Yehuda Bauer. In several of his published works Bauer situates the uniqueness in the deliberate and conscious decision by the Nazi leadership to move towards the total extermination of the Jewish people.[3] No calculated plan of that kind had ever been put forward, with respect to Jews or any other people. The Nazi ideologues had become convinced that it was impossible for humankind to advance to a "higher" human plateau without the complete disappearance of Jews from the face of the earth. They were "vermin" whose continued presence within the human family threatened its biological stagnation if not actual retardation. The Jews were regarded as the central barrier to the Aryanization of Europe, which would in turn bestow upon the Nazis absolute control over the world.

Bauer also adds a religious component to his understanding of the Holocaust's uniqueness. While this "sacral" element has definite ties to the long history of Christian antisemitism it takes on for the Nazis a "demonic" quality that gives the antisemitic tradition new force. As Bauer sees it, there existed a "quasi-apocalyptic" dimension to the Nazi embrace of the classical antisemitic legacy found in the Christian tradition.[4] This had never occurred prior to the emergence of the Nazis, nor has it happened since.

Bauer has also engaged in public discussions regarding the relationships between Jews and other Nazi victims, especially the Gypsies. During the International Scholars Conference in Oxford in July 1988 Bauer appeared to concede, in a session on Holocaust and genocide, that there was growing documentary evidence that the Nazis aimed to exterminate all the Gypsies. He

---

[2]Berenbaum, "The Uniqueness", 26.

[3]See Y. Bauer, "Whose Holocaust?." *Midstream* XXVI:9 (1980) 34-43; *A History of the Holocaust* (New York/London/Toronto/Sydney: F. Watts, 1982); and "Is the Holocaust Explicable? in *Remembering for the Future: The Impact of the Holocaust on the Contemporary World* (Papers from the International Scholars' Conference, 10-13 July, 1988, Theme II, 1967-1975).

[4]Berenbaum, "The Uniqueness" 88.

argued that they were in fact well on the way to realizing their goal by the end of the war. Several days later, in a more public session in London, Bauer seemed to return to his earlier view that the Holocaust's uniqueness results from the totally special character of the attack on the Jewish people.

Bauer's stress on *intentionality* as the root of the Holocaust's uniqueness is shared in some measure by several other scholars, including Uriel Tal, Steven Katz, George Mosse, and Lucy Dawidowicz. Tal, for example, whose views we shall examine in greater detail shortly, argued for an understanding of the Holocaust as the end result of distinctly modern philosophical and scientific theories emerging in Western Europe throughout the century or so preceding the emergence of the Nazi movement. Central to this modern consciousness was a strong belief in the possibility of genuine human progress and in the importance of biological "cleansing' in promoting such progress.

The most thorough articulation of the *intentionality* perspective to appear of late is the first of a projected three-volume work by Steven Katz.[5] As Katz interprets the Nazi phenomenon, Hitler suffered from an obsession with racial views that pitted the Aryan race against Jews, whom he regarded as a parasitic people that fed on the lifeblood of Germany. Katz clearly differentiates Hitler's belief in the Aryan myth and the struggle for world domination between Aryans and Jews from the classical Christian myth that portrayed the Jews among the minions of the devils and the Antichrist. For Katz Nazi racial ideology represented a step beyond the traditional Christian approach to the Jewish people. The Church, he argues, was content to persecute and proselytize. It left Jews the option of conversion. The Nazis eliminated any and all options for Jews to survive. That was the fundamental difference. Katz defines the Holocaust as "phenomenologically unique by virtue of the fact that never before has a state set out, as a matter of intentional principle and actualized policy, to annihilate physically every man, women, and child belonging to a specific people."[6]

In discussing the uniqueness of the Holocaust, Katz deliberately refrains from any theological conclusions. In his judgement both the theological "radicals" (e.g. Rubenstein, Cohen, Fackenheim, Greenberg, the Eckardtsm, and to a degree Moltmann, Littell, Sherman, van Buren, Cargas, Tracy, Thoma and Pawlikowski) and the theological "conservatives" (e.g. Berkovits, Neusner, Barth, Schneerson, and Journet) have all exceeded the available evidence in arriving at their conclusions.[7] In his view they are extrinsic to the experience of the death camps

---

[5]S.T. Katz, *The Holocaust in Historical Content*, Vol. 1. The Holocaust and Mass Death before the Modern Age (New York/Oxford: Oxford University Press, 1994).

[6]Katz, *The Holocaust*, 28.

[7]I do not agree with Katz's assessment in this regard. It is somewhat difficult to argue the issue with him, however, since he has failed to offer any of his criteria for "authentic" theologizing. The Eckhardts have written a strong response ("Steven T. Katz and the Eckhardts: Response to a Misrepresentation"), originally presented to the Christian Study Group of Scholars, which will appear in a forthcoming issue of *Shofar*.

and depend largely on prior theological positions. It is interesting in this context that he ignores the writings of Elie Wiesel, who, while not a theologian in a formal sense, has deeply influenced the formulation of both Jewish and Christian post-Holocaust theologies. Katz concludes with the following observation.

> Any theological position, at present, is compatible with the singularity of the Sho'ah. Religious conservatives who intuitively reject the uniqueness of the Holocaust on the usually implicit grounds that such an unequivocal conclusion would *necessarily* entail ominous alterations in the inherited normative *Weltanschauung* are simply mistaken....Conversely, the theological radicals who hold that the singularity of the Sho'ah necessarily entails religious transformations, and within Jewish parameters halakhic changes, have not shown that to the case. They have merely assumed it to be so, positing the "required changes" they take to be obligatory without providing either halakhic or philosophical justification for such innovations. It may be that one of these alternative positions is true, but so far neither has made a convincing case for itself. Therefore, I avoid all theologizing in this study.[8]

On the question of the non-Jewish victims of the Nazis and the implications of their deaths for Katz's theory of the Holocaust's uniqueness, he offers only a skeletal outline in volume one. The issue, he says, will be discussed at length in the final volume of his projected trilogy. Katz concedes that the slaughter of the Nazis' non-Jewish victims was "abhorrent," and formed an integral part of the overall plan of Nazism. It was a distinctive part of that plan, however, which in the final analysis differed from the plan directed against the Jews, who alone were singled out for total extermination.

Though Katz displays considerable familiarity in his bibliographic citations with the growing body of literature on the non-Jewish victims, his overall provisional conclusions do not quite measure up in my judgement. I have questions with respect to his conclusions regarding the treatment of the Roma, the disabled, and the Poles. Some distinction still needs to be drawn among the victim groups because the Nazis drew them. Growing evidence, however, suggests that the plan of total extermination, in principle, might well have included several of the other groups at some future date. In fact, in the case of the Gypsies and the disabled, it may have already begun.

The *results* perspective on the Holocaust's uniqueness is advanced by several important scholars. Raul Hilberg, whose work *The Destruction of the European Jews* still remains the most comprehensive study on the Nazis' systematic extermination of European Jewry certainly stands out in this group. In a special way Hilberg has highlighted the central importance of the German railroad system that transported Jews to the death camps on a daily basis in a highly efficient manner. Other prominent names associated with this viewpoint are Lawrence Langer, Hannah Arendt, Joseph Borkin and Emil Fackenheim.

---

[8]Katz, *The Holocaust*, 30-31.

For Fackenheim, who in some ways could also be included with the *intentionality* advocates, the uniqueness of the Holocaust is multi-faceted. Its scope was unprecedented when compared to other instances of the mass slaughter of human beings. The Nazis aimed at eliminating every Jew alive on the basis of their Jewish parentage. Faith and ideology played no role in determining the fate of a Jewish person. Ultraorthodox Jews died alongside atheistic Jews and Jews who had converted to Christianity. Liberal and Socialist Jews were killed together with socially conservative Jews. For the Nazis, says Fackenheim, the destruction of the Jews was an end in itself. The death camps were not accidental by-products of the Nazi plan but part of its very essence.

Joseph Borkin and Lawrence Langer are both struck by the way in which the Holocaust totally deprived its victims of any meaningful choices. Langer describes the world of the death camps as a universe of "choiceless choices." It is nearly impossible for us to imagine how this world was experienced in terms of inner consciousness by those who found themselves confined within its perimeters. Borkin, focusing much more on the objective level, sees the death camps as the perverse perfection of slavery where the human being was reduced to raw material. The only value attached to the camp inmates by the Nazis related to their hair, gold teeth, ashes, etc., which could be converted into profit.

Michael Berenbaum and Richard Rubenstein, in different ways, each advocate a position that affirms the uniqueness of the Jewish experience under the Nazis but insists on relating that experience to a larger context. For Berenbaum that context is primarily the victimization of the Poles, the Gypsies, the disabled and the other victim groups. For him Jewish uniqueness relative to the Holocaust consisted in the Nazi view of Jews as not merely symbols of evil but as its actual embodiment, coupled with the universal death sentence pronounced upon them as a consequence of this perspective. Berenbaum is convinced that this Jewish uniqueness can be preserved while fully acknowledging the victimization of the other groups under the Nazis. The imagery Berenbaum finds most appropriate (drawn from Dante's *Inferno*) has been suggested by philosopher Bohdan Wytwycky. It depicts the Nazi victims in terms of concentric rings extending out from the center of hell, which is occupied by the Jews.[9]

Rubenstein shares Berenbaum's conviction that the Holocaust is a distinctly modern phenomenon that cannot be seen as merely the continuation of historic anti-Judaism/antisemitism. He too is unwavering in seeing the Jewish situation under the Nazis as unique because of the Jews' status as permanent Nazi targets who lacked any options whatsoever for ameliorating their situation and whom the Nazis envisioned as "disgusting parasitic vermin and at the same time the embodiment of absolute evil that must be eliminated to complete the Nazi drama

---

[9]Berenbaum, "The Uniqueness," 95-96. Also see B. Wytycky, *The Other Holocaust: Many Circles of Hell* (Washington: The Novak Report on the New Ethnicity, 1980).

of salvation."[10] But he joins Berenbaum in stressing the broader implications of the Holocaust and points to the insights it can provide into modern socio-political life. He focuses on ways in which those who control the use of violence in a given society can go quite far in acting with impunity against others under their control. The Holocaust enables us to understand better the world in which we live as a "world more complex, more obsessed with power, more difficult to humanize than one might have guessed before."[11]

The forces that combined to make the Holocaust such a devastating reality remain at large in contemporary society. Some have acquired even greater strength in our day. The real challenge is whether there are countervailing powers with sufficient force and authority to prevent the Holocaust from being not merely the "Final Solution," but in fact the prelude to something considerably worse. Unlike Berenbaum, Rubenstein does not address the issue of the other Nazi victims in any depth, though he does acknowledge their presence at certain points of his analysis.

The "Other" Victims

Writers on the Holocaust who have addressed the specific situations of the non-Jewish victims, such as Richard Lukas for the Poles and Ian Hancock for the Roma, have tended to underline the links between Jewish victimhood and the Nazi attack against other "social undesirables." In general, while these writers make some extremely telling points about the situation of their respective victim groups during the Holocaust, they tend to suffer from a lack of proper nuancing in important areas.

There also exists a significant group of Jewish authors who downplay the significance of the Holocaust, whether for contemporary Judaism or for society as a whole. Most of them (e.g. Ismar Schorsch or David Hartman) have their roots in more conservative sectors of the Jewish community. They fear that an overfocus on the Holocaust may take contemporary Jewry away from the covenantal emphasis, which they deem vital for its continued survival.

I cannot in this brief essay detail my argument for a close affinity at least in principle between the Nazi attack on the Jews and at least some of the other victim groups, particularly the Poles, the Gypsies, the disabled, and to some extent the homosexuals. What I will do is present a short synopsis of the attack on the Poles together with a few highlights of the victimization of the other groups in order to make clear the basic thrust of my argumentation.

---

[10]R.L. Rubenstein and J.K. Roth, *Approaches to Auschwitz: The Holocaust and Its Legacy* (Atlanta: John Knox Press, 1987) 17.

[11]Rubenstein and Roth, *Approaches to Auschwitz*, 20.

The Attack on the Polish Nation

On September 1, 1939, Poland was invaded by one of the world's strongest and most modern armies. Over 1,800,000 soldiers, representing the elite of the German army, took part in the campaign against it. The German army was vastly superior to any counterforce Poland could mount in its defense because of its tremendous fire-power and mobility enhanced by its motorization. On September 3, 1939, in fulfillment of their treaty obligations to Poland, Great Britain and France declared war on Nazi Germany.

From the very outset of the German invasion of Poland, it was apparent that the Nazis were not engaged in a conventional war to defeat the Polish military nor even to subdue the state politically. Instead, as the contemporary Polish-American historian Richard Lukas puts it, "the Germans waged war against the Polish people, intent on destroying the Polish nation."[12]

This is a very crucial point, one that is often overlooked in writings on Polish victimization under the Nazis. Poles were not killed first and foremost as individual dissenters, whether religious or political. Nor did the Nazi leadership wish only to conquer Poland in a military or political sense. Rather, the Polish nation as nation fell victim to the same basic ideology that eventually turned its attention with even greater fury to the annihilation of the entire Jewish population of Europe.

The Nazi theory of racial superiority totally dehumanized the Polish people. In the Nazi perspective, Poles were considered *un-termenschen* (subhumans) who lived on land coveted by the superior German race. Poland was not simply to be defeated and occupied, the primary goal of the subsequent Nazi invasions of other Western European countries. "The aim is not the arrival at a certain line," declared Hitler, "but the annihilation of living forces."[13]

Even prior to the actual invasion of Poland, Hitler had authorized on August 22, 1939, killing "without pity or mercy all men, women, and children of Polish descent or language. Only in this way," he insisted, "can we obtain the living space we need"[14] And the person placed in charge of implementing Hitler's Polish "plan," Heinrich Himmler, said outright that "all poles will disappear from the world. It is essential that the great German people should consider it as its major task to destroy all Poles."[15]

---

[12]R.C. Lukas, *Forgotten Holocaust: The Poles Under German Occupation 1939-1944* (Lexington, KY: The University Press of Kentucky, 1986) 1.

[13]See E. Duraczynski, *Wojna i Okupacja: Wrzesian 1939-Kwiecien 1943* (Warsaw: Wiedza Powszechna, 1974) 17. Also See N. Levin, *The Holocaust: The Destruction of European Jewry 1933-1945* (New York: Schocken, 1973) 163; 193; and L. Poliakov, *Harvest of Hate: The Nazi Program for the Destruction of the Jews of Europe* (New York: Holocaust Library, 1979) 263.

[14]J. Gumkowski and K. Leszczynski, *Poland Under Nazi Occupation* (Warsaw: Polonia Publishing House, 1961) 59.

[15]See K. Popieszalski, *Polsaka pod Niemieckim Prawem* (Posnan: Wydawnictwo Instytutu Zachodniego, 1946) 189.

From the above quotations it becomes amply evident that key Nazi operatives, including Hitler himself, seriously contemplated the total extermination of the Polish population in due time. Whether they would have carried out this plan fully if they had been given the opportunity is a matter of conjecture at best. The annihilation of Jews is a fact, not merely a possibility. But on the level of theory, in trying to understand where Poles fit into the Nazi victimization scheme, no other conclusion can be drawn except that they belonged with the Jews, Gypsies, the disabled, and, to a degree, the homosexuals in the category of candidates for eventual total extinction in the gradual emergence of the new Aryan humanity.

The Nazi policy of imposed "Germanization" in the annexed territories relied upon four strategies: a campaign of widespread and unmitigated terror; expropriation of land and possessions; deportations; and enslavement. The terror, designed to be harsh enough to mute all possible resistance, began immediately after the invasion in 1939. Virtually every city, town, and village in western Poland witnessed wholesale massacres and executions of the leading citizenry. In the city of Bygoszcz, for example, some 10,000 people perished, out of a population of 140,000 during the first four month of occupation. But even the regions designated as falling under the "General Government" were subjected to much the same treatment.

The terror employed by the Nazis to pacify the Polish population included an extensive use of torture. One of the most notorious sites was the training school for the Gestapo at Fort VII in Poznan. Famous as an institute of sadism, Fort VII drew its victims from the ranks of clergy, university professors, and politicians. It experimented with every conceivable form of torture, from massive beatings to the inflation of prisoners' intestines to the point of bursting.

The Nazi policy of destroying the Polish nation focused (though not exclusively) upon eliminating anyone with even the least political and cultural prominence. But the Nazis has a wide definition of those falling under the rubric of "elite." The category included teachers, physicians, priests, officers, people in business, landowners, writers, and extended even to anyone who had completed secondary school. As a result, millions of Poles qualified for liquidation in the Nazi effort to reduce Poland to a nation of indentured servants in the first instance and, perhaps in due time, to wipe it off the map completely.

There are some other ways in which the experience of Poles approximated that of the Jews during the Holocaust. Lukas points, for example, to the fact that Poles had one of the lowest food rations in Nazi-occupied territories next to the Jews.[16] Polish children, though in far lower numbers (along with those from the Gypsy community), were subjected to the horrid medical experiments and immediate death inflicted upon Jewish children. Polish clergy and nuns were also singled out for incarceration and execution.

---

[16]Lukas, *Forgotten Holocaust*, 30.

The Nazis realized they would have to break the back of the Catholic church in Poland if their plan of national annihilation was to succeed. When the Nazis partitioned Poland after the invasion, they seriously undercut the church's own territorial structures by dividing up historic dioceses. Thus weakened, Polish Catholicism, especially in the annexed areas, lost most of its hierarchy and clergy. Only in Poland did the Nazis systematically arrest and imprison bishops. By the end of the war many cities had suffered major losses in the ranks of the clergy: Wroclaw, 49.2 percent; Chelmo, 47.8 percent; Lodz, 36.8 percent; and in Poznan, 31.1 percent. Overall 1,811 Polish diocesan priests perished under the Nazis out of the total of 10,017 in 1939. Many church buildings were also destroyed. In Posnan, for example, only two out of the pre-war thirty churches remained at the end of the war.[17]

The Roma, the Disabled, and the Homosexual Victims

In recent years a number of important scholars such as Sybil Milton, Henry Friedlander, Gabrielle Tyrnauer and Ian Hancock have begun to challenge the prevailing view set by pioneering Holocaust scholars such as Yehuda Bauer and Raul Hilberg that the victimization of the Jews and the Roma is to be substantially differentiated. These scholars insist that there exists a close affinity between the Nazi treatment of the Roma and the parallel effort to "purify" German society of Jewish blood and influence. The attack on both Jews and Gypsies was rooted in biological interpretation.

Upwards of 250,000 Gypsies died in the process, including half of the community in Eastern Europe. The Nazis regarded the Gypsies as *artfremd* ("alien" by blood to the German species), a term also applied to the Jews. Additionally, the Roma were termed "parasites," "congenital criminals," and "asocial." Beginning in 1933 they were increasingly subjected to harassment, arrest, and involuntary sterilization based on the miscegenation clauses of the Nuremberg laws and other legislation. By 1936 local and national laws for "eliminating the gypsy plague" became commonplace. In concentration camps neither Gypsies nor Jews had any legal rights. They could be killed at will. I believe scholars such as Milton and Friedlander are on the right track in positing the eugenic factor, rather that antisemitism, as the core of Nazi ideology.[18]

The Nazi attack on the disabled began slowly in 1939 with the killing of a few individuals. Hitler issued an order, which he dated September 1, 1939 (the day

---

[17]Lukas, *Forgotten Holocaust*, 13-14.

[18]S. Milton, "The Context of the Holocaust," *German Studies Review* 13 (May 1990) 270-271. Also see G. Tyrnauer, "Holocaust History and the Gypsies," *The Ecumenist* 12 (September-October, 1988) 90-94. I. Hancock, "Uniqueness, Gypsies and Jews," *Remembering for the Future* Vol. 2 (ed. Y. Bauer et al.; Oxford: Pergamon Press, 1988) 2017-2025 and H. Friedlander, *The Origins of Nazi Genocide: From Euthanasia to the Final Solution* (Chapel Hill: University of North Carolina Press, 1995).

286 Biblical and Humane

World War II commenced), that authorized the process of executing anyone deemed unfit to live by reason of physical or mental condition. The effort escalated rather rapidly into a fullscale euthanasia program directed against those defined as unfit to live by psychiatrists or physicians. Gas chambers first appeared in the process of exterminating the disabled. So too the use of burning to dispose of bodies. During the thirties a series of laws were enacted against the disabled, which Sybil Milton again maintains closely resemble the anti-Jewish legislation.[19] I sense a growing view among Holocaust scholars that at least for the Gypsies and the disabled we have no choice but to speak of their planned extermination *in toto* by the Nazis.

Finally, when we come to the homosexual victims, we are on much more uncertain ground. This is especially the case for the lesbian community, though some new research is beginning to develop. No much solid inquiry has been done on homosexuals until fairly recently, in part because survivors from the gay community were extremely hesitant to identify themselves publicly. There is also some initial evidence that he Nazis generally confined their attack to German homosexuals (although the U.S. Holocaust Memorial Museum now has testimony from at least one Polish gay victim)) and that they believed that at least in some cases "rehabilitation" might be a possibility. The question, let me emphasize, is not whether gay people suffered brutal treatment under the Nazis inside and outside the concentration camps. A play such as *Bent* has captured well the depth of their pain. The principal issue here is whether they were intentionally included in the Nazi plan for human purification. It is hard to say with certainty at this point whether the attack on the gay community was seen primarily as one effort to rid German society of the liberal culture associated with the Weimar Republic and to overcome the lack of "manliness" that led to the devastating German surrender at Versailles or whether the Nazis regarded it as integral to the plan for biological cleansing. In my judgement this remains an open question at the moment, though the *existing* evidence would seem to push us towards a "social parasite" interpretation of the Nazi attack on gay people rather than an "eugenic" interpretation.[20]

In addition to the required data regarding homosexuals, we must stand ready to adjust our perspectives on all groups involved because of the massive amounts of archival materials recently made available from central and eastern Europe. We have discovered a text, for example, that seems to indicate that at least one

---

[19]Milton, "The Context of the Holocaust," 270-271. Also see R. Proctor, *Racial Hygiene: Medicine Under the Nazis* (Cambridge: Harvard University Press, 1988), R.J. Lifton, *The Nazi Doctors: Medical Killing and the Psychology of Genocide* (New York: Basic Books, 1986), Friendlander, *The Origins of Nazi Genocide*, and *Medicine, Ethics and the Third Reich* (ed. J.J. Michalczyk; Kansas City, MO: Sheed and Ward, 1994).

[20]See R. Plant, *The Pink Triangle* (New York: Holt, 1986), R. Lautmann, "The Pink Triangle: The Homosexual Male in Concentration Camps," *The Journal of Homosexuality* 6 (1981) 35-51, and *Hidden Holocaust? Gay and Lesbian Persecution in Germany, 1933-45* (ed. Gunter Grau; London & New York: Cassell, 1995).

(unidentified) Nazi leader explicitly rejected the idea of the eventual total extermination of the Polish people. And there is need to pursue the question of the Nazi attitude and policy towards Black people, who may have to be added to the list of "biological" victims despite their small numbers.

The Uniqueness of Jewish Victimization

My basic assertion that the Jewish victims can no longer be regarded as totally unique in their victimization does not mean I eschew all important differences between them and the other victims discussed in this study. There are indeed differences, and these should not be lost in the process of reworking our more fundamental descriptive categories. First of all, to repeat what has been emphasized earlier, European Jewry nearly disappeared as a result of the Nazi attack. While this may have been the ultimate goal of the Nazis for some or even all of the other groups we have considered, it was never realized to the same degree. This is a difference we can never forget.

Secondly, there was both a "sacral" and a historical dimension to the Nazi hatred of Jews. Antisemitism had not only been around for centuries, it had become an integral part of religious tradition. This clearly added a distinctive dimension to the victimization of the Jews, as richard Rubenstein has emphasized of late. Ian Hancock and others have shown the existence of a continuing pattern of discrimination against Gypsies for most of the second millennium of European society. While this discriminatory pattern somewhat parallels that developed in relation to the Jews, it lacks any corresponding "sacral" dimension. This "sacral" dimension clearly rendered Jewish victimization distinctive. It accounts for the selection of the Jews as the primary victims who always received the harshest treatment in the camps. It likewise accounts for the considerable popular support, or at least indifference, that the Nazi attack on the Jews generated among the masses, even among other victim groups. This religious antisemitism combined with political nationalism during the period between the two world wars to produce an intense religio-political nationalism that came to regard Jews as the pre-eminent "outsiders," who constituted a grave threat to authentic political and cultural sovereignty. Some feelings along these lines were sometimes manifested against Gypsies, but without quite the same intensity because the religious compulsion was missing.

In short, then, the need obviously remains to maintain a clear measure of distinctiveness relative to the attack on the Jewish people. But no longer can we regard Jewish victimization as without parallel. We must begin to acknowledge, far more than we have thus far, that the Jews, Gypsies, Poles, and the disabled (and perhaps homosexuals) fell under the same umbrella, namely, the Nazi desire to purify humanity and raise human consciousness to a new, supposedly higher level of maturity. The best paradigm for doing this in my judgement remains the proposal of Berenbaum and Wytycky referred to earlier, which is highly dependent on theological understandings (contrary to Katz). In a word, the non-Jewish victims must now be seen as integral, not peripheral, to our basic understanding of the Holocaust.

Understanding the Holocaust's Ethical Significance

In light of the above analysis we can certainly continue to assert that the Holocaust was indeed a "war against the Jews" so long as we acknowledge that it was something more as well. The ethical significance of the Holocaust emerges from understanding the full dimensions of the Holocaust, not the Jewish experience alone, as critical as that is. While antisemitism had a direct impact on the moral response to the Holocaust within the Christian churches, and while it continues to be a pre-eminent moral challenge that demands a bold response, our understanding of the ultimate ethical significance of the Holocaust will remain truncated if we confine ourselves to its antisemitic dimensions.

Recognition of the integral links among those victims who in one way or another qualified in Nazi thinking as "biological parasites" enables us to appreciate better the basic correctness of those scholarly viewpoints that posit the Holocaust as a distinctly modern phenomenon. In these perspectives the fundamental moral challenge of the Holocaust lies in the Nazi effort to create the "superperson," to develop a truly liberated humanity, in which only a select few (i.e., the Aryan race) could participate. This new humanity would be released from the moral restraints previously imposed by religious beliefs and would be capable of exerting virtually unlimited power in the shaping of the world and its inhabitants. In a somewhat indirect, though still powerful, way the Nazis had proclaimed the death of God as a guiding force in the governance of the universe.

Uriel Tal captured well the basic theological challenge pre-sented by the Holocaust. In his understanding, the so-called "Final Solution" had as its ultimate objective the total transformation of human values. Its stated intent was liberating humanity from all previous moral ideals and codes. When this process had reached completion, the human community would be "freed" once and for all from the imprisonment of a God-concept and its related notions of moral responsibility, redemption, sin, and revelation.[21]

Michael Ryan has also underlined this direction of Nazism in his analysis of Hitler's *Mein Kampf.* For Ryan, the most striking aspect of this work is Hitler's willingness to confine humanity in an absolute way to the conditions of finitude. But this resignation is accompanied by the assertion of all-pervasive power within those conditions. In the final analysis, says, Ryan, Hitler's worldview "amounted to the deliberate decision on the part of mass man to live within the limits of

---

[21]U. Tal, "Forms of Pseudo-Religion in the German *Kulturebereich* Prior to the Holocaust," *Immanuel* 3 (1973-197) 69.

finitude without either the moral restraints or the hopes of traditional religion–in this case, Christianity."[22]

The Holocaust thus can be said to have unleashed a totally new era in which the growing capacity to use power brought on by technology and bureaucratic efficiency was directed towards the transformation of humanity itself. As Robert Jay Lifton has put it, this was the first time that mass killing was undertaken in the name of "healing" the human community. Eugenics had become a new form of "baptism."

Understanding the Nazi attack on thee non-Jewish victims helps us to appreciate more deeply this goal as the ultimate thrust and threat of Nazism. Antisemitism certainly remains a persistent moral challenge facing the Christian West in particular. It is something we need to confront continually through acts of repentance and educational programs. But, in the end, we will fail to understand the full moral impact of the Holocaust if we do not deal directly with the challenge of the enhanced realities of human power and its growing potential for destructiveness revealed by the Holocaust through the Nazi attack on the Jews first and foremost, but also through the attack on the other victim groups we have examined in this study. Pastor Martin Niemoller was right in the end, the Holocaust ties the survival of all, Jews and non-Jews, inextricably together.

[22]M. Ryan, "Hitler's Challenge to the Churches: A Theological-Political Analysis of *Mein Kampf*," *The German Church Struggle and the Holocaust* (eds., F.H. Littell and H.G. Locke; Detroit: Wayne State University Press, 1974) 160-161.

Genocide in Rwanda

Michael Berenbaum
United States Holocaust Research Institute

It is a privilege to write this essay in honor of Professor John Priest, who was my teacher and a mentor, and who as chairman of the Department of Religion and Director of the Humanities Doctoral Program handled problematic times and difficult issues with tact, wisdom, and fairness. He is a scholar of distinction and a teacher's teacher. I am honored to have his signature affixed to my dissertation and pleased to enjoy his friendship. At three score and ten, he has lived quite a life. I wish him strength in the future and the blessing of a long and even more fruitful life.

In November 1995, I was invited, as a representative of the United States Holocaust Memorial Museum, to a conference entitled "Impunity and Accountability: Dialogue for National and International Response," sponsored by the government of Rwanda. In anticipation of the trip, I inquired about the government of Rwanda. Was it totalitarian, democratic, or authoritarian? Were its leaders good guys or bad? Were we about to enter a situation on the side of one of the two warring parties without knowing who they were and what positions they held? No matter who answered, the response was uniform, the judgment quite simple: these people in power stopped the genocide.

Naturally, that did not answer the questions I had asked, but it did say much about the regime. Even after returning from Rwanda and spending six long days with top governmental leaders face-to-face, I still do not know the answer. Perhaps the answer cannot be known because they have not yet fully governed.

The government is composed of the children of those Tutsi who went into exile in 1959.The only comparison that seems to shed some light on this unusual circumstance is a hypothetical one. Imagine that Fidel Castro were overthrown and the people who came back to run Cuba were the now middle-aged sons and daughters of those refugees who had escaped in 1959 and who had grown up in Southern Florida and elsewhere.

Tutsi refugees of 1959 were able to maintain a deep national consciousness in exile for an entire generation. So intense was the Tutsi consciousness that this elite group of diaspora Rwandese were capable of supporting a military operation on a voluntary system of taxation. The sons and daughters of these refugees, who were willing to come back to a homeland in which they had never lived from prestigious positions all over the world, fought a war against the Hutu. Victorious, they took charge of the government. They had not planned for the positions they were to hold, for the life they were to lead. The Secretary of Defense and Vice-President is a physician. The Secretary of Transportation was a Professor of Mathematics at Howard University. For the most part, they had the linguistic background in the native language in order to be able to function. As to Western languages, some speak French and others English, depending on the countries where their parents found refuge and where they received their education.

On the day of our arrival, we were taken to the Mugombwa Genocide site, which is an open mass grave with some 26,000 dead–at least that is the number reported to us. For years, I had read descriptions of the smell soldiers encountered when they liberated the concentration camps. It is a theme common to all accounts of liberation. Yet anything I had read about physically encountering the stench of such massive death is an understatement. I now know in the deepest recesses of my being what these liberators meant. I could not get that smell out of my nostrils; I could not get it out of my system. Being in the presence of so much death is an overwhelming physical experience. And the odor beggars description. I might have presumed that after all these years of study of the Holocaust and working with the documentary and photographic evidence, my encounter with this site would make me feel a bit more distant or jaded. When we returned from Mugombwa, we not only drank and drank but we kept taking perfume and putting it in our nostrils, trying to substitute another odor for the one we kept smelling. Within the pits of our physical being, we felt nauseous, a physical nausea. I could not shower myself clean.

I also understood anew the systemic wisdom in the Nazi system, which required that the Sonderkommando, rather than German personnel, be forced to work with the bodies of those who were gassed.

I do not know African burial practices well enough to explain why the fields are still open. Our hosts were not clear–perhaps they did not know–whether this site was where the killing took place or whether the bodies were gathered from the surrounding area and brought to this central burial site. One of the very important questions they asked us is what they should do with the physical evidence.

We advised them what to photograph and document, to resort to attestations and affidavits. Those of us who come from western traditions kept entreating them to complete the process–put the sand and dirt over the graves, so that people would not be forced to live in the vicinity of that odor and children would not have to grow up in an atmosphere where that smell is commonplace, a part of their ordinary, daily environment.

As a student of the Holocaust, I had the sense of traveling back in time to 1946, right after the end of World War II. The Genocide of Tutsis in Rwanda is not identical to the murder of Jews, but it is similar enough to offer parallels, to echo another time, another place. Meeting Tutsi survivors, I understood that they could describe details of their own experience with precision, but the general course of events is not yet understood. Rwandese survivors can give you the general outline of what happened: between April and July of 1994 there was the wholesale slaughter of massive numbers of Tutsi by Hutu.

The precipitating event for the genocide was the shooting down of the Air Force airplane carrying the President of Rwanda and Burundi. Before his death, the President of Rwanda had long exercised an authoritarian rule, which with each passing month is remembered with greater appreciation. The plane was hit by a surface to air missile, a sophisticated weapon that requires advanced training to operate. Someone knew that the two leaders were together, that they were flying that route, on that specific plane. The Hutu used the interim period even before the next president was sworn in to have their way and to settle old scores.

The moment the President was shot down, there were radio appeals to initiate the killings, and there was a systematic organization, so the claim was made, of these killings. Radio propaganda played a very important role in calling for and in organizing the genocide. A systematic replaying of these broadcasts, monitored and recorded by Western intelligence will be required if we are to comprehend fully the role of propaganda in the genocide.

Rwandan officials speak of 500,000 to 1,000,000 dead. The figures themselves indicate the magnitude of the deaths. They may not however be accurate. We were told that the bulk of the slaughters were done by machete. However, a comparison with the German killing operations makes these numbers seem high. The Nazis were not unskilled at killing, but even they were not able to slaughter 500,000 to 1,000,000 people in a two or three month period. Mobile killing units, *Einsatzgruppen*, operating in the conquered areas of the Soviet Union in the summer and fall of 1941 used machine guns and were still unable to kill such numbers in three months. The death camps utilized stationary killing facilities–gas chambers and crematoria–and mobile victims, transported from ghettos by trains. And yet, at the height of the murder, the Nazis deported 437,402 Hungarian Jews on 148 trains to Auschwitz between the 15th of May and the 8th of July, killing almost 90% of all arrivals. They were unable to kill one million in three months.

One must better understand the killing process to come up with an accurate understanding of numbers. How many people can be killed in one day by a soldier with a machete before the killer's arm gets tired, before he gets bloody and says, "the hell with it, I'm going to take off, I'm going to leave, I'm going to give up!" Killing by machete is not exactly the type of physical activity that one can sustain over a long period of time. It's also a singularly direct method of engagement with the victim and takes its toll on the killer. The killer gets bloody; bodily fluids are splashed. How tiring is such killing? Is killing by machete the equivalent of slicing bread or chopping trees? These are unpleasant questions, but not unessential ones.

When Heinrich Himmler, whom Richard Breitman masterfully describes as the "architect of the Holocaust," visited the killing fields in Minsk, one of his senior officers complained: "Look at the eyes of these men, they are destroyed. What are we creating, a nation of savages or neurotics?"[1] So the German killing process had to take a toll on the killers, and one must understand the nature of that toll to comprehend what truly happened.

Lest I be misunderstood, this caution is neither an appeal for sympathy for the killers nor is it a denial of the genocide, rather it is an attempt to confront and comprehend what actually happened.

It was also unclear to the officials with whom we met why killing took place in some regions and not in others. Unlike the Germans, the Hutu did not keep meticulous paper records, so our understanding of the killers can only come from interrogating them and their victims, trying to understand what decisions were made by whom and when. Oral history will be invaluable–indispensable–in understanding what happened and why.

Numbers are an issue; so too are the modes of killing. More intriguing, is the nature of the relationship between Hutu and Tutsi. We were told that tribal identity in Rwanda is patrilineal. In the case of an intermarriage between Hutu and Tutsi, the identity of the children is determined by the father. Thus, in some instances, Hutus were not only killing neighbors but also nieces and nephews, and children of those related by blood. Those who rescued and sheltered Tutsis were rescuing not strangers but kin.

The most electric moment of the conference was provided by Professor Gunnar Heinsohn, of Rafael Lemkin (the man who invented the word "genocide") *Institut für Xenophobie und Genoziforschung* at the University of Bremen in Germany. Heinsohn, the author of a new book entitled *Why Auschwitz? Hitler's Plan and the Perplexity of the World Since Then,* broke a total taboo by speaking about the Hutu. Sitting next to me on the panel he said, "I am a Hutu and as I put my arm around Michael Berenbaum, who is a Tutsi . . .. My father was a submarine Captain, who patrolled the Atlantic and my uncle was an SS officer of high rank. Michael Berenbaum is a Jew. My uncle and his fellow Hutus wanted to

---

[1] As quoted in R. Breitmat, *The Architect of Genocide: Himmler and the Final Solution* (New York: Alfred A. Knoff, 1991), 196.

kill all the Jews, including Michael and his family, yet Michael and I are good friends."

He then asked: "What must happen over the next 50 years that will allow a Hutu to put his arm around a Tutsi and a Tutsi to feel comfortable, to claim friendship and intellectual kinship?" He then had the extraordinary wisdom to allow the audience to remain silent. The German scholar gave a wonderful paper on what steps had to be taken between the first and second generations and what had to take place over a long time.

Understanding the killer is essential to reconstruction; so too the self-understanding of the victim. The unmastered trauma will come back to haunt again and again. Tutsi leadership needs to understand the difference between those who collaborated and those who did not, between those prefectures where the killing took place and those prefectures where it did not. They need to understand why some people rescued and why some people killed. My training as a Holocaust scholar had taught me the questions, some of which could not be answered during the conference. Historians ask for understanding. Lawyers ask what is to be done with the perpetrators?

One major segment of the conference was devoted to the question of how to rebuild a shattered legal system and how to deal with the perpetrators. American human rights lawyers were invited as advisors. They were joined by lawyers from Argentina who reconstituted their legal system after Desperados, Ugandese lawyers who rebuilt the system after Idi Amin, and South African lawyers rebuilding their system post-apartheid. In the remarkable developments of the late 1980s and early 1990s many different countries have moved from totalitarian rule to democratic rule. Representatives of Ethiopia, Latin America, Uganda, South Africa, Chile, and Germany could speak from experience of the transition of power from governments that massively violated human rights and human dignity, to successor regimes. Under totalitarian rule–even under authoritarian rule–those who were left in positions of power often were part of the system, most especially judges, prosecutors and the police.

Lawyers were also asked how to get testimony and how to gather material evidence. American lawyers recommended an Amnesty program to deal with the 56,000 people under arrest. In fact, as the conference progressed, they became convinced that such a progrm was the only option. Otherwise, 56,000 prosecutions would be required, 56,000 investigations, 56,000 separate judgments. They suggested that a pyramid be developed wherein the foot soldiers could be freed *if* they confessed and informed on the officers. Low-ranking officers who *confessed and informed* on higher-ups could be set free, until the chain of responsibility is established and a more complete picture of the whole emerges. Those in power would be held accountable.

We spoke a bit about the difference between gathering legal evidence and gathering historical evidence. The trials at Nuremberg provided the first understanding of the scope of German crimes, the first definition of what had actually happened. Yet, even there evidence was taken out of context. A lawyer removes documents from the file in order to use them as evidence. A historian wants to see documents in context, to know what other items were under consideration by an official at the time. Efraim Zuroff, whose wonderful memoir, *Occupation Nazi Hunter*,[2] depicts his passionate pursuit of the remaining war criminals, was just as vehement in pursuing the Hutu war criminals. Only thus can justice be restored, he argued. Alan Ryan, former director of the Office of Special Investigation, was equally adamant. He applied his training as a prosecutor to help shape the investigations in Rwanda.

Our hosts initially proposed that they establish 147 different trial centers; their reasoning was charming and fascinating. Many of the potential witnesses have never left their homes except to places they walk to by foot.They had never traveled by wagon, car, truck or bus yet alone train or airplane.

The first task facing the conference was how to deal with the perpetrators, but an equally important second task was how to heal the survivors. What mental health services are needed? What positive vision can be encompassed in the aftermath of all that has been experienced? What can give them the capacity to go on and to invest in the future and rebuild. How is trauma recognized and acknowledged? What is to be done with the orphans?

In 1945, Jewish survivors faced a difficult problem. They had no home to which they could return, and there was no where else in the world where they could go. Thus, many continued to live in the camps where they were incarcerated and among the people who had until recently sought their destruction. Rebuilding their interrupted and shattered lives was their first priority. Of equal importance was the national solution found in the establishment of a Jewish State in Palestine. The vision itself provided some healing and a measure of consolation. What comparable sense of vision can be offered to the Rwandese?

Jonathan Lemberger, the Israeli director of AMCHA, the group of mental health professionals who work with survivors of the Holocaust, cautioned our hosts that the effects of the trauma would express itself differently at various stages of life. Mourning and acknowledgement were essential if the impact of the trauma was to diminish over time. He also spoke of what has now been recognized as Post-Traumatic Stress Syndrome. He was forced to extrapolate from working with survivors forty years after an event as to how to heal in the first year after the genocide.

I presented a paper on the question of how to commemorate genocide. For Rwandese the real parallel was not to the American experience but to the Israeli one. National Days of Remembrance in the United States are designed to teach the American people about an event that happened to someone else, a continent away and half a century ago. In Israel, a nation of survivors, the Holocaust is not

---

[2]E. Zuroff, *Occupation Nazi-Hunter: The Continuing Search for Perpetrators of the Holocaust* (Hoboken, NJ: Ktav Books, 1994).

something that happened to others. The Israelis see themselves as the successor to the victims, their heirs, their kin. In Israel on Holocaust Memorial Day a siren is blown and two minutes of silence are observed. All traffic comes to a halt, even buses and trucks stand still, places of entertainment are closed, television and radio programming is solemn. Both in the United States and in Israel, the Holocaust is taught in schools and civic observances are held.

Rwandese were interested in how to remember genocide in a religious setting. While the observances of the Holocaust in Israel are mostly secular, including the Memorial ceremony at the sacred shrine of Yad Vashem, in the United States, Days of Remembrance are observed in synagogues and churches throughout the land. Rwanda is a Roman Catholic country with very heavy African elements shaping its Roman Catholicism. Religious leaders reacted differently to the genocide. Some assisted those in need; others were complicitous. One fiery Priest called for excommunication of the priests and bishops who had condoned, participated in, or advocated the genocide; he has written to the Pope. Others were cautioning against excommunication, arguing that the church is necessary as a support mechanism for reconstruction.

Hutu and Tutsi were divided neither by religion nor by language. There are recognizable physical characteristics that distinguishe between Hutus and Tutsis; as a rule, Hutu are short and squat, Tutsi tall and lanky. There is a striking beauty to some of the Tutsis you meet, yet there is so much intermarriage that the physical characteristics are less striking with each passing generation.

We also discussed other elements of the United States Holocaust Memorial Museum including its education department, archival documentation, and exhibitions. We described in detail the Oral History program and how essential a similar program will be to documenting the genocide.

We experienced the power of one such testimony. When a survivor of the genocide spoke, one could hear in the voice, the intonation, the language, the imagery she used echoes of Holocaust Testimony. When we described the National Registry of Jewish Holocaust Survivors, documenting the eye witnesses to the event, by cities of birth, camps of incarceration, places of liberation, town of post-war resettlement, and new country where life was rebuilt, our hosts became intrigued. We also described Yad Vashem's Pages of Testimony, which gathers by affidavit the names of all those killed–one by one, person by person.

The Rwandese were quite interested in the issue of reparations. Yet, from whom would they receive such reparations? Naturally, they had the tremendous desire to receive generous reparations for the maximum numbers of people. They were unmindful of who was going to have a stake in providing the reparations and where the funds were going to come from. They presumed that the genocide was an embarrassment to France and Belgium, whose soldiers had left just as the killing began and who had some colonial responsibility. They should be willing to make some amends. The Jews who attended the conference had to deflate exaggerated expectations. We told our hosts that the reason the German government offered reparations was to buy back international standing for Germany in the aftermath of the Holocaust. The only way it could recapture the good name of the Germany people was to differentiate the successor government from the perpetrator government. The Rwanese could not assume that Belgium felt embarrassed or that France felt humiliated or that the United States felt responsible, and, therefore, the chances of getting any significant sum of reparations were slim. There was a possibility of getting relief and development money but certainly not commensurate with expectations or needs.

A word about foreign governments and genocide: while military forces left, non-governmental organizations engaged in humanitarian relief efforts remained. The leaders of the NGO's were often young people, college students and post-graduates. Care, UNICEF, Save the Children, Doctors without Borders–all these remained to rescue, to relieve, to alleviate pain and suffering, while soldiers who were trained for combat were called home by their governments, governments fearful of the political repercussions that would result if some harm befell their soldiers.

There is a price to be paid for combatting genocide, but the West was unwilling to pay it. Western countries feared losing the life of a heavily armed volunteer soldier and thus turned and ran when the first signs of massive murders were perceived. Even the United States AID program is headed by a contract employee, a Canadian, who if taken hostage would be less politically embarrassing to the Administration than an American hostage.

Our hosts were convinced that the genocide in Rwanda could have been stopped by hundreds, not thousands, of heavily armed, well trained Western soliders. I suspect that they may be right. But the combination of the failed Western Imperialist tradition and the desire for political cover made Western governments reluctant to remain on the ground. American soldiers came in but only to get Americans out. They did not come in to restore order. A young researcher is currently working to trace the State Department documents dealing with the American decision not to intervene and not to use the word "genocide." We await the results of his work.

I returned from Rwanda impressed by the integrity and dedication of all the aid groups and their wonderful volunteers. I wish that I felt half as good about our soldiers and our leaders.

I returned from Rwanda with a greater belief in the necessity of a judicial response in the aftermath of genocide. I had judged Nuremberg cynically because its outcome seemed futile. Only a few were held accountable, too few. My own research had discounted the principle that proximity to the crime was a measure of responsibility. I now have a greater understanding of what is at stake for the Rwandese in bringing the perpetrators to justice and what is at stake for the world so that at least some measure of justice be achieved. If we cannot prevent genocide or alleviate the plight of its victims, we must at least be dedicated to prosecuting its perpetrators.

Many years ago, when I first started working on the creation of the United States Holocaust Memorial Museum, I was worried that the Museum might become irrelevant over time. I returned from Rwanda with a rather different fear. The Museum may be all too relevant. Such is the tragedy of our world.

Religion and the University:
In Honor of Her and Him

Robert A. Spivey
Virginia Foundation for Independent Colleges

John Priest's professional odyssey, beginning at a denominationally related undergraduate liberal arts college, Ohio Wesleyan, moving to an institution engaged in professional education of ministers, Hartford Theological Seminary, then teaching in a developing department of religion at a burgeoning state institution, Florida State University, closely parallels the story of religion in American higher education. Thus a retelling of the story of the academic study of religion (her) presents an opportunity also to honor John Priest (him).

Religion in American Higher Education

Early on religion permeated church-related colleges. These institutions were openly committed to education that was basically Christian; they required chapel, saw the president as a moral philosopher, and taught religion courses reflective of the Christian faith. When these phenomena became more problematic, the place for the fullest embodiment of religion became the theological seminary, for theology as queen of the sciences was pursued only in that special segment of the university, the divinity school. Even in the seminary, there were forces at work to decrease the role of theology, namely the increasing professionalization of ministerial education. Moreover, seminaries were either isolated by or separated from mainstream American higher education in the university. During the latter part of the twentieth-century, religion found a place in major public universities through the establishment of departments of religion–religious studies as one academic program among numbers of others. To most observers, the above describes the decline of the role of religion in higher education–from religion's permeating the essential character of the university, to a role of increasing confinement, first in a school or college, next in a seminary, and finally in an academic department.

Two recent books address the question, "What happened to religion in the American university?"–George M. Marsden's *The Soul of the American University: From Protestant Establishment to Established Nonbelief*[1] and Douglas Sloan's *Faith and Knowledge: Mainline Protestantism and American Higher Education.*[2] In each case the surprising culprit responsible for the diminished role of religion in higher education is Protestant religious thought.

George Marsden, faculty member first at Calvin College then at Duke University and now at Notre Dame University (representing three powerful segments of American religion, namely conservative Protestantism, liberal Protestantism, and Roman Catholicism), describes the demise of religion in education in terms somewhat similar to Stephen Carter's *The Culture of Disbelief.*[3] Beginning with the early academies for training of church and civic leadership in Puritan New England, Marsden characterizes three major periods for religion in higher education: the first, until 1850, was a period of explicit commitment to learning as preparation for Christian service; the second, till the end of the nineteenth century, featured universities following the dictates of liberal Protestantism, including demand for tolerance, distaste for sectarianism, and emphasis on professionalism according to the German model of the professor as embodiment of academic freedom and natural knowledge; and in the third period, the twentieth-century, we witness universities abandoning explicit religious considerations in order to champion the modern secular university.

According to Marsden, most people think that the demise of religion in the university was caused mainly by the rise of public state universities, following the Morrill Act of 1862, and the emergence of dominant secular intellectual theories, such as Darwinism and Freudian psychology, plus political pressures to disavow church affiliation, following strict interpretations of separation of church and state (e.g. the Carnegie retirement system, forerunner of TIAA/CREF, which required participating colleges to disavow controlling religious affiliation). Marsden, however, insists on identifying the major culprit as religionists themselves. The commitment to openness and toleration by the Protestant establishment led higher education inevitably down a slippery slope of secularization neither foreseen nor desired by nineteenth- and twentieth-century Protestantism. In essence, no good deed went unpunished.

For Marsden the loss of any significant Christian presence in colleges and universities was ironically the result of the Protestant project to create a Protestant

[1] New York: Oxford University Press, 1994.
[2] Louisville, Kentucky: Westminster John Knox Press, 1994.
[3] New York, Basic Books, 1993.

America. As long as America functioned culturally under Protestant auspices, such a project seemed coherent; however, with increasing twentieth-century pluralism in American culture, especially after World War II, the Protestant worldview simply functioned to undermine any particular expression of strong religious convictions. The very logic of the non-sectarian ideal that the Protestant establishment promoted against Catholicism, Judaism, and religious sects finally dictated that liberal Protestantment itself should move to the periphery along with other religious perspectives.

The heart of Marsden's argument occurs in Part II, "Defining the American University in a Scientific Age," which describes the transformation of the Protestant college into the modern research university. According to Marsden, the creation of Johns Hopkins under the leadership of Daniel Coit Gilman became the norm for all higher education, in part because it was the first institution to make graduate and professional education the center of the academic enterprise. From the day Johns Hopkins opened its doors in 1876 until Gilman retired in 1901, the institution reflected the words of its first president:

> The Institution we are about to organize would not be worthy of the name of the University, if it were to be devoted to any other purpose than the discovery and promulgation of the truth; and it would be ignoble in the extreme if the resources which have been given by the Founder without restrictions should be limited to the maintenance of ecclesiastical differences or perverted to the promotion of political strife.
> As the spirit of the University should be that of intellectual freedom in pursuit of the truth and of the broadest charity toward those from whom we differ in opinion it is certain sectarian and partisan preferences should have no control in the selection of teachers, and should not be apparent in the official work.[4]

Strangely the building of such institutions was assumed to be Christian, for it was presumed that the best hopes of America were equivalent to what it meant to be a Christian. Even "methodological secularization" drew its inspiration, according to Gilman, from the Christian attempt to uplift humanity. Gilman assumed "science" was the expression of Christianity because the aim of science was progress in the development of humankind.

The second recent analysis of religion and higher education–Douglas Sloan's *Faith and Knowledge*–narrates a story similar to that of Marsden, namely the twentieth-century failed attempt of mainline Protestantism to make a significant impact on American higher education. According to Sloan, the primary area for religious influence in the developing university was the faith and knowledge relationship. Such was pivotal not only for the place of religion in higher education but also for the role of religion in modern culture generally:

> The conception of knowing and of knowable reality that has come during the past centuries to dominate modern culture and education has left little place for the concerns and affirmations of religion. The dominant conception of knowing that has shaped

---

[4]Cited in Marsden, *Soul*, 151.

modern consciousness and culture, while quite powerful, has been extremely narrow. In the prevailing modern view of how and what we can know, the quantitative, the mechanical, and the instrumental are accorded full standing. All those things, however, that involve–as Huston Smith has put it–values, meaning, purpose, and qualities are regarded as essentially having little to do with knowledge, except as they can be reduced to more basic and more material and mechanistic entities.[5]

Responses by religionists to this materialist, mechanistic worldview were, according to Sloan, of three types: an anti-modern fundamentalistic alternative drawn from a literalistic reading of the Bible; a scientific naturalism which smuggled in a value dimension; and a two-realm theory of truth with knowledge based on science and empirical observation on the one hand and on the other hand truths of meaning, morality, feeling.[6] Each was found wanting, even the third response of mainline Protestantism.

In summary, Sloan judges that the theological renaissance of Protestant thought failed to penetrate the cognitive center of the modern university, with the result that "religionists" were left with fractured "special interest theologies" (similar to political interest groups), loss of an objectivistic conception of knowing without any suitable replacement (symbolized by the development of the multiversity over against the university), and a resurgence of fundamentalism as dogmatic as the worst aspects of modernism.

Against the backdrop of Marsden and Sloan, the story of religious studies at Florida State University both reinforces and challenges the overall portrayal of the role of religion in the American university.

The Florida State University Department of Religion

The immediate background for the 1965 establishment of the Department of Religion at Florida State, and those at numbers of other state universities, such as the University of California at Santa Barbara, Indiana University, the University

---

[5]Sloan, *Faith and Knowledge*, viii. Support for this characterization of the university comes from J. Fried, "Monocultural Perspectives and Campus Diversity," *Higher Education Exchange* (Dayton, Ohio: Kettering Foundation, 1995) 18:

American higher education has been dominated by scientific paradigm since the mid-nineteenth century. This paradigm influences all dimensions of our colleges and universities, including teaching, learning and research. The paradigm assumes the superiority of reason over emotion; objectivity over subjectivity; the independent, noncontextual existence of empirical data; the irrelevance of the observer's perspective to that which is observed; the existence of universal, noncontextual truths; and the primacy of technical and operational concerns over issues of belief or meaning.

Manifestations of the paradigm can be seen in a variety of institutional practices. In teaching, learning, and research we can see the enhanced prestige of the "hard" disciplines, i.e., data based, laboratory focused over the soft or economically marginal disciplines like the human services or many social sciences. Faculty seem to prefer cognitive instructional methods over methods which involve either emotion or discussion of multiple interpretations as revealed by students' differing perspectives.

[6]Sloan, *Faith and Knowledge*, viii-ix.

of Virginia and the University of Tennessee at Knoxville, was the Supreme Court decision, *Engel v. Vitale* (1962), in which state-sponsored prayer in the schools of New York State was declared unconstitutional by a vote of eight to one, and the *Abington School District v. Schempp* (1963) decision, in which the Court ruled, also by eight to one, that the Pennsylvania public school practices of devotional Bible reading and recitation of the Lord's Prayer were unconstitutional.

While recognizing implicitly the pluralism of American society, both Supreme Court decisions affirmed the validity of the academic study of religion in public education at all levels. The court declared in the Schempp case:

> It might well be said that one's education
> is not complete without a study of religion. . . .

And Florida State, along with a number of other state universities, took that dictum seriously.

One way of characterizing the FSU Department of Religion makes use of the Harvard psychologist Carol Gilligan's *In A Difference Voice,* which posits a difference between the moral development of men and women.[7] She explores the paradox that the very traits that have traditionally been associated with women's goodness–their concern for others and what she calls an ethic of care, of *relationships*–are the very qualities that have led psychologists to describe women as morally inferior to men, who are instead occupied with an ethic of fairness and justice, of *principles*. Gilligan does not argue, as one might expect, that women's morality is better than that of men, or that men's morality is wrong or deficient. The vision of maturity that she proposes is one that requires both male and female–the male ethic of justice and the female ethic of care. She illustrates these two views of moral discrimination by describing an argument between two four-year-olds; the one, a girl, wanted to play "neighbor," and the other, a boy, wanted to play "pirate." In the course of the disagreement, the boy proposed a fair solution: each game should be played in succession–equal time, first playing "pirate" and then playing "neighbor." Thus, each wins in succession. The four-year-old girl proposed a different solution to the dilemma: "No, you can be the pirate who moves in next door." In effect, she advocated that both win together.

To clarify her distinction (happily more directly related to religion-study), Gilligan borrows from Robert Alter's *The Art of Biblical Narrative*[8] to emphasize the indeterminate meaning of narrative. As an example, she cites the two creation stories of Genesis, to be seen as complementary rather than contradictory.

In my judgment, the formation and development of the Department of Religion at Florida State University reflects, in the main, this different voice–a

[7] C. Gilligan, *In a Different Voice: Psychological Theory and Women's Development* (Cambridge, MA: Harvard University Press, 1982). Cf. Carol Gilligan, "In a Different Voice: Women's Conception of the Self and Morality," *Harvard Educational Review* 47, (1977) 481-571.

[8] R. Alter, *The Art of Biblical Narrative* (New York: Basic Books, 1981).

featuring of both/and (not either/or), a stress on relationships, connections, Though from the beginning the department consisted of faculty with various specialties, there was an overriding concern for wholeness. Such was worked out in the basic curriculum structure of the department: the history and literature of religion, religious thought, and religion and culture. Note the dominance of *and*: history *and* literature of religion, religion *and* culture. Even in the second category, religious thought, the department embraced not only philosophy of religion but also theology, the form of religious thought associated with a confessional, religious community. By this decision, the department opted for continuity, rather than discontinuity, with the pattern of religion-study associated with church-related colleges and universities and with the prevailing pattern of religion doctoral study that featured graduate education built upon a seminary degree–a study in which theology remained queen.

Two books were symbolic of the nature of the religion program at Florida State, Mircea Eliade's *The Sacred and the Profane*[9] and Martin Buber's *I and Thou*[10]. Until the 1980's, they were *the* heart of the introductory course. In addition to each title's use of the conjunction *and*, Eliade's phenomenological work points to the transcendent, sacred dimension so that no particular religious phenomenon is excluded or judged superior or inferior. Thereby, Eliade's viewpoint furthers the essential pluralism of the study of religion in a state university context. In the other writing, an example of religious thought, Buber stresses the   connectedness of fundamental reality: "In the beginning was relation."

This awareness of connections became an obvious characteristic of the department, first of all through affirming linkage, in both undergraduate and doctoral studies to the humanities, the latter once headed by John Priest. Secondly there were impressive indicators of connection and relation by means of the quantity and quality of religion department faculty involved in interdisciplinary endeavors: the Humanities Institute, once co-chaired by Richard Rubenstein; American Studies, headed by Leo Sandon; Black Studies, led by Bill Jones; Asian Studies, chaired by Bill Swain; Peace Studies, directed by John Carey.

Other connectional efforts included the short-lived Institute for Continuing Studies in Religion, which affirmed the relationship of the university to the church; the Institute for Southern Culture and Religion, Richard Rubenstein's creation of connection with the region; and linkage to government and church in Leo Sandon's Institute for Social Policy Studies. Moreover, Larry Cunningham and Charles Wellborn were involved with the formation and development of FSU's Florence and London interdisciplinary centers for study abroad.

---

[9]M. Eliade, *The Sacred and the Profane: The Nature of Religion* (trans. Willard R. Trask; New York: Harper & Row, 1959).

[10]M. Buber, *I and Thou* (trans. Walter Kaufman; New York Scribner, 1970).

Two other developments bear singling out, because of the FSU department of religion's national leadership in emerging areas of religious studies. In Florida State's major project for the development of learning about religion in the public schools (almost half a million dollars in grants over an eight-year period), we were aided not only by the distinguished historian of American religion Edwin S. Gaustad, but also by social studies education faculty, principally Rod Allen and secondarily Joann Dye, in developing materials for making religion-study an integral part of the regular social studies curriculum of the schools. The project, curriculum materials for religion study from the first through the twelfth grades (plus a teacher education component), was incredibly ambitious–and almost succeeded. Unfortunately, for a number of reasons, including a long history of the secularization of public education, reach did exceed grasp. Though FSU broke ground, the planting did not occur. Some day, though, religion will be a natural, regular subject for study in the schools. Ken Kesey provides an appropriate epitaph for that project in the comment about his novel, *One Flew Over the Cuckoo's Nest*, "It's the truth even if it didn't happen."

Another significant role for the department of religion was its early leadership in the national professional organization of academic religion study, the American Academy of Religion. The move of the AAR's headquarters from its long-time site at Wilson College, a small, liberal arts, church-related, private college, to the large, public university of Florida State University and to the leadership of myself, Walter Moore, and John Priest symbolized the phenomenal growth in quantity and complexity of religious studies on the national educational scene in the 1960's and 1970's. From a quaint, informal organization, the National Association of Biblical Instructors (NABI), which met during the Christmas break at Union Theological Seminary in New York City, to the programmatic array of a multi-faceted academy of religion meeting in major hotels, nationally and regionally, represented a coming of age of religious studies.

The journey of the department was also symbolized by one of its first visiting scholars, Marburg University Professor Ernst Benz–an internationally acclaimed eclectic scholar of a variety of religious phenomena (for example, his fascinating articles on spirit phenomena in the Tallahassee area[11]), and by another visiting scholar, one of John Priest's humanities Ph.D. students, The Right Reverend Marjorie Matthews, the first woman bishop of the United Methodist Church. We had come full circle–an international German scholar engaged with living religious stuff and a national denominational leader reflecting on and making use of critical, constructive study of religion.

This narrative on some aspects of the story of the department of religion is not so much for purposes of self-congratulation, though that could well be the tenor of a *Festschrift* for John Priest. Rather the story is intended to point out the character of what has occurred. When one looks at the way the department has

---

[11] E. Benz, *Der Heilige Geist in Amerika* (Düsseldorf-Köln; Eugen Diedericks Verlag, 1970).

infiltrated, combined with, permeated the life of the Florida State University, then it is difficult to imagine the institution without the department. 1965 was a good year for FSU in particular and for religion-study in general.

Eliade has a way of speaking in which he says, "And then they believe and then they do this. . . ." We believed that there should be academic study of religion at FSU, and we did these things. One knows more about the nature of academic religion study by looking at what was and is being done–a department that was and is solid in academic credentials and also reaching out with shoots into the life of the university in myriad ways, even more than have been named here.

In honor of the academic study of religion, I say, well done–well done, faculty, students, staff, friends, who have been part and parcel of the FSU Department of Religion during its thirty year history.

Her Future

I realize that predictions or prescriptions for the future are basically futile. Mort Sahl said the last word in his indisputable aphorism, "The future lies ahead." Another comment is also appropriate, "To prophesy is very difficult, especially about the future." At the same time, I recognize that we not only can but also must reckon with the future. René Dubos comments wisely:

> Persons and societies do not submit passively to the surroundings and events. They make choices as to the places where they live and the activities in which they engage–choices based on what they want to be, to do, and to become.[12]

So I now speak about a possible future for religious studies, starting from the perspective of biblical studies. The title for this section originates from Elizabeth Schüssler-Fiorenza's fascinating study, *In Memory of Her: A Feminist Theological Reconstruction of Christian Origins*.[13] In this work, she uses the traditional academic disciplines of theology, ethics, church history, and biblical studies in order to pursue a knowledge of Christian origins that will empower women. In the course of the investigation she builds upon mainstream traditional scholarship and yet calls into question its uncritically accepted presuppositions, particularly patriarchal and androcentric contexts. Schüssler-Fiorenza's imaginative, comprehensive effort offers a critique of traditional male scholarly interpretation about the emergence of the Christian movement around Jesus. In her search for a resting point for faith–in her case, the life and ministry of Jesus–she claims that Jesus is inherently feminist, that his message, "Call no one father among you on earth" (Matthew 23:8-9 and parallels), is an authentic saying of Jesus that consciously repudiates patriarchy.

---

[12] R. Dubos, *Celebrations of Life* (New York: McGraw-Hill Book Company, 1981) 6.
[13] New York: Crossroad, 1983.

Yet, her criteria of authenticity and her search for Jesus' message demonstrate vividly the inescapable danger for each biblical interpreter. As Albert Schweitzer instructed in *The Quest for the Historical Jesus*, every application of criteria of authenticity invariably concludes with that which accords most with one's own presuppositions–ironically, Schweitzer himself was guilty of that error. Most often, Jesus and the scholar sound remarkably alike.

One consequence of her depiction of Jesus as feminist, even though Schüssler-Fiorenza is conscious of the danger, is anti-Jewishness. Her push for the uniqueness of Jesus in the first-century Jewish world results in an opposition between patriarchal Judaism and feminist Christianity. The oversimplified message is as follows: Even though Christianity takes on androcentric, patriarchal trappings early in its history, Jesus and *earliest* Christianity are pure feminism. . .to be contrasted with androcentric Judaism.[14]

As the late Erwin R. Goodenough showed time and again, the Christian sweep of the Greco-Roman world in the first centuries was prepared for by the phenomenon of heterodox, Hellenistic Judaism concurrent with and informative of Jesus and the early church. As tempting as it may be for the Christian scholar, there is little solid evidence for a feminist Jesus apart from an emerging feminism of heterodox Judaism.

This criticism of Schüssler-Fiorenza does not detract from *In Memory of Her* as an invaluable contribution to the interpretation of the origins of the Christian faith. Especially noteworthy is her avoidance of the danger of some feminist "early-Christian-origins" interpretation that relies excessively on extra-canonical texts as embodying the truth of Christian faith–interpretation that creates a canon beyond the canon. It is possible to elevate peripheral writings, like the Gnostic texts, only if one is prepared to ignore their context as offshoots of an emerging mainstream Christian tradition.

Apropos of the last remark, another scholarly work of quite a different sort, Brevard Childs' *The New Testament as Canon: An Introduction,*[15] avoids the usual historical critical approach to biblical materials in which the interpreter first establishes the original setting and then, if so inclined, attempts to show the contemporary theological relevance of that original setting. Instead Childs begins at the other end and attempts to "discern the canonical shape of the present text." By implication his way of viewing the canon offers the intriguing possibility that imaginative efforts like those of Schüssler-Fiorenza become themselves part of the canonical tradition. Instead of a search for feminist evidence beyond the canon, the feminist interpretation of the biblical text extends the canonical shape of the Christian tradition.[16]

---

[14] See R. S. Kraemer's review in *RSR* (1985) 8. It should be noted that Elizabeth Schüssler-Fiorenza does take account of this criticism in her later work.

[15] Philadelphia: Fortress Press, 1985.

[16] See G. T. Sheppard, The Use of Scripture within the Christian Ethical Debate Concerning Same Sex Oriented Persons, " *USQR* 40 (1985) 19-23.

In summary, future religion-study will both benefit from radical interpretation, in this case feminist, and also gain from fresh ways of looking at traditional conservative issues, in this case the canon.[17]

Any projection of the future of religion study in a state university setting as distinct from private church-related colleges, must begin with the rather obvious observation of her past: the development of departments of religious studies in state universities was prepared for by church-related departments of religion moving away from confessional, doctrinal, dogmatic study. Moreover, over the years, due to cultural and religious shifts, there has been a gradual salutary movement away from the notion that inclusion of the study of religion stems primarily from the religious character of the institution. Instead, at present, nearly everyone agrees that the study of religion finds its validation and justification in the concept of religion as a legitimate humanities and social sciences subject matter. Indeed most church-related colleges and universities reject the view that religion's sphere of scholarly activity is circumscribed by the sponsoring church's religious doctrine; the aim is to be critical, not catechetical. Nationally, then, the study of religion is pursued in departments of religion either as one of the humanities, or in some cases as one of the social sciences–without, on the one hand, the need for apology, and without, on the other hand, claiming a privileged position. In short, the study of religion whether in a church-related college or a state-supported university draws its identity from already existing academic disciplines, whether in the humanities or in the social studies.[18] Such basic, minimal justification, may, however, serve to obscure the full role of religion study for the future. I agree with Wilfred Cantwell Smith, the Harvard historian of religion, who in his American Academy of Religion presidential address pointed to a more demanding and difficult role for religion-study.[19]

Smith's argument goes something like this. From a certain perspective, the emergence of departments of religion in state universities may be seen as the culmination of the secularizing process that is part and parcel of modern Western history. Specifically, the modern West, unlike other civilizations, has postulated that human nature is fundamentally secular and that religion is to be conceived as an addendum. Thus, Western education at all levels interprets religion as some sort of extra in human life. Against that view, the historian of religion, like Smith, asserts that it is not religion that is the addendum, but secularism. The vast majority of human beings, including the intelligent and perceptive among them, in all times and places and in all cultures, civilizations, and ages other than our

[17] For a critical summary of recent trends in New Testament scholarship see R. A. Horsley's "Innovation in Search of Reorientation: New Testament Studies Rediscovering its Subject Matter," *JAAR* 62 (1994) 1127-66, arguing for an agenda whose goal is historical, rather than theological, understanding. My paper argues against such an either/or viewpoint.

[18] See L. J. O'Connell, *Bulletin of the Council on the Study of Religion* 15 (1984) 144.

[19] See "The Modern West in the History of Religion," *JAAR* 52 (1984) 3-18. Compare W. A. Nord, *Religion and American Education: Rethinking a National Dilemma* (Chapel Hill, NC: University of North Carolina Press, 1995) 304-319.

own Western one, have recognized that there are three levels in the environment: what the West calls the natural world around us; the human world in which persons are both social and individual; and a higher realm to which we humans, indeed to which both the other two levels, are related. The third, the transcendent realm, is the most important, the most ontologically firm, the most valuable. Just because it is transcendent, it cannot be talked about, spoken of, in the normal way; moreover, to speak of the transcendent *as religion* is a distortion, as is clearly evident in most world religions. To perceive of the Hindu religion as an addition to what it is to be Indian is to miss the fact that Hindus do not try to be Hindu. They *are* Hindu. The case is similar with Islam. To be a Muslim–the word in Arabic is a common noun, not a proper noun–is to act out of a certain set of Islamic ways. Similarly, the Buddhist, the Christian, and the Jewish are salient ways of being human. The innovative secularist way is at most one more such experiment. To talk about *homo religious* is misleading; there is only *homo sapiens*–and Smith quips, "a minority (those in the West) are not quite *sapientes* enough to have sensed what kind of universe we live in and what kind of being we are."[20]

This fundamental error of the contemporary university (and the church-related college) has, according to Smith, negative consequences for the modern West. Secularism, which began by rejecting certain particular items in the religious complex, has proceeded to reject transcendence across the board and, when transcendence as a dimension of everything is denied, then everything is affected, including the basis of community and the worth of the individual.

For example, in *Habits of the Heart*,[21] the authors speak of the fact that Americans have lost the language they need to make moral sense out of their private and public lives. Walt Whitman heard America singing; the authors of *Habits of the Heart* hear America stuttering. Our excessive individualism and self-actualization deny us the language that can satisfactorily articulate the reasons for our deeper commitments–to our friends, our families, our public life. As a people, we have largely lost what Bellah and others call the "communities of memory," namely, the traditions of civic republicanism, service in the pursuit of the common good, and biblical faith, the religious heritage of our ancestors.

In this context, religion study is more than hunt and gather, show and tell. Indeed, information without purpose is part of the narcissism, the extreme individualism, that permeates American society. The growth of the religious right is only one, though highly visible, evidence of the inevitable misguided reactions to the dominance of the secular. Wilfred Cantwell Smith concludes that the West must "'rejoin the human race' after the isolationist detour, with a renewed enhancement of the sense of what it means to be truly human. Modern secularism

---

[20] Smith, "Modern West," 9.

[21] R. N. Bellah, R. Madsen, W. M. Sullivan, A. Swidler, and S. M. Tipton, *Habits of the Heart: Individualism and Commitment in American Life* (Berkeley, CA: University of California Press, 1985).

is an intellectual error. It is so important an error as to be socially and historically disruptive; not to say, disastrous. And as an intellectual error, it is the task of intellectuals to correct it."[22]

Following Smith, how then can scholar/teachers in the academy of religion join in that correction? In my judgment, we will best serve by working with human problems, seeing the depth and breadth of *homo sapiens*. Theology in its more traditional sense, especially as dogmatics, will continue to be nourished by particular communities of faith. In the state university context, the scholar of religion will be concerned less to systematize and defend ecclesiastical statements and more to focus, especially within the setting of the humanities, on common human problems such as gender, birth, death, politics, human creativity, and destiny.[23] These themes are obviously not the province of the religion scholar alone; therefore the shoots of inter- and cross-disciplinary endeavors will flourish.

Conclusion

In these last comments it is obvious that we have moved from the nature of the department of religion to the nature of the university. To return to the beginning is to address the fundamental questions that have always puzzled religion scholars.

One further recent wide-ranging and suggestive analysis of religion and the university, namely Warren A. Nord's *Religion and American Education: Rethinking a National Dilemma*, declares our national battleground as rooted, first, in religious conservatives' belief that America is a Christian (or Judeo-Christian) nation, which has been captured by the forces of secularism and must be restored by a return to religious practices, goals, and teaching in public education and, second, in liberal humanists who see the "Religious Right" as dangerous intruders into secular public education. Nord admits to truth on both sides: public education is hostile to rather than neutral to religion, and public education cannot promote religion or the practice of religion. Thus Nord proposed a third alternative, a "Reasonable Center."

Indeed the beauty of Nord's thesis, buttressed by a thorough study of the origins and development of the current dilemma, is that his study views higher education in the larger context of school education. Thus the curriculum question–What is the proper role for religion in learning?–begins with the start of formal education, at the kindergarten level, and continues till the end, through doctoral study. Particularly illuminating is one of Nord's closing comments, which I cite rather fully:

---

[22] Smith, "Modern West," 18. For a different perspective, namely a contrast between "religious study of religion" and "academic study of religion," see S. Gill, "The Academic Study of Religion," *JAAR* 62 (1994) 965-75.

[23] See W. F. May, "Why Theology and Religious Studies Need Each Other," *JAAR* 52 (1984) 751.

We modern-day Americans have a spiritual problem. There is something fundamentally wrong with our culture. We who have succeeded so brilliantly in matters of economics, science, and technology have been less successful in matters of the heart and soul. This is evident in our manners and our morale (*sic*); in our entertainment and our politics; in our preoccupation with sex and violence; in the ways we do our jobs and in the failure of our relationships; in our boredom and unhappiness in this, the richest of all societies.

How did this come to be? Maynard Adams has argued that our tragic flaw "lies not in the failures of modern Western civilization but in the condition of its success."

Too much we have come to define our lives in terms of the paradigm values of modernity–liberty and individualism, rights and self-fulfillment, economic success and technological progress–and we have lost our spiritual balance. We badly need to reassert the importance of duty and virtue, tradition and community, passion and sacrifice, reverence for nature, and even, perhaps, sin and guilt.

I do not want to overstate my case. As I argued in chapter 11, significant forms of moral progress–particularly those that result from the assertion of liberty and rights–are characteristic of modernity. We do live in a world which, in very important ways, is much to be preferred to any traditional (religious) society. We have righted old wrongs. But we have also run roughshod over ways of thinking and feeling that merit renewed attention. Once again we need to *restore the tension*, taking our spiritual well-being as seriously as our search for material well-being.

Our educational system nourishes the temper of our times and in so doing exacerbates our problems. Needless to say, the reforms I have proposed are not going to rejuvenate our culture spiritually. But then that has not been my purpose. I have argued for taking religion seriously on secular (philosophical, educational, political, and constitutional) grounds. Nonetheless, by requiring students to study religion we can give them something of the intellectual and imaginative resources necessary to acquire critical distance on the relentlessly materialistic thrust of modern culture and think in a relatively informed way about our spiritual situation. Surely religion focuses on many of the right questions whatever one thinks of the answers. Our inability to see this betrays a lack of depth in our thinking about education.[24]

The wave of the future, unlike the *soul-less* contemporary American university, must consist of *learning from religion* as an indispensable, inevitable accompaniment of the human adventure.

So in honor of her–the past, present and future of the study of religion–and of him–John Priest, scholar, teacher, *homo sapiens*–we can seek the truth wherever truth may be found. Like him, we can study and learn–without apology and with rootedness in the biblical and the humane.

[24]Nord, *Religion and American Education*, 380f.